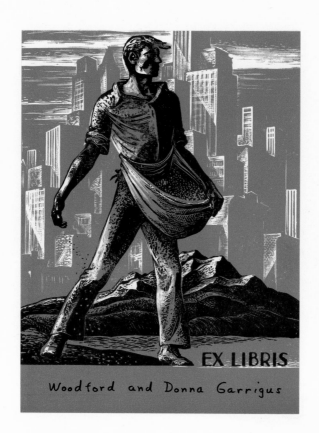

EX LIBRIS

Woodford and Donna Garrigus

George Perkins Marsh

VERSATILE VERMONTER

George Perkins Marsh

VERSATILE VERMONTER

By David Lowenthal

Columbia University Press   New York   1958

TO MERLE CURTI

Preface

"IN REVIEWING THE LIFE of this eminent man, who studied languages while he practiced law, who divided his time between business and politics, who wrote books and delivered lectures on literary subjects, and who investigated geographical problems while he elevated diplomacy, one cannot fail to be impressed with the breadth of his interests and the variety of his activities and duties on the one hand, and on the other hand the high degree of specialization and the necessary narrowing of interests and activities which has characterized [modern scientists]." So spoke William Morris Davis in praise of George Perkins Marsh, half a century ago at the National Academy of Sciences. "One can hardly fail to question," Davis went on, "whether advice on the treatment of national scientific problems can be as well given by intensive specialists of the modern school as by men of a wider experience, of whom Marsh was so admirable an example." To survey Marsh's life and achievements in the light of his "wider experience" is the aim of this book.

The career of George Perkins Marsh spanned most of the nineteenth century, and there were few aspects of his era on which he did not leave a mark. Lawyer, editor, farmer, manufacturer, congressman, diplomat *par excellence,* Marsh was the broadest American scholar of his day. He was at home in twenty languages, became the country's foremost authority on both Scandinavian and English linguistics, made important contributions to comparative philology, helped to found and foster the Smithsonian Institution, served as arbiter of public taste in art and architecture, established principles for railroad regulation, provided new insights into the nature of the history of man and of the earth. And from his pioneer work in geography developed the American conservation movement.

In the quality as in the diversity of his undertakings, Marsh exemplified the creative, utilitarian spirit of his times. He will be remembered best for the unique historical and geographical insights —his awareness of ecological relationships, his extraordinary study of man's transformation of the environment, his blueprints for resource husbandry—set forth in his book *Man and Nature*. But the clue to Marsh's versatile scholarship lies in his variety of activities, wealth of practical experience, and passionate involvement in the life of his times.

Marsh's manysidedness has made the preparation of this book both a challenge and an adventure, in which I have had help from many sources. My appreciation goes first to Carl Sauer, who introduced me to Marsh's work and who has done more than anyone else to give Marsh proper recognition for his study of man's role in changing the face of the earth. I am particularly grateful to John Leighly, who stimulated me to explore the background of Marsh's penetrating and comprehensive insights. In that exploration I was fortunate to have the guidance of Merle Curti, whose perceptive counsel and sympathetic encouragement have been a constant support and inspiration. To Fulmer Mood I am indebted for pointing out some of the pitfalls and promises of biographical investigation. Richard Hartshorne and Andrew Clark helped me place Marsh in the framework of the history and philosophy of geography, and James C. Malin and J. Russell Whitaker have given me the benefit of their pioneer work and friendly advice. Special thanks go to John K. Wright, who has been most generous with his time and experience in historical and geographical research.

For specific information and help about Marsh's background and life in Vermont, I should like to thank the following: in Woodstock,

Elizabeth French Hitchcock, Margaret L. Johnson, John H. McDill, Loren R. Pierce, Rhoda Teagle, E. E. Wilson; in Burlington, Dr. Lyman Allen, Leon W. Dean, Paul D. Evans, Gladys Flint, John C. Huden, Laura M. Loudon, Sidney Butler Smith, Frank D. Spaulding; in Montpelier, Harrison J. Conant, Elizabeth W. Niven, the late Arthur Wallace Peach. For advice and assistance of every sort, I am also indebted to Selig Adler, Richard Beck, Saul Benison, Jan O. M. Broek, Francis Brown, Laura C. Burgess, the late Aurelia E. Crane, the late Caroline E. Crane, A. Hunter Dupree, Robert F. Durden, Senator Ralph E. Flanders, Frank Freidel, Charles C. Griffin, John P. Harrison, Einar Haugen, Charles B. Hitchcock, Sexson E. Humphreys, Donald Q. Innis, Edward C. Kirkland, Mary Raymond Lambert, Carl L. Lokke, John Lowenthal, Edmunds Lyman, Howard R. Marraro, Lewis Mumford, G. Bernard Noble, Chalmers Roberts, Ishbel Ross, Margaret Sheppard, Elisabeth L. Shoemaker, William L. Thomas, Jr., and Glyndon G. Van Deusen.

Vernon Carstensen, Andrew H. Clark, Merle Curti, Wilma B. Fairchild, John C. Greene, Norman Hood, Robert Reynolds, and John K. Wright kindly commented on various drafts of the manuscript; and I am especially obliged to my father, Max Lowenthal, for his detailed and searching criticism of the penultimate draft.

I am happy to acknowledge permission to quote from manuscripts in possession of the Annmary Brown Memorial in Brown University; the Boston Public Library; the Calais Free Library, Calais, Maine; Mrs. William Clough, Woodstock, Vermont; Dartmouth College (by permission of the Trustees); Harvard University; Sexson E. Humphreys, Ohio University; the Huntington Library, San Marino, California; the Library of Congress; the Massachusetts Historical Society; the Minnesota Historical Society; the National Archives; the New-York Historical Society; the New York Public Library; Dr. Marsh Pitzman, St. Louis; the Smithsonian Institution; the University of Vermont; the Vermont Historical Society; John K. Wright, Lyme, New Hampshire; and Yale University.

For their courteous and painstaking assistance, I am deeply indebted to the library staffs and archivists of the institutions listed above, as well as of the following: Allegheny College; the American Geographical Society; the Boston Athenaeum; Columbia University; Cornell University; the Elm Tree Press, Woodstock, Vermont; the Free Press Association, Burlington, Vermont; the Asa Gray Herbarium, Harvard University; Harper & Brothers; the Historical Society of Princeton, New Jersey; Hobart College; the Oliver Wendell Holmes Library, Phillips Academy, Andover, Massachusetts; the Maryland Historical Society; the University of Maryland; the Missouri Historical Society; the State Historical Society of Missouri; the University of Missouri; the New York State Library; New York University; Northwestern University; the University of Pennsylvania; the Enoch Pratt Free Library, Baltimore; Princeton University; Charles Scribner's Sons, New York; Charles E. Tuttle Co., Rutland, Vermont; the U. S. Army Adjutant General's Office Records Administration Center; Vassar College; the Vermont State Archives; the Norman Williams Public Library, Woodstock, Vermont; the Wisconsin Historical Society; the University of Wisconsin; and the offices of the town clerks of Burlington and Woodstock, Vermont, and of the county clerks of Chittenden and Windsor counties, Vermont.

I am grateful to the American Geographical Society, which, by releasing me from other duties, has expedited completion of the book.

The patience, discernment, and sense of humor of Dorothy M. Swart have made the final editing of the manuscript a pleasure. To her, to Helene K. Marer for preparing the Index, and to many others at Columbia University Press I express my gratitude.

My wife, Jane Lowenthal, has helped throughout with typing, perceptive criticism, and countless constructive contributions to this book.

DAVID LOWENTHAL

American Geographical Society,
New York, September, 1958

Contents

CONTENTS

ILLUSTRATIONS

George Perkins Marsh

VERSATILE VERMONTER

❧ I ❧

Woodstock

*We have a tradition in our family that sometime in the past century,
one of our ancestors crept out of the ground in Lebanon, Connecticut,
and as soon as he got enough money together to run away with, came
up to Queechy Vermont, where we have remained ever since.*

MARSH AT MIDDLEBURY, VT., DEC. 2, 1859

GEORGE PERKINS MARSH was born on March 15, 1801, in
Woodstock, Vermont. It was a hard and bitter winter, this first of
the new century. Typhus raged in the village of Woodstock, along
the flats and swamps of the Quechee River, but the family of
Charles Marsh, Esquire, Woodstock's leading lawyer and United
States District Attorney for Vermont, fortunately escaped the
malady.

Comfortably isolated in his home across the river on the lower
slopes of Mt. Tom, Marsh could look down on the whole village
below. Here he brought up his large family, entertained visiting
dignitaries, and managed his estate, the choicest in the township.
He owned most of Mt. Tom, and his well-tilled fields and meadows
covered the whole of the rich intervale in the great bend of the
Quechee. The new turnpike from Royalton, in which Marsh held
a half interest, skirted the Marsh mansion and entered Woodstock
by a bridge over the Quechee built by Marsh in 1797. Across this
bridge to Elm Street, which he himself had planned and laid out,
Charles Marsh used to walk to his law office.

From the summit of Mt. Tom young George Marsh could survey
the entire cosmos of his early years. The main range of the Green
Mountains, far to the west, was dark with spruce and hemlock and
white pine. But thirty years of clearing and planting had converted
the lower, gentler hills surrounding Woodstock into a variegated
pattern of field and pasture, while pioneer profligacy and the need
for fuel had already destroyed much of the forest on the steeper
slopes. In the summer of 1800 a great fire accelerated the denuda-
tion of Mt. Tom; the summit as Marsh knew it was treeless and
windswept, affording a magnificent view of the village of Woodstock, more than five hundred feet below. Seven miles to the east
lay Hartford, the home of George's grandfather, Colonel Joseph
Marsh. A few miles further down, the Quechee joined the broad
Connecticut River, spanned not far upstream by a bridge linking
Norwich, Vermont, where young Marsh was to teach school, and
Hanover, New Hampshire, the site of his alma mater, Dartmouth.

I

*A Petulant, Pettefoging, Scribling sort of Gentry, that will keep any
Government in hot water till they are Thoroughly brought under by
the Exertions of Authority.*
                    ETHAN ALLEN, DESCRIBING THE MARSHES AND THEIR FRIENDS

Revolutionary Vermont usually calls to mind Ethan Allen and the
Green Mountain Boys, reckless, unschooled, ultrademocratic; but
the Marshes were emphatically not Vermonters of this type. Indeed,
for years they strove desperately not to be Vermonters at all. They
sought instead to set up a Puritan commonwealth of their own between the Green Mountains and the White Mountains, a Dart-
mouth-dominated New Connecticut. Their political utopia unreal-
ized, the aristocrats of eastern Vermont concentrated on inculcating
the young with all the proper virtues. So it was that in frontier
Vermont George Marsh was brought up to be a Calvinist, a conservative, and a gentleman.

For a long time the Green Mountains separated two different and hostile worlds. To the west, from Bennington and Rutland north through the fertile Champlain Valley, came men from the western Connecticut hill country. Many of them were religious dissenters, revivalists, or freethinkers, refugees from Congregational conformity; among the faithful, western Vermont was notorious as the abode of atheists, who chose to have "no Sabbath—no ministers —no religion—no heaven—no hell—no morality." [1]

East of the mountains, along the upper Connecticut River and its tributaries, settlers came from more conservative central and eastern Connecticut. Orthodox in religion and Federalist in politics, many of them were college graduates and men of wealth. The Marshes and other residents of the upper Connecticut Valley were infamous for their niggardliness and their "puritanical gravity, that shrewdness and Connecticut peddler's air, which enables them to drive a lucrative business in the humblest and most unpromising pursuits." On the other hand, they were reputed to be honest and "punctual to a fault." They lived well and comfortably; the roads in eastern Vermont were fine (in contrast to those west of the mountains), the fences in good repair, the houses neat and weatherproof. "Steadiness of character, softness of manners, a disposition to read, respect for the laws," noted Timothy Dwight approvingly, "are all exclusively predominant in this region." [2]

Such were the traits of George's grandfather Joseph Marsh, who —together with his mother, wife, nine children, three brothers, two cousins, and their families—emigrated from Lebanon, Connecticut, in the early summer of 1772. Hartford, their destination, was one of many townships along the Connecticut chartered by Governor Benning Wentworth of New Hampshire at the close of the French and Indian Wars a decade earlier. In these wars Joseph Marsh had served briefly as an officer. He became a town proprietor at least six years before emigrating to Hartford, so presumably poverty was not the reason he left Connecticut. Although he had little formal education, Marsh's military training, sizable family support, and powerful six-foot frame made him prominent in the frontier community. Hartford throve on trade in timber, potash, and wheat, and so did the Marsh family.

Over the years Joseph Marsh acquired wealth and influence. Colonel of county militia, representative to provincial conventions, unquestioned leader of eastern Vermont during the American Revolution, Marsh was elected first lieutenant governor of Vermont in 1778. But he distrusted the radical Green Mountain Boys, and his so-called "Dartmouth College party" tried every conceivable scheme to gain autonomy for the upper Connecticut Valley. In the end he failed. The towns east of the Connecticut—including Dartmouth—rejoined New Hampshire, and Marsh and his friends capitulated to Vermont in 1784. Although the radicals controlled the state, Marsh again became lieutenant governor, and later served for many years as chief justice of the Windsor County Court, where his remarkable memory, keen logical mind, and equable temper offset his lack of education. Meticulous in dress and manner, he remained a perfect Federalist gentleman to the last. "He was of the pure Washingtonian school," wrote a doting grandson, "and trained his children in it." [3]

2

Vermont (The Green Mounts) is as famous for her Marshes as her mounts.

REV. JOHN WHEELER TO J. H. GREEN, FEB. 16, 1843

Charles, eighth of Joseph Marsh's twelve children, was graduated from Dartmouth, attended Judge Tapping Reeve's law school at Litchfield, Connecticut, and began to practice law in Woodstock in 1789—the first lawyer there and the third in Windsor County. It is said that Charles Marsh reached Woodstock without a penny in his pocket beyond the purchase price of the first fifty acres of land he bought; but with his undoubted talents—and an influential father who was head of the county court—professional success and prestige came rapidly.

Marsh's increasing properties soon had to support a growing family. In 1790 he and his wife, Nancy Collins, moved out of the Eagle Hotel into the big frame house Samuel Winslow had built for them at the foot of Mt. Tom. Here Nancy Marsh gave birth to Charles, Jr., in 1790, and Ann Collins in 1793, the mother dying in childbirth. Five years later Charles married Susan Perkins Arnold, also recently widowed, who brought with her a two-year-old daughter. Charles and Susan had five more children: Lyndon Arnold, 1799; George Perkins, 1801; Joseph, 1807; Sarah Burrill, 1809; and— the eldest son having died—Charles, 1821.

As an educated man and a trained advocate, Charles Marsh was at first an anomaly in the Vermont bar. Charles's young cousin Jeremiah Mason found the courts "badly organized and usually filled with incompetent men. Most of the members of the bar were poorly educated, and some of vulgar manners and indifferent morals." Legal training scarcely mattered. "I certainly knew very little law," Mason recalled, "but that was the less necessary as my opponents knew not much more, and the judges I addressed none at all." Still worse, "a large portion of the inhabitants were new settlers and poor, and of course not desirable clients." Mason departed to hang out his shingle in New Hampshire, where lawyers were gentlemen, judges were scholars, and clients were wealthy.[4]

Charles Marsh was made of sterner stuff—or perhaps he agreed with his colleague Royall Tyler, who considered Vermont "a good place for lawyers" just because "all the rogues and runaways congregated" there. Woodstock became the county seat in 1790, and Marsh superintended the building of the new courthouse. For a whole decade he monopolized the legal business of Woodstock, and for many years he led the Windsor County bar. Severity and quick temper made him widely feared in court. But he generally spoke in a dry, restrained manner, his low-pitched voice forcing everyone to pay the closest attention. Brief and pungent, he was notorious for his ability to limn the repulsive and detestable. He also browbeat juries. He won one case by agreeing with the prosecutor that his clients were "poor and mean, wicked and criminal," and that they ought to be hung. But the jury should attend only to the evidence. If they were swayed in the slightest by his clients' reputation, Marsh warned them, "you will as richly deserve the state prison as they deserve the gallows." [5]

During the War of 1812, when the Federalists temporarily controlled Vermont, Charles Marsh was twice elected to public office. He made himself highly unpopular each time. In the Vermont Council of Censors, a body which met once every seven years to suggest revisions of the state constitution, Marsh advocated a Senate elected by the propertied class to counterbalance the "hasty, inconsiderate, violent rabble" in the Assembly. In the United States Congress Marsh also behaved like a proper Federalist, and took a grim pleasure in supporting unpopular measures. He not only favored a raise in Congressional pay—similar demands proved disastrous to the political fortunes of many of his colleagues—he had the temerity to ask for ten dollars a day! [6]

Charles Marsh never gained renown in public life. Better educated and more brilliant than his father, he did not make the most of his talents, perhaps because he was the son of a famous and popular man. Echoing his father's political and social views, he lacked the disposition and the desire to make them palatable to others. Seldom a seeker after office, he generally rejected it when it came his way. [7] He had a gift for self-deprecation—which his son George inherited; but he applied it only to his relations with God. To most mortals he saw himself unquestionably superior. He felt that he never lied or acted unjustly; nor did he permit anyone else to do so without mercilessly pillorying him. His portrait shows a man one would not care to meet in an argument: a spare, wiry, six-footer with a strongly lined, lean, handsome face, thin lips, and derisive smile.

Reared in a harsh religious tradition, Charles Marsh remained a strict Calvinist throughout his life. He helped found the Congregational Society of Woodstock, and donated the land for the Meeting House. A pioneer officer of the American Bible Society, the American Board of Foreign Missions, the American Education Society, the American Colonization Society, and the American Society for the Promotion of Temperance, Marsh never wearied of supporting these good works. Yet he was besieged by doubt and despair. "My faith (if any I have) is so weak," he confessed, "my hope so faint, that . . . I am dumb before my Judge. . . . 'How shall I answer Him for one of ten thousand of my transgressions?'"[8] The main prop of Marsh's piety was not faith but his concept of divine justice, and he taught his children to fear God as a stern and righteous Judge.

Charles Marsh was gentler at home than in the courtroom, but a tyrant none the less. George's father was as quick to condemn stupidity as to denounce any lapse from obedience or moral rectitude; a young Marsh had to know as much as possible about everything. This was a lesson George learned early in life. Making the daily rounds with his father, he "never forgot the stern rebukes administered to the laborers when their work was found to be ignorantly or carelessly done."[9] Those who learned slowly, or who made careless mistakes, took a back place in the family circle; George was impelled by more than mere curiosity to devour the encyclopedia at the age of five. His family considered him a paragon because he knew almost everything from ethics to needlework. At the age when most children begin to learn the alphabet, George Marsh was well on the way to becoming a pedant. The results of this rigorous childhood training were lasting. Marsh always prided himself on his encyclopedic knowledge; versatility was a striking characteristic of this learned man, whose productive scholarship encompassed so many fields. His passion for information of all sorts continued to appear in the recondite bits of learning which Marsh was fond of interjecting into conversations and into his letters and writings, sometimes by way of illustration, often as an exercise in virtuosity. Marsh never quite got rid of the notion that facts are virtues in themselves, and that the knowledge of a great many of them is conducive to happiness. For in the home of Charles Marsh, such was indeed the case.

3

Other communities . . . may glory in the exploits of their fathers; but it has been reserved to us of New-England to know and to boast that Providence has made the virtues of our mothers a yet more indispensable condition . . . both of our past prosperity and our future hope. MARSH, *Address Delivered before the New England Society of the City of New-York,* DEC. 24, 1844

Unlike his father, George's mother was brought up in an atmosphere of pleasant, even quixotic, sentiment. Susan Perkins was born in Plainfield, Connecticut, in 1776, one of the nine children of Dr. Elisha ("Terrible Tractor") Perkins, a noted and prosperous physician. Convinced that electric currents could relieve rheumatic and other pain, Perkins invented, about 1790, his famous metallic tractors, tadpole-shaped pieces of brass wire and steel, with which he stroked pain out of the afflicted part of the body.

Dr. Perkins was a practical humanitarian. He sold his tractors (cost, one shilling) for five pounds each; and millions bought them. The Connecticut Medical Society denounced his "bare-faced impositions" upon the public and expelled him as a user of nostrums. Perkins had apparently deceived himself as well as others, for he conceived a similar remedy for yellow fever, went to New York in 1799 to test it—and died there of the disease.[10]

Some years before her father's martyrdom to medical science, black-haired, black-eyed young Susan Perkins, the belle of the family, rejected handsome, haughty Charles Marsh in favor of the romantic lyricist and lawyer Josias Lyndon Arnold (son of Dr. Jonathan Arnold, of Rhode Island), who had migrated to St.

Johnsbury, Vermont. At the time of her marriage in 1795 Susan was "a splendid woman" of nineteen. "Her beauty was of the queenly type," a contemporary later reminisced, "Juno and Venus in one." Susan was well equipped to cope with frontier hardships in the northern wilderness, but within a year her husband fell ill and died.[11] Susan left St. Johnsbury, Charles Marsh soon renewed his wooing, and this time she accepted him.

No account remains of Susan Perkins Arnold Marsh's long and useful life after her second marriage, or of what manner of mother she was; George himself rarely wrote about her. Mental and moral training she left to Charles, contenting herself with the roles of housewife and comforter. Sympathy, sensitivity, common sense: these are the qualities that stand out in her relationships with husband and children alike.

4

Woodstock—an elegant little place.
      c. w. ELDRIDGE, *Journal of a Tour through Vermont* (1833)

The Woodstock of Marsh's boyhood was an attractive village. In 1800 it numbered only forty or fifty frame houses and two hundred and fifty inhabitants—but there were more than two thousand people in the township, at that time the fourth most populous in the state. Scores of small farms were scattered over the neighboring hillsides; the migration that later swelled the villages and the fertile lowlands and left the hills deserted had hardly begun. Woodstock at the turn of the century was chiefly a center for local trade, where farmers could ship their wheat and other produce to the Connecticut River and points south and east, buy store goods, and pick up the news of the day.

Crossing his father's bridge to tree-shaded, and muddy, Elm Street, young George would first pass the small schoolhouse; just beyond was his father's law office, then Charles Dana's dry goods store,

John Carleton's brick shop and saddlery, and Amos Cutler's shoe-
store. The village fanned out northeastward beyond the rickety
county jail, along the Quechee, and southward past the Green.
Originally a "savage-looking spot," the Green had been cleared
of its heavy growth of spruce and white pine and was now a rough,
treeless eyesore. Around it stood the principal buildings of the
village: the splendid new courthouse on the riverside, Benjamin
Swan's pearlash factory at the upper end, and across the road the
shop and home of young Isaiah Carpenter, *bon vivant* and bass
violist, who operated a printing press and published the *Northern
Memento,* Woodstock's first weekly paper.[12]

Directly opposite the courthouse was the two-story Eagle Hotel,
large enough to lodge half the state legislature when it convened in
Woodstock in 1807. It served as the rendezvous for farmers, merchants, and the courthouse crowd. All imbibed quantities of Woodstock's famous cider brandy, gin sling, maple rum, potato
whisky, and countless varieties of punch, toddy, and eggnog,
supplemented with free salt cod and gingerbread. In Vermont at
the turn of the century distilling was a major industry, and liquor
flowed freely. Other types of license flourished too; Woodstock
was infamous as a place "where the greatest indecorum between the
sexes, is habitually practiced and countenanced. "-[13] It is safe to say,
however, that George's morals were not sullied by any association
with the young bloods at the Eagle Hotel, or with those who congregated late at night in Samuel Chandler's countinghouse. Not
only did the Marshes keep the Sabbath strictly, they sought to preserve the Sabbath atmosphere throughout the week. And the young
lawyers whom George met at his father's house and office bore little
resemblance to the unlettered fellows Jeremiah Mason had complained of; most of them were college graduates, well versed in
English literature, their courtroom style modeled after the prose of
Addison, Swift, Steele, and Johnson.

George had no lack of companions; there were children everywhere. His elder brother Lyndon was an inseparable playmate.
Hiram Powers, the future sculptor, grandson of Dr. Thomas Powers,

often played with the Marsh boys, and George Marsh and Hiram
Powers remained lifelong friends. Young Danas, Swans, and
Churchills were numerous, while a score of cousins lived near by at
Quechee.

The Marshes often visited their close friends, the Paines, at
Williamstown. Elijah Paine was one of the most remarkable men
of his time. United States Representative and Senator, then forty
years a Federal judge, Paine built a turnpike across the Green
Mountains, promoted the introduction of Merino sheep into Vermont, and saw wool become Vermont's major industry. His full
and careful daily weather records provided vital material for Zadock Thompson's pioneer *Natural History of Vermont*. Scientist,
statesman, farmer, Paine served George Marsh as a model in his
own career. Of Paine's four children, Caroline was just George's
age and his particular favorite. Charles Paine, two years older, was
later a governor of Vermont and involved Marsh in railroad speculation.

George and Lyndon and their young friends roamed far and wide
around Woodstock, stretching willows for whistles, reconnoitering
the vacant rooms of the new Marsh mansion, "climbing high rocks,
ascending Mt. Tom, losing ourselves in the woods or strolling
through the meadow, never forgetting the orchard from the first
formation of apples till the ripe fruit was ready for gathering."
George explored the Quaking Pogue, a fear-inspiring bog of unknown depth on the far side of Mt. Tom; he learned marksmanship
from Revolutionary War veterans, went fishing in the Quechee,
watched wrestling matches, barn-raisings, and sheepshearings, and
horse racing on the smooth, straight river road below his father's
house. Other festive occasions were the regimental musters after the
fall harvest. Ripe fruit, cider, gingerbread, cakes, and pies filled
booths along the roads and on the parade ground in the meadow
opposite the Marsh place, while the militia marched out from the
Common.[14] During the War of 1812 zealous patriots paraded with
snare drums and fife; but the Charles Marsh family, good Federalists and lovers of peace, held aloof from such foolishness.

5

Most rubato *of Vermont rivers.*

Vermont, AMERICAN GUIDE SERIES, 1937

The river itself was always the focal point. Like its sister tributaries to the Connecticut, the Quechee is nowhere navigable, but
it was full and swift enough in George Marsh's boyhood to provide
water for a score of mills. The river was the font of farming as
well as of factories. The light-brown, fine, sandy loam of the fluvial
terraces, on one of which lay the Marsh farm, is the most productive
and easily worked soil in eastern Vermont.

Rising high on the eastern slopes of the Green Mountains, the
Quechee alternately dashes over rapids and meanders along fertile
intervales, here roaring through a deeply incised gorge, there moving
placidly past alder-covered banks. Icebound during winter, the
river opens up again in April and overflows the wet meadows
beyond its banks. In summer the river shrinks to a mere trickle;
until the fall rains set in, the mills formerly shut down for lack of
power to turn their wheels.

Turbulent even before white men came to the valley, by George
Marsh's youth the Quechee had already become more erratic.
When farmers cleared their fields and cut spruce, white pine, and
hardwoods for timber, fuel, and potash, the denuded hillsides failed
to absorb rain and snow. Instead of percolating through the soil,
water rushed unchecked into the stream; the snows melted pre-
cipitously in the spring thaws; floods came more frequently. And
in summer the river sometimes dried up entirely. Even as a youngster Marsh took note of these changes and was aware they were
man-made.

Freshets often destroyed dams and mills. Charles Marsh's bridge
across the Quechee had to be rebuilt three times in a decade, and
it shook so severely when the coach from Royalton passed over it
that passengers breathed sighs of relief when they reached the

safety of the Eagle Hotel. The most disastrous flood in Marsh's boyhood, in July, 1811, breached the bank and destroyed his father's high stone wall and the sawmill above it. Despite such vicissitudes, Woodstock's mills were numerous and flourishing. In addition to Jabez Bennett's sawmill and gristmill in the center of the village, Woodstock boasted a flaxseed oil mill, carding machines, a fulling mill, clothier's works and a dyehouse, and a gin distillery and malt-house; while in West Woodstock Moses Bradley manufactured cream pots, pitchers, and milk pans.

Woodstock's surplus grain, ash, timber, and maple sugar were carted over the plank turnpike to Windsor or on the common road to White River Junction, thence across the Connecticut and down one of the New Hampshire turnpikes to Hartford or Boston. The Connecticut River offered another way out, after canals had been built around Quechee Falls at Hartland and Olcott's Falls south of Hanover. By 1810, huge log rafts and flatboats fitted with main-sail and topsail navigated all the way from Wells River, Vermont, to Hartford. The riverbank scene was enlivened at landings and canal sites by flatboat crews and by the exchange of goods. Tea, coffee, salt, condiments, molasses, rum, and household furnishings found their way into rural Vermont and New Hampshire in payment for farm produce, wool fleece and cloth, timber, potash and pearlash, ginseng, maple sugar and syrup, and copperas.[15]

As a farmer, Charles Marsh was vitally concerned with all this. Although he left most of the farm work and road and bridge building to hired help, the smallest agricultural details interested him keenly. So did cooking and eating. George's account makes it plain that there was more to home life than the cold comforts of Calvinism and litigation:

That I am addicted to the pleasures of the table I utterly deny, but I confess I am a little critical in roast ham & pork & beans. This however is but a proof of my filial affection. I have to thank my parents both for my taste & my knowledge. . . . My mother . . . considered within her-self the nature & capabilities of pork, & the exigencies of the human

palate, and she created, evolved out of the depths of her own consciousness, the splendid result—roast ham. . . . Well, of course my father could
not be otherwise than a lover of baked pork & beans. What good man is?
Some there may be who never tasted them, having been cursed with a
birth out of N[ew] E[ngland]. Others there can be none. . . . But as all
wise men know, there are varieties of beans, some good, many indifferent,
more bad. My father emigrated from Connecticut. His first crop (all the
seed he carried from C) was cut off by a late frost. He tried the neigh-
bours, sent hither & thither, bought Shaker seed beans, but all to no
purpose. A baking bean he couldn't get. . . . In this extremity what
did he do? Did he turn Jew, or Mohammedan, & forswear pork? Did he
profess himself a Pythagorean & renounce beans? Not a bit of it. He
just sat down & invented a new bean for himself. . . . My father's bean—
it is a bush bean, of course; everybody knows that—is a small white bean,
of regular shape & proportions, nearly cylindrical, with hemispherical
ends, skin as thin as Mrs. ——'s cuticle, & flesh when baked as soft as
her hand. No damned crust, no globular segregation into indigestible
pellets, but a carnation to the eye, homogeneous to the touch, ambrosial
to the palate.[16]

6

*I know no more important practical lessons . . . than those relating
to . . . the study of nature.*

MARSH, *Man and Nature* (1864)

Not until he was about ten did George pay much attention to
the world of nature. Timid and gentle, he preferred to play indoors
with girls, and most of all to be alone and read. He was a strange-
looking child, with a large, preternaturally adult head, and an
habitually serious, even sad, expression. George's young friends may
not have been particularly delighted with so pensive a companion,
but in the family circle his precocity aroused admiration and his
exemplary conduct exempted him from criticism. At the age of five
or six he began to study Latin and Greek, tutored by his brother
Charles; George Marsh later asserted that he owed much to this
brother, "who excited my curiosity about books, when I was not
much more than an infant, and who kindled my love of knowledge

to a passion." [17] This passion remained with Marsh throughout life.

George's mother occasionally tried to pry him loose from his books, but the boy continued to read everything he could get hold of. His particular favorites were the large volumes of Reese's *Encyclopaedia,* which were so heavy he could barely lift them. Thanks to the pithy articles in the encyclopedia, George was able to astound his father with the scope and quantity of material he had absorbed. The praise he received encouraged Marsh to feel intellectually superior; this perhaps explains the rather haughty tone of much of his later work.

In the end, the encyclopedia was young George's undoing; days of leaning on the floor, poring over the pages in poor light, injured his sight so severely that at the age of seven or eight he almost went blind. For the next four years he could not read at all, and for months the slightest amount of light caused him intense pain.

Marsh gained something, however, from this terrible experience. Unable to read, he learned to depend on direct observation, to rely upon other people. And he acquired a love of nature which never failed to sustain and reward him. When he left his darkened room Marsh's vision was at first so blurred that he could scarcely make out familiar landmarks; but as his sight improved, the boy went exploring among the trees, flowers, animals, and birds in the hills and fields with the same zeal and thoroughness he had shown in his wanderings through Reese's *Encyclopaedia.*

Marsh was fortunate that his affliction came at an age when his experience of nature could be direct, intimate, naïve, and vivid. He grew up a practical-minded Yankee who prided himself on his devotion to utility and reason, but he was also a romantic. He was attracted by Thoreau and by the eccentric Transcendental poet Jones Very, whose lyrics reawakened "the sense of the delight of life in close contact with nature"; the sonnet "Nature" carried Marsh back to his childhood in Woodstock: "The bubbling brook doth leap when I come by/ Because my feet find measure with its call." Marsh was "forest-born," he asserted in his old age; "the bubbling brook, the trees, the flowers, the wild animals were to me persons, not things." At the end of his life he recalled that as a lonely boy he had "sympathized with those *beings,* as I have never done since with the *general* society of men, too many of whom would find it hard to make out as good a claim to *personality* as a respectable oak can establish." Marsh could not understand why others did not share his intense pleasure in nature; he considered his friend Rufus Choate's "want of sympathy with trees and shrubs and rivers and rocks and mountains and plains" a distinct character defect.[18]

Young Marsh would have been false to his father's training had he neglected to take a scientific interest in nature. He later recalled jolting along ridge-top roads in a two-wheeled chaise. "To my mind the whole earth lay spread out before me. My father pointed out the most striking trees as we passed them, and told me how to distinguish their varieties. I do not think I ever afterward failed to know one forest-tree from another." His education in physical geography began when his father "called my attention to the general configuration of the surface; pointed out the direction of the different ranges of hills; told me how the water gathered on them and ran down their sides. . . . He stopped his horse on the top of a steep hill, bade me notice how the water there flowed in different directions, and told me that such a point was called a *watershed.*" [19] Marsh never forgot the form of the land, or the forces that shaped it.

7

Very much narrowness of mind and very great soundness of faith do sometimes go together.

RUFUS CHOATE TO JAMES MARSH, NOV. 14, 1829

George's early formal schooling was sporadic and inconsequential. Latin and Greek with his brother, geography and morality with his father, and his own encyclopedic reading were far more important than the little he learned from intermittent attendance at the rickety, unpainted, two-room common school on Elm Street. George missed a lot of school, for even after he regained his sight his eyes remained weak and his hearing poor, and he was often ill or too frail to go out. At other times, sickness shut down the school altogether; in some winters contagion was so prevalent that it never opened. In 1811, for example, Woodstock suffered an epidemic of "spotted fever" (cerebrospinal meningitis), and George was sent to school in Royalton, ten miles north.

Marsh's religious instruction, though stern, was as trivial as his formal secular education. The Congregational meeting houses were little more than temporary bases for itinerant ministers until in 1810 Charles Marsh persuaded the Rev. Walter Chapin, a young Middlebury College graduate, to fill the Woodstock pastorate. The amiable Chapin told his congregation that the forms of religion were as important as the spirit, and gave them a lot more of the former than of the latter. Rigid adherence to doctrine was essential, for, as Chapin was fond of saying, "morality without religious principle was but the 'ghost of departed virtue.'"[20] Chapin was also a missionary, but his success among the heathen required frequent jaunts all over New England, and interfered with his work in Woodstock. This mediocrity could not have had much effect on George Marsh; perhaps Chapin's sermons inured him against the persuasions of more accomplished ministers in the religious revivals at which so many of his Andover and Dartmouth fellow students succumbed to prosyletization. Marsh never made the confession of faith necessary for a full communicant in the Congregational Church; but there were, of course, more serious reasons for his doubts than the roving Rev. Chapin can be held responsible for.

In his twelfth year his parents thought of sending George to North Yarmouth, Maine, as a pupil in the home of the Rev. Francis Brown, later president of Dartmouth College. "Master George is very impatient for the time I shall send him to your care," wrote Charles Marsh. He added that "the poor boy . . . reads more hours every day, besides going to a common school, than anyone in the family." [21] George's health did not permit, and the plan came to nothing.

Charles Marsh was determined, however, to train his son in the conservative orthodox tradition, so in 1816 George went to Phillips Academy at Andover, Massachusetts. He boarded in town with three future ministers and two more who did not live to finish their schooling. Along with ninety other students Marsh endured the prison-like existence which passed for education in New England schools of the time. The curriculum consisted principally of training in Latin and Greek, which George already knew, and religion and morals, in which he was not too delinquent. In addition to their daily prayers, the boys recited on Saturday a ten-page lesson from Mason's *Self-Knowledge,* spent all day Sunday at church and Bible classes in the dilapidated, unheated South Parish Meeting House, and on Monday abstracted Sunday's sermons.

The headmaster was the stern and efficient John Adams, who was chiefly noted as a disciplinarian. "He was very religious, but had no literary tastes . . . an excellent man with no distinguishing traits"; so was he characterized by the cultivated Josiah Quincy, who suffered Adams's rule a few years before Marsh did. Adams thought it more essential to secure a boy's religious faith than to instill zeal for knowledge. In almost every class there was a revival, and Adams's dramatic techniques converted scores of youths. "There will be a prayer-meeting," he would thunder out as the regular services ended; "those who wish to lie down in everlasting burning may go; the rest may stay." George spent only a few months at Andover, but got a full dose of the Adams treatment. It immunized him against religious authoritarianism for life. "The sons of schismatics," he later wrote, "let us not dishonor our parentage by anathematizing schism among ourselves." [22] Obedience without reason brought only conformity without conviction.

8

It is, sir . . . a small college, and yet there are those who love it.
DANIEL WEBSTER BEFORE THE SUPREME COURT (1818)

It was foreordained that George Marsh should go to Dartmouth. Brother Charles had attended; brother Lyndon had entered the year before; cousin James was a senior. That a Marsh should desert Dartmouth in her darkest hour was not to be thought of. A year before he entered, the board of trustees had deposed President John Wheelock, son of the founder, and offered Francis Brown the presidency of the college. "Should you disappoint us," wrote Charles Marsh for the board, "we shall be thrown into a state of absolute despair, and the College, I believe, must sink . . . into a seminary of Socinianism." Meanwhile, former President Wheelock charged Marsh and his fellow "aristocratic" trustees with bigotry and persecution, and persuaded the dominant New Hampshire Democrats to amend Dartmouth's charter. Charles Marsh, Daniel Webster, and the other trustees refused to give way to "mob tyranny," and when George Marsh arrived at Hanover in the fall of 1816 he found the College quarreling with a new state university on the same campus.[23]

Before Marsh was graduated, the United States Supreme Court had vindicated Dartmouth College; but the students derived small advantage from the decision, for the curriculum remained as narrow and humdrum as it had been at the start of the controversy. Dartmouth studies were hardly more than a continuation of those at Andover, and George Marsh got little pleasure or profit from them. What he learned of value he picked up independently. He seldom referred to his college days later in life, except to blame himself for having wasted time.

At fifteen, George Marsh was younger than most of his thirty-three classmates; several were past twenty, and the average age was eighteen. Diffident, shy, studious to excess, Marsh had no close friends except his cousin James Marsh, a senior, and Rufus Choate, who was a sophomore; they were his only intellectual equals. Far ahead of his class from the start, he was interested neither in sports nor in most social affairs, and had little to do with his schoolfellows. They, in turn, found him aloof. They admired his scholarship and appreciated his dry, quiet humor, but did not warm to this solemn, bespectacled young man who "was indifferent to all external objects, save some book, and then he placed the book very near his eyes." [24]

Few of Marsh's fellow students shared Daniel Webster's love for Dartmouth. Undergraduates complained then, as they have ever since, of the absence of social attractions in Hanover. It was a small town; some sixty white houses stood around the Green, with three-storied Dartmouth Hall on one side of the square. Marsh lodged in the village his first three years, and during his senior year in Dartmouth Hall. Tuition amounted to $21 a year, and there were incidental expenses: $2 a year library tax, 25¢ for a copy of the laws, fines for minor infractions of rules—amounting to 60¢ in Marsh's case. All told, he paid only $117.22 for the four-year course, a sum his father could easily spare, with pocket money besides; Marsh was known as one of the "richer" students.[25]

For most of his classmates, going to college was a much more formidable experience, both financially and scholastically. Frugality and plain dress were the rule; most students had to eke out their allowances by teaching school. Nor was there an aristocracy of learning. Some boys entered Dartmouth by way of preparatory schools, but most had spent their formative years on New Hampshire and Vermont farms. In contrast to men from Harvard and Yale, Dartmouth graduates were reputed to be rough-and-ready fellows of little learning and culture. This reputation was on the whole well-merited; discipline was extremely strict, but scholastic requirements were low. No matter how lazy or incompetent a student might be, if he could pay his bills and keep out of trouble he almost always got his degree.

Students assembled in the chapel daily at five in the morning, or "as early as the President could see to read the Bible," for neither light nor heat was provided. This may well have contributed to President Francis Brown's premature demise. After chapel, students dispersed to recitations, each of the four years in a separate room. Breakfast followed this class, then a period of study—or slumber— then a second recitation; after dinner, study again, and an afternoon class at three or four. Evening prayers were at six, "or as late as the President was able to see." Sunday was a day of enforced rest; students went to morning and evening chapel, twice to church, and except for meals were otherwise forbidden to leave their rooms.[26]

In their few hours of recreation students swam in the Connecticut River and played football on the Green; in the winter there was ice skating. Gambling was not allowed, but even Marsh sometimes took a hand at whist. Marsh's indulgence in this frivolity, like Timothy Dwight's, taught him a lesson; when asked fifty years later to join a game, he replied: "No, I believe not. I did too much of that in my college days, and I have never taken a card in my hand since." Timothy Dwight bemoaned his own card-playing as a lapse from moral rectitude; Marsh merely regretted the waste of time.[27] There were few pleasant ways to waste time at Dartmouth. Two literary societies, the United Fraternity and the Social Friends, maintained libraries and engaged in debates; membership in one or the other was mandatory, and Marsh was assigned to the Social Friends at the beginning of his sophomore year. Phi Beta Kappa, to which Marsh of course belonged, a theological group, to which he did not, and a sporadic Handel and Haydn Society were the only other organized student activities.

The college year began in September and did not close until August; the long vacation came in midwinter. Commencement Day was the big holiday of the year; parades, fireworks, and refreshment booths and sideshows around the Green gave the college the aspect of a county fair. The trustees held their annual meeting, some celebrity gave an address, and everyone endured hours of pompous student oratory.

For the fatuity of the students' thinking and the insipidity of their style, the narrow, rigid curriculum of the college was largely to blame. All courses were compulsory. The first three years were mainly devoted to Greek and Latin and mathematics; in the senior year a liberal dose of metaphysics, theology, and political law was administered out of Edwards, Locke, Dugald Stewart, and Paley. Of natural science there was virtually none; like most New England colleges, Dartmouth still held such studies subversive of religion, morality, and good government. Not until 1836 were chemistry, mineralogy, and geology added to the curriculum. The little astronomy that Dartmouth thought safe to impart in Marsh's student days was taught by Ebenezer Adams, a stubborn, lusty-voiced ignoramus who relied mainly on what Marsh told him; indeed, Marsh was "not corrected," according to a classmate, "for any mistake or fault" during his entire college career.[28]

The natural history in Paley's *Natural Theology* and *Evidences of Christianity,* which Marsh read in his junior and senior years, was designed to buttress Biblical history and Protestant dogma. One of Paley's major doctrines was geological catastrophism, the theory that the earth had actually undergone all the violent revolutions delineated in the Bible. Another Paley premise was that only a purposeful Creator could have made the wonderful forms of nature; a third was that God created everything in nature for man. Like most students, Marsh at first believed all this as a matter of course, but in time he discarded much of it.

The only Marsh composition surviving from his college days is a manuscript entitled "Zoology: Linnaeus's system," a detailed, forty-six-page classification of the vertebrates. The pages are long, the handwriting small and cramped, the list of animals unending, and we sympathize with young Marsh when halfway through his list of birds he writes "Ordinis Picarum finis Huzza!! Huzza!! Huzza!!"

College training in languages was little better than that in science. In Greek and Latin, Marsh went far beyond the curriculum. He joined Choate and James Marsh in a club for extra study of the classics, and "when he left college," reported a classmate, "he read the Greek poets and historians with as much ease as an ordinary man would read a newspaper." Not all the work at Dartmouth was routine and second-rate. "President Brown hears us in Horace," wrote Rufus Choate, "and it is our own fault if we do not make progress." [29] But there were no courses in modern languages, and Marsh acquired the Romance tongues entirely by himself, studying Spanish and Portuguese as well as French and Italian.

Pedagogy as well as subject matter left much to be desired. There was little actual instruction; recitations were held to test how much the students—called on in alphabetical order—had managed to memorize. But if the teaching was inferior and the classes were dull, the three-man faculty—Brown, Adams, and the pious Roswell Shurtleff, who taught theology, moral philosophy, political economy, and mathematics—were not wholly to blame; never well paid, they were now receiving no salary at all, their library was taken from them, they had to teach in hastily improvised, inadequate classrooms, and should the trustees lose to New Hampshire they would have no jobs.

The situation of the college was indeed "critical in the extreme." During the midwinter vacation in Marsh's freshman year the students were dispossessed; the rival state university preempted all the college buildings. Undaunted, President Brown summoned the scholars to meet at dawn in the Rowley Assembly Rooms above Stewart's hat shop. "It was a pleasing tho solemn sight," reported the *Dartmouth Gazette*, "to see the students, who before had been accustomed at the return of a season of study to flock to the chapel at the welcome sound of the bell, now punctually flocking to this retreat of persecuted innocence." [30]

Meanwhile, the faculty and trustees were having a desperate time. In November, 1817, the New Hampshire Supreme Court decided against the trustees, and Charles Marsh made plans to transfer George and the other students to Middlebury if the appeal failed. Not until February, 1819, did Chief Justice Marshall read his historic decision prohibiting interference by New Hampshire: "The college is a private . . . institution, unconnected with the government . . . the charter of such an institution is plainly a contract"; such contracts were inviolable.[31] The rival university disbanded, and delighted Hanoverians celebrated by firing off cannon.

So intimately involved, Marsh always thought the Dartmouth College case "vitally important to the cause of education." He felt that the controversy had "excited a sympathy between the two vocations before thought antagonistic—the academic and the forensic,—which was not without favorable results to both of them." Years later, however, when corporations claimed immunity from legislative interference on the basis of Marshall's decision, neither filial nor collegiate loyalty prevented Marsh from condemning this interpretation of the sanctity of contracts as "an old legal superstition." [32]

Marsh's senior year was relatively uneventful. With the excitement of the case past, student morale declined and disciplinary problems arose. Marsh's classmates were repeatedly fined for being absent and for not doing their work; the situation became so serious that in May, 1820, Rufus Choate, now secretary of the faculty, warned that "if any member of the Senior class hereafter . . . habitually neglect any of the exercises of the college he [shall] be refused examination with his class." [33] But they all managed to squeak through to the Commencement exercises on August 20.

As the band played, students paraded to the meeting house under the direction of Colonel Amos Brewster, Grafton County high sheriff, whose stentorian voice, pompous swagger, cocked hat, sword, gold lace, and sash were indispensable accouterments of the annual festival. Then the audience settled down to an orgy of speeches, which began with an oration on "The Decline of Eloquence," proceeded solemnly through disquisitions on the moral and religious character of the first settlers of New England, the expulsion of the Moors from Granada (poem), and the influence of moral and religious sentiments upon genius and the fine arts. It ended, hours later, with Marsh's English oration and valedictory address: "The Characteristick Traits of Modern Genius, as Exemplified in the Literature of the North and of the South of Europe." [34] Marsh's style was considered plain, direct, and unornamented in comparison with his classmates', but posterity will not miss his Commencement address.

9

I hate boys, hate tuition, hate forms.

MARSH TO SPENCER BAIRD, 1859

Two short weeks after graduation Marsh returned to Norwich, Vermont, across the Connecticut River from Hanover, to begin his first job, as a teacher. The salary was poor, but the title splendid for a young man of nineteen: George Perkins Marsh, A.B., Professor of the Greek and Latin Languages at the American Literary, Scientific, and Military Academy.

Norwich Academy, as it was generally called, was new and emphatically experimental. It was modeled after the eccentric ideas of its founder, Captain Alden Partridge, ebullient former superintendent of the U.S. Military Academy, who believed that all men of "cultivation" needed a military education. Citizens with "a systematic knowledge of fortifications and tactics" would be better equipped to understand history, "a large portion of which is made up of descriptions of battles and sieges." Another argument wooed Calvinist morality: military training, Partridge assured parents, would prevent their sons from falling into evil habits by eliminating their leisure time; at Norwich, drill and exercise occupied "those hours of the day which are generally passed by students in idleness, or devoted to useless amusements." [35]

During the time which might otherwise have been misspent on vacations, Partridge arranged "excursions" for the cadets, marches all over northern New England. The captain was an experienced surveyor, and during summer trips with the cadets he took altitudes of many of the Green Mountain peaks. Marsh went along in the summer of 1821, learned how to use a barometer, and became more familiar with local land forms.[36]

If the summer jaunt in the Green Mountains appealed to Marsh, nothing else about the Academy did. The brick barracks, surrounded by a high fence and guardhouses, seemed depressingly gloomy; the blue-coated, high-collared cadets, depressingly stupid; and Marsh lacked the patience and perhaps the skill necessary to pound the ancient languages into their heads. Never a man to suffer fools gladly, from early childhood Marsh preferred educating himself, not others. Later in life he became less self-centered and misanthropic, and gave generous help to a number of bright young protégés, but a teaching career never appealed to him. Disgusted by his classes at Norwich, bored with the society of the pompous Partridge and his family, he spent most of his leisure time in the Dartmouth library, reading German and Scandinavian until late at night. Owing to this regime, Marsh's eyesight and the school year came to an end at the same time; he gave up his job and left in search of a good oculist.

Marsh's eye trouble was the same he had suffered earlier, but he could find no cure for it, and in the next few years was able to read very little. He spent futile winters in New York, Philadelphia, and Providence, visiting physicians who blistered and cupped him but failed to improve his vision. Marsh returned to Woodstock weak and thin, depressed and discouraged. At home he prepared for the law by being read to and by listening to cases in court.

Marsh's horizon at this time was almost entirely bounded by family life. During the worst months, when he was in constant pain and scarcely able to see, his mother or one of his cousins from Quechee cared for him. Meanwhile he relieved his misery by giving vent to mordant repartee and fearful puns. In better hours he talked law with his father and his elder brother Lyndon—also practicing in Woodstock—and played with the new baby, Charles. Unable to work at anything that mattered to him, he sought no friends, and spent solitary days roaming the countryside. Thanks to prolonged abstinence from the printed word, his eyes gradually improved; and Marsh afterward looked back on this period of his life, which at the time had seemed so barren and sad, as one of growth and maturation, a coming-of-age which developed his powers of observation and increased his capacity for reflection.

Four years passed quietly in this way, enlivened for Marsh by few contacts outside the village. He did undertake one small job— an investigation of deaf-mutes. Vermont had many of these unfortunates, and Marsh—owing to family connections with Governor C. P. Van Ness—was asked to see what the state could do for them. He inspected the new Connecticut state school for deaf-mutes in Hartford, visited institutions in New York City and Philadelphia, and corresponded with officials at Canajoharie, New York, and Danville, Kentucky. Marsh recommended to the legislature in 1824 that, rather than build an expensive asylum for the forty deaf-mutes of educable age in Vermont, the state should pay for those who wanted to go to asylums in other states. Vermont made arrangements with Connecticut, and two years later nineteen Green Mountain deaf-mutes went to Hartford.[37] Otherwise of no interest, Marsh's report was characteristically thorough, and showed the early development of what James Russell Lowell later complained of as his "Congregational" style.

Happier in making lofty generalizations than in studying petty legal details, Marsh nevertheless persevered in his preparations for the bar. A committee of three, including future Senator Jacob Collamer, examined and admitted him as an attorney of the Windsor County Court in the September term of 1825.[38] Shortly afterward Marsh set out for Burlington, on the other side of the state, where he was to make his home for the next thirty-five years.

❧ II ❧

Burlington

THE EIGHTEEN YEARS between Marsh's arrival in Burlington and his election to Congress in 1843 were full of grievous discouragements. After sampling at least a dozen professions, Marsh was no nearer a decision about what to do with himself than he had been at the beginning; indeed, not until a second eighteen years had gone by and he was a man of sixty was his course clear before him. Meanwhile, he vacillated between law and politics on the one hand and the life of a scholar on the other, always finding the former obnoxious, dull, or degrading, and the latter unremunerative. Business for its own sake never suited Marsh; he disliked dealing with people whose chief interest was making money. Forays into finance, manufacturing, railroad and land speculation, intended to eke out enough to give him leisure for study and other "useful" activities, invariably turned out disastrously, and forced him back into occupations he disliked. He felt that an evil genius pursued him everywhere; it is no wonder that he shifted his course so often. In law, a calling which he came to abhor, he suffered the untimely death of his first partner, and his second later enmeshed Marsh in calamity. In politics he made two false steps before finding his way; in business, wherever Marsh took a hand all went wrong; and his personal life was mutilated by tragedy.

Only in the realm of scholarship did the satisfactions outweigh the reverses; the pursuit of knowledge compensated somewhat for material losses. It was during this troubled time that Marsh began to build up his magnificent library, found the leisure to study art, music, languages, and history, and laid the foundations for the chief works of his later life.

I

B. F. Bailey & G. P. Marsh, attornies at law, Have formed a co-partnership under the firm of BAILEY & MARSH, *and will attend to the business of their profession at the office hitherto occupied by B. F. Bailey, in Pearl-Street.*

BURLINGTON *Northern Sentinel,* OCT. 28, 1825

It was a good partnership, successful from the start. Handsome, popular, brilliant—at twenty-nine Burlington's representative in the Assembly and leading attorney in Chittenden County—Ben Bailey brought in most of the business and appeared before juries, where his breezy wit served him to excellent advantage. Meanwhile the serious, standoffish young Marsh did most of the dull office work.

Bailey & Marsh's business was chiefly civil law. The firm argued fifty or sixty cases a year before the county courts, the state supreme court, and the Federal circuit court. Bankruptcies, trespasses, estate claims, foreclosures, damage suits—some involved tens of dollars, some thousands, but they all bored Marsh thoroughly.

Thanks to his partnership and his political connections, Marsh began to take part in public affairs soon after he arrived in Burlington. Town leaders admired his literary skill, and he wrote many of their petitions for legislative favors. Marsh delivered the Burlington Independence Day oration in 1829, and was chosen town selectman for 1831–32; his only surviving decision in that office was that citizens might be inoculated against smallpox at public expense.[1]

Politics occupied as much of the partners' time and energy as their legal practice. Ben Bailey was a perennial candidate for office. Both Marsh and his partner were protégés of Governor Cornelius P. Van Ness, Vermont's strongest political figure in the mid-1820s; but Van Ness, an old friend of Martin Van Buren, doomed himself by supporting Andrew Jackson in 1828. Jackson was highly unpopular in Vermont, because Vermont sheep raisers relied upon the high protective tariff on wool which they believed he opposed. Marsh's political debut as Bailey's campaign manager was also made miserable by the Anti-Masons, who aroused so much feeling against the "Masonic aristocracy" that they carried Vermont for William Wirt in the 1832 presidential election.

Bailey ran for Congress in 1830. His bitter battle against the incumbent, Benjamin Swift, and Heman Allen, the Anti-Mason candidate, consumed two years and eleven elections. As editor of the Burlington *Northern Sentinel,* one of the town's two weeklies, Marsh heaped insults on Bailey's opponents, while in the columns of the Burlington *Free Press* the Anti-Masons reviled Bailey and Marsh for their connection with Van Ness and the Democrats. According to the *Free Press,* Bailey was a depraved loafer who swaggered about on public house piazzas cracking smutty jokes with hostlers, while George P. Marsh was a stuck-up aristocrat, a nobody who gave himself airs because of his illustrious grandfather. After the fifth inconclusive ballot, when Marsh excoriated the opposition for calling eight thousand men from their labors to vote at the busiest season of the year, the *Free Press* jeered that "no person, unless nurtured in the lap of a purse-proud insolent overbearing aristocracy, or made mad by despair, would undertake to thus wantonly insult and revile a large portion of the community." The man responsible for the disruption of the district by this long campaign, claimed the *Free Press,* was Marsh, who "prostituted himself soul and body to pander for the inordinate and shameless lusts of his partner." "Petty cabal of Burlington intriguers!" shouted Marsh; "Base calumniator!" retorted the *Free Press*.[2] In May, 1832, Ben Bailey suddenly died of measles, and Heman Allen was at long last elected. Marsh went to look for a new law partner and a new political alliance.

2

Only odd or perverse people go to law.
                MARSH TO LUCY WISLIZENUS, ROME, FEB. 14, 1875

Marsh's political career died with Benjamin F. Bailey, and his law
practice also suffered. The quantity of legal work Marsh undertook
fell off sharply after Bailey's death. Before 1832 Marsh argued half
a dozen cases annually before the Vermont Supreme Court, but he
appeared only once or twice a year thereafter and not at all after
1835.

In 1833 Marsh formed a partnership with Wyllys Lyman, husband
of his sister Sarah, a Hartford, Vermont, man who had studied law
in Woodstock. Theirs was primarily a business rather than a law
partnership; most of Marsh's appearances in court now concerned
his own rather than clients' troubles. Ever more averse to legal
work, he began to close off his practice and planned a trip to Europe. Prior to 1835 he had regularly served the county bar as justice
of the peace and in other capacities, but now he relinquished all
such obligations. His last legal office was as County Commissioner
of Bankruptcy in 1842. The following year, the last before Marsh
went to Congress, the firm of Lyman & Marsh handled just five
cases on the county court docket and one in the supreme court.

Why did Marsh quit the law? For one thing, his clients disgusted
him. He complained that law had forced him into "constant association with low, ignorant, and even depraved men . . . against
which I have, for several years, enjoyed almost no counteracting influences." [3] Because their interests were selfish and material, he felt
they were evil. Such people not only robbed him of his time, they
also, he thought, ruined his character. But the main point was that
Marsh considered legal practice as likely to pervert as to promote
justice. Educated to believe it wicked to be wrong, he could scarcely
abide defending a guilty man. He shared his father's aversion to
"animal sympathy," as he called it, and would have been shocked

to know that his own speeches were more persuasive to the heart
than to the head.

At times Marsh felt less bitter; in certain ways law was "the best
of professions." Since it required constant mental agility, it was
"the calling in which men . . . retain their mental faculties the
longest." Marsh enjoyed legal problems in the abstract. And despite
its usual grimness, the law had its brighter side; "the strange people
[lawyers] come in contact with," he later reminisced, "the strange
language they hear, furnish countless occasions for mirth." [4] A
grudging tribute to his clients! In general, Marsh lacked sympathy
for the mundane concerns of ordinary men.

Marsh's own reputation as a lawyer was considerable. He was too
idealistic to be practical, but clients found him diligent and thorough. One of his colleagues, impressed by Marsh's "strong will . . .
obdurate firmness . . . fearless and effective" exposures of evil,
claimed that "as an advocate and debater, he ranked with the foremost of his age." A more judicious appraiser found Marsh "not
exactly fitted for country law, as he knew too many precedents"
and was addicted to a "laboriousness" and regard for logic "that
could never adapt itself to a country court." Marsh himself later
confessed that he "lacked the special gifts of the profession, & [was]
but an indifferent practitioner." [5]

3

In the light of Marsh's tragic personal life during these first years
in Burlington, any occupation would probably have seemed un-
satisfying to him. Lonely and reserved, he had none the less found
congenial people at the university, in law, and in the business community, and soon built up a circle of friends. And not long after
his arrival he fell in love.

In April, 1828, Marsh married the vivacious, high-spirited Harriet Buell. He was twenty-seven, she twenty-one. Cheerful and
even-tempered, Harriet made an excellent foil for her serious hus-

band. Her father, Colonel Ozias Buell, was a pillar of Burlington commercial and social life, a founder of the Congregational Church, and treasurer of the University of Vermont. Thanks to his profitable agricultural machinery and dry goods store, Buell could be generous to his new son-in-law; Marsh left Sion Howard's hostelry and moved with his wife into a small house Buell gave them at 12 Maiden Lane. A few years later he bought a wisteria-covered cottage at Church and Pearl streets. This pleasant, if cramped, dwelling, together with a shed put up to house his library, was Marsh's home for the remainder of his life in Burlington.

Marsh was content in his marriage. Within a year a son, Charles Buell, made his happiness complete. But it did not last long. Even before the child was born, Dr. Benjamin Lincoln warned Marsh that Harriet had a heart condition which might prove serious. Marsh worried about this constantly, but he did not tell Harriet, who appeared to be well. Young Charles, fair and sturdy, big for his age, seemed to his father "extremely gentle & affectionate . . . & of very good promise, intellectually." Marsh cultivated that promise. By the time Charles was four and a half "he read very well. This I had taught him, by carefully printing, with a pen, letters, words, & little stories, in parchment books." Marsh's pedagogy was carefully thought out: "Children are most interested in that which is done expressly for themselves, & I have no doubt that the manufacture of the books under his own eye, & for his use . . . stimulate[d] his zeal to master their contents." [6]

Harriet became pregnant again in 1832, and had a difficult time both before and after the birth of a second boy, named George Ozias. By the following winter Marsh could no longer conceal from her that she was very ill. Doctors in New York and Philadelphia confirmed his worst forebodings, but Harriet was more concerned about young Charles, who had suddenly contracted scarlet fever. The Marshes hurried back to Burlington to find their son apparently past the crisis. But the trip had been too much for Harriet's strength. She failed fast, and died on August 16, 1833.

Exhausted and grief-stricken, Marsh now had to care for Charles, who had had a relapse. Deafness followed the fever, and Marsh had to write out answers to the boy's questions on a slate. Eleven days after the death of his mother Charles was dead.

Marsh was overwhelmed by the double blow. He sent his younger son to Woodstock, and went to stay with his sister and her husband, Wyllys Lyman. "It was well for me," he later concluded, that business "drove me into a constant succession of severe labors, of a very engrossing character. This only saved me from madness, for I was never alone . . . for more than a year, without bursting into a fit of uncontrollable grief. Every night was one long wail of the deepest sorrow, for even my dreams were full of death." For several years he lived alone, boarding at a hotel and sleeping in his own desolate house. His expression became graver than ever, his bearing more somber. Solace of any sort he rejected; well-meaning friends "almost drove me mad by their ill-judged attempts to console me. They told me 'my wife and child had been taken away for *my* good.' The idea that the young mother had been snatched away from her helpless children, and our boy from the light of life, for the *good* of such a one as I, implied to my mind a horrible injustice. . . . Such an interpretation . . . was to me blasphemous, and I could not bear it." [7]

4

When Marsh first came to Burlington it was a rapidly growing village of 1,650 souls. Settled since the time of Ethan Allen, it was still a "savagely raw and shabby" town, or rather a collection of small settlements, separated by large tracts of wild country and poor, gravelly farms and divided down the center by a steep, wooded ravine. But Burlingtonians were compensated by the grandeur of the site: the broad sweep from the university at the top of the ridge down through the town to Lake Champlain, 250 feet below, and across that wide expanse of water to the steady azure wall of the

Adirondacks. Far to the east was the other rim of the Burlington world: the shredded dark peaks of the Green Mountains, from Mt. Mansfield to Camel's Hump. Where Woodstock's enfolding hills isolated and preserved the rural patterns of Marsh's youth, the greater ranges which bounded the vistas of Burlington formed natural highways to the outside world and promised more spacious horizons.

It was the "delightfully free, noble, and open" Lake Champlain, with waterway connections to New York City, Quebec, and the West, that made Burlington the Queen City. With the finest port and best-protected harbor in Vermont, Burlington had for years sent Vermont timber to Quebec, and now shipped Canadian lumber to New York through the new Whitehall-Albany canal connecting Lake Champlain with the Hudson. Burlington-owned canal boats and schooners thronged the docks, wharves, and mooring places. Above them, sixteen English and West India dry goods stores, as well as seven blacksmiths, six taverns, five mantua-makers, four tailors, five joiners, three masons, three saddlers, two barbers, two watchmakers and jewelers, and a tobacconist catered to the needs of much of Chittenden County. Two banks, two meeting houses, a courthouse, and a stone jail rounded out the institutional landscape.

Seventeen attorneys practiced in the local courts; within twenty years Marsh had forty-eight county colleagues, not all so ignoble as might be supposed from Marsh's strictures against the legal profession. Indeed, a few of Marsh's closest friends were lawyers, especially the able, cultivated John Norton Pomeroy. Heman Allen, Wyllys Lyman, another Marsh brother-in-law, James W. Hickok, Albert G. Whittemore, Asahel Peck, Alvan Foote, Charles D. Kasson, David Read, and Jacob Maeck, the gadfly of the county bar, were all associates of Marsh at one time or another.

It was not among these legal colleagues, however, that Marsh spent his leisure hours; he turned rather to the scholars at the university on College Hill. Here, in what Henry James later described as "the most truly charming of . . . New England country towns," education flourished under the guiding genius of James Marsh. "The son of an intelligent farmer," George wrote later of his cousin, "rural . . . labors continued to have so strong a charm for him that . . . he entertained the project of retiring permanently to his father's farm"; he went instead to Dartmouth, then to Andover Theological Seminary, and at length to Burlington in 1826.[8] Tall, feeble in appearance, with a weak, high-pitched voice that students could hardly hear, James Marsh revolutionized New England college instruction no less profoundly than he transformed New England philosophy. He liberalized admissions, made instruction less formal, abolished petty disciplinary regulations, reduced textbook study to a minimum, and encouraged the widest latitude of thought; he reconstructed buildings (burned to the ground in 1825); and his aides filled the college coffers with hard-won Vermont dollars. Within a few years the University of Vermont had attained a national reputation.

The Marsh cousins profoundly influenced each other. Soon after they came to Burlington they revived their Dartmouth club, and spent one or two evenings a week reading and discussing Greek, German, and English philosophy. Each stimulated the other, but James Marsh, who had already embarked on "that ocean of German theology and metaphysics," probably led the way. Few Americans at that time knew German or cared about abstract philosophy. But Marsh's interpretations of Kant and Coleridge became the philosophic basis of American Transcendentalism. James Marsh never approved of his Cambridge disciples. He was an idealist and mystic; but he was also a hard-headed Vermonter who loathed sham and self-deceit and held out no hope for the perfectibility of man. He laughed at Brook Farm reformers who hoped "to redeem the world by a sort of dilettante process, to purge off its grossness, to make a poetical paradise in which hard work shall become easy, dirty things clean, the selfish liberal, and the churl a churl no longer." And he thought their scholarship as shoddy as their morality. George Marsh shared his cousin's principles and prejudices, and lamented when

James's death in 1842 bereft him of a friend of "philosophical genius and culture." [9]

On the university medical faculty was another cousin, Dr. Leonard Marsh, whom George Marsh considered "the profoundest thinker, by many degrees, in my knowledge." But shyness hid most of Leonard's talents—he was "a little like the iron steamer *Great Britain* in being built in a dock with gates so small, that it can't be got out, except in fragments." [10] These fragments were explosive; scathing Marshian invective fills the pages of Leonard's *A Bake-Pan for the Dough-Faces* and *The Apocatastasis; or, Progress Backwards,* the latter a splendid satire against the proslavery arguments of John Henry Hopkins, Protestant Episcopal Bishop of Vermont.

Bishop Hopkins himself was an interesting neighbor, whose beliefs George vehemently opposed. Hopkins was High-Church, anti-democratic, proslavery; nevertheless, Marsh admired this ecclesiastic who was also an accomplished musician, a skilled artist, and an excellent practical architect. In later years Marsh wrote poems for Hopkins's journal, *The Churchman.*

Marsh also saw much of the colleagues his cousin had brought to the university. He took delight in botanical outings with sociable George Wyllys Benedict, the popular new science professor who later entered politics, became a state senator, and promoted telegraph communication between Boston and Burlington. With Dr. Benjamin Lincoln, well-known reformer in medical education, Marsh enjoyed long discussions on music and mathematics. The conservative Rev. John Wheeler, James's successor as president, shared George Marsh's interests in agricultural research and fruit-growing in the Champlain Valley. A more fascinating companion, and the university's most productive scholar, was Zadock Thompson, geologist, statistician, historian, writer of textbooks, compiler of gazetteers, maker of almanacs, keeper of weather records, Episcopal minister, and editor of the *Iris,* a "Literary and Miscellaneous" periodical. In his spare time Thompson ran a seminary for young ladies, and with Marsh founded the Burlington Lyceum.

This was the Burlington circle in which Marsh took intellectual refuge, and which held him in highest esteem. Referring to Marsh's accomplishments in law, in history, in literature, President Wheeler judged him "possessed of more talents, not creative genius, than any man I ever knew." [11]

5

Marsh possessed little but talents during his first years in Burlington. After the deaths of his father-in-law (1832) and wife, however, he inherited considerable property. Five years later he had real estate valued at $7,500 as well as $10,000 in cash and stocks; by 1843 his real estate alone was worth more than $16,000.[12]

Allied by family and fortune to Burlington's leading enterprises, Marsh was a strong advocate of sound money policies. Ozias Buell had been a director of the Burlington branch of the United States Bank, and when the Jackson Administration attacked the bank, Marsh, as spokesman for local business interests, deplored the threatened withdrawal of deposits as "impolitic and unjust."

When the Burlington branch was about to close, Marsh, Lyman, and the John H. Peck firm asked the Vermont legislature for a private bank charter. "Business of every kind grows with the facilities for its transaction," argued Marsh in his petition; in five years the branch bank had promoted a fivefold increase of capital in Burlington. The stodgy old Bank of Burlington was owned by a few "older merchants" so conservative they would not grant short-term loans. Burlington needed a new bank "with a capital sufficiently large to . . . furnish those means of exchange, discount, & negotiation of bankable paper, which the business of the country requires." [13] Marsh and his associates were permitted to buy the defunct United States branch bank in 1835 for $142,000.

Marsh's real estate included the large Castle Farm overlooking Shelburne Bay south of Burlington, where he owned a big flock of Merino sheep. Wool was much in demand. The high tariffs of 1824 and 1828 on wool and woolens and the depredations of the wheat midge after 1825 had revived the Vermont craze for sheep raising, particularly for light-fleeced Saxony Merinos. The heavy, well-drained clay soils of the South Burlington–Shelburne region produced good grass and pasture, and Marsh developed one of the finest purebred flocks in the Champlain Valley. His farm was run by tenants, but Marsh was keenly interested in stockbreeding, and drove out Spear Street to Castle Farm almost every summer day.

Another valuable Marsh property was a narrow strip of land along the Winooski River north of town, including its 38-foot lower falls. In possession of both raw wool and water power, Marsh decided to combine his assets. Why ship wool all the way to Boston when it could be manufactured into broadcloth, just as easily and with far more profit to Burlington and to himself, on the Winooski River falls? Joined by his brothers-in-law Lyman and Hickok and other local businessmen, Marsh started work on the plant in the autumn of 1835.

The Winooski (formerly called the Onion) is the longest, most useful river within Vermont. Narrow, rocky, often precipitous, it is nowhere navigable, but has etched out the only convenient route, from Montpelier southwestward to Burlington, across the Green Mountains. Vermont's major east-west transport arteries—Williston Turnpike, Vermont Central Railroad, modern highway—have all used its valley. At the falls Ethan and Ira Allen had early dammed the river, put up a forge and furnace, and built the schooner *Liberty*. A freshet destroyed all this in 1790, but Ira Allen rebuilt, allegedly saying, "There, old Onion, I defy you to move that dam for forty years!" Just forty years later, after heavy rains, the river rose twelve feet and wrecked the dam, two bridges, and several mills.

Marsh's woolen mill was the first new enterprise since this disaster. The legislature readily granted a charter to the Burlington Mill Company; as a member of the Legislative Council in 1835 Marsh saw to that. Raising money for the factory and getting a good road across the pine plain to the falls were more formidable jobs. Marsh planned the road and superintended the work, "often lifting heavy logs and stones with his own hands," it was said, "in order to quicken the zeal of his Irish laborers." Not content with the usual practice of merely bridging the ravine, Marsh had it filled with earth and a substantial stone culvert, which can still be seen below Pearl Street. The panic of 1837 slowed the project, but a year later the locust-shaded road (now Winooski Avenue) was opened. Four yards wide and turnpiked, it was of great importance for trade to St. Albans and the north, as well as for the Burlington-Winooski connection. The local press applauded the civic virtues of Marsh and Lyman (the road had cost them much more than the $1,500 they had received for the job); "few men among us," commented the *Free Press,* "have contributed more liberally . . . to promote the substantial interests of the town." The Burlington *Sentinel* envisaged the day "when the *loom, shuttle,* and *mechanical arts* will arrest the now waste of waters of that noble river [the Winooski], and, like another Lowell, a busy and active population spring into existence." [14]

The completed seven-story mill comprised sixteen sets of machinery, dye, stapling, and drying houses, a storehouse, machine shop, packing house, and twenty tenements, all steam heated. But trouble began almost before manufacturing got under way. There was a bad fire in 1838, and the following spring the ice pack burst through and battered the factories. Fire and flood were minor irritants, however, compared with Congressional tariff cuts. In 1839 the price of wool sank so low that many farmers let their sheep perish rather than feed them through the winter. Lower duties on foreign woolens forced manufacturers like Marsh to sell their cloth for less than they had paid for the raw wool the summer before, and the Winooski factory lost over five thousand dollars a week. The tariff of 1842 gave partial relief, but that of 1846, which again removed protection from domestic woolens, while retaining a 30 percent duty on raw wool, put Marsh out of business. Along with mill owners throughout New England, he sold out at a ruinous loss. Sheep raisers soon felt the pinch, and land values around Burlington dropped sharply; once again, thousands of Vermonters emigrated westward.

6

He [Marsh] was a potent member, tho rather young for such a place.
JAMES BARRETT TO S. G. BROWN, NOV. 10, 1884

Banker, farmer, manufacturer, public-spirited citizen, Marsh was sufficiently rehabilitated in the eyes of the community to be chosen in 1835 to run on the state-wide Whig slate for the Supreme Legislative Council, Vermont's upper chamber. The Anti-Masons had triumphed in most state elections since 1831, but the new Whig party attracted many of their conservatives. And it was an Anti-Mason–Whig coalition that put Marsh, who ran one to two thousand votes ahead of the rest of his slate, into office in October, 1835.

Marsh's first task as councilor was to try to elect the state governor. Neither the Anti-Mason, Palmer, nor the Whig, Charles Paine, had a popular majority, and for the fifth year in a row the election was thrown into the Joint Assembly. For a month Marsh and his colleagues descended two or three times a day from their small third-floor room in Montpelier's State House, "hardly less inaccessible than Camel's Hump," as one councilor grumbled, down two flights of winding, narrow stairs to the Representatives' hall, a dark, grim chamber indelibly stained with tobacco juice.[15] After casting a few futile ballots, the Council trudged wearily back upstairs again to attend to such business as it could without a governor.

The site of these deliberations was not impressive. A small village strung out along the Winooski River, Montpelier was of little consequence except as the seat of the state capital, which it remained only because of rivalries among more suitable towns. It was extraordinarily isolated; "turn the eye in whatever direction," commented a traveler, "and mountains, like modern Alps towering in the air, obstruct the view. You almost feel shut up from the world, imprisoned." Legislators who had to travel weary miles along mountain roads to reach Montpelier spoke bitterly of its notorious unfitness as a capital. "If the State House had not been here," complained Speaker George F. Edmunds some years later, "no man who was not fit for a place in the insane asylum, would believe that its location in Montpelier could be thought of." [16]

Marsh stayed at the Pavilion, largest of Montpelier's four hotels, kept by Mahlon Cottrill, known as the "Prince of Landlords." Cottrill provided liberally for his boarders, who made the most of their vacations from farm and family. While legislators passed laws conceding local option to temperance societies in their home towns, they continued to enjoy their liquor in Montpelier, out of sight of their constituents.

On account of the election imbroglio, the legislative session endured a record thirty-five days but accomplished even less than the normal slim quota of work. There was some question whether the legislature could function at all, until Marsh, as chairman of the Judiciary Committee, decided that the state constitution permitted the appointment of the lieutenant governor as acting governor. The measures Marsh had to deal with in the Legislative Council were mostly private bills: charter requests for new railroads, canals, manufactures, private schools, insurance companies, roads, and banks; quarrels over town boundaries; petitions for state manifestoes on slavery, tariffs, the national bank; appeals from prisoners for pardons, and from the poor for charity; and demands for the preservation of fish in Lake Memphremagog and smaller ponds.

The only item of real significance in the legislative agenda concerned imprisonment for debt. The abolition of this old penalty, which put 4,000 Vermonters a year in jail, had been defeated at every session since 1820; Vermont lagged far behind the other New England states in this respect. Agitation for reform was strong in Burlington, where in one nine-month period 13 men were jailed for all other crimes and 487 were locked up for debt. "The voice of the people is against the law," exclaimed the *Northern Sentinel,* "why then is it not repealed? The answer is this—a few cold-hearted, miserly men control the elections of the freemen of Vermont." Arguing that "imprisonment for debt can be justified only on strong presumption of fraud on the part of the debtor," Marsh early became a leader in the reform movement which forced the state legislature to ameliorate the law in 1830 and 1834; [17] household goods were now exempted from seizure, and debtors were to be freed after surrendering their property.

Others continued to press for total repeal, and a bill abolishing debtors' prisons passed the House in 1835. As a creditor and as a lawyer, Marsh felt this was going too far. Abolition, he told the Council, "would be injurious to the class which it is intended to relieve, by increasing the difficulty of obtaining credit." The bill furnished no "satisfactory substitute for the security to the creditor which justice requires, and the arrest and imprisonment of the person supply." [18] Marsh's argument was persuasive; the youngest member of the Council, he had become its commanding figure. The Council refused to concur with the House—an extremely rare event—and thus killed the reform measure for the time being.

This defiance by the upper chamber, together with the legislature's failure to elect a governor, brought about the demise of the Legislative Council. The Septennial Council of Censors of 1834–35 had, as usual, proposed a bicameral legislature, and at last received popular support. "The Council suspended three bills at the late session," complained an influential Whig paper. "Why not give us a Senate, and do away with this *half way* business of legislation?" [19] Elected six days after the end of the session, the Constitutional Convention promptly abolished the Council in favor of a Senate by a vote of more than two to one.

Thus ended Marsh's second political career; in rejecting relief for debtors, he had in effect eliminated his office.

7

Despite his many occupations, Marsh still felt dissatisfied and un-happy. In this mood he briefly considered leaving Vermont for good. A trip to the South in the winter of 1836–37 proved fruitless; the following year Marsh decided to explore the great West. He went as far as the Falls of St. Anthony on the Mississippi, then a lively place on the lumber frontier. In small but bustling Chicago his friend William Butler Ogden, who in two years had made a fortune in real estate and railroad promotion, and was mayor of the city, offered Marsh a partnership. The Vermonter was amazed by the fertility of the prairies and the speed with which newcomers amassed wealth. But he found the flat Middle Western landscape monotonous, and the absence of an active cultural life west of the mountains persuaded him that he should stay home and sustain the virtues of New England.

After his return to Burlington in January, 1838, Marsh joined more in the social life of the town and spent evenings with friends rather than in solitary reading. He soon rejoiced that he had not moved to the West, for he met and fell in love with Caroline Crane, a slim, serious, dark-eyed girl of twenty-two. The daughter of a retired Massachusetts sea captain turned farmer, Caroline lived with her brother, the Rev. Silas A. Crane, and had been for three years a student and then a teacher in his boarding school for young ladies.[20] That Marsh had never before met her in a town as small as Burlington shows how much of a recluse he had become since Harriet's death.

Caroline's suitor, now thirty-seven, looked more like a farmer than a lawyer or a scholar. Tall and slender in his youth, Marsh had filled out, but his weight was well distributed; road building and mountain climbing had kept him in excellent condition. Marsh's "firm step and erect bearing" impressed Caroline. "His habitual expression was grave," she wrote; "the firm-set mouth might even be called stern; and his earnest grey eyes always seemed to look through the object they were resting upon." [21]

This intense and serious man did not immediately inspire Caroline with love, however. The following winter she went to New York to teach school. Marsh was determined to marry her; he came to see her as often as possible, wrote her ardent, amusing, and doleful letters every day; he could not get along without her, he claimed: "I believe no man was ever so constituted as to require the society of a sympathizing friend more imperiously than I. . . . I not only feel the necessity of communicating my thought and feelings, but it seems to me I cannot even *see* sightworthy objects alone." [22] In a few months he gained Caroline's consent. Silas Crane married them in New York at six o'clock in the morning—Marsh detested ceremony and chose the hour for the sake of privacy—on the twenty-fifth of September, 1839.

Caroline was fifteen years her husband's junior, but neither this difference in their ages nor Marsh's immense erudition made her play a passive or subordinate role. She admired her husband's work and shared his intellectual and artistic interests, but also kept up her own pursuits—chiefly literary—and friendships. Her main influence on Marsh, however, was social, not intellectual. Marriage made Marsh, never a gregarious man, more genial, relaxed, receptive. From Caroline he learned to expect less of other people and to enjoy them more. He even came to expect a little less of himself, to accept some of his limitations. Though brought up like Marsh in a conservative Congregational home, Caroline had a faith both more evangelical and more practical than her husband's. Her charitable attitude toward the weaknesses of others tempered Marsh's rigorous standards of morality. He was well aware of her benign influence; she responded to and magnified his enthusiasms, minimized his misfortunes, enhanced his pleasure in success, and even taught him a little patience.

At first all went happily for the couple. Marsh brought back his son George, now a boy of seven, from Woodstock; the cottage at Church and Pearl was more lively than it had been for years. Save for Marsh's books and engravings, Caroline found the furnishings plain, even bare; but this was from choice, not poverty.

Marsh seldom departed from his settled daily routine. An early riser, he was at work in his study by five, winter and summer. His desk was piled high with papers and books in five or six languages, and he turned first to one and then to another, seldom spending more than an hour at a time on any subject. He breakfasted at eight, then went to his office. In the office, as at home, time was precious. Callers were urged, sometimes not gently, to come to the point, and Marsh would get up impatiently when he considered the interview over. (The unfortunate client who came to his house after hours met with so cool a reception that he never repeated the visit.) Sleep was imperative after the heavy midday meal, which Marsh enjoyed at home. He returned to the office about two, spent a couple of hours there, and devoted the rest of the afternoon and evening to his family, playing with his son and reading aloud to his wife. Serious in public, he was drily humorous at home.

But family troubles interrupted this pleasant regime. Never very strong, young George fell seriously ill, and Marsh—who would allow no one else but Dr. Leonard Marsh to care for the boy—had few nights of unbroken rest. In 1841 and 1842 Marsh sustained grievous losses. A sister, Susan Arnold, and a niece succumbed to tuberculosis; his favorite sister, Sarah, Wyllys Lyman's wife, died after a long and painful illness; then his younger brother, Joseph. And the following year James Marsh died. Not long afterward Caroline was afflicted by ailments that left her unable to walk for many years and so affected her vision that she could read for only a few minutes a day. Marsh, too, in tracing a map of a proposed Vermont railroad route, again damaged his eyes. Meanwhile, business troubles increased, and the losses at the woolen factory forced him to give up his long-cherished visit to Europe.[23] Pessimistic about his future, he turned again to scholarly studies, and pursued them with energy.

❦ III ❦

Puritans and Goths

"MY EARLY INTELLECTUAL ADVANTAGES," Marsh complained when he was thirty-eight, "were of the commonest description. . . . Between weakness of sight, business cares, and domestic sorrows, I have had absolutely no time for regular study or thought since I left college." As a result, he concluded, "I have lost much of the precision and accuracy, and much of the extent of the general knowledge, of my youth; my powers of observation have been weakened by disease, my enthusiasm cooled, and my spirit sobered by labors, disappointments, and griefs." [1]

Marsh gave himself too little credit. His education was indeed narrow, but he took pains to widen his range of proficiency and to enrich academic studies with reflection. He did not lose old skills, but gained new insights in observing nature; "sight is a faculty, seeing is an art," he remarked frequently, and in the art of seeing he schooled himself thoroughly. Finally, consider Marsh's complaint that he lacked time for study; what would this man have done with *more* time, who without it studied architecture and art, practiced carpentry, measured mountains, learned languages, wrote an Icelandic grammar, translated German verse, Danish law, and Swedish belles-lettres, and gave recondite lectures on topics so various as to defy classification? To discuss all these interests would be to write an encyclopedia; two or three of Marsh's avocations will show the range of his early interests.

I

From childhood, when he watched the building of his father's new house, tools and materials had fascinated Marsh. Wood, glass, steel, stone, brass, were a pleasure for him to handle and to fashion, and he was fond of saying—only half in jest—that his father "spoiled a good tinker when he made a bad scholard of me." Fortunately for Marsh's vanity, he never had to put his mechanical skills to an economic test. His later inventions and designs for mathematical instruments came to nothing; his triumphs were practically confined to his own household. Marsh's notion that every man should be his own architect proved costly, as he confessed: "Persons have ridiculed some of my highest flights of architectural genius as clumsy, awkward, disjointed; and a carpenter, though in my pay, ungrateful varlet! once told me that every dollar of money I expended on my old den added a new blemish." [2] But where others executed what Marsh planned the results were better. Many a monument and many a public building—including the Vermont State House and the Washington Monument—owe much to his learning, taste, and judgment.

The graphic arts engrossed Marsh even more than the mechanical. He delighted in his collection of prints, etchings, and engravings; he also thought art a praiseworthy avocation. "I fear you will think I am becoming *pazzo per l'arte*," he wrote Caroline; "but when you consider from what lower professional cares and business perplexities it partially withdraws me, you will rejoice that I am now making art, in its higher manifestations, my principal hobby."

Art was also his principal luxury; he was buying Titians, Guidos, Reynolds, Rubens, along with miscellaneous books about painting, wood engraving, and printing; he later estimated he had spent more than four thousand dollars on the collection. He guarded his pictures jealously from clumsy Burlingtonians, resolving after a few mishaps that "visitors who see with their fingers' ends . . . shall cultivate their sense of *touch* at the expense of my engravings no longer." [3]

Marsh expressed his tastes in moral rather than aesthetic terms. He preferred classical and idealized portraits, works by the sculptor Hiram Powers and the engraver Danforth. The actual human figure is full of imperfections; artists should provide exemplars, show what it ought to be, for physiognomy, Marsh thought, reflected moral character. In landscape he preferred realism and precision. The natural world had no ideal form; the best that one could do was to copy it faithfully—which most artists, for lack of training in botany, geology, geography, and simple observation, failed to do to Marsh's satisfaction.

When he went to Washington in 1843, Marsh became intimate with a number of young American artists. The Marsh home was a rendezvous for G. P. A. Healy, Thomas Crawford, Eastman Johnson, and Charles Lanman. Both Johnson and Healy did portraits of their host; Marsh admired Healy's use of color in limning the semitransparency of skin and his skill "in seizing & portraying the best characteristic expression of his sitter." He considered Healy's "portrait of myself (the greater the subject the greater the work) . . . his *magnum opus.*" By the mid-1840s Marsh's private collection, notable for its etchings, was one of the finest in the country; there may have been larger ones, but none, Marsh thought, approached his "in *historical* value and interest." [4] And his reputation in the artistic and scholarly world was measured accordingly.

Judged by modern standards, Marsh's training was superficial, his taste little more than conventional. That he was so highly regarded as a connoisseur suggests how few Americans were interested in the study of art and how dominant were purely traditional attitudes. When Marsh's friend Charles Coffin Jewett bought his collection for the Smithsonian Institution in 1849 for three thousand dollars, he paid worshipful tribute to the "educated eye . . . cultivated taste . . . earnest study of the history of art," and diligent searches which had enabled Marsh to bring it together. Indeed, Marsh was generally considered "the only authority in this country on the art and history of engraving." [5]

Utility and patriotism reinforced Marsh's pleasure in art and mechanics. He habitually justified his hobbies by emphasizing their usefulness. Knowledge of the fine arts, for example, spurred social and technological progress. Understanding of mechanical processes reinforced Marsh's conception of himself as democratic, egalitarian, practical-minded. In praising technical arts and crafts, Marsh also exalted America, where invention and social improvement together banished ignorance, backwardness, and political and religious tyranny. His worship of technology, which he linked to Puritan ideals and frontier necessities, gave Marsh a measure of faith in progress.

2

An acute ear, a superb memory, and a capacity for sustained effort enabled Marsh to speak a foreign language almost as soon as he could read it, and he prided himself on his precise pronunciation. Having picked up most of the Romance languages along with his Greek and Latin in college, he turned to German and began Danish and Swedish at Norwich in 1820. Although eye ailments and legal work allowed him little time for study during the next decade, he occasionally bought Scandinavian books.

Shortly after the death of his first wife and son in 1833, when he desperately needed something to occupy his mind, Marsh wrote to the eminent Danish linguist and antiquary, Carl Christian Rafn, for advice on the study of Scandinavian languages and literature. As a lawyer, Marsh explained, he had "often had occasion to trace principles to a northern origin"; he grew "strongly interested in the history and character of the Scandinavian people . . . and determined to become acquainted with the languages and literature of Northern Europe." But the obstacles were "insuperable"; nothing in Icelandic, Danish, or Swedish could be found in America, and it was difficult to know what books to buy from abroad. Would Rafn

MARSH, 1844. PORTRAIT BY G. P. A. HEALY
Original at Dartmouth College

CAROLINE CRANE MARSH

"excuse an obscure stranger" and oblige Marsh with some suggestions? [6]

Eager to promote Scandanavian studies, Rafn overwhelmed the American attorney with books and periodicals. At the start Marsh ordered fifty to a hundred volumes every month, "but *proh dolor!* (Anglicé—alas for my dollars!) the prices of some of them are such as astound even me, accustomed as I am to be fleeced in this way." He decided to confine himself chiefly to the literature and history of Iceland and ancient Scandinavia, but within a couple of years was again buying everything he could get. By 1849 he possessed most editions of the Icelandic Eddas and sagas and almost all existing works on Icelandic history, mythology, law, and travel; on Scandinavia proper, his collection was little inferior. According to a modern Icelandic scholar, "it was, in the day of its owner, in a class by itself in America, and it still remains [in the library of the University of Vermont] one of the most significant collections of its kind in the United States." [7]

Marsh's fascination for the northlands had as many roots as the great tree Yggdrasill. Some grew out of studies of German and Coleridgean philosophy carried on with James Marsh. Another source was Marsh's interest in legal, linguistic, and racial origins. Ethnocentrism nourished other roots; fancied resemblances between Scandinavian and New England landscapes, and between the moral excellences of the Goths and the Puritans, encouraged Marsh to steep himself in Scandinavian lore. A few other Americans shared Marsh's enthusiasm. A summer in Sweden, Walter Scott, and the Icelandic sagas gave Henry Wadsworth Longfellow a taste for Scandinavian imagery. The poet James Gates Percival sought spiritual and linguistic guidance from Scandinavian mentors as early as 1834. The pacifist blacksmith Elihu Burritt learned and translated Old Norse while librarian of the American Antiquarian Society after 1837. Emerson contributed his deification of Swedenborg; and a host of scholars were excited by supposed relics of the Viking discovery of New England. Marsh and these contemporaries transformed Scandinavia in

American eyes from an "Ultima Thule of ice, snow, semi-barbaric folk, and militarism" into a romantic land of heroic fortitude, faith, and freedom.

Above all, the Viking voyages fascinated Americans. Danish linguists and historians, led by Rasmus Christian Rask, had rediscovered the Viking virtues in the great Icelandic Eddas and sagas. Rask rescued old manuscripts, demonstrated the importance of Icelandic for comparative philology, and in 1825 founded, with Rafn, the Royal Society of Northern Antiquaries. The major work of the society was the *Antiquitates Americanae,* a fine collection of sagas, codices, and other materials relating to the Iceland-Greenland-Vinland voyages.

Impressed with Marsh's ability and interest, Rafn enlisted the Vermonter's aid, and in 1834 made Marsh the Royal Society's American secretary. Marsh's main job was to arouse interest in, and financial support for, the *Antiquitates Americanae.* Work had been held up three years for lack of funds, but Rafn told Marsh that if he could sell 200 subscriptions (at $12 each) printing would be resumed. Marsh distributed the Society's annual report, searched for subscribers, contributed $500 from his own funds, and fostered interest in runic stones and other presumably Viking artifacts. Rafn praised Marsh for these efforts and relied on him more and more; "we chiefly build our hopes of a favorable result," he wrote Marsh a year later, "on your exertions." [8]

Finally published in 1837, *Antiquitates Americanae* fared better than Marsh had anticipated, and was highly praised by such eminent men as George Folsom, Edward Everett, and Henry Schoolcraft. The sagas, the Fall River skeleton, and the inscriptions on Dighton Rock and on the old stone tower at Newport convinced many New England scholars of that time that the Vikings had indeed landed along that coast. (Most of these relics have since been dated as Indian or colonial.) Everyone was talking about Scandinavia, and Marsh was proud that "the *Antiqs. Amer.* have done more to create this interest than any other means." [9]

3

Widespread interest in the *Antiquitates* encouraged Marsh to spur publication of his *Compendious Grammar of the Old-Northern or Icelandic Language: Compiled and Translated from the Grammars of Rask,* the first ever prepared in English. He had proposed the idea to Rafn as early as 1834, when the Danish scholar taught Marsh how to learn Icelandic pronunciation. The work was done soon afterward, but Marsh's frequent absences from Burlington and the difficulty of obtaining type for the Runic characters held up publication. Three hundred copies were finally printed early in 1838.

Marsh designed the *Grammar* both to "facilitate access to [Icelandic] literary treasures" and to awaken interest in the origins of English. A copious, flexible, forceful tongue, Icelandic was unrivaled for "spirited delineations of character, and faithful and lively pictures of events, among nations in a rude state of society." And as the closest surviving relative of Anglo-Saxon, Icelandic was of great importance to etymologists. While most of the book is taken from Rask, Marsh's own comments occur on every page. For example, he advocated a science of pronunciation: "Many of the sounds generally supposed to be simple may be resolved into yet simpler elements." When all these were known, "phonology may to a certain extent be taught by books." Marsh also did original work on inflections and syntax.[10]

Other translations followed the grammar. The Swedish scholar Carl David Arfwedson, American Consul in Stockholm, who regularly sent Marsh books and journals, prompted him to translate articles from them. Dealing with every aspect of Scandinavian life, Marsh's translations included such diverse topics as practical résumés of Swedish trade and abstruse juridical dissertations on toll rights in the Danish Sound.

Marsh set himself high standards in translation. Thanks to its "piebald and Babylonish composition," English could, he believed, express the thought and feeling of most foreign languages; it was "sufficiently flexible to imitate the emasculated delicacy of the Italian, the flippant sentimentality and colloquial ease of the French, the stiff and unbending majesty of the Spanish, and even the Protean variety of the German and the Greek." But it was not easy to do this properly. A faithful translation, Marsh believed, should reflect the style and manner of the original. Foreign literature of the past should be rendered, not into modern English, but into "a dialect used in England in the period of a corresponding degree of artificial cultivation and polish." [11] In this way one obtained both historical perspective and accuracy of mood and thought.

Marsh practiced his theory in his own translations. His abridgment of Molbech's life of the painter Hörberg and his samples from the sagas are quaintly archaic. More idiomatic is Marsh's version of parts of Olof Rudbeck's *Atlantica,* the famous work of the seventeenth-century physician-historian who sought to prove that Sweden was the cradle of all mankind. Marsh's occasional sorties into verse were also faithful to the originals. Dissatisfied with Longfellow's tame translation of Claudius' "Rhein Wine Song," Marsh produced his own version of the German drinking song:

> The Rhine! the Rhine! leaf, tendril, grape, there flourish!
> Shower blessings on the Rhine!
> His rugged banks they overhang, and nourish
> Us with this genial wine.

The editor of the *American Review* justly remarked that Marsh's is "a more literal, if not a more finished version" than Longfellow's. Less halting are Marsh's translations of Matthisson's slight but charming "The Fairies" and "The Gnomes"; the following is a selection from the latter:

> Elf, night-mare, goblin-sprite,
> Through caves of pitchy night,
> We glare with emerald eye,
> And smallest mote descry.
> There we nectareous naptha drink,
> With vitriol blue our visage prink,

Then down on puff-ball pillow sink.
No music know but Satan's choir,
Tickling the ear with discords dire.
Such are the Gnomes, if you inquire.[12]

But Marsh's command of vocabulary and of German idiom is more conspicuous than are his poetic talents.

Marsh translated, alone and with his second wife, Caroline, several works by the great Swedish poet and Gothicist Esaias Tegnér, among them the long narrative "Axel." He found Longfellow's well-known translations of Tegnér faulty. Marsh's 1841 version of Tegnér's "The River" is a painstaking job; the meaning is accurately caught, there are no misinterpretations such as Longfellow made. But one cannot praise the Vermonter's effort as poetry. The language is derived from the German and English nature poets whom Marsh admired; it is, in fact, stilted, watered-down Wordsworth. Tegnér's original is taut and economical of words; Marsh's translation lacks these qualities.[13] Unlike Longfellow, Marsh understood what he was reading, but he was not poet enough to put it into English verse.

The *Antiquitates Americanae* and his translations introduced Marsh by reputation to American and European men of letters. "Are you acquainted with Mr. Marsh?" one Danish visitor asked Longfellow. "He is the most eminent Scandinavian scholar I have met with in America." Travelers from Scandinavia were told that Marsh was "the most learned man in the United States," and made Burlington their Mecca. Marsh's correspondence with Rafn continued until the latter's death more than thirty years later, in 1864. In his last letter—written in impeccable Danish—the Vermonter told Rafn that "business and many deep sorrows have now for several years swallowed up my time . . . but I have never entirely given up my love for Scandinavian literature." He still bought Scandinavian books, but "leafed rather than read" them. And he had to content himself with viewing the North from afar. "A journey to Scandinavia," he wrote C. C. Andrews, United States Minister to Sweden, years later, "had always been one of my strongest desires," but he had neither the time nor the money for the trip.[14] Though Marsh did little further work in Northern studies, his efforts and counsel inspired a new generation—Willard Fiske, for example, was particularly indebted to Marsh.[15] Through Fiske and others he exerted a lasting influence on Scandinavian scholarship in America.

4

As with his other avocations, Marsh justified his interest in Northern studies by proving it morally worth while. Antiquarian pleasure in Icelandic and Old Norse led him to affirm the innate superiority of Germanic languages and peoples. Seeing the same virtues in his fellow New Englanders, Marsh connected the two:

The intellectual character of our Puritan forefathers is that derived by inheritance from our remote Gothic ancestry, restored by its own inherent elasticity to its primitive proportions, upon the removal of the shackles and burdens, which the spiritual and intellectual tyranny of Rome had for centuries imposed upon it. . . . The Goths . . . are the noblest branch of the Caucasian race. We are their children. It was the spirit of the Goth, that guided the May Flower across the trackless ocean; the blood of the Goth, that flowed at Bunker's Hill.[16]

In *The Goths in New-England* (1843) and in his *Address delivered before the New England Society* (1844) Marsh ascribed to the Goths and their descendants virtues that far exceed those cited in E. A. Freeman's later panegyrics of the Anglo-Saxons. Marsh traced New England institutions back to Gothic origins, in the same fashion and for the same reasons that American historians half a century later sought the sources of American democracy in the German forests. Marsh's Nordic myth embodied many passions: a new nationalism; an idealized pagan past; a search for pure racial inheritance; a militant anti-Catholicism; a reaction against Lockean realism in favor of German idealism; nativism; praise of rural virtues and contempt for urban life. These prejudices were em-

braced by many Americans of the mid-nineteenth century, who regarded Marsh as their spokesman.[17]

Marsh maintained that a desire to stimulate American patriotism
led him to ennoble the Gothic past: "The love of country . . . next
to self-respect, is the most important ingredient in the character of
a virtuous man. It is to the want of an intelligent national pride
. . . that we must ascribe the non-existence of a well-defined and
consistent American character." Marsh urged his fellow countrymen to emulate "the phlegmatic Northman, the ardent son of the
fervid South, the philosophic German, the mercurial Frenchman,
and the semi-oriental Sclavonian [sic]," who had explored their
ancestries, purified their vernacular tongues, and reawakened national zeal. The best way to foster love of country was to learn
its history; if they knew the origins of their institutions, Americans
might appreciate them more. Most Americans were too busy making history to study it, but Marsh warned that it would soon be too
late to recover the past. Those who discounted American history
because it was so brief forgot that "we were a nation a century before
we became an empire." Let us spend less time in school on Greece
and Rome, Marsh proposed, and more on our own past.[18] And
study especially the Puritans; in their history we can take the greatest pride.

The latter-day Puritan should be proud, said Marsh, that he was
a Goth, a descendant of those hardy, freedom-loving peoples whose
moral purity, fearless strength, and democratic tribal life had re-
juvenated the decadent Roman world. Even if the Puritans were
not pure Goths racially, they still had all the Gothic spiritual virtues.
The Goths in New-England is a succession of antitheses, with the
Protestant, democratic, fine-natured, hard-working Goth forever
battling against the evil forces of the Catholic, despotic, sensuous,
lazy Roman.

5

The moral superiority of the Gothic race Mr. Marsh attributes to . . .
a bad climate and a bad soil.
    EPISCOPUS, *Remarks on an Address . . . by George P. Marsh* (1845)

To explain the sterling character of his Goths, Marsh employed
a type of environmental determinism he learned from Herodotus.
"Soft countries breed soft men," Cyrus warned the Persians, who
on his advice "chose rather to dwell in a churlish land, and exercise leadership, than to cultivate plains, and be the slaves of others."
Marsh had likewise chosen the rough hills of Vermont in preference
to Western prairies. And he had nearer authority than Herodotus
for his argument. His friend Peter Force had recently republished
John White's eloquent *Planters Plea,* in which that seventeenth-
century Puritan leader replied to those who would give up harsh
New England for a life of ease in the West Indies:

The overflowing of riches [is] enemie to labour, sobriety, justice, love and
magnanimity: and the nurse of pride, wantonnesse, and contention. . . .
If men desire to have a people degenerate speedily . . . let them secke
a rich soile, that brings in much with little labour; but if they desire that
Piety and godlinesse should prosper, let them choose a Country such as
this is . . . which may yield sufficiency with hard labour and industry.[19]

In other words, not necessity alone, but stern necessity, was the source
of virtue.

Marsh's reasoning closely paralleled Montesquieu's theory that
"the barrenness of earth renders men industrious, sober, inured to
hardship, courageous, and fit for war."[20] His Goths were so good
because nature had been so harsh to them. Too much sun, Marsh
believed, bred stagnation; life in "the sunny climes of Southern
Europe" was lazy and out-of-doors; "the charms of domestic life
are scarcely known." In "the frozen North," by contrast, the short,
wintry days were no inducement to outdoor indolence; there was
nowhere to go but the domestic hearth. "Secure from the tempest

that howls without, the father and brother here rest from their
weary tasks; here the family circle is gathered around the evening
meal, and lighter labor, cheered, not interrupted, by social intercourse, is resumed." This was an idealized picture of Marsh's own
childhood. "Here the child grows up under the ever watchful eye
of the parent . . . lisping infancy is taught the rudiments of sacred
and profane knowledge, and the older pupil is encouraged to con
over by the evening taper, the lessons of the day, and seek from the
father or a more advanced brother, a solution of the problems, which
juvenile industry has found too hard to master." Reverence for
"home" and "woman," family life and education, affection and cooperation: civilized morality owed much to these Gothic domestic
virtues. The environment also had aesthetic impact; the sweet
solitude of nature in the Northlands predisposed the Goth to
patience, serious thought, spiritual contemplation, and self-reliance.
And "the necessity of waging a perpetual war with a sterile soil and
an angry sky" taught him independence and "a fixed habit of un-
tiring industry."

Such was the influence of environment upon character. "These
hereditary propensities," Marsh asserted, "our ancestors shared in
common with all the descendants of the Gothic stock. . . . So long
as the great features of nature are unchanged, so long as the same
mountains and plains and stormy shores shall be exposed to the
same fierce extremes of cold and heat, so long," he promised, "will
the character of New-England be conspicuous for the traits which
now distinguish it." [21]

To show a Gothic ancestry for his Novanglian forebears, Marsh
traced the Goths from Scandinavia through all the vicissitudes of
English history. According to the sixth-century history of Jordanes,
embellished by later legend, the Anglo-Saxon-Jutish (i.e., Gothic)
conquest brought the roots of democracy to Britain, and planted
Gothic virtues so firmly that even the Norman Conquest could
not uproot them. The English language, Marsh stated, likewise
survived the "mass of alien words, that monkish superstition, Gallo-

Norman oppression, scholastic pedantry, and the caprice of fashion, have engrafted upon it." [22] And in the sixteenth and seventeenth centuries—the age of Cromwell, Milton, and the King James Bible—the "Goths" rose against their "Roman" rulers to purge England of foreign influence.

This epoch of Gothic hegemony also witnessed the migration to New England. The Founding Fathers, Marsh believed, "belonged to the class most deeply tinctured with the moral and intellectual traits of their Northern ancestry." Persecuted by tyrants, "our forefathers were 'harried out of the land,' before that [noble Gothic] character had become enervated, or its lofty energies spent," and thus "freed themselves from the last remnant and most offensive peculiarity of the Roman spirit, religious intolerance." [23]

6

A tall old codger . . . came to Burlington, and gave himself out for a prophet. . . . He selected me for his interpreter, and gathered his flock in a large room. . . . He placed me in a chair where I could see both his audience and him, and commenced his revelation, but stopped suddenly, came up to me, put his hands under my knees, and said, "you solemnly swear to be my deacon forever." So said I, "I shall swear to no such thing!!" At this, he flew into a violent passion, and said, "Then I turn you out of my church and anathematize you!" "Well," said I, "you old scoundrel, turn me out then." He then began to curse, whereupon I took up the puddling stick my mother had to mix hasty pudding with, and gave him a pair of as sound blows on the ear as you shall see of a summer's day. MARSH DREAM RELATED IN LETTER
TO JOHN N. POMEROY, DEC. 16, 1844

As his dream suggests, Marsh had scant respect for institutionalized religion. Above all, he was alarmed by the revival of Catholicism. He blamed the Catholic Church for the political reaction which had engulfed Europe since Waterloo, and viewed with fear and loathing the efforts of the Holy Alliance "to rebuild not only what Napoleon, but even what Luther overthrew." [24] To evangelical Protestants like Marsh, the Oxford Movement and the growing influence of Pusey, Keble, and Newman in England presaged the Romanization of the Anglican Church.

Worst of all, to Marsh's mind, Catholicism was winning converts in America. Episcopalians, like Bishop Hopkins of Vermont, adopted High Church liturgy; several prominent Vermonters, following the example of Ethan Allen's daughter, went over to Rome. Catholicism had almost become respectable. Only a year after Marsh's fervent address there, Philip Hone was shocked to hear that the New England Society, with the militant Catholic Bishop of New York, John J. Hughes, in a seat of honor, had toasted "Pius IX, Pope of Rome. . . . What strange changes of late have come over the spirit of the times! . . . The sons of Pilgrims toasting the old lady, whom their fathers complimented with the titles of 'whore of Babylon' [and] 'red harlot'!" Marsh had reason to fear that "even with us . . . the evil leaven is at work." [25]

"It is from England, that this poison mainly distils," Marsh wrote; but the chief carriers were the Irish. There was no people whom he disliked so much as these most militant Catholics. Annual emigration from Ireland numbered fifty thousand by 1842, and by 1851 there were over a million Irish in the United States, half the foreign-born. It was the Irish, not the Oxford Movement, that aroused anti-Catholic feeling culminating in the Know-Nothing and other nativist organizations. The Irish community became more aggressive as its numbers increased, and Protestants expressed more hostility, not only in impassioned orations like Marsh's, but also in acts of violence, among them the burning of St. Mary's Church, in Burlington.

Equating religious and civic virtue with rural simplicity, Yankee opponents of Irish Catholicism also assailed the fast-growing seaboard cities where most of the immigrants settled. "Every foreign heresy or folly in religion and in government finds a congenial soil in that corrupted [urban] mass of outlandish renegades and adventurers," Marsh charged. What an indigestible mess simmered in the American melting pot! Marsh feared that "the infusion of ex-

traneous elements will cause a fermentation, which can only end in
their own violent expulsion, or the corruption of the whole mass."
Nine months after this speech, March vainly tried to get the House
of Representatives to lengthen residence requirements for naturalization from seven to twenty-one years.[26] Evidently he lacked faith
that his Puritans could prevail against these latter-day Roman legions.

Marsh's eulogies of the Goths and the Puritans were generally
well received, though the *New Englander* regretted that he had
been so harsh to Romans and city dwellers. The citadels of Con-
gregationalism supported Marsh, but an Episcopalian attacked him
as a dangerous radical who had "interwoven . . . sheer rationalism
in religion, and sheer Jacobinism in politics." The same critic
derisively punctured Marsh's climatic hypothesis. Why were the
natives of Kamchatka and Labrador uncivilized? "Mr. Marsh's
explanation would be . . . that whenever bad weather fails of
developing Puritanism, it is not the kind of bad weather which his
theory requires." [27]

The most trenchant criticism came from Marsh's good friend the
Rev. George Allen, former disciple of James Marsh and later a
Catholic convert. "You have started," Allen charged Marsh, "from a
petty sectarian prejudice—such as one picks up in a little village—
such as the half-educated son of a narrow-minded Calvinistic deacon
might be expected to entertain," and had been blinded by bias ever
since. "You credit the Puritans with your own modern Rationalism,
and you charge upon Episcopacy what is not just even of Popery."
It was absurd for Marsh to glorify the Puritans, the most illiberal
of religious factions. "If you were compelled to live with the *real*
Puritans, George Marsh, you would be driven to hang yourself
—to escape being burned by them." [28]

7

Most of these strands of Marsh's thought are aspects of romanticism. He was often self-contradictory: in the same paragraph, for

example, he praised the Industrial Revolution and condemned cities; he saw no reason why he should not enjoy simultaneously the comforts of the present and the virtues of the past. But inconsistency is the essence of romanticism; such discrepancies did not disturb Marsh.

Romantic idealism supplied Marsh's antithesis between Goth and Roman: "The Goth is characterized by the reason, the Roman, by the understanding; the one by imagination, the other by fancy; the former aspires to the spiritual, the latter is prone to the sensuous." The distinction between *reason* and *understanding*—developed by Greek philosophers, revived by the seventeenth-century Cambridge Platonists, rediscovered by Kant and Coleridge, and reinterpreted in America by James Marsh—was the central theme of New England transcendentalism. Man learned the facts of material existence through the *understanding; reason* supplied inspiration beyond all worldly experience. The essential point Coleridge and the Marshes make is that religion and the real meaning of life cannot be comprehended by experience and logic, as Locke and his school preached; they can be understood and justified only through intuition.[29]

Marsh's metaphysics was monistic in theory but profoundly dualistic in feeling. He tried to think of the world as a unity, but his background made him fiercely partisan; he could not help seeing things in terms of good and evil. He elevated mind above matter, the spiritual as against the sensuous, the ideal as opposed to the real, the "indwelling, life-giving principle" rather than the form, the human against the animal, the organic over the inorganic, truth above utility. These are the values of the Cambridge Platonists, whom Marsh lauded as "most pious and learned"—a significant juxtaposition of values. For Marsh, metaphysics was a branch of ethics. His credos in politics, religion, science, and art all derived from morality.

In art and literature, according to Marsh, the realistic Romans excited admiration by outward form and sensuous display; the Goth "pursues the development of a principle, the expression of a thought, the realization of an ideal." [30] Differences between Puritan (Protestant) and Catholic also fitted Marsh's philosophic scheme; one was concerned with inner meanings, the other with the outer trappings of religion; one considered spiritual freedom the essential and welcomed discussion, diversity, individuality, the other prescribed arbitrary ritual and ecclesiastical authority.

Marsh exalted deeply felt and suprarational religion. With other conservative neo-Calvinists he censured the "sensuous philosophy of Locke, and its wretched corollary, the selfish morality of Paley," which had long dominated American thought. The cool, rational approach to religion neither appealed to the heart nor touched the spirit. Still worse was Paley's *quid-pro-quo* doctrine, "which solves all questions of duty by a calculation of the balance of profit and loss":

> Whatever, Lord, we lend to Thee
> Repaid a thousandfold will be;
> Then gladly will we give to Thee . . .

This was "fatal in religion, and . . . degrading and demoralizing in ethics." [31]

Marsh's expressed philosophy was not consistent with his way of life, even with his fundamental beliefs. The disparity is most apparent in his professed contempt for material values. Because he despised mere expediency, and wished to refute it as a motive for action, he was driven to denounce the materially useful. Yet in practice Marsh was a devotee of utility; everything he undertook he had to justify to himself, if not to others, as advantageous to his family, the community, the nation, or posterity.

Marsh's idealistic, semimystical doctrines of the 1840s scarcely influenced his later studies on man's relationship to nature. When he realized—perhaps through both "reason" and "understanding"—that he had mistaken the relations of society and environment, he reversed his ideas of causality. By the time Social Darwinism and a newer nationalism had made racism and environmental determinism attractive to other scholars, Marsh had dropped them from his philosophy. His mature scholarship is the better for being in part a refutation of his old ideas.

❧IV❧

Congress and the Smithsonian

MARSH'S CELEBRATION of the Gothic migration to New England coincided with his own departure for Washington as a member of the House of Representatives. He had reentered politics in 1840 to support William Henry Harrison for the Presidency. In the Whig party, Marsh was on the side of the angels. The Anti-Masons were extinct; the Democrats had all but ruined Vermont by abolishing the protective tariff on wool. As county keynoter, Marsh scored the twelve years of Democratic misrule which had left the "country depressed . . . industry prostrated . . . political rights & sacred barriers of the constitution trodden underfoot, by an imbecile & intriguing administration." [1] And at the Whig State Convention in June, 1840, Marsh helped to draw up resolutions in favor of protective tariffs, progress, and reform. On this invincible platform Harrison swept Vermont by almost two to one, and paved Marsh's way to Congress.

The 1840 census led to a Congressional reapportionment that cut Vermont's strength in the House from five to four; the new Congressional district for northwestern Vermont, of which Burlington was the focus, thus contained parts of two old districts. One had been served in Congress by the scholarly Augustus Young, who now retired; the other, by fiery William Slade, a popular, outspoken abolitionist who, as a resident of Middlebury, was unacceptable to the upstate men in the new combined district. In Marsh, Burlington leaders (notably his old opponents Heman Allen and *Free Press* editor Henry B. Stacey) thought they had found a spokesman for the area's business and farming interests. Marsh's "age, in the very bloom and vigor of life and the palmy state of his intellectual usefulness . . . his high personal character, his unimpeachable integrity, and the acknowledged purity of his life," according to the *Free Press,* made him the perfect candidate. And yet just a dozen years before, the *Free Press* had stigmatized "Squire Marsh" as "a man whose veins are bursting with the insolence of aristocracy." [2] The Whigs nominated him—by a fairly narrow margin over Slade —in June, 1843.

Marsh promised to fight hard for economic freedom from England, sound currency, and a protective tariff, but he refused to be bound by instructions or "to sacrifice the general good of the whole . . . country, to promote the interests of his own" section. Marsh's poor opinion of the common man bolstered his determination to be his own master. All men were equal under law, but it did not follow that all men should *make* laws; very few were "both *competent* and *prepared* to decide upon all questions." Elect me, said Marsh, and then leave me alone. The Democrats denounced him as "high-toned . . . and aristocratic," and within his own party Marsh faced accusations that he was weak on slavery. But he "avowed himself to be every inch a whig, a whig protectionist, a whig abolitionist," and campaigned strenuously throughout the summer. In the September election, running ahead of his ticket, Marsh defeated John Smith, of St. Albans, by a 1,600-vote margin.[3]

Marsh was in no condition to celebrate. In the midst of the election battle Caroline suffered a stroke, and soon afterward young George caught typhoid; both required full-time nursing. Worn out by these and other burdens, Marsh himself fell ill. It was a sick and woebegone Congressman who—after a three-day journey by steamer down the Champlain and the Hudson and by railroad from New York—reached Washington in December. The unfamiliar city was wet and disagreeable; dirty slush covered the streets outside the Exchange Hotel on C Street, where Marsh found a suite of small, untidy rooms. He was "weak and lame," he complained, "sadly dispirited about my family . . . & I ought honestly to be in bed, but I keep about, & am trying to learn my trade, as well as I can." But, he wrote glumly, "every step I have taken has been met by some disappointment that has thwarted every calculation I had made." [4]

I

The Twenty-eighth Congress, wrote John Quincy Adams, was "the most perverse and worthless . . . that ever disgraced this confederacy." [5] This is hardly a fair appraisal. Adams himself was a potent member of the House, and there were other Whigs of whom he might have been proud: from his own state, John G. Palfrey, noted antislavery leader and historian; studious James Dixon of Connecticut; powerful Hamilton Fish of New York; from Pennsylvania, brilliant Joseph R. Ingersoll and the dynamic Lewis C. Levin; and from the South, Alexander Stephens, Henry Foote, magnetic Robert Toombs, and the young orator Thomas L. Clingman.

Marsh came soon to share Adams's view, however; for the performance of Congress did not live up to the prestige of its members. But perhaps little constructive action could have been expected, with the House Democratic, the Senate Whig, and John Tyler, President after Harrison's fatal illness, at odds with both parties.

As a member of the minority party in the House, Marsh prepared to sit back and enjoy an obstructionist role. He was encouraged by symptoms of a schism between followers of former President Van Buren and the friends of Calhoun. There seemed to be little danger that the divided Democrats could push through any of the measures feared by Vermont Whigs. So Marsh devoted himself to becoming familiar with procedure, meeting other members, exploring Washington's social life, and finding a decent place to live.

Marsh's Congressional colleagues from Vermont were all Whigs but one, and all new to Washington. Tall, beak-nosed, magisterial Jacob Collamer, the incarnation of Yankee common sense, in his time became Vermont's favorite politician. In the House and later in the Senate Collamer sat "quietly chewing his tobacco and looking as much at home as if he were sitting on his own hearthstone." Marsh had known Collamer for years, but there was little love between them. Collamer had no interest in Marsh's science, art, and literature, while the latter despised Collamer's stag parties. Marsh thought him an opportunist, too often on the winning side. "He is an able man," Collamer's lifelong colleague Solomon Foot said of him, "but so selfish & so disgustingly conceited, as greatly to impair his influence." [6] Representative Foot himself, generous and unassuming, a schoolteacher from Rutland who had advanced by hard work to a position of national importance, was Marsh's fast friend for a quarter of a century. With Vermont's senators, William Upham of Montpelier, an excitable abolitionist, and talented but bibulous Samuel S. Phelps of Middlebury, Marsh had less contact.

Marsh's closest associates on Capitol Hill were Rufus Choate and Robert C. Winthrop, of Massachusetts. Choate he had known since Dartmouth. Winthrop appealed to Marsh as a fellow scholar. Personable, eloquent, with a wide-ranging but somewhat superficial mind, Winthrop became influential in the House, where his mellifluous moderation endeared him to Southern Whigs. At first political allies, Marsh and Winthrop later diverged; Winthrop became the leader of the Cotton Whigs, Marsh a flaming Republican. But they remained close friends, and corresponded for years about art, architecture, literature, and history.

With John Quincy Adams, Marsh enjoyed easy and friendly relations. Marsh admired his fight for the right of petition, and committee work often brought together the Vermonter and the pungent old former President. Marsh respected Webster, whom he saw a good deal of socially. But he maintained only a superficial relationship with him and with Clay. He shrank from heroes and hero worship; the adulation these two men received disgusted him.

When Clay came to Burlington during the 1840 campaign, Marsh remarked sourly on the "great shouting, throwing up of caps, and blowing of brazen instruments," and promised to save Clay "one shake by keeping out of his reach. I hate man-worship in all shapes." [7]

Marsh went often to Presidential levees, teas, dinners, even balls, this first winter in Washington. The Exchange Hotel had few charms, and it was pleasant to move in a wider social circle than Burlington offered. The Vermonter's flair for languages gave him entree to the diplomatic corps; his interest in science and technology led to friendships with such men as James M. Gilliss, of the Naval Observatory, Alexander Dallas Bache, of the Coast and Geodetic Survey, and Joseph G. Totten, of the Corps of Engineers.

The physical as well as the social climate helped Marsh to enjoy life. He regained his strength in the mild Washington winter, in early spring took long walks with friends and family, and later relished the roses, green peas, and strawberries of a luxuriant summer. All in all, Washington pleased him. True, the slave mart still functioned, almost within sight of the Capitol; but the city as a whole was no longer the abode of vice it had been when Charles Marsh was in Congress; "no disgusting sights of beggers or prostitutes met the eye." [8] Although much of Washington was still raw, ugly, squalid, Marsh was grateful for the warmth of the sun.

2

Not all was sunshine and magnolias, however. A Congressman had to hustle for his eight dollars per diem, especially if he came from Vermont, where constituents worried about what the Southerners and the free traders were up to, and expected to be told what was going on. Even though Marsh had made it plain that he would take no "instructions," he was bound to keep an eye on the next summer's election. "My correspondents are very numerous," he complained; "the day that I do not receive ten letters requiring replies is an easy one." [9] A rheumatic arm made writing more difficult.

Hundreds of miscellaneous matters engrossed his time. Committee meetings were at nine in the morning; the House met weekdays, and frequently Saturdays, at eleven or twelve. Marsh ate nothing between breakfast and dinner in the evening, which made for a long, fatiguing day. He found "confinement to the House tedious" and increasingly irksome. "It is indeed a disorderly body," reported the orderly Collamer. "It is difficult to hear & very few men or subjects will engage attention. Most of the members are engaged in reading, writing letters, franking documents or in private conversation, not generally in whispers." [10] Ladies crowded the galleries to hear their favorites abuse each other. But Marsh was punctilious in his attendance. Even toward the end of the session, when Congress met nights as well as afternoons, he seldom missed roll call. Other members were less scrupulous; it was often hard to get a quorum.

Though present, Marsh took little interest and almost no part in the debates. He wrote all his official letters at the House, and then relaxed. "It became . . . almost a standing pleasantry among some of the frequenters of the galleries, to predict when J. Q. Adams and G. P. Marsh" would doze off; "it was amusing to see them both quietly alert until they saw who was to have the floor for the next hour, and then . . . dropping at once into a profound sleep, broken simultaneously by the sound of the Speaker's hammer." [11] Thanks to these midday naps, Marsh could attend social functions past midnight and still get up to work at four-thirty in the morning.

The crucial issues in the House concerned slavery, notably the notorious gag rule, which permitted the Speaker to table, unread, any petition concerning abolition. Fighting at first alone, John Quincy Adams ceaselessly attacked the rule as unconstitutional; other members eventually joined him, and although the gag rule remained in force, many Southern Whigs were among the minority that voted, in February, 1844, to repeal it.

Their stand made Marsh optimistic about emancipation. The South now elected only two fifths of the House of Representatives, and could no longer coerce the country; its "better elements" seemed willing to give in. "Slavery is on the defensive," Marsh judged. "Slaveholders find themselves overborne by the force of public opinion through the civilized world." Southerners assured Marsh that emancipation was imminent in the border states. He agreed with Southern friends like Clingman and Berrien that violent Northern abolitionists only made it harder for the South to eradicate slavery. Vermont voters who never left their narrow valleys were dissatisfied, however, with Marsh's diplomatic silence in Congress, so Marsh explained why "I can[not] satisfy myself or my constituents, without giving offense in quarters which it would now be bad policy to stir up the animals." Why irritate the South unnecessarily, when "they are preparing (with the exception perhaps of the extreme South) . . . to abolish slavery"? The Whigs "did not wish to provoke those who are already giving up." [12]

Nor did Marsh worry about Secretary of State Calhoun's plan to annex Texas; he believed that the Southern Whigs would hold firm against Manifest Destiny. Marsh proved to be right; in April the Senate defeated annexation by a vote of two to one. The immediate future seemed safe; the leading Presidential candidates, Henry Clay and Martin Van Buren, had both declared against annexation. But Van Buren's stand doomed him. The Democrats nominated James K. Polk instead, and fears concerning Texas and a possible war with Mexico haunted Congress from this time forth.

The tariff was as bitterly debated as Texas and the gag rule. In 1842 the Whigs had barely succeeded in raising duties on materials manufactured in the North—wool, glass, iron. But Southern planters complained that they had to pay too much for Northern goods, and the Democrats now agitated to reduce imposts and end protection. With the tariff, as with Texas, Marsh was at first confident of Whig victory, but by April, 1844, his optimism began to wane. A known moderate, Marsh thought he might sway the decision, and on April 30 he delivered his maiden speech. In quiet, even tones, he rebuked low-tariff Northern Democrats who "prefer the supremacy of their party to their own solemn convictions of what belongs to their country's good." Marsh was terse, strong, sarcastic. Free traders professed constitutional qualms on protection, but, Marsh pointed out, the same men who would now deny Congress the power to tax had themselves restricted rights of petition expressly guaranteed by the Constitution! "Gentlemen who swallowed those camels will [n]ever be strangled by so small a gnat as this." Appeals to the Constitution were lightly made:

The constitutional cholic is, indeed, a grievous complaint, oftentimes an excruciatingly painful disease, but, happily, it is never mortal. Gentlemen are frequently attacked by it, they sicken, they suffer . . . but die never. In the long rows of our departed predecessors, in yonder cemetery, you find the monuments of those who have fallen a prey to death in all its varied shapes. Gout, apoplexy, consumption, fever, and even the hand of violence, each hath its victims, but constitutional scruples, none.[13]

All this was sheer bombast. Marsh went on, however, to explain his faith in protective duties. Only a protective tariff was steady, and stability was essential to prosperity. "Myself unhappily a manufacturer, I know too well the indispensable necessity" of estimating profit and loss in advance. A small reduction of duties, which "shall scarcely save a penny to any individual consumer, may work utter ruin to the manufactering capitalist, and the hundreds who depend upon him." Those who claimed that Northern industrialists were prosperous did not know about the costly fiasco on the Winooski. "There is scarcely a woolen factory in New England," Marsh assured the House, "which has not lost a sum equal to its entire capital, since 1837."

Protection was vital to impoverished Vermont. "We of the extreme North . . . contend with physical difficulties to which the more favored South and West are strangers. Our territory is mountainous—our soil rugged and comparatively unthankful. . . . Our climate is of even fearful severity." The 1842 tariff would not make Vermont manufacturers rich, but it would keep the mills rolling. Fear that Congress might remove this slim protection "has already produced a panic, whose influence upon the price of our only staple

will cost the wool growers of Vermont not less than half a million.
. . . Prostrate our manufactures, deprive us of this one resource, and
you plunge us into absolute, hopeless, irretrievable ruin." [14] Evidently the author of *The Goths in New-England* felt that further
adversity would not improve Vermont's Puritans.

Marsh's constituents applauded his "rare rich racy style" and were
delighted "that our mountains can breed a lion." Perhaps frightened
by Green Mountain lions, the House rejected tariff reduction ten
days after Marsh's speech, by the close margin of 105 to 99. To be
sure, this was but a temporary respite; two years later, despite
Marsh's indictment of free trade as an "unholy combination between our own Government and the capitalists of Europe," [15] Congress passed the Walker tariff, which ruined Marsh's woolen interests. But when it adjourned in June, 1844, Congress had post-
poned Texas and tariff alike until the election should provide a
clear mandate.

3

It was high time for Marsh to be home. The Presidential campaign was in progress, and as a candidate for reelection to Congress,
Marsh had his own fences to mend. At first he had "no fear, or next
to none," that Henry Clay would not be elected President, but as
Clay wavered on Texas and slavery, Marsh began to despair of
victory. "Mr. Clay is infatuated," he reported from Washington in
October; "he believes he shall carry *every* state but *two!* If there
were a few weeks instead of days between this and the election, I
verily think he would manage to *lose* every state but *two.*" Marsh's
own campaign was effective, however. The Whigs swept Vermont
in September, and Marsh topped the ticket with double his previous
majority. Vermont also held firm for Clay, but, as Marsh forecast,
Polk won the Presidency by a large electoral margin. Apprehensive,
Caroline Marsh viewed the Washington scene:

An hour after midnight, a yell of triumph, protracted, hideous, demoniac, rang out from one end of the city to the other. . . . Early the next morning [November 10] Mr. Marsh called a friend to the window and pointed out a huge flag floating over a distant quarter of the town. "Do you know what that flag is waving over?" he asked, with an excitement of manner very rare with him. "There is the *Slave Market* of Washington! and that flag means *Texas;* and *Texas* means *civil war,* before we have done with it." [16]

Texas was the topic on every mind. The Democrats considered the election a mandate for annexation, and Marsh thought the prospect "gloomy in the highest degree." Aware that the decision depended "upon no debate within doors, but upon appliances without," he nevertheless hoped against hope that by plain speaking he might change a few minds. What was the use of Texas? he asked in the House. Would it furnish Northern manufacturers a great new market, as some Southerners promised? Hardly likely; Texas was poor and thinly populated. Would acquisition "extend the area of freedom"? Texas was freer now than she would be with slaves. Would Texas help relieve the dense slave population of the South? Such relief would be temporary at best. These so-called "reasons" were mere rationalizations, Marsh concluded: the expansionists' real goal was political power—Texas would assure Southern hegemony in Congress.

The South need not be anxious, Marsh asserted. The North had no power, and moderate Northerners no desire, to interfere with slavery. But Southern slaveholders in Congress had intemperately "stigmatized the people of the North . . . as abolitionists, fanatics, incendiaries . . . with a reckless hatred of the South and its institutions." This Southern obsession about Northern enmity might lead, Marsh warned, to a dissolution of the Union and civil war, which would be "hailed by the despotic governments of Europe . . . as the signal of a richer partition than the dismemberment of Poland." It was not to destroy slavery, but merely to stop it from spreading, that Marsh opposed the acquisition of Texas. "While we of the North repudiate and disclaim all purpose of impairing the moral or legal right of the South, we are yet resolved that the extension and perpetuation of an evil which is its misfortune should not be our fault." [17]

For all of Marsh's moderation, five days later the House voted annexation by 120 to 98. Texan Representatives sat next to Marsh the following winter.

4

Committee work seemed to Marsh far more constructive than speeches to closed minds. The Naval Affairs Committee, his first assignment, dealt with pension claims, complaints about discipline, dockyard management, procurement of supplies, and experiments in naval architecture. "All mechanical matters in my committees are referred to me," Marsh remarked; "hosts of projectors" were constantly at his heels.[18] He paid scant heed to most lobbyists, but technical inquiries engaged Marsh's interest and brought him into contact with scientific Washington.

A typical case was that of two Navy machinists who had invented a rope-making machine which produced a superior rope at half the former cost. The Navy had denied the inventors compensation, on the theory that since they were Navy employees whatever they made was government property. But Marsh ruled they had been paid only for building the machine, and not "rewarded for the exercise of mechanical ingenuity." The distinction between brains and brawn was characteristic of Marsh. "The petitioners were employed, not as *inventors,* but as labourers—not to *contrive,* but to *build* machinery." He awarded them $500, which was what he estimated the machine saved the government each year.[19]

Simple sailors fared less well than inventors at Marsh's hands. A strict disciplinarian, he sought unsuccessfully to prevent the abolition of corporal punishment in the Navy. He also endorsed the moral crusaders who petitioned his committee to do away with the

Navy liquor ration. The Navy itself did not favor separating sailors from their grog; seamen the world over, it reminded the committee, "are particularly tenacious of all established customs." Such a drastic step would cause widespread discontent, smuggling of liquor, constant violation of discipline; recruits would balk at the prospect of so dry a service; and hardened veterans would be seduced into foreign services where Bacchus still reigned. But Marsh ruled that "the advantages to health, discipline, efficiency of the crew, important saving in stowage and freight, removal of temptation from apprentices and other young persons on board ship, and, above all, the moral bearing of the question, are more than sufficient to counterbalance the arguments" of the Navy Department.[20] Despite his committee's approval, Marsh's bill died in the House. Not until the Civil War did a New England-controlled Congress finally commute the Navy liquor ration, at the rate of five cents a day.

Marsh also served on the Joint Committee of the Library of Congress. The Library of a century ago would have been lost in today's mammoth establishment. Congress was not very book-minded; Marsh had to reject one fine, inexpensive collection because he could not get "so large an appropriation for the purchase of *any* library, let its character be what it might." [21] But he and his colleagues did cajole Congress into raising the Library's annual budget from $2,500 to $5,000.

The Library Committee's most important task was the disposition of scientific specimens brought back by Commodore Charles Wilkes's exploring expedition, the largest government survey since that of Lewis and Clark. The committee had to decide what was to be done with the mass of geological, botanical, and zoological material collected during the expedition's five years in the Southern Hemisphere. The solution of the problem helped the government assume its future role in science, and involved Marsh in the founding of the Smithsonian Institution.

Specimens had thus far been cared for by the National Institute for the Promotion of Science, a private group of scientists and gov-

ernment officials founded in 1840 by Secretary of War Poinsett.
Concerned because Congress had made no provision for the collection, the National Institute took over the Wilkes Expedition material as it arrived, and incorporated it with other government
collections which had moldered for years in Washington storerooms
and attics—odds and ends from the Lewis and Clark Expedition and
from explorations by Lewis Cass, Henry Schoolcraft, Stephen Long,
and the indomitable Pike. By 1842 a trained staff, ably directed by
Charles Pickering, was classifying and cataloguing, and late in 1843
the National Institute asked Congress for a grant to continue its
work. The request precipitated a fight. Senator Benjamin Tappan
of Ohio, amateur scientist and chairman of the Library Committee,
attacked the National Institute for usurping the functions and funds
of the Library Committee, officially charged with the collections.

Such was the situation when Marsh came to Congress. The outraged Tappan headed one strong bloc; on the other side were the
Institute scientists, supported in the Library Committee by Rufus
Choate. A third group suspected the motives of both parties and
wanted the government to stay out of science entirely. It seemed to
Marsh that the National Institute was doing the job far better than
the Library Committee could, and he pushed its request for an appropriation of $12,000. Reporting for the Library Committee in
June, 1844, Marsh urged Congress to give the National Institute
superintendance of the specimens and also to accept federal ownership of all the Institute's property. From this the government might
build a great national museum and "give character, consistency, and
unity to national science." Successful American promotion of the
"liberal arts," Marsh added, ought to be "a leading example of the
benefits of free and popular institutions." [22]

But despite the efforts of Marsh and John Quincy Adams in the
House, and Choate and Levi Woodbury in the Senate, Congress
refused to support the Institute or even to recognize its trusteeship,
and after a time it ceased operations. The collections lay idle and
homeless until the Smithsonian Institution took them over in 1857;

eventually, as Marsh had hoped, they formed the nucleus of the United States National Museum. Marsh and other Congressional friends of the National Institute had meanwhile turned their attention to the new Smithsonian. In the debates on this organization, though party feuds and personal ambitions continued to complicate the issues, the lines between the scholars and the frontiersmen, the anti-intellectuals of that era, were for the first time sharply drawn.

5

A laboratory is a charnel house—chemical decomposition begins with death, and experiments are but the dry bones of science. . . . Without a library . . . all these are but a masqued pageant, and the demonstrator is a harlequin.

MARSH, *Speech on the Smithsonian* (1846)

Marsh spent the long summer recess of 1845 trying to recoup his personal fortunes. Nothing went well: the woolen works at Winooski continued to lose money; the firm of Lyman & Marsh made several unfortunate investments and had to borrow heavily. Marsh's one triumph was finding "some remarkably fine engravings, which I could not resist." [23] Culture was his only extravagance. In this realm, he was convinced, the nation as well as the individual deserved the best. An occasion for deciding what might be best arose, shortly after Marsh returned to Washington in December, in the debates on the Smithsonian Institution.

Denied recognition at home on account of his bastard birth, James Smithson, English chemist and physicist, had willed his fortune "to found at Washington, under the name of the Smithsonian Institution, an establishment for the increase and diffusion of knowledge among men." In 1838, to the dismay of many legislators, $508,318.46 in gold was deposited in the United States Treasury. Some Congressmen mistrusted Smithson's motives, suspecting a British effort to regain ascendancy in America. Others considered it an insult to accept money from abroad, and advocated its immediate return.

Even legislators who willingly accepted Smithson's bequest did not know what to do with it. Few cared about the purpose, and the terms of the grant were so vague that no two men agreed on how to dispose of it. John Quincy Adams persistently urged Congress to build an astronomical observatory. Many educators favored a national university. Others wanted agricultural schools, popular lecture series, educational pamphlets and periodicals, nautical almanacs, prizes for essays, experimental farms, basic research, and applied technology.[24]

Out of this welter of schemes for the disposal of Smithson's money, two chief camps emerged by 1844: the practical and the intellectual. The former—Democrats and Westerners like Senator Benjamin Tappan of Ohio and Representative Robert Dale Owen of Indiana—wanted to use the bequest for agricultural schools, popular lectures, chemical experiments, and other projects of immediate value to the common man. The intellectuals, notably Adams, Choate, and Marsh, favored a big museum and a great national library for basic research and the diffusion of knowledge among scholars. "Nothing is more imperiously demanded by all great American interests," Marsh asserted, "than enlarged, multiplied, & diversified collections of books." [25]

Skirmishing between the scholars and the devotees of utility was particularly fierce in the Joint Library Committee, to which Congress referred the Smithsonian problem. Here were the leaders of the two factions, the militantly practical Tappan and the erudite Choate and Marsh. Tappan had just routed the National Institute; he now won the first Smithsonian battle. Why create a big library, he asked, when the Library Committee itself bought all the books worth having for $5,000 a year? Approved by the committee majority, Tappan's bill for a Smithsonian Institution devoted to education and agricultural experimentation barely failed to pass the Senate. But Choate's countermeasure, authorizing the Smithsonian to spend $20,000 a year, most of its income, for books, was beaten in the House.

As a freshman member Marsh had little to do with the Smithsonian; in the Twenty-ninth Congress he played a more active role. With John Quincy Adams, Marsh served on a seven-man Select Committee on the Smithsonian Bequest, of which the radical Democrat Robert Dale Owen was chairman. A redoubtable minority of two, Adams and Marsh stood their ground; after weeks of argument the committee produced a compromise bill: the library was to receive $10,000, the rest of the income to go for other purposes. But when the bill came up in the House, Owen sought to halve the library appropriation. What was the good, he asked contemptuously, of a huge library, designed to emulate the "vast and bloated book-gatherings . . . of European monarchies?" [26] The money should be used, he maintained, for a graduate normal school, an agricultural experiment station, and the printing of popular scientific tracts.

To save his books from the Philistines, Marsh answered Owen in his longest, most effective Congressional speech. His main argument was pragmatic. An advocate of utility, Marsh recognized the importance of experimental research. But true science "must be drawn from deeper sources than the crucible and the retort." Americans who worshiped technology failed to realize, Marsh charged, that technical skills flowed from pure research; excessive zeal for practicality was itself impractical. Marsh cited examples from astronomy, chemistry, music, and optics to show how applied science depended upon abstract knowledge. "Higher knowledge" not only catalyzes physical science, it "serves to humanize, to refine, to elevate, to make men more deeply wise, better, less thoughtful of material interests, and more regardful of eternal truths."

Marsh refuted Owen's anti-intellectual arguments by appealing to national pride. Most great statesmen were learned; all the founders of the Republic, who had helped "establish principles that have left their impress for ages, have spent some part of their lives in scholastic retirement." Virtue and freedom could never coexist with ignorance; far from being "intuitive or even instinctive," as Owen claimed, our American liberties had "necessitated the labor of successive generations of philosophers and statesmen." Marsh also appealed to Anglophobia: "There are other sources of instruction than the counsels and example of our ancient mother." A great library would be "the most effective means of releasing us from the slavish deference, which, in spite of our loud and vaporing protestations of independence, we habitually pay to English precedents and authorities, in all matters of opinion." [27]

Owen claimed Americans did not need most books; "shall we grudge to Europe her antiquarian lore, her cumbrous folios, the chaff of learned dullness that cumbers her old library shelves?" [28] We should indeed begrudge this, replied Marsh: just "because a newer, or better, or truer book, upon a given subject, now exists, it does not necessarily follow that the older and inferior is to be rejected. It may contain important truths or interesting views that later . . . authors have overlooked—it may embody curious anecdotes of forgotten times—it may be valuable as an illustration of the history of opinion, or as a model of composition." No man could synthesize all knowledge even in one field; "every good book supposes and implies the previous existence of numerous other good books."

Libraries in the United States, Marsh charged, were in a pitiful condition. Göttingen had six times as many volumes as the largest American collection. The Library of Congress, with forty thousand volumes, was "miserably deficient" in every field; it had fewer than a hundred books in German, out of a million and a half printed in that language. Again, perhaps twenty thousand books on American history existed, "every one of which it would be highly desirable to possess"; the Library of Congress had less than a tenth of them. A really first-rate library, on the order of Göttingen's, could not be built up within a century on an annual appropriation of $10,000 for books. Marsh recommended that for thirty years the entire income of the fund be spent on books, a museum, and an art gallery. [29]

John Quincy Adams thought Marsh's "one of the best speeches

ever delivered in the House," and the *New Englander* wished him a long life in Congress, so that he might continue "to present before the eyes of . . . our western members, what many of them have never seen, the spectacle of a living scholar." But the rough, un-lettered Westerners remained largely unconverted to book-learning. Representative Isaac Morse, of Louisiana, believed Smithson was far more "practical" than Marsh had depicted him; what stimulated the Britisher to give all his money to the United States was achievements like the steam engine, the cotton gin, and the telegraph. Such inventions were far more useful than a library full of musty books.[30] And other Westerners solemnly agreed.

A week later, aided by warnings in the press that Owen's scheme to set up experimental and agricultural schools was a "diabolical plot to spread Fourierism," the scholars in the House again attacked the practical men. J. Q. Adams decried Owen's plan to educate teachers for the normal schools, and self-educated Andrew Johnson of Tennessee found it "farcical and amusing." He would like to see a young man, "educated at the Smithsonian Institution and brought up in all the extravagance, folly, aristocracy, and corruption of Washington go out into the country to teach the little boys and girls to read and write!" Few would ever become teachers: "ninety-nine out of a hundred . . . who received the benefit of this Institution would hang about a law office—get a license—become a pack of drones." [31]

The House clearly opposed Owen's educational schemes. Section after section of the bill was struck out, and finally William J. Hough, of New York, offered a substitute, to which Marsh moved several amendments, "all with a view . . . to direct the appropriation entirely to the purposes of a library." One of Marsh's amendments did away with lecturers; another raised the annual appropriation for the library to $25,000; another provided for the publication of scientific treatises. The House accepted the Hough-Marsh bill on April 29 by the close vote of 81 to 76.[32]

6

Despite the adoption of Marsh's plan, he was not one of the three Representatives initially named to the fifteen-man Board of Regents which ran the Smithsonian Institution. Instead, Speaker John W. Davis selected his fellow Hoosier and Marsh's most hostile adversary, Robert Dale Owen, along with New Yorker William J. Hough, and Henry W. Hilliard, of Alabama. Marsh's legislative victory seemed doomed to administrative defeat; for although Senator Choate was a regent, friends of the library plan were outnumbered on the Board by Owen's supporters. Backed by Alexander Dallas Bache, Owen persuaded the Regents to choose as Secretary— a full-time director—"a man capable of advancing science and promoting letters by original research." [33] This was a blow to Choate and Marsh, who had hoped to appoint Charles Coffin Jewett, librarian at Brown University. The Board instead elected the eminent Princeton physicist Joseph Henry; Jewett became Assistant Secretary and librarian.

Manipulated by Bache, Owen had undone himself, however. Henry's closest friend, Bache urged him to accept the secretaryship in order to "save this great National Institution from the hands of charlatans." By "charlatans" Bache meant not the pro-library men but the Owenites, whose support he had used to elect Henry. Like Bache, Henry thought Owen's schemes for an imposing building, education, and the publication of cheap instructive tracts ridiculous. The austere Henry and the ebullient Owen had nothing in common. As Owen saw "all vestiges of interest in the common man" vanish, he lost influence on the board, and when the Indianan left Congress in December, 1847, Winthrop (now Speaker of the House) appointed Marsh regent in his place. [34]

Marsh's appointment followed a compromise between the library men and Secretary Henry. Henry was not against the library as such, but he doubted that the entire income would suffice for one of the size Choate and Marsh planned, let alone pay for cataloguing, binding, storage, and upkeep. He interpreted the enabling act as permitting the expenditure of $25,000 a year on the library, but he considered the permission discretionary, and threatened to resign unless he were given a free hand. He and Bache compromised with Choate, however, agreeing to use roughly half the annual income for the library and museum, the other half for research, publications, and lectures.

Marsh at first opposed the compromise "as a departure from the spirit if not the letter of the law," and intended to expose the matter in Congress. After several conferences with Henry, however, Marsh decided it was more politic to sustain the compromise to split the income "equally between the Library and what were called the active operations"; Congress was not likely to give the library more. Marsh later wrote that "our action was entirely harmonious during my continuance on the Board." [35]

Unfortunately, the compromise was not to take effect until the building was completed. Bache spread construction costs over four or five years, reducing other expenditures to a minimum so as to increase the endowment. He recommended that in the meantime the only books bought should be "such valuable works of reference as . . . may be required." Although Marsh and Choate opposed this scheme, and the Regents never officially approved it, retrenchment nevertheless became Smithsonian policy. Nothing like $12,000 a year ever was spent on the library; in 1847 book purchases cost only $545.99, the following year still less, despite what Marsh considered exceptional bargains in European libraries. The height of extravagance came in 1849 and 1850, when $6,100 went for books and pictures, most of it for Marsh's own collection of prints and engravings.[36]

Marsh made one more effort to restrain Henry and Bache. He backed Andrew Johnson's proposal, in December, 1848, for a special investigation of the Board of Regents. This "would serve as a most wholesome and necessary check" upon Smithsonian operations. "The Board of Regents," Marsh protested, "ought to have been long since made acquainted with its direct responsibilities to the power which had created it." [37] But Johnson's motion failed, and controversy over the Smithsonian died down for a number of years. Marsh had not realized his dream of a great national library. He played a major role, however, in establishing an institution devoted to basic scientific research.

7

Although the Regents devoted much time and energy to internal squabbles and to defense against outside attacks, they accomplished considerable constructive work. Marsh's associates on the Board were men of wide experience in science and administration. Secretary Henry, discoverer of self-induction and a pioneer in electromagnetism, proved a forceful, honest administrator of the government's first venture into science, though he was too stubborn and sensitive in relations with his staff. The most powerful regent for two decades was Alexander Dallas Bache; some even said that Henry was no more than a rubber stamp for Bache, whose imperturbable good humor and tact seldom failed of their objectives. An enthusiast for applied science, Bache investigated weather and magnetism and directed the Bureau of Weights and Measures as well as the Coast Survey; no one was better placed to organize scientific work in the capital. Bache's mentor, and chief of the Corps of Engineers, was General Joseph Gilbert Totten, who made every subject from conchology to crystallography his concern—a catholicity particularly attractive to Marsh. The elderly Richard Rush, veteran diplomat and cabinet officer, was another regent of broad scientific and scholarly interests. William W. Seaton, co-editor of the Washington *National Intelligencer* and mayor of Washington, served as chairman of the Executive Committee while Marsh was on the Board. All in all, it would have been hard to find a more distinguished group in Washington.

The minutes of a typical meeting of the Executive Committee

illustrate the scope of the matters dealt with by the Regents. Present on August 10, 1848, were Henry, Seaton, Totten, Marsh, and Jefferson Davis. The committee decided not to buy G. Nye's collection of paintings, but would purchase three copies of Skinner's *Farmer's Library and Journal of Agriculture*. They agreed that the first volume of the "Smithsonian Contributions to Knowledge" should sell for thirty-five cents. Marsh reported that Henry Stevens, the Vermont-born bibliophile and bookdealer, was preparing a bibliography of Americana before 1700, and wanted to publish it in the "Smithsonian Contributions to Knowledge"; there were many supporting testimonials. Philadelphia brewer Dr. Robert Hare, inventor of the compound blowpipe, had given the Institution enough chemical apparatus to "fill a canal boat." Other gifts included a paper-holding press from N. P. Trist; a bronze bust of the Danish classic sculptor Thorwaldsen; volumes of etchings; a rare Bible. Henry presented a meteorological progress report: James P. Espy had devised a scheme for reporting weather data, and the Smithsonian was sending instruments to volunteer observers as far away as California. Marsh mentioned an offer "to sell to the Institution a collection of shoes, illustrative of the changes of form in this article of dress. The purchase was declined; the article would be accepted as a gift." [38]

Scattered among these minutiae were the germs of some significant enterprises. The United States Weather Bureau was foreshadowed in the Smithsonian's venture into climatology, directed by Arnold Guyot with the advice of America's leading meteorologists. By 1852 over two hundred weather stations all over the United States were supplying temperature, pressure, precipitation, and wind data to the Smithsonian.

Another new Smithsonian service was the publication of scientific monographs. Owing to the high cost of stones for lithographic plates and for engraving and reproducing maps and drawings, many scholars could not afford to have their researches published. The "Smithsonian Contributions to Knowledge," large, handsome volumes published annually, gave American scientists, explorers, and naturalists a chance to bring their work to the attention of a wider public. The Smithsonian not only published findings but also advised, promoted, and directed expeditions, anticipating the future Bureau of Ethnology. Papers on a variety of subjects appeared in the series, but the geography and ethnography of the trans-Mississippi West received special attention.

Marsh himself chose the first volume to be included in the "Contributions," E. George Squier's and Edwin H. Davis's *Ancient Monuments of the Mississippi Valley*. Squier, a twenty-five-year-old teacher and journalist who had been digging in Indian mounds along the Mississippi, showed Marsh some of his work in 1846, and Marsh persuaded Joseph Henry that the Smithsonian should publish it. Sparing no effort, Marsh read proof, raised money, calmed Squier's fears about royalties, and publicized the work. "It is fortunate for the cause of American ethnology," he wrote in support of the volume, "that the first systematic attempt at its elucidation should have been conceived and executed in so truly philosophical a spirit." [39]

In private, Marsh was more critical of the work. Though without experience in archaeology, he understood field techniques better than Squier, who had described neither site locations nor floristic associations. What was the character, Marsh wanted to know, "of the forest growth on and near the works as compared with that in localities not likely to have been inhabited? The primitive forest is probably different," he explained, "from that now growing on grounds once cleared." Squier replied casually that so far as he recalled, vegetation was identical both near and remote from the ruins. Marsh regretted that so important a fact, "the most important with regard to their chronology," should have been omitted.[40] Marsh's emphasis on plant succession as a clue to settlement history was remarkable, if not unique, in the mid-nineteenth century.

Published in 1848, *Ancient Monuments* was well received by

American scholars. Marsh tried unsuccessfully to get the Smithsonian to finance another expedition headed by Squier. But he did help him obtain the post of United States Chargé d'Affaires in Central America, where Squier negotiated for a Nicaraguan canal route and did valuable work in Latin American archaeology.

8

Marsh's major contribution to the Smithsonian was perhaps the appointment of his protégé, the young naturalist Spencer Baird, as Henry's assistant. It was the efficient Baird who, as curator of the museum and later as Henry's successor, built up the Smithsonian's great collections, established exchange relationships all over the world, and trained and sent into the field the young geologists, zoologists, and botanists who made the first systematic explorations of America.

When Marsh met him in 1847, the twenty-four-year-old Baird, an indefatigable collector and a keen ornithologist (Audubon had wanted to take him on a Western expedition), was Professor of Natural History at Dickinson College, Carlisle, Pennsylvania. Baird had married a daughter of General Sylvester Churchill, of Woodstock. Marsh had been extremely fond of Mary Churchill, a bright, talkative girl who "never laid any claim to beauty"; and he took an instant liking to Baird, who asked Marsh to help him get a curatorship at the Smithsonian. There were other deserving, well-placed aspirants, notably the geologist David Dale Owen, Robert's brother. But by the following year Owen was out of power, and Marsh was able to exert more influence for Baird. He got support from other regents and found Henry favorably disposed to Baird. But the Secretary did not want to appoint a curator "until the building is in proper condition to receive the specimens of Natural History and this will probably not be the case under five years." As a scientific amateur, Marsh had to handle Henry in gingerly fashion; he suspected that the Secretary considered him "strong in punctuation, & not wholly ignorant of Low Dutch, but in 'science' a dummy." He urged Baird to come to Washington and plead his own case, *"provided* that you will, for the time, lay aside a little of your modesty, and swagger enough to make a proper impression." Marsh also advised Baird to cultivate Bache as "a man more prompt . . . in action" than Henry.[41]

Meanwhile, Marsh proceeded to educate Baird. He gave him the run of his library, criticized his researches, tutored him in German, and stimulated him to study Scandinavian languages. Samples of Marsh's advice indicate what Baird was up against: "You'll have no trouble with Danish. . . . Study the language *per se,* and the analogies will come fast enough to embarrass you, without being sought. Dutch can be learned by a Danish & German scholar in a month," he wrote, advising Baird to read Tieck's *Kaiser Tonelli* and Conscience's *Eenige Bladzyden uit het Bok der Natuer.*[42] Study, study, study.

In 1848 Baird was able to put some of this hard-won knowledge to use. The New York bookdealer and publisher Charles Rudolph Garrigue asked Marsh to translate and edit the immense Brockhaus *Bilder-Atlas;* Marsh turned the job down, and recommended Baird. Baird would get a dollar a page, Marsh told him, invaluable editorial experience, and an international reputation. He accepted and went to work. "How many pages can you do in a day?" inquired Marsh, astounding him with some tale of his own prowess; Baird's life became "regular almost to monotony."[43] When the *Iconographic Encyclopaedia* appeared in 1852, even the perfectionist Marsh rejoiced at its success. The hard work helped to form Baird's judgment and enlarged his perspectives, brought him in touch with eminent scholars, and trained him in what was to be his lifework.

Meanwhile, Baird wrote Marsh of "the consummation of what you, more than anyone else, have put into train"; Henry had appointed him Assistant Secretary to the Smithsonian, in charge of museum, collections, and natural history.[44] Baird was to remain thirty-eight years, ten as Secretary; for all but the last few he and the Smithsonian continued to benefit from Marsh's sagacious advice and sympathetic aid.

The Smithsonian story illustrates the kind of role that Marsh was to play again and again. He was not a great statesman; aloofness and provincialism prevented him from playing a prominent role in national affairs. Nor was he a scientist of the first rank; he made no original discoveries. But in the borderlands linking science and the public weal Marsh made lasting contributions. He applied science to life, not with the disinterested precision of an engineer, but with the aims and methods of a humanist. Marsh was, indeed, a superb promoter of knowledge. The Smithsonian—its aims, its activities, its personnel—was in large measure the result of Marsh's efforts as an impresario of ideas.

❧ V ❧

American History and Manifest Destiny

MARSH'S ASSUMPTION of Smithsonian responsibilities coincided with an enlargement of his personal and social life. No longer were the Marshes transients in the nation's capital; they were acclimatized veterans. After two years of boarding, Marsh rented a small house between 19th and 20th streets on the south side of F Street. Here they lived from 1845 until 1849. To begin with, the new home badly needed repairs and had no furnishings whatever. But after everything had been bought, fixed, or made comfortable, they "never for an hour regretted trying the experiment of housekeeping," according to Caroline, and had "never been so happy in Washington before." [1]

I

More than a mile from the Capitol, Marsh found his daily walk down elm-shaded Pennsylvania Avenue invigorating, the distance great enough to discourage the office seekers and lobbyists who had stolen so much of his time the first winter. Out in the west end, near Georgetown, life was calm and quiet. Marsh went less often to political gatherings, but found congenial friends among the administrative officials and foreign diplomats who lived near by. One of Marsh's favorites was the liberal German scholar Baron Frederick von Gerolt; he was also friendly with the Russian Minister, elderly

Count Alexander de Bodisco; the literary Chevalier Calderon de la Barca of Spain; Colonel Beaulieu of Belgium; Steen Billë of Denmark; and the Austrian Chargé, Chevalier Hülsemann.

Marsh's closest friend was Colonel James Bucknall Estcourt, British Commissioner for the settlement of the Maine-Canada boundary. Cultured, sensitive, Estcourt was for Marsh the Anglo-Saxon *par excellence*. Curiously, this friendship made Marsh more an Anglophobe than ever. That England produced such men as Estcourt made it all the worse, to Marsh's mind, that her affairs were directed by a haughty, ignorant aristocracy. In Washington the presence of the able Estcourt made more glaring the inadequacies of Fox, a dissolute gambler, and stupid Pakenham, Fox's successor as British Minister.

The Estcourts shared the Marshes' passion for all things German: the two couples passed many evenings reading aloud German philosophy, poetry, and natural science. In his speech on the Smithsonian Marsh claimed German scholarship had "done more to extend the bounds of modern knowledge than the united labors of the rest of the Christian world. Every enlightened student . . . will readily confess [the] infinite superiority" of German to all other literatures. He became familiar with the philological work of Grimm, the new geography of Humboldt and Ritter, the historical insights of Niebuhr; for relaxation he turned to the delicate comedies of Ludwig Tieck, the brilliant romances of Jean Paul, and German poetry of every kind, from the *Nibelungenlied* to the latest romantic ballad. Sundays he attended the German Evangelical Lutheran Church, whose Göttingen-educated pastor, earnest young Adolf Biewend, frequently came and read to Caroline, or joined the Estcourts, von Gerolt, and others in the Marshes' German discussions.[2]

On the outbreak of European revolutions in 1848 many of Marsh's diplomatic friends left Washington, some to defend their governments, others to join the rebels. Soon afterward refugees fled to the United States, particularly from Germany; many scholars and scientists appeared in Washington, where they came within Marsh's compass. Sympathizing with liberal revolts against absolutist governments, Marsh denounced the Holy Alliance as a "most flagitious betrayal of human liberty," and, on behalf of the House Committee on Foreign Affairs, expressed good will toward the revolutionists. He also welcomed them in defeat. Adolph Louis Köppen, a Danish professor of history, stayed a month at F Street, an exhausting guest "by reason of the multitude of his talks." Another *intime* was "one Lischke," a Prussian "deplorably given to the shooting of little innocent . . . birds, impaling of insects, disembowelling of fish, and pickling of crustaceans," whom Marsh put in touch with Baird "to exchange bloody trophies." The most frequent visitor was Dr. Frederick Adolph Wislizenus, Thuringian-born naturalist and physician, who "hath wandered in New Mexico, and written a book, and is very full of prickly pears, burs, and cacti *überhaupt.*" [3] Wislizenus was both Caroline Marsh's doctor and her sister Lucy's suitor.

Marsh was a good host, within the limits of his modest budget and household. Dining there one Christmas Eve, Jacob Collamer found the quarters cramped: "half-a-dozen gentlemen [were] as many as his rooms will accommodate at one time." On the other hand, young Donald Grant Mitchell, whose bachelor reveries later made him famous as Ik Marvel, regarded the "cosey, modest" Marsh home as "one of my pleasantest eating places," an oasis in the prevailing dullness of Washington social life. Marsh was "a thorough scholar" with "a splendid library and fine old engravings"; Caroline was an engaging and accomplished woman, whom Mitchell thought exceptionally pretty.[4]

Caroline's ill-health made it simpler for them to entertain at home than to go out. Among the visitors at F Street, Mitchell particularly noticed Robert Winthrop, who talked "of Texas and Houston"; Rufus Choate, chatting "of old days at Dartmouth"; Matthew Fontaine Maury, the Virginian director of the new Naval Observatory, who was charting ocean currents and sea lanes; the artist G. P. A. Healy, fresh from successes in the courts of Europe; and young Charles D. Drake, future Missouri senator. Marsh's strictures against intoxicants in the Navy and the halls of Congress fortunately did not apply at home; quantities of liquor lightened these learned gatherings. Drinking his excellent wine, the guests paid tribute to their generous host, "the stout master flanked by a modest Bocksbeutel, expressing his old Teuton love for the modest juices of the Stein-wein." [5]

Except for occasional headaches and neuralgic attacks, Marsh's health was good. Sedentary life had added several inches to his girth—he now weighed more than two hundred pounds—and his face had filled out. His dark brown hair was plentiful, and he wore it long, brushed back over a high forehead; the massive brow, the heavy spectacles, the firm lips, and the determined chin all gave an impression of force and forthrightness.

Marsh's intense and reserved expression did not put strangers at ease. Shy young George F. Edmunds, the future Vermont senator, who married Marsh's niece, was at first "greatly awed" by the Congressman, "a very dignified man with great glasses, and surrounded with an army of books." But Marsh's "gentleness and kindness" soon reassured Edmunds, who left "with a sense that my own importance had increased from the interview." In an unobstrusive way Marsh generally made his presence felt. He never swore, seldom raised his voice, but exerted a persistent, quiet authority, particularly at home. Only children were not inhibited by him, for Marsh treated them with mature gravity; one or another of his neighbors' youngsters would often accompany him solemnly, hand in hand, on his way down F Street toward the Capitol.[6]

Caroline, though happy, was more than ever an invalid. She could no longer see well enough to read, her back troubled her whenever she walked, and she suffered a series of minor miscellaneous ailments. Despite doctors' care, seabathing, and nursing by her husband and sister, she lost weight alarmingly. Marsh feared that she had some incurable spinal disease. In the long evenings he read aloud to her, or Lucy acted as amanuensis. Though in pain much of the time, Caroline kept her spirits up amazingly and hid her illness from visitors.

After the first winter, young George did not stay with his parents in Washington. The schools were inferior, and Washington slave society had a bad influence on an impressionable boy of twelve with "the faults of an only child, and a delicate one at that," as Marsh put it. He decided George needed firm handling. Partial to the old New England virtues, Marsh favored for his son "a satisfactory place . . . in the family of some clergyman." The unhappy boy was shifted from place to place. For two years he boarded in Burlington with his aunt and uncle Hickok, who found him disobedient, stubborn, unfriendly. Marsh then found a school at Newton Centre, Massachusetts, run by a Herr Dr. Siedhof, who could teach George a good vernacular German. "I hope," he concluded a typical letter to his son, "while your organs of speech are flexible, and your ear delicate, you will practice the analysis of sounds." He sternly cautioned George to make the most of this superb educational opportunity, as financial embarrassment "may very probably put it out of my power ever to afford you hereafter advantages so great as you now enjoy." [7]

Unappreciative of Dr. Siedhof and his school, George wrote his father that he had been "imposed upon." He knew less Latin and Greek than ever, arithmetic was not given, "and all the English branches are miserably taught, now how shall I ever enter college from a school where there is such teaching." George complained that the rooms were small, crowded, and unventilated, and the food inadequate and miserably cooked; "yesterday the meat was so, excuse the term, *rotten,* that you could smell it." Other parents assured Marsh that his son had just cause for complaint; Siedhof underestimated the requirements of American boys, while "Mrs. Siedhof has been *very unfortunate* in her cook and help generally the winter past." And though he was a profound scholar, Siedhof was "capricious, irritable, & furious in temper." [8]

Worse followed. Unaware that the school forbade the boys to spend money, Marsh told George to buy himself some clothing, *"viz., three pair of thin pantaloons, & two thin coats, & in procuring them, I hope you will consult economy;* & particularly that you will not have them made so tight as to expose them to wear out too fast, & above all, that you will have them made as gentlemen, and not as loafers, wear them." When George bought these clothes, Siedhof accused him of breaking the rules; George called him a liar, and was expelled. Marsh was furious, both with Siedhof, who had previously said he was *"vollkommen zufrieden"* with the boy, and with his "insolent and improper" son's "impertinence and disobedience." [9] George tried to convince his father that he had "not abused the confidence you 'imprudently' reposed in me but that I have only done what was due to *your* own dignity & mine." But Marsh was having too much trouble finding another school for his son—an institution "where he can't *help* learning, if there be such" —to forgive him for the episode. Finally he sent George, now a slight, dark-haired, rebellious boy of fifteen, to the Kimball Union Academy in Meriden, New Hampshire. There George made fair progress in Greek and mathematics, but remained, according to the headmaster, "a little too independent in his bearing—indulges in the foolish habit of smoking—does not love to be constant at church." [10]

George was bright and high-spirited, but, in this and other episodes, argumentative and outspoken. He did not hesitate, for instance, to find fault with his father's business affairs. When a tenant who had long owed Marsh money returned to Burlington, George wrote his father: "Hadn't you better pitch into him for some of that rent?" [11] But Marsh was unjust with the boy. More anxious than affectionate, he was quick to find fault; too often he considered his son disrespectful when he was perhaps only tactless.

2

*Wherever I go, I find the mudpiles better worth study than the super-
structure of the social edifice.*

MARSH TO WILLIAM T. SHERMAN, FEB. 27, 1872

Marsh's summers away from Washington were also pleasant.
There were leisurely visits from Baird and Estcourt, labors of love
on the board of governors of the indigent University of Vermont,
stimulating trips to Massachusetts. Marsh praised Burlington to
Baird, but his own heart was in Boston; only there could one find
the "best aspects" of American society. In the summer of 1847 he
spent enjoyable days there with Choate, with his old uncle Jeremiah
Mason, and with George Ticknor, whom Marsh thought "one of
the most thoroughly well-educated and well-informed men I have
ever met . . . though not *deeply* learned after the German model."
He also hobnobbed with Charles Sumner, William H. Prescott,
George Hillard, and John Lothrop Motley. Sumner, ten years
Marsh's junior, was a scholar-politician after his own heart, and the
two became firm friends. Marsh also met the famous botanist Asa
Gray, who impressed him as "a man of great learning, of a high
order of intellect, and of a truly noble and generous character"; [12]
and the young Swiss zoologist and geologist Agassiz, whose pious
exuberance had made him a Cambridge favorite.

Sumner arranged for Marsh to deliver the Phi Beta Kappa address at Cambridge in August on any subject of his choice. He
warned his friend that "one who speaks beyond an hour and a
quarter, speaks at a venture," but added graciously that "*you* can
speak as long as you wish." Marsh's *Human Knowledge* was a
rambling, abstract speech, "elaborate and instructive," thought Edward Everett, but "dull." Choate, Sumner, Mason, and Ticknor all
lauded Marsh, while the press pronounced "every sentence . . . an
essay" and suggested that any hearer who failed to enjoy Marsh's
masterly performance was simply not used "to having valuable
truths presented to him in such rapid succession." [13]

After a week at Cambridge Marsh went to speak at Union College, Schenectady, on American history. Together with *Human Knowledge,* this lecture (*The American Historical School*) earned him the *New Englander*'s accolade as "one of the ripest scholars of the age." Marsh gave still another lecture at the Rutland County Agricultural Fair in September, where he judged oxen, swine, and maple sugar, lauded the progress of agriculture, and cautioned against the depletion of natural resources.[14]

"I shall hardly have leisure," Marsh wrote bibliographer John Russell Bartlett, "to prepare an article for the Eth[nological] Soc[iety]." He proposed instead, "if I can find time," to translate the Danish geographer and historian Joakim Frederick Schouw's *Skandinaviens Natur og Folk,* "combating the common notion that national character is influenced by physical causes, which might be interesting." [15] Marsh was also writing about the sands of the sea, the proper proportions of pyramids, and the explorations of Steenstrup and Tschudi. It is hard to imagine where he found time to prepare three such lectures as he delivered in the summer of 1847. Together with his Congressional speech on the Smithsonian, these lectures are a great improvement over his earlier impassioned addresses.

Central to all the 1847 essays was the very idea of *utility* which he had so strongly rejected a few years before. In *Human Knowledge* Marsh expanded his Smithsonian thesis that all knowledge is useful, that applied science cannot exist without pure science. In his *American Historical School,* Marsh dwelt on the utility of history. He had already shown, in the *Goths in New-England,* that Americans lacked a proper "reverence for antiquity" because of their optimism and social and geographical mobility. He now called for new historical insights. To emphasize what was best in their tradition and national character Americans needed a new kind of history, one which would explain peculiarly American institutions. European historians dealt with the pomp and circumstance of armies and aristocracies, remote and meaningless to Americans. History for citizens of a republic should concentrate on the common man; scholars should delve into such mundane sources as municipal proceedings, records of internal trade, education, living standards, health and welfare, private correspondence, leisure activities, ephemeral popular literature, and "the private biographies of the humble as well as the great." This type of data, which historians had previously "scorned to record, as beneath the[ir] dignity," revealed more of "the true history of man than the annals of ages of warfare, or the alternate rise and fall of rival dynasties." [16]

The unique nature of American democracy required new perspectives of the past, Marsh believed; barren political chronicles must give way to comprehensive social histories embracing the everyday life of the people. "We must know what have been the fortunes of the mass, their opinions, their characters, their leading impulses, their ruling hopes and fears, their arts and industry and commerce; we must see them at their daily occupations in the field, the workshop and the market." [17] History *for* the people should be *about* the people, not just about their rulers.

A few European historians were beginning to break ground with social history, but no one had yet tried the kind of comprehensive study Marsh envisaged. In America, few cared. Most New England historians of his own era were so biased against the common people that they left them out of their chronicles. Only Bancroft attempted to fuse nationalism with American democracy, and he was more concerned with glorifying the present than with portraying reality. Like most others, Marsh believed history should be purposive and transcend mere objective truth. But his quest for historical facts— notably in his *Man and Nature*—was more comprehensive than theirs. Professional American historians, except for McMaster and Henry Adams, long ignored the history of civilization and society. Only a comparative amateur like Edward Eggleston could plead, half a century after Marsh, for "the history of culture, the real history of men and women." It required a new century for Mr. Dooley to demand a "real" history: "If any wan comes along with a histhry iv Greece or Rome that'll show me th' people fightin', gettin' dhrunk, makin' love, gettin' married, owin' the grocery man an' bein' without hard-coal, I'll believe they was a Greece or Rome, but not befure." [18] Not until eighty years after Marsh's *American Historical School* did his precepts become a standard of the "New History." In history, as in geography, Marsh was almost a century ahead of his time.

So much for his view of the past. What of the future? Marsh thought that progress was possible, but by no means inevitable, despite modern technology. He hoped that his kind of history would show some of the pitfalls ahead. Material progress, he warned, could not sustain itself alone; social foresight was essential. A special aspect of this concerned Marsh in his Rutland address, where he set forth a program for the management of natural resources. Showing how past mismanagement of the land diminished present prosperity, and recommending that care be taken for the sake of the future, Marsh presaged his most significant work in conservation. [19]

3

Why conquer or buy provinces which will be but an apple of discord?
MARSH, *Speech on the Mexican War* (1848)

The pleasure that Marsh took in his social and intellectual life could not sweeten the political scene. President Polk's ambitious program was making history. In the winter of 1845 Congress completed the annexation of Texas, and in May, 1846, the United States embarked on war with Mexico. During the same period "Fifty-four forty or fight" threatened conflict with England over the Northwest. Growing party and sectional discord marked the first session of the Twenty-ninth Congress; unrivaled acrimony, the second session. Marsh drew apart not only from Southerners, but also from Northern Democrats. By the time the Thirtieth Congress assembled, General Scott had occupied Mexico City and fighting had ended. But the Washington battle over the fruits of victory was hotter than ever.

When Robert C. Winthrop, "a fine fellow and a true Whig," was elected Speaker of the House by a one-vote majority on the third ballot, Marsh's party ruled the lower chamber the first time since he had come to Washington.

To end the war speedily and without territorial expansion was now the aim of Marsh and like-minded Northern Whigs. Marsh was a leader in the Whig propaganda crusade. In and out of Congress he spotlighted the costliness of the war and the worthlessness of Mexican territory that the expansionists proposed to acquire. Marsh also promoted Albert Gallatin's peace pamphlet, a passionate exposé of the financial crimes of the Administration. The indefatigable Marsh supplied Gallatin with statistics, government documents, maps; he did much of the research himself; he persuaded the Whig steering committee to order thousands of copies of the pamphlet and bring it "within the reach of every person in the U. S." [20] Marsh hoped that an aroused public would then force Congress to withhold further war appropriations.

To defeat the Administration's request for an $18,500,000 loan, Marsh delivered a scathing speech in Congress in February, 1848. The Administration proposed to raise this money by taxing tea and coffee, bank stock, gold and silver. Should the North, Marsh asked rhetorically, pay for a war that benefited only the South? These goods were used almost exclusively in the North. "How much tea and coffee are consumed by the three or four millions of Southern slaves? . . . How many of them consult gold and silver watches, to know their hours of labor, refreshment and repose?" Marsh played on antislavery sentiment to show Northerners that principles as well as pocketbooks required them to reject these taxes.

While Marsh castigated everyone connected with Texas and Mexico, his chief targets were the "contemptible" Northern Democrats. Southerners sincerely believed that annexation would materially aid them, but no such excuse could palliate the sins of Northern expansionists:

He who would write the blackest page in American history must ferret out the secret and long continued intrigues, by which the Texas Revolution was fomented; uncover the hollow duplicity with which our neutral relations with Mexico were violated; disclose the Machiavellian diplomacy by which opposite and inconsistent arguments were made to influence different sections of this country, and the arts whereby annexation was made the policy of the Democratic party, in spite of the deliberate and solemnly expressed convictions of the entire North; depict how the hopes of Texan stock-jobbers fell and rose as this or that Northern Democratic member exhibited tokens of rebellion, or meekly gave in his adhesion to the slavish policy of his party . . . explain how that contemptible faction, that so long swung here like a pendulum, between the law of conscience and the dictate of party, alternately betraying each, was at length fixed; and, in fine, tell what votes were extorted by craven fear, and what purchased by damnable corruption.[21]

Having demolished the politicians, Marsh next excoriated the soldiers who had sacked cities and slaughtered Mexican civilians. To dismember Mexico further would not only be morally reprehensible, it would yield no profit. Marsh would even refuse Mexico as a gift. America would lose in stability more than it could gain in resources by the accretion of so alien a land. Acquisition of the Mexican provinces would merely inflame sectional hatred; for the North was bound to prohibit slavery and the South to insist on it there.

Marsh arrested "the profound attention" of the House,[22] but he could not arrest Manifest Destiny. Within a month the Senate ratified Polk's treaty with Mexico, and the United States acquired California and New Mexico. Meanwhile, old John Quincy Adams succumbed at his seat in the House. With the expansionists victorious in the South, and the stanchest champion of freedom dead in the North, Marsh foresaw trouble for the Union.

Party and sectional leaders found another source of discord in the Northwest. Wanting a *quid pro quo* for Texas, many antislavery Congressmen had bolstered the expansionist demand for fifty-four forty. Marsh cared little for Oregon, however, and was immensely relieved when Polk finally compromised the boundary at the forty-ninth parallel. But the question of freedom in the newly acquired territories revived Congressional discord. In a bitter speech, Marsh insisted that Congress explicitly and immediately forbid slavery in the Northwest.

Southerners claimed that slavery could never be profitable in New Mexico, California, and Oregon; nature forbade it. Why, then, demanded Marsh, should the South "insist . . . on a barren, disputed right, which it is never intended to exercise?" But slavery was not in fact confined to any particular environment; it had flourished in Greece, Rome, Anglo-Saxon Britain, Scandinavia. Marsh contended that slavery was "everywhere profitable under the management of a prudent master," especially in new colonies where labor was scarce. He was certain slavery would come to the new territories unless it were specifically prohibited; indeed, he had evidence that there were already slaves in Oregon.[23]

In his previous speech on the Mexican War, the Vermonter had attacked the whole credo of expansionism. Why annex Oregon, California, and New Mexico? Even if these lands were flowing with milk and honey, laden with gold and silver, rich in wheat and cotton, Marsh would not want them. Nations, he believed, should grow by slow development, not by sudden accretion. Hasty acquisition of great chunks of land dissipated national energies, sacrificed the maturation of the old to the heedless exploitation of the new domain, and generated new discords among factions.

Marsh's thesis that countries should include only areas inhabited by like-minded citizens of similar culture was a typically partisan bit of political science. As in the *Goths in New-England,* he extolled racial, linguistic, and cultural homogeneity. The happy nation was the one that was unified, however small. "The citizens of the little republic of San Marino, and of the duchy of Tuscany, are as happy and as prosperous as if they were annexed to the kingdom of Sardinia, or even enjoyed the paternal discipline of the gentle Metternich," declared Marsh. There was, in short, nothing to be gained by increase in size, much to be lost. The price of expansion was loss of freedom. The larger the country, the more difficult it was to defend—the greater the need for standing armies, centralized power, and executive patronage, all dangerous to liberty. America faced the fate of the Roman Empire: "the soldiery raised to protect the frontier may supersede your electoral colleges, and impose upon you a Dictator."

Since there was no merit in size as such, Marsh continued illogically, the United States would be better off without *any* territorial additions. He doubted that it had even been wise to venture into the Mississippi Valley; the original thirteen states met all national needs. The Old South would regret the competition of Texas sugar and cotton; farmers in the Genesee Valley would be poorer when Western wheat captured their markets; Boston would lose the China trade when shipping went to San Francisco. It was geographic nonsense, Marsh maintained, to include the West in the United States. Impassable mountains and sterile deserts separated East and West: "they can never have a common interest with us." Besides, the Far West and Southwest were inhabited by Spaniards and Indians, "of habits, opinions, and characters incapable of sympathy or assimilation with our own . . . unfitted for self-government, and unprepared to appreciate, sustain, or enjoy free institutions." [24] Geographic determinism, partisan politics, and New England provincialism combined anew in Marsh's assult upon the West as "unsuited to the genius of the people of the United States" and as bound to weaken the nation. "Why should not the unnatural connection between us and these remote regions be severed?" he asked. [25]

Marsh's Novanglian prejudices may explain his dislike for the Western territories; but it is remarkable that a man so interested in technological developments, so certain of man's power to subdue nature, should have regarded easy contact between East and West as chimerical. Marsh was continually surprised by miracles of transport engineering. And his dim view of the West's resources was as unreasonable as his exaggeration of the difficulty of getting there.

Ever since his 1837 trip he had been prejudiced against everything west of the Hudson. His notions of Texas and northern
Mexico came from General Churchill ("no sensible or northern man
would desire to live in [Mexico]"), Lieutenant William H. Emory,
and naturalists like Wislizenus, who all considered the whole area
worthless for farming. New Mexico and California, Marsh supposed, were even less pleasant; "the best informed explorers" told
him they were mainly "unsuited to agriculture, unable to sustain
a dense population, adapted only to the lowest form of semi-civilized
life—the pastoral state." [26] Not even Oregon was much good, Marsh
surmised.

He was guilty of unusual lack of insight in his low estimate of
the West. To be sure, few then suspected the potentialities of the
region, save visionaries who thought to people the deserts of the
New World. But Marsh, who had just lectured on man's ability
to transform nature in Vermont, should have displayed more imagination about the possibilities of California and Oregon. Marsh
sometimes envisaged spectacular achievements in the conquest of
nature; but his descriptions of man's errors are much more graphic.
He was better as a critic than as a planner.

4

How could Vermont Whigs stomach a Lousiana planter and
slaveholder, a Mexican War hero, as their Presidential candidate!
When the Whigs nominated General Zachary Taylor in 1848, Marsh
found himself in serious trouble at home. While Congress dragged
on wearily through the summer, Marsh recognized "symptoms of
rebellion" in Vermont; [27] two days before he reached Burlington
the Free-Soil Convention in Utica nominated Martin Van Buren.
Radical Democrats constituted the core of the Free-Soil party, and in
New York they were a threat to the Democratic party; but in Vermont—where there was little Democratic strength—Free-Soilers
made serious inroads in Whig strongholds. Vermonters felt strongly

about slavery and were tired of being told to be moderate; the Free-Soil party provided an outlet for their impatience.

Like most Vermont Whigs, Marsh was a Free-Soiler at heart; but party loyalty, political realism, and distrust of Van Buren and David Wilmot kept him in Taylor's camp. Marsh feared, however, that the Southern general's ticket was "so unpalatable to my constituents that my support of it may put an end to my political life." His margin of victory in 1846 had dropped to a mere 900 votes. Fortunately for Marsh, his opposition was now divided between the regular Democratic candidate, Asahel Peck, capable Burlington lawyer, and Free-Soiler Stephen S. Keyes, "who was a Texas proslavery man," accused Marsh, "until he was nominated for Congress by the Van Burenites." In the September election Marsh led but did not get the required majority. "I am not *Free-soil* enough," he mourned, "and many of my old friends are going for a Loco." In two other Vermont districts three-cornered fights also failed to produce a winner. Marsh shuddered at the prospect of a prolonged battle like that between his partner Bailey and Heman Allen back in 1830–32. He wished the next ballot were final; whoever had the most votes should win the seat, whether or not he had a majority. "It would be a serious inconvenience," he wrote Collamer, who was in the same predicament, "to have three-fourths of the state called out again in January, & I am moreover persuaded that the sooner this question is decided, the better are our chances of success." [28] Collamer and Marsh persuaded the Whig-controlled state legislature to change the election law so as to permit victory by plurality.

Marsh redoubled his campaign efforts, speaking "sometimes seven hours in a day, and shall speak more, yea, I shall reason with them continually until Nov. 7th." But Taylor made little effort to conciliate Northerners, and Free-Soil orators were "active, unscrupulous, and numerous"; Marsh's opponents even charged him with being *pro*-slavery. The real issue was not slavery itself, Marsh explained patiently, but the extension of slavery, which Taylor promised to oppose. In resisting Texan annexation, the Southern Whigs had displayed "generosity, an incorruptible firmness, and . . . political virtue." Many Southerners, Marsh assured his constituents, thought slavery morally wrong and economically inexpedient; "no man can pass a winter at Washington on terms of familiar intercourse with Southerners without finding that . . . it is in general only political demagogues who seriously defend the institution." [29] Time, calm, and the Whig party would bring emancipation.

Marsh's defense of the Whigs was less effective than his denunciations of their opponents. Here he was on firm ground, the outraged Puritan lustily condemning the iniquitous, "a great master of strong and condensed expression." He reserved his choicest epithets for Democrats turned Free-Soil: "They profess reformation without repentance, glory in their shame, and with hands still . . . red with the blood of an unholy war, they proclaim themselves the chosen apostles of human liberty. Out upon the bald hypocrisy of these whited sepulchres! The sacred cause of freedom needs no such allies as these." [30]

Election Day set Marsh's fears at rest. Though the Free-Soilers made their best showing in Vermont, Taylor carried the Green Mountain state by a comfortable margin. Marsh ran well ahead of his ticket with an absolute majority of 1,554. Exhausted but happy, he hoped for a return to "political virtue." [31]

Reaching Washington after being delayed three weeks by snowstorms and other mishaps, Marsh found the weather balmy, roses still in bloom; the archivist Peter Force, "a great crony of mine, had saved several bunches of catawba grapes for me and they were still hanging on the vine until I plucked them." But his euphoria lasted no longer than the roses and the grapes. Marsh served now on the important House Foreign Relations Committee as well as on the Smithsonian, and had never been busier. "There isn't any Christmas vacation for us poor dogs now a days," he complained. "Our mill goes, whether there is any water or no. We . . . work like horses." [32]

5

Though Taylor's inauguration was still two months off, by New Year's the capital was thronged with office-seekers. Marsh himself was one of them. " 'Some of my friends,' " he wrote facetiously, "think it possible I may be sent abroad in some diplomatic capacity. . . . I have had a puff in a Boston newspaper recommending me as Minister at Berlin on the ground that I *can speak German like a brick.*'" Contacts with European diplomats had increased Marsh's lifelong desire to see the Old World, and he was anxious to find a climate that would help Caroline. But the Winooski mill failure and other financial vexations had reduced him "from affluence to comparative poverty"; only a diplomatic post would enable him to go abroad. Before the 1848 election, Rafn in Copenhagen heard rumors that Marsh was to be Minister to Denmark, but this was a minor job with a meager salary.[33] The logical posts in the light of Marsh's interests and abilities were Frankfort and Berlin. Marsh placed his chief hopes on these missions.

Whig and Democratic papers alike in Vermont touted Marsh's claims, even the Burlington *Sentinel* supporting him as "an act of simple justice—to which the uniform courtesy of Mr. Marsh . . . to his political opponents, adds obligation." The nation's press generally agreed that Marsh's great scholarship, linguistic skill, "modest and winning manners," gentlemanly polish, and influence in Congress entitled him to a place abroad. "Gen. Taylor might ransack universal Whiggery with a lantern," concluded the Boston *Courier,* "without coming across a man better fitted" for the Berlin post.[34]

Marsh's chances were seriously undermined, however, by outgoing President Polk's appointment of Senator Edward A. Hannegan, of Indiana, an expansionist Democrat noted for lack of tact and of sobriety, as Minister to Berlin. With Berlin gone, Marsh could hardly expect anything but a second- or third-rate post. Another blow was Taylor's choice of Jacob Collamer as Postmaster-General; little Vermont could hardly expect two major appointments. Los-

ing hope, Marsh considered other political prospects: there was the
Senate, where he might take Phelps's place; or, if he stayed in the
House, he might become Speaker. Winthrop had lost favor in the
North, and a caucus of Whigs and Free-Soilers had agreed to push
Marsh for the Speakership.[35]

In the end, what enabled Marsh to get what he most wanted was
the friendship of Colonel William Wallace Smith Bliss, Taylor's
chief of staff in the Mexican War and now the President's son-in-law
and private secretary. Within a few weeks, Marsh and the brilliant
young "Perfect" Bliss had discovered mutual interests in languages,
philosophy, and mathematics. This companionship gave Marsh
easy access to Zachary Taylor, whom he found "honest, upright,
and genial," partial to high tariffs, to freedom in the territories
—and to Vermonters in the diplomatic service. The President would
be delighted to give Marsh a post. There was only one obstacle. The
Whig majority in the House was extremely small; Adminstra-
tion leaders were loath to risk losing a Whig seat. Could Marsh
guarantee that a Whig would be elected in his place? Vermont
Whigs assured the President that if Marsh were rewarded his
district would be "safe beyond peradventure by more than *800*
over any combination." [36]

Thanks to these testimonials, on May 29, 1849, Taylor appointed
Marsh United States Minister to Turkey. Green Mountain Whigs
were overjoyed; the President had honored Vermont "AS SHE WAS
NEVER HONORED." Marsh himself was pleased though surprised; the
post was "not that which I would have selected nor that where
I should expect to be most useful," but the exoticism of the East
appealed to his romantic imagination, the climate of the Bosporus
would be good for Caroline, and he would have plenty of time for
travel; he had heard the duties were "very light," and supposed "I
shall be at liberty to be absent from Constantinople a considerable
part of the year." [37]

Marsh planned to sail in July, but Caroline, bedridden in New
York, was too ill "to travel ten miles, or even five, by coach." He took

advantage of the enforced delay to make sure that a Whig, James Meacham, would replace him in Congress. Campaigning throughout Vermont's hottest summer in half a century, on August 29 he delivered "a parting word of counsel" to his constituents, promising that the Whigs would protect Vermont's industry, repeal the sub-treasury law, promote internal improvements, and prevent the extension of slavery.[38]

There were many other matters to settle. Marsh had to pack household equipment and baggage—including scientific paraphernalia for collecting flora and fauna to send to Spencer Baird—for an indefinite stay abroad. What with traveling expenses, and scores of debts to pay before leaving the country, Marsh was in desperate need of money. As a last resort he sold portions of his library to friends, and to the Smithsonian his collection of engravings and prints and some books to the value of $3,000. Marsh stored most of his remaining books in the Smithsonian vaults. Unfortunately, the purchase by the Smithsonian was of little immediate aid; the parsimonious Joseph Henry delayed full payment for three years.

Finally, Marsh had to decide who should accompany the family to Constantinople. In addition to himself and Caroline, her sister Lucy, and young George, the party comprised Marsh's niece Maria Buell and his old friend Caroline Paine, sister of former Governor Charles Paine.

Just before leaving, Marsh visited Woodstock, where his father had died the preceding January at the age of eighty-four, to say good-by to his mother, whom he was not to see again. Afterwards Susan Marsh speculated about the difficulties her son had overcome and those he had yet to meet. "His trials have been peculiar," she concluded, "& I often feel comforted with a hope that we shall live to see him not only a professor but a possessor of that faith & the love of the saviour of sinners, which will lead to happiness." [39]

❧ VI ❧

Constantinople and the Desert

THE MARSH SAILING PACKET took a full month to reach
Le Havre. Head winds buffeted the ship back and forth for eleven
days in the Channel. Marsh was seasick the whole voyage, confirm-
ing his view that "ocean, in all its phases, is an uninviting object."
After this rough voyage, the railroad trip to Paris was a series of
delights: terraced foothills approaching the fertile valley of the me-
andering Seine; thatched, tree-shaded cottages with "a sort of out-
door look, not pleasing at first sight"; long, narrow, variegated strips
of field—"everything . . . as unlike America as can well be im-
agined." [1]

The ocean trip seriously weakened Caroline, who had to re-
cuperate for three weeks in Paris. Marsh was not at all unhappy
about the delay. He visited bookstores and libraries; he marveled
at churches and statuary, at streets and people, at the absence of
vice and misery: "no drunken men, no brawling, no squalid poverty,
and scarcely a beggar," wrote the astounded Marsh; "how they can
earn their bread I do not know, for one sees few tokens of industry."
He was delighted with Paris prices; "a single man," he estimated,
may "enjoy all the advantages of the place" for a thousand dollars
a year, "provided he is able to speak the language well enough to
make his own bargains." [2] In the midst of sightseeing Marsh did a
little diplomatic work, discussing with the Turkish envoy at Paris
means of increasing American trade to Black Sea ports.

In mid-November the Marshes resumed their leisurely trip south by railroad and stagecoach, by steamer down the Rhone to Avignon, by *vetturino* along the Riviera and across the Apennines. Italian evergreens captured their attention: ash-green olives, cork oaks, dark cypresses, palms, umbrella pines, citrus groves. Marsh did not regret missing summer foliage; he could "see the configuration of the surface much better as it is—our geology and geography [are] the stronger for the winter frosts." [3] The alternation of level green plain, blue Mediterranean, and barren or snow-covered mountains made a landscape far more vivid than the ubiquitous greenery or bleak browns of New England.

At Florence, Marsh met his boyhood friend, the sculptor Hiram Powers, long resident in Italy; under Powers's guidance he spent two weeks "luxuriating . . . among paintings and sculpture." Then on to Rome, where Marsh saw the Colosseum, in the shadow of which he was later to live, and visited St. Peter's "often, and always with renewed admiration, though disgusted with the wretched superstitions of which it is the seat." Naples offered a full-scale eruption of Mt. Vesuvius, two days after they arrived. Despite the suffocating vapor and the noise, "appalling beyond any sound I ever listened to," Marsh got within a hundred yards of the source on the northern side of the volcano, in order to measure the rate of flow of the fifteen-foot-high cherry-red lava current. Marsh returned to Vesuvius several days running, and sent his notes on the eruption to the Smithsonian.[4]

After a week aboard the frigate *Mississippi* in the smooth waters of the Mediterranean and the Aegean, the Marsh entourage steamed through the Dardanelles and the Sea of Marmara, rounded Seraglio Point, and entered the Bosporus and the Golden Horn. Before them were the domes and minarets of Constantinople, romantically lit by the morning sun. Frigate and fort gave salute and countersalute, echoes reverberated in the encircling hills; Turkish and American officers came aboard, and the new United States Minister ceremoniously disembarked. It was the twenty-third of February, 1850, almost half a year since he had set sail from America. What with Paris and Florence, Avignon and Rome, pictures and statues, ruins and volcanoes, he had "enjoyed more during the winter, than I thought I could in the rest of my life." [5]

I

After these European pleasures, Marsh found Turkey a disappointment. The weather changed suddenly; bright sun gave way to snow flurries and cold winds. Constantinople itself was barred to Europeans by the Turkish government; foreign diplomats lived in less picturesque Pera, across the Golden Horn. Quaint-looking from the waterfront, Pera's squalid cobblestoned alleys rose so steeply that horses could not maneuver them, and the Marshes had to finish their journey to Dubois' Hotel on foot.

This hostelry proved to be cold, damp, and practically unfurnished. The large drawing room had neither stove nor fireplace; after one freezing day Marsh obtained a large, charcoal-burning brazier, around which crouched the seven shivering members of the Ministerial party. Incense failed to dissipate the vertiginous effect of the coal gas. There were only two sheets among all of them; the beds were filthy, the privy out of order. The meals were miniscule and "so wretched," Marsh complained, "that we neither did nor could swallow them." After two weeks "in this idle and useless condition," Marsh moved to a warmer but equally depressing hotel, opposite a great cemetery full of decaying turbaned tombstones; in a near-by parade ground soldiers drilled from daybreak until late at night to the penetrating accompaniment of fife and drum.[6]

Marsh knew no comfort until late April, when he took a house at Therapia, a small Greek village twelve miles from Constantinople on the European side of the Bosporus. The three-story house, perched twenty feet above the landing quay, had ceilings ornamented with intricate mosaics, a Turkish bath, a piano, and a formal terraced garden in the rear, with fragrant pomegranates, jasmine, and passionflowers. Broad steps, lined with crimson dahlias in great stone vases, led to a second terrace where berries and fruit trees grew, and to a vineyard above. In summer the garden yielded melons and quinces. Later, the figs ripened, small but sweet, and grapes, abundant and delicious, though not superior, Marsh judged, to those of New England.

In the villa at Therapia pleasant days slipped past without incident. Caroline remained in good spirits, though constantly ill. They had an army of servants: a maître d'hôtel who "progresseth continually in the ways of perfection," a cook, a waiter, a gardener, a washerwoman and her maid, a seamstress, a Turkish officer who accompanied Marsh when he went out, and another who carried messages to the Sublime Porte. Marsh devoted days of leisure to horseback rides and to excursions to Bebek or the Golden Horn, stopping sometimes to take coffee and sherbet with a Turkish friend.

June brought a surprise visitor, Doctor Wislizenus; won over by this intrepid suitor who had followed her halfway around the world, Lucy married him at the Legation, and they went off to Germany and the United States. With Lucy gone, Therapia was quieter than ever. Few visitors ventured out from Constantinople; the Marshes saw no one except missionaries and the British and French Ministers, who vacationed near by. Here the Marshes remained throughout the long, equable summer and fall, listening to the wind sighing through pines and cypresses, the nightingales singing in their branches, the bleating of goats; and watching the flux of travel: women shuffling along the quays, donkeys loaded with panniers of black bread, effendis with their pipe-bearers. Below, the laurel-fringed Bosporus was flecked with lithe, fragile caïques, darting over the transparent surface to Constantinople or to the Black Sea.

2

In the narrow bottom of one of these caïques—rowed by six oarsmen for an extravagant fee—Marsh crouched uncomfortably on his way to Teheragan Palace for his first call, March 11, 1850, on his Imperial Majesty, twenty-seven-year old Sultan Abdul-Medjid. The reception was an imposing spectacle, for a Vermonter unused to the ceremonious East. Marsh presented his credentials, congratulated the Sultan on the recent birth of twin princes, and expressed hopes that Turkish-American relations would remain friendly; the Sultan, wearing plume, fez, and diamond agraffe, responded formally in French, and the new Minister bowed out.[7]

There could have been no more fascinating place to serve a diplomatic novitiate than Turkey, long famous for international intrigue. Now on the brink of the Crimean War, Turkey had for years been rent by internal dissension, civil violence, economic distress, social and religious turmoil. When young Abdul-Medjid came to the throne in 1839, Turkey was harassed by the powerful Mehemet Ali, rebellious Viceroy of Egypt; but with help from England and France, Abdul-Medjid reestablished suzerainty over Egypt. Encouraged by the able British Ambassador, Stratford Canning, who virtually dictated Turkish foreign policy, the Sultan established a modicum of civil order, granted religious liberties, safeguarded Christian missionaries and foreign residents, and initiated economic reforms intended to break the hold of the aristocracy on land and people.

Marsh thought the Sultan just and generous; "unlike . . . a long line of cruel predecessors," he was "almost worshipped . . . throughout his empire . . . excess of liberality indeed seems to be almost his only fault." But Abdul-Medjid, though "a most excellent and well-meaning man," was too gentle and amiable to be effective—and he was "alone in his empire." Marsh feared, he added, that the venality of the Sultan's advisers, the wealth of his opponents, the intractability of reactionary Moslems, and above all the malignant activities of the Greek Orthodox minority on behalf of Austrian or Russian ambitions, would nullify Abdul-Medjid's program. "Enormous frauds and peculations of the officers of Government" imperiled finances. The Armenian tax farmers took half of what they received, and were bribed to persuade the credulous Sultan to grant remissions of levies. The previous ruler had a remedy for these evils, "rude indeed, but effectual. The Pacha who had grown rich by bribery, or the Armenian who had swindled the government, was strangled or banished, and the treasury replenished by the confiscation of his spoil." But the present Sultan, Marsh concluded sorrowfully, "has renounced this just, though summary, means of redress, and has provided no substitute . . . and the government is robbed and cheated with shameless openness, and perfect impunity." [8]

With a government "characterized on the one hand by helpless imbecility, and on the other by open and unrebuked corruption," only the "mutual distrust and hatred" of racial and religious factions stifled domestic revolution, and only "commercial and political jealousies . . . among European Powers" prevented external aggression. As the Crimean War drew nearer, Marsh feared that even this last security would vanish. Turkey was "in a shocking state," he wrote; "it is a house of cards, & the smallest power in Europe could overthrow it, if the rest would not interfere." The government was "little better than bankrupt . . . the whole Empire is in a state of complete disorganization, and there is no security for life or property anywhere." [9]

3

Pera, the city of diplomats, epitomized the inadequacies of Turkish reform. It was "a wretched place," Marsh complained, "full of villains of every description—outcasts from European civilization"; rape, murder, robbery, and religious vendettas were everyday affairs. Among the annoyances of his "ticklish" post, Marsh noted "fleas and scorpions, fellows watching you or following you with an ugly stick or worse; . . . loud screams at midnight . . . from a neighbor's house, that a band of armed robbers was plundering . . . a report of a gun and then another report that a neighbor's wife had been shot at her window, the assassin expressing much regret at his mistake, having taken her for another lady." [10] In this atmosphere the foreign ambassadors lived and worked. Whatever their political differences, they were, as Christians in a Mohammedan land, socially close-knit. Marsh found the diplomatic corps, as a whole, superior to that in Washington, and thanks to his command of languages he got on extremely well from the start.

For the most part Marsh worked with the great Stratford Canning. He was also on good terms with the Russian Ambassador, Titoff, who shared his interest in ancient Scandinavia; General Aupick, the French Ambassador, and his clever Consul-General, Eugène Poujade; Count Portales, Prussian Minister and friend of Humboldt; Count de Souza of Spain; Baron Tecco of Sardinia; and Count Stürmer, Internuncio from Austria.

In this assemblage no one ranked lower than the American Minister; at an official dinner Marsh's place was seventy-second. He was not even a plenipotentiary but a mere Minister; every minor European power maintained an envoy of higher diplomatic grade. Marsh felt sure that his low status degraded the United States in Turkish eyes.

Another vexation was the poor personal reputation of American diplomats in Turkey. Marsh's immediate predecessor at the Sublime Porte had been the bellicose Maryland politician Dabney Smith Carr. French was the essential diplomatic language, but Carr knew no French; he "was almost never seen in society," Marsh related, "unless in that of some drunken Englishman, & had no better diplomatic position than his horse." Carr's recall had removed "a load of infamy . . . from the shoulders of the Christian community here." Not yet recalled was George A. Porter, Consul at Constantinople, "an idle, ignorant, weak, and dissolute person," reported Marsh, and "a discredit to the country that employed him." [11] Other consulates were as badly staffed; J. Hosford Smith at Beirut was a person of "doubtful competence" and "little ability"; E. S. Offley at Smyrna was a disagreeable and stubborn fellow who gave Marsh endless trouble. The majority were unable to cope with the simplest commercial or diplomatic problems. The voluminous consular correspondence shows that Marsh continually had to come to their aid. There was much room for improvement in American foreign service and prestige in the Levant.

Marsh also wished to promote Turkish-American trade. As Turkey's self-appointed guardians against Russia and Austria, England and France took the lion's share of Turkey's commerce. But Britain's adoption of free trade opened Black Sea ports to American vessels; American machinery and hardware, or British goods purchased with American cotton, might be exchanged profitably for commodities from the Levant. Turkish duties on American goods were very low. If the United States reciprocated by reducing tariffs on olive oil, wine, silk, raw wool, and dyestuffs, and set up a proper consular system, March envisaged "a very great and profitable trade with the East." [12] Aali Pasha, the Turkish Foreign Minister, was ready to meet Marsh halfway; anxious to reduce her dependence on England, the Sublime Porte welcomed *rapprochement* with the United States.

The first result of Turkish-American accord was the visit to the United States of Emin Effendi, better known as Amin Bey. This Turkish naval officer was to report to his government on American ships, docks, and Navy yards, and to survey American resources to determine the most desirable type of trade. Marsh had induced the Porte to choose the right man for the job, "a genuine Turk," he explained, rather than one educated in Europe who "would have acquired prejudices in favor of England or France." [13]

Amin Bey was accompanied to America in 1850 by John P. Brown, Marsh's hard-working though somewhat obtuse dragoman, or translator. At first all went well. "Emin Bey proves to be an intelligent fellow," Brown wrote Marsh from shipboard, "out of whom I hope to make something useful." The Turk had a brilliant reception. Feted in New York, he moved on in a glow of good feeling to Washington, where Fillmore and Webster honored him, and Congress allotted $10,000 for his expenses. Brown was "de-

lighted at the success of our little scheme." But there was a worm in
the apple of American generosity. Rumors spread that Turkey had
never accredited Amin Bey, and that Congress had been duped by an
impostor. Despite denials by the State Department, which "never for
a moment . . . doubted" the official character of the mission,[14]
several journals—particularly the New York *Tribune*—accused
Marsh and Brown of foisting a spurious envoy on the American
people.

Public affection for Amin Bey cooled rapidly; the rest of the trip
was a dreadful failure. Poor Brown grew excessively weary of drag-
ging him around the country; he no longer sang Amin Bey's praises
but spoke of him contemptuously as gross, ill-mannered, ignorant,
obstinate. The Sublime Porte's reaction to the mission was mixed.
The practical results were of moderate scope, and if the Sultan saw
in the official "brilliant reception" of the naval officer "a new proof of
the friendship of the American government for the Sublime Porte,"
he was "surprised and incensed" at the unwarranted attacks in the
public press.[15] Commerce between the two countries remained
negligible.

Marsh also tried but failed to promote American trade with
Persia. The Persian Chargé d'Affaires at Constantinople proposed a treaty of commerce, and Marsh drew one up, gaining considerable concessions for the United States. The whole affair was
carried on in secrecy, for fear of interference by France, which
monopolized Persian trade. The United States Senate ratified the
treaty in 1852. To Marsh's dismay and anger, however, the news
had leaked out to the press, and France prevailed upon the Shah
of Persia to reject the treaty.[16] This was not the only time the State
Department was careless with Marsh's confidential communications.

4

Marsh's regular duties were, as he had hoped, not terribly onerous;
but there were some responsibilities he had not anticipated. The

most agreeable of these was protecting the dozen Protestant missionaries who ran a seminary at Bebek on the Bosporus. Brought up, Marsh told them somewhat pompously, "to form a fit estimate of your personal characters, [and] to feel a strong interest in the success of the great objects you are . . . promoting," the Minister aided the missionaries in their frequent brushes with the Sublime Porte. For instance, after they got official permission to build a mill and bakery to provide their poor disciples with food and employment, the bakers' guild protested and the Porte stopped the work. But "it was not found wise," commented one of the missionaries, "to make a direct promise to Mr. Marsh, and then attempt to evade it." He went to the Grand Vizier and settled the affair successfully "without any harsh words, and without any Oriental *lubrication*." [17]

Far more difficult for Marsh were the complex problems of extraterritoriality. Since the Middle Ages, European traders in Byzantine and Turkish Constantinople had received certain privileges in return for the commerce they brought. Foreign companies were given sections of the city where they carried on their economic, social, and religious life without interference. Residents of such enclaves, exempt from local taxes and immune from the laws of the land, were subject only to the rule of their own communities. In Turkey, where most foreign commerce was in European hands, and where the dominant religion and the social code differed markedly from European practices, such privileges and immunities were highly prized by foreign residents and deeply resented by natives.

The American Minister had not only to protect American citizens in Turkey, but also to judge disputes between Americans and others. All apart from the enormous amount of work entailed, Marsh found his duties irreconcilable: how could he defend American interests and at the same time be an impartial magistrate? Exceptions to the general rule complicated matters. American diplomats had authority in criminal but not in civil matters involving Americans. Thus Americans and Turks could sue each other in Turkish courts, but if a Turk won a civil case and the American refused to pay, nothing could be done, for American consuls could not enforce Turkish decisions. In retaliation, Turks often refused to execute just American claims. Pending abolition of all extraterritoriality, Marsh asked for authority in civil cases as well as criminal, but the Senate Foreign Affairs Committee turned down his proposal.[18]

The cases Marsh had to hear posed intricate questions of jurisdiction; he found the forensic labor arduous and time-consuming. For example, an English firm sued the dragoman of United States Consul E. S. Offley in Smyrna; Offley claimed jurisdiction and decided against the British, who appealed the case to Marsh. In another case, two Armenian protégés of the British Consul in Jerusalem claimed that the American Vice-Consul at Jaffa, a Turk, owed them $100,000, and demanded that Marsh dismiss him from his post so that they could try him in Turkish courts.[19]

Differences between American and Turkish law made matters worse. Marsh was loath to enforce Turkish prison sentences for non-payment of debts, because he did not see how the Legation could "exercise so broad a power, which the American government does not exercise in its own territory." But if he occasionally strained a point for Americans, on the whole Marsh was eminently fair. He had "no wish to shield American citizens," as he told the Porte, from the just consequences of their misbehavior. Marsh was extremely severe with abuses of privilege. When he caught Offley trying to leave Turkey without giving surety for his considerable debts, the irate Minister warned the would-be decamper that "I cannot suffer the interests of our citizens in Turkey to be hazarded by any attempt to deprive the Turkish tribunals of the jurisdiction which belongs to them." Unless Offley satisfied his creditors, Marsh would "notify the Porte that neither you nor your interests are any longer under the protection of this Legation." [20] The Consul decided not to leave.

Extraterritorial privileges, Marsh realized, were actually detrimental to American interests. "The whole practice of foreign protections," he wrote the Secretary of State, "is a mischievous anomaly." [21] It aroused hostility and suspicion among the Turks, who were reluctant to enter into business which might subject them to foreign jurisdiction. The entire fabric of privileges and immunities encouraged Europeans to think themselves superior to the Turks. Such arrogant ethnocentrism, Marsh recognized, might have disastrous results. It was many years, however, before extraterritoriality in Turkey came to an end.

5

The poor Hungarians the martyrs of so saint a cause [sic] *are about to be cast out helpless, with no other choise than to shot themselfs* [sic], *to perish by hunger or to gain a miserable life by unlawful dishonest means.*   KOSSUTH TO MARSH, JAN. 1, 1850

Among the thousands who asked help from the American Legation, the great majority were foreigners—the political refugees, escaped convicts, and human flotsam and jetsam of Constantinople. Their numbers had recently been augmented by hundreds of exiles who had fled from Italy, Poland, and Hungary after the failure of the 1848 revolutions. All these people circulated from one legation to another, begging for protection, for work, or simply for food.

Christian legations in Turkey traditionally took care of Europeans who had no diplomatic representatives of their own at the Porte. Following this principle, Marsh issued a number of passports to refugees from the Papal States. But the problem grew out of hand as increasing numbers sought American aid. While some were really political refugees, the majority turned out to be "men of depraved and desperate characters," as Marsh described them, "who ask for protection only as an immunity for crime." Many passports had been issued blank in Rome and acquired by criminals. Furthermore, Marsh's predecessor, Dabney Carr, had sold passports to non-Americans; some consuls still did so. This prevented Turks and Europeans from punishing or extraditing their own nationals. Marsh finally refused to shield any except bona fide American citizens, but continued to be plagued by "Americans" who displayed "passports," placed themselves under his protection, demanded money, and often had to be shipped away at legation expense.[22]

One group of refugees, however, Marsh helped to the limit of his powers. This was Kossuth's band of Hungarians, who had fled to Turkey in August, 1849. Austria demanded their extradition, but the Sultan—supported by Britain—refused to yield them. Marsh congratulated Turkey and on his own initiative offered Kossuth and his followers asylum in the United States. Many high American officials had publicly lauded the Hungarian revolutionists, and Austria complained of the hostile tone of President Taylor's 1849 message to Congress. The famous Mann Report enraged public opinion against Austria; a real break threatened. Instructing Marsh to do what he could for Kossuth and his followers, the State Department approved his offer of asylum.

In March, 1850, Marsh asked Turkey to let Kossuth and his chief compatriots go to the United States.[23] But Turkey had promised to detain the Hungarians a full year, and refused to release them now, fearing Austrian reprisals. Austria wanted to keep Kossuth from reaching England or America, where he might enlist support for incendiary movements.

Meanwhile, Kossuth was in constant communication with Marsh. Pouring his heart out in weekly letters from the Anatolian interior, the Hungarian leader complained that his 1,200 men were ill-treated and neglected. Still more pitiable were the bulk of the former soldiers in and around Constantinople, who could not get work and were not allowed to join the Turkish army. Could not these men, asked Kossuth, be brought to the United States and given land? Marsh was pessimistic. He thought Congress would offer the refugees land once they reached America, but could "hold out very little encouragement" that the government would give them transport across the ocean.[24]

Marsh assured the impatient Hungarian that he had interceded for him time and again with the Porte, and would continue to advance "the interests of that great cause which has excited so strong a sympathy in my own breast, as well as in that of the entire body of my countrymen." In July, 1850, Aali Pasha, as anxious as Marsh to rid Turkey of the refugees, offered to pay their passage to England if Marsh guaranteed that the United States would take them the rest of the way; unfortunately, Marsh lacked "authority to accept this liberal proposal." Meanwhile he needled his government, emphasizing how important it was to maintain America's reputation for aiding the oppressed.[25] But Congress, now embarrassed by the controversy with Austria, made no appropriation for the refugees.

Their plight grew desperate by winter. American newspaper sympathy, past government promises, and Marsh's own conscience "compelled me to go much beyond my means in supplying the wants of these suffering outcasts"; they could hardly be allowed to die at the legation door. Webster acted at last in February, 1851. Commending Marsh for having fed so many refugees, the Secretary of State offered passage to Kossuth when his year of detention was over.[26] Overjoyed, Kossuth boarded the *Mississippi* with his family and fifty associates on September 10.

This was by no means the end of American difficulties with the noble Magyar. Certain that Kossuth had no intention of keeping his promise to go directly to the United States, Marsh warned Captain Long and Commodore Morgan to give the Hungarian patriot no chance to leave the *Mississippi*. Marsh's suspicions were borne out. When Kossuth discovered no stopovers were scheduled, he complained that he was "still a prisoner." At Spezia, where the squadron put in for supplies, excited crowds thronged the *Mississippi* day and night; Kossuth alternately harangued his sympathizers and begged the Commodore to let him leave the ship and go to England. In desperation Morgan finally acceded; Kossuth toured France and England in triumph before reaching America in December, 1851. Captain Long did not "wish to hear the name of Kossuth ever again," but word spread that the Hungarian had been horribly mistreated aboard the *Mississippi;* American papers condemned Long for his brutality. Marsh valiantly defended Long, "one of the most valuable officers, I have known in the course of my life," and took to task his friend H. J. Raymond, of the New York *Times,* whom he assured that Kossuth was lying: "It was notorious, from the moment he went on board the ship, that he did not mean to proceed to America in her." [27]

Others came to share Marsh's view that Kossuth's liberation was almost more trouble than it was worth. As the Hungarian marched from one ovation to another, preaching revolutionary doctrine, denouncing various governments, and asking for aid against Austria, American political leaders became increasingly constrained. Despite Kossuth's eloquence, the government was not moved to meddle in European affairs; "many of the politicians," a Washington friend reported to Marsh, "have been merely coquetting with him." [28] Kossuth soon fell from favor. Some were disgusted by his bad manners, arrogance, or equivocal attitude toward slavery; others wearied of his exhortations and appeals for money. In the end he gave a greater impetus to nativist sentiment than to the cause of world liberty.

Marsh was disappointed that Kossuth had failed to strengthen American sympathy for European political freedom, but he was not surprised. For Kossuth personally he had no use whatever. He considered the Hungarian's selfishness and egotism boundless; to these traits he now added ingratitude. Kossuth "never . . . had the decency," Marsh observed bitterly, "to utter a word of thankfulness for the unceasing exertions of every member of this Legation in behalf of himself & his associates, or even for the bread which hundreds of them have eaten at the cost of the ill-furnished pockets of myself & my secretaries." [29]

Marsh was always amazed when people were ungrateful, and simply dismissed such men as contemptible. It was worse when his own government treated him in what he thought a mean and stingy way. Patriotism did not permit him to condemn America, but he did complain bitterly.

6

I never lived in so poorly a furnished house (we have not a foot of carpeting), never fared so badly, never enjoyed so few luxuries or even comforts as here. I have given no entertainments of any sort . . . yet my household expenditures have exceeded my salary.

MARSH TO CHARLES D. DRAKE, AUG. 3, 1850

November cold drove the Marshes from Therapia back to Pera. But they could not find a house there fit to live in. None had fireplaces or stove chimneys, although Pera was colder than New York; no houses were available for less than a full year, and rents were enormous. Other necessities were correspondingly expensive; most food had to be imported. Meat was wretched and costly, fruit inferior; Marsh found even the famous Smyrna casaba melons poor.

Food, rent, and the high price of fuel made Pera, Marsh claimed, "the most extravagant city in the world"; he lived less well on his $6,000 salary than he had as a $2,500 Congressman. Ministers were expected to keep large retinues; every Turkish official expected a present on each visit; impecunious Hungarians always needed help.[30] Marsh's dispatches were studded with complaints about the insufficiency of his salary.

It was for the good of his country, Marsh insisted, that he wanted more money and a higher rank. "The Turks are a rude people," he explained, "and measure the consequence of foreigners by the style they live in." The Austrian Internuncio got a salary of $80,000; the British Ambassador, $60,000; most envoys had winter palaces in Pera and summer places on the Bosporus. "I *know* that if I had the means of living like a gentleman," wrote the paupered American Minister, "if I could now and then ask a Turk to dinner, if I could make him a present of a rocking chair, or some other trifle . . . I could accomplish more for the extension of our commerce

. . . in *one year,* than my 'competent' predecessors have done . . . to this hour." [31]

Marsh's complaints did not fall on deaf ears. Colonel Bliss alerted the President, and Marsh was awaiting his promotion to Minister Plenipotentiary when he was stunned by news of Zachary Taylor's death. This "deep calamity" elevated to the Presidency Millard Fillmore, whom Marsh despised; it also doomed his chance for an increase. The friendship of the new Secretary of State, Daniel Webster, availed him little. According to Marsh's friend Francis Markoe, now the department's Chief Clerk, Webster was "crazier than ever for the Presidency [and] would not recommend an unpopular measure to save the soul of his best friend." Webster did recommend "some augmentation" of Marsh's salary, but was "very gruff and ill-natured" about the matter, Solomon Foot told Marsh; "his disparaging remarks in reference to yourself, led me to suppose, you had in some way given the old fellow some offense." [32]

Instrumental in Marsh's disappointment was the campaign Horace Greeley waged against him in the New York *Tribune*. "Greeley," declared Marsh, when the *Tribune* began to attack him, "is an old, and so far as I know, unprovoked enemy of mine, and no new evidence of his malice toward me can surprise me." The two men first met in Burlington in 1848; in December Greeley had come to Washington as a Congressman. The crusading editor flayed his fellow Representatives for wasting time and money, tried to cut their salaries, and published statements showing how they cheated the government by charging for excessive mileage to their homes. Marsh was one of a small handful who had opposed the mail-route mileage bill as petty and degrading. Like his father, he refused to support piddling Congressional economies; time and again he voted for additions to diplomatic bills, improvements of the White House and of public grounds, and other items that seemed to Greeley mere ostentation. "The best-hated man" in the House, Greeley made certain of Marsh's dislike: "One day, when a vote was to be taken on a question in which Greeley felt an inter-

est, but apparently Marsh did not, the zealous new member, notic-
ing that the latter made no sign, pulled him by the sleeve and said;
'Why don't you vote? Why don't you vote? This is a question on
which you ought to vote.'" Marsh resented being told what to do
and abhorred personal familiarity; he made some cold and cutting
reply. Wounded, Greeley "never after missed an opportunity of
manifesting strong hostility toward his recalcitrant colleague." [33]

Marsh's request for a raise was just what Greeley expected from
"a man of fortune, an advocate of High Salaries generally, and a
deadly foe to retrenchment." Who cared, asked Greeley, if an American Minister's "parade and glitter of ostentatious display" did not
measure up to the Russian Ambassador's? The mission to Turkey
had been "competently filled" by Porter and Carr "without any
complaint as to salary," noted the *Tribune* editor. "If Mr. Marsh
is sick of it, let him drop off and some good man will be found to
take his place for the $6000." [34]

Greeley's "malicious falsehood" infuriated Marsh. Both Porter
and Carr had repeatedly complained about their salaries, and prices
in Constantinople had since doubled. Greeley did not care about
truth; "he thought his assertion . . . would be believed, & that it
would injure me." [35] And it did injure Marsh. He had some friends
in the press, but they were outshouted by Greeley.

There was one solution for Marsh's financial problems. If he spent
the winter in the provinces, he could avoid the ruinous expense of
taking a house at Pera. Marsh figured that they could "spend three
or four months travelling in Egypt, Arabia, and Syria, with every
convenience, for less money than we can stay here." Caroline's
health was worse than ever; Marsh wanted to get her away from the
cold, wet Bosporus. Such a trip, Marsh explained to the Secretary
of State, would further American interests in the Near East. Satisfied that an "escape from the miserable inconveniences of life at
Constantinople" was indispensable, Marsh had already set sail for
Alexandria when his *congé* came at last, with Webster's "hearty
sanction." [36]

7

The Austrian steamer *Schildt* tossed in the heavy Mediterranean swells; Marsh was sick during the whole week's voyage. "Truly," he wrote, "I hate the sea, and would be well content to pay my share of the cost of filling it up altogether." Alexandria seemed scarcely worth the trip; modernized by Mehemet Ali, it was flat, dull, uninteresting. Marsh conferred there with Said Pasha, Mehemet Ali's son and future Viceroy of Egypt. At Cairo he saw Viceroy Abbas Pasha. Far from finding Abbas "foolish and brutal," as he had been told in Constantinople, Marsh was impressed with the Viceroy's intelligence and candor. The conflicting interests of his own subjects, the Sublime Porte, and European powers put the Egyptian ruler in a precarious position. As Viceroy under the Turkish Empire, Abbas had to administer the Sultan's religious and social reforms, which were highly unpopular—and potentially dangerous to Christians—in Egypt. If he defied the Sultan, Abbas asked Marsh, would England help Egypt? Fresh from talks with Stratford Canning, Marsh said he thought the Viceroy could count on British friendship.[37]

This was strange counsel, coming from the American Minister to Turkey, particularly in view of Marsh's general disapproval of Britain. A year's contact with Canning had temporarily converted Marsh to a qualified admiration of British foreign rule. "All the great interests of humanity, our own included," Marsh asserted, "will be best advanced by an extension of British sway in the Levant"; he hoped Egypt and Turkey would become English protectorates! [38] What concerned Marsh most, however, was the danger of Russian hegemony, against which he thought Britain the only bulwark.

Early one January morning the Ministerial party sailed up the Nile from Cairo. It was a carefree expedition, with George making jokes, Caroline Paine "clean daft" in the study of Italian, and Marsh

sunning himself on the deck. Date palms and an occasional syca-
more and mimosa fringed the banks of the turbid river. Rice, wheat,
sugar cane, and cotton filled the narrow valley, with here and there
a village of dried mud huts. Everywhere bullocks drew up water
for irrigation in endless chains of buckets; Marsh heard the creaking
of these norias from early dawn till late at night. Waterfowl—
herons and cranes, geese, ducks, cormorants, and pelicans—festooned
the shores, and near Aswan Marsh glimpsed crocodiles.

Above the First Cataract to Wadi Halfa the trip surpassed all
Marsh's expectations. The Nubian desert reached almost to the
river, leaving a mere thread of arable land; the days grew warmer,
the air soft and mild, with a steady north breeze. Their broad,
shallow-bottomed, lateen-sailed vessel contained cabins, hammocks,
a fireplace, and a caged ostrich; their cook concocted magnificent
meals from dainties furnished by Cairo bazaars, and sheep and
poultry garnered from the countryside. "We have a good boat,"
exulted Marsh, "most excellent servants, dragoman and crew, and I
have no where enjoyed so many of the pleasures, alloyed with so few
of the ordinary discomforts, of travelling, as in this visit to the
Nile." [39] Not even the bites of Nubian flies and the piercing demands of Nubian natives for baksheesh diminished Marsh's enthusiasm.

On the leisurely journey down the Nile, they stayed twelve days
at Thebes in a house of "unburnt Pharonic bricks, mummy cases, &
dead men's bones," and then in an "incredible mud hovel . . . on
the roof of a temple at Luxor." At Karnak, carrying Caroline
through the temple, Marsh sprained his ankle. He hobbled into
Cairo at the end of April still incapacitated. But a one-eyed, shriv-
eled Arab physician put Marsh's badly swollen foot and ankle in
warm water, dipped his own fingers in olive oil, and rubbed,
pressed, and pulled; Marsh put on his shoe and walked away without pain.[40] After this miraculous cure, Marsh decided to go into the
desert, hoping that warm sand and dry air would benefit Caroline.

They left Cairo on May 7, with a caravan of twenty-six camels, under the guidance and protection of the doughty Sheik Hussein of Aqaba and his sizable retinue.

Like the ancient Israelites, the Marshes took forty days to reach the Holy Land. They traversed almost the same route—east to Suez, down the eastern shore of the Gulf, over the central ridge of Sinai, through precipitous wadis and across barren plateaus to Aqaba and the Red Sea, thence across Arabia Petraea to the red ruins of Petra itself, up Mt. Hor, and along the Wadi El Araba to the Dead Sea and the pleasant groves of Hebron. Here they exchanged their camels for mules and went on into Jerusalem. The route was formidable, the heat intense—110° or more in their tents—but all went well: "any forty days of *stage* travelling in the United States," Marsh reassured his mother, "would involve more of fatigue, danger, and discomfort of all sorts, than this trip has done." [41]

Marsh was particularly pleased with the adaptable camels. Sure-footed, dependable, not choosy as to food, the camel could carry heavy loads and travel great distances without drinking. His nose kept out sand, his stomach retained water, his hump stored fat and secured the saddle. One could bestride a camel "sidewise or backwards," Marsh wrote, "with legs crossed or dangling, and arms folded or akimbo, with no fear that your beast will kick up or stumble and pitch you over his head, or rear and throw you over his tail, or shy out from under you at the sight of an old woman or the bow of a country school-boy, or take the bit in his teeth and run to Quoddy with you." [42]

His fondness for camels, with their rolling gait, evil disposition, and terrible smell, seems perverse considering his dread of the sea. But the affection was real and, Marsh claimed, reciprocated. He once encountered a camel "in a great rage, making threatening sounds, blowing a sort of bladder out of its mouth, snapping at other people, but didn't bite *me*." To the uninitiated, breath jerked out of his body, limbs aching and sore, throat parched, the jolting step of the camel might seem wearisome, but a few days' practice, Marsh promised, would make it most relaxing. Indeed, the camel's back was so comfortable that robbers lurked waiting for travelers to fall asleep on their steeds. Arabs ground grain and baked bread while in motion; others asserted they could look through telescopes, sew, knit, darn stockings, or draw, and Marsh boasted that "by resolving myself into a set of animated gimbals, I contrived to take and record compass bearings." [43]

Marsh and his party started early, by two in the morning when there was a full moon, to avoid riding in the heat of the day. On the way, Marsh devoted himself to scrutiny of the desert landscape, now bounded by the narrow defile of a dry wadi, now a broad stretch of firm hamada with clumps of dwarf acacia and stunted tamarisk. There was little conversation; camels were tempted by near-by thistles, which made it difficult to ride abreast and enforced solitude on the travelers.

At the end of the day's journey the Marshes threw themselves exhausted on the sand; while men unloaded camels and pitched tents, Hussein's servant offered small cups of coffee spiced with cloves, with the Sheik's compliments. This refreshing and delectable gift was, in fact, Marsh discovered, "a portion of what he [Hussein] daily robbed from our stores for his own use!" Then came dinner; after writing their journals, the party settled down for the night, grateful for cool breezes after the scorching desert day. The evening silence was broken only by camels crunching their meal of beans and by the Bedouins quietly quarreling over the division of expected profits. Sleep came soon—barring incident: Marsh recalled one fearful night with "no water—thermometer at 110°, air deathly still, and camels *very* near." [44]

After resting several days at Hebron, the party went on to Bethlehem and Jerusalem. Marsh swam in the Dead Sea, but did not find "the extraordinary buoyancy, stickiness, and other odd qualities" he had expected.[45] The road north to Nazareth was long and tiring. Fever had weakened Caroline at Sinai and Bethlehem, young George had been sick in Jerusalem, and Marsh himself now felt ill.

A few hours after they reached Nazareth Marsh lost consciousness. An old Spanish priest at the convent bled him—with the result that Marsh seemed to stop breathing. The anxious priest squirted liquid ammonia directly in his face, which revived the patient but scalded him badly.

After a week's recuperation at Mt. Carmel, the Marshes set out for Damascus. By the time they reached Magdal on the Sea of Galilee, both were again desperately ill. Despite the urgings of their guide, who feared attacks by robbers, they could not go on, and stayed helplessly in the ancient birthplace of Mary Magdalene, a mud village in a low, marshy plain, which seemed to Marsh "one of the most horrible places imaginable." [46]

They were saved by the arrival of the Rev. John Bowen, an Arabic-speaking Welsh minister and physician. Bowen persuaded Arabs in the vicinity to help him build stretchers and move the invalids twelve miles to high, cool Safed. There in an old olive grove Bowen and the Nazareth priest, aided by Caroline Paine and Maria Buell, nursed the Marshes back to health. After nine days the expedition got under way once more, with Marsh on a litter, exhausted and feeble, but enjoying to the utmost the wild grandeur of little-known southwestern Lebanon. Twelve days more brought them to Beirut, and they reached Constantinople on August 31, after an absence of eight months.

Rumor had spread back home that they had all perished in the desert—one friend recalled that he had always "had very little expectation of ever looking upon *her* [Caroline's] sweet face again." [47] Caroline was, in fact, still seriously ill. At Constantinople only the British Embassy physician, young Humphrey Sandwith, gave a hopeful prognosis, and gradually brought her out of danger. Marsh's own reserves were low after his bout with fever. He came down with erysipelas, then jaundice, and did not recover until spring.

None of this diminished Marsh's ardor for exploring. He had liked Palestine even better than Egypt, and looked forward to further trips. "My anticipations of pleasure and instruction from travel have been much more than realized," he wrote in retrospect. He had experienced "great enjoyment, great sufferings, and great mercies." [48]

8

Let us faithfully record the impressions of the day, and depend upon it, both we and the world shall be the wiser for it.

MARSH, *The Camel* (1856)

Marsh's travels were enhanced by his exceptional powers of observation and his breadth of interest. Every aspect of the landscape, natural and human, fascinated him; geology, climate, flora, and fauna competed for his attention with ruins and relics of antiquity and peoples and cultures of the present. He approached all facets of existence, animate and inanimate, as an intelligent amateur; he was the first to admit that he was no scientist. But while Marsh deplored his lack of special training and ignorance of natural science, these failings detract little from his accounts of places and people.

His letters and journals display a naïve yet profound realism, a fusion of all the elements of landscape into unified description, that is rare among men trained in narrow specialties. His pictures are most vivid and meaningful just where they are least analytic, least learned, least encumbered with scientific paraphernalia. To Marsh, as to others in his day, "science" meant the detailed cataloguing of facts; the sort of synthesis he performed was not considered "scientific."

Marsh's exhortations on "the extreme importance of keeping a most full and minute record of every observation and every noteworthy occurrence" are gems of good sense, as his own journals and letters are models of their kind. Marsh recorded what he saw, carefully, systematically, and industriously. Claims that travelers remembered more, and better, without the aid of diaries were "all moonshine," Marsh warned; "you remember no whit the worse, and you observe vastly better, for the practice of full, clear, and accurate description." One could recall only a small part of what one saw in strange lands, "where all—nature, art, man—is new." Journals served to "refresh and revive the fading pictures" that could hardly be duplicated. "Let no excuse of lassitude, no impatience of the inconveniences of writing on your knee in the open air, with insects buzzing about your ears, and the wind scattering your papers and sanding your page before it is filled," deter the traveler from putting everything down. "Trust nothing to the memory. Make no vague entries, such as 'fine scenery after sunrise,' 'remarkable rock far off to the right,' 'singular appearance in the sky this morning,' and so forth, foolishly imagining that you will remember the details, and have the energy to write them out tomorrow." Today's energy must suffice; "tomorrow will bring with it new observations to record, new inconveniences to surmount, new weariness to combat." [49]

Lack of systematic training did not deter Marsh from conscientiously recording basic geographical data. He took compass bearings, measured altitudes, registered temperatures and rainfall, estimated wind direction and force, computed stream widths and rates of flow, and noted such aspects of terrain and climate as volcanic eruptions, earthquakes, lunar eclipses, northern lights, mirages, typhoons, and landslides. Two of Marsh's fact-filled letters to Joseph Henry appeared in the *American Journal of Science*. He enlisted missionary support for the Smithsonian weather research program; he had the Institution send meteorological instruments to the missionaries at Bebek and in the Turkish interior.

Most of Marsh's own instruments, he continually lamented, were of poor quality, unreliable, badly scaled, so cheaply and carelessly made as to be useless for precise measurements. A famous Paris firm had "shamefully cheated" him with defective barometers; a level and compass Wislizenus sent from Germany proved equally bad; a thermometer from the renowned firm of Troughton and Sims had "so large an air bubble in the tube as to be quite worthless"; a pair of eighteen-inch globes from Malby of London were "rude enough to disgrace an apprentice of two months' experience."

Marsh grieved that European artisans had fallen upon such evil days, but found the American thermometers and barometers Baird sent him no better.[50]

Marsh collected flora and fauna as assiduously as he took temperatures. On the Nubian trip, for example, he gathered specimens of some eighty plant species for Wislizenus. It was not easy to dry them properly; consequently, they arrived in poor condition. Proper preservation was even harder to achieve with the animal specimens which Marsh sent to Baird at the Smithsonian. Casks leaked, spirits evaporated, specimens spoiled, again and again Marsh's labors went for naught. Finally, he urged Baird to send from America spirits, casks, and strong, wide-mouthed glass vessels with good corks. When these came Marsh was able to make shipments more successfully.

Baird had asked particularly for fish. Marsh sent him twenty species from the Bosporus in the fall of 1850, along with crabs, tree frogs, and lizards; a "charming variety," Baird commented. From the Nile, Marsh collected asps, cerastes, "two pelicans' heads with the sacs and the parasitic animals that inhabit them, also the neck and other curious respiratory apparatus"; beetles, ostrich heads, innumerable lizards, fish, scorpions, bats, frogs, and toads. Baird craved crocodiles, and Marsh hoped "to make some additions to your snakery," but "could get neither eggs nor young [crocodiles]. It is a dangerous diversion," he explained, "to look for the nest of this bird." In the desert, leopards larger than Bengal tigers lurked about the camp "and uttered the fearfullest roar I ever heard." Jackals were common; one broke into Hussein's hen coop one night and killed forty-five chickens, "with the blood of which he was so puffed up that he couldn't get out." Marsh ordered him killed and prepared for Baird, "but he escaped, treacherously let off no doubt by the Arabs, who are very reluctant to kill any animals, except for food."[51]

Back in Constantinople, Marsh gathered grasshoppers, coleoptera, mantes, and other insects for the Pennsylvania entomologist S. S.

Haldemann, and at Hunkiat Skeleosi discovered a new species of salamander, which he christened *Salamandrosus Maribus* in honor of Mary Baird. Nor did Marsh neglect birds; he promised to send Baird "enough [eggs] for an omelet" and a few more for Haldemann to hatch. But the Minister hesitated to pilfer a stork's nest, fearing "a bullet through me in spite of diplomatic privileges were I to climb the chimney to rob it." [52] He did persuade his niece, Maria Buell, to plunder the nest of the rare *Jeb*. Marsh was not able to send the camels, aurochs, or dinosaur skeletons which Baird yearned for, but he put the Smithsonian in touch with the Grand Duke of Tuscany, the Emperor of Russia, and various German zoos to that end.

Nothing gave Marsh more pleasure, or so stimulated his sense of humor, as these collecting excursions. At Agrigento, in Sicily, he reveled in sarcophagi and tried to "recover . . . the bones of Empedocles" to send Baird for dissection, so that the naturalist might "see whether the Greek philosopher and the American savant be of one species." Marsh's research in vertebrate paleontology culminated in the discovery of "fine osteological collections in the convents and churches" of Italy, notably of "a bicipitous variety of the human family." Many saints, he observed, belonged to this race; John the Baptist was "cited as having . . . no less than three heads," but Marsh could not ascertain "whether these heads were successive or contemporaneous." [53]

Marsh also advanced American science in more humdrum ways. He made a point of visiting museums and arranged with their directors to exchange duplicates of specimens and publications with the Smithsonian Institution. From these small beginnings Baird developed the world-wide system of exchanges which helped to make the Smithsonian's National Museum the greatest repository in America.

Man's works fascinated Marsh as much as nature's. It was an unending pleasure for him to be in the Old World, where the human past was so much in evidence, and where so many aspects of life—

styles of clothing, modes of architecture, agricultural tools and processes—remained "just what they were in the time of the patriarchs and prophets." Marsh had read Wilkinson, Martineau, and Burckhardt, and was familiar with the then "startling conclusions" of the great German historians, Lepsius and Bunsen, about the antiquity of the upper Nile relics. The Minister made detailed studies of Egyptian architecture, sculpture, design, and coloration. Archaeology, like zoology, was so young a science that even an amateur might find something new; on the way to Palestine, in a desolate ravine near ancient Petra, Marsh found numerous Greek and Sinaitic inscriptions and, still more exciting, a three-hundred-foot tunnel cut through rock, designed to prevent the stream from flooding Petra during high water.[54]

Marsh sensed man's antiquity in every quarter. "Not the pyramids and temples and tombs only—but the very earth . . . the meadows levelled and the hills rounded, not as with us by the action of mere natural forces, but by the assiduous husbandry of hundreds of generations . . . have a hoary and ancient aspect that seems to belong rather to an effete and worn-out planet than to . . . the thousand fresh existences of the new world." [55] It was here Marsh first realized that man had everywhere left his mark; in time he saw how far that touch had transformed nature. The mangled forests and disrupted rivers of New England had already shown Marsh the immediate impact of human improvidence; the deserts of the Levant demonstrated the ultimate consequences of the same processes. Thousands of years of history intervened, to be sure; but to Marsh the connection was abundantly clear and heavy with portent.

✠VII✠

Diplomatic Problems and Pastimes

DURING MARSH'S ABSENCE in Egypt and Palestine a furor arose at the legation. Italian-born Francis Dainese, acting United States Consul at Constantinople, had early impressed Marsh as helpful, zealous, and intelligent. Marsh had wanted to make Dainese Consul in place of Porter, absent in Washington. But the legation dragoman, John P. Brown, then warned Marsh that Dainese was "notoriously fraudulent." Marsh withdrew his previous recommendation, explaining to the Secretary of State that Dainese's appointment would be "prejudicial to the public interests." [1] Dainese nevertheless remained acting Consul.

When Marsh departed for Egypt in January, 1851, he left as Chargé d'Affaires Henry A. Homes, a scholarly, Turkish-speaking American missionary who had served sixteen years in the Levant. Homes at once came into conflict with Dainese, whom he accused of cheating travelers, taking bribes for illegal passports, and passing merchandise through customs duty free. In July Porter dismissed Dainese and made Homes acting Consul, but Dainese denounced Homes as a "proselytizing priest" and refused to yield the consulate or the legation archives. With the help of guards from the Austrian Legation, Homes and Brown broke into the consulate, removed the legation seals, and locked the place up. Deprived of diplomatic immunity, Dainese escaped his creditors by fleeing to Syria, and at length made his way to the United States. Once in Washington, he broadcast accusations against Brown and "Mr. ex-Reverend Homes," who had burglarized his office, "trampled the American flag, & affixed the seals—the double-headed eagle of Austria—to the doors and windows of the American consulate!!!" Had Marsh been where he belonged, Dainese told Secretary of State Marcy, the Minister "might have prevented the perpetration of these outrages by his subordinates," but he was "almost constantly absent from his post." [2] Dainese also fed material to the press on the Amin Bey "fraud" and other matters supposedly discreditable to Marsh and Brown.

Back in Constantinople, Marsh learned that everyone except Dainese's creditors was relieved he was gone; the legations expressed "astonishment that such a swindler should ever have been in our government employ." But Marsh was thousands of miles from Washington, Dainese right there; in March, 1852, President Fillmore appointed Dainese Consul at Constantinople. (Strange to say, the official dispatch never reached Marsh. He heard of the appointment only through the press and consequently did not honor it.) Urging revocation, Marsh sent strongly worded dispatches detailing Dainese's infamies, together with a confidential note of protest from Aali Pasha, Turkish Minister of Foreign Affairs.[3] The appointment was finally revoked October 26, 1852—never having been operative—but Dainese remained in Washington to make more trouble for Marsh.

Owing to the Dainese affair, Marsh almost became *persona non grata* at the Porte. Dainese somehow gained access to Aali Pasha's confidential note and threatened to sue the Turkish Minister for libel. Not knowing whether Dainese had stolen his dispatch or received it as a gift from the State Department, the embarrassed Marsh was forced to leave Aali "at liberty to suspect, that the communicating of his note to [Dainese] was an indiscretion of my own." [4]

Throughout his long diplomatic career, Marsh suffered again and again from humiliating disclosures of his confidential dispatches. Then, as now, Americans mistook frankness for honesty and imag-

ined secrecy incompatible with democracy; American diplomacy
was weaker as a result. "Important intelligence has often been with-
held from our government," Marsh contended, "because it is notorious that there is no safety in making confidential communications
to it." Washington's betrayals embittered Marsh. "Perhaps it is best
as it is," he wrote sardonically. "The contrary rule [i.e., secrecy]
would sometimes deprive officials of the pleasures of blabbing a
secret, and then, great & good men might sometimes be exposed to
the great & severe trial of their manhood, independence, and moral
courage, if they were expected to . . . refuse to answer impertinent
questions." Marsh's reflections against the State Department were
"as just as they are severe," replied Chief Clerk Markoe to an
earlier, similar charge. But what could one expect? "I have been
nearly 20 years in this Dept.," he added dolefully, "and I despair of
ever seeing anything done in it as it ought to be, unless by accident." [5]

What with the Dainese difficulties, the Kossuth imbroglio, financial vexations, and poor health, the winter and spring of 1851–52
were difficult months for Marsh. At Therapia—to which he had
returned with enough stoves to make the villa habitable—he went
over his travel journals and began to write "some loose babble about
the Desert." His prolixity worried him; "the moment I begin to
treat any particular point, it swells up like a bladder, and I am fearful I shall make a volume on a grain of sand." Finally he sent off
an article about camels, "the silliest thing I ever wrote" [6]—but he
had enjoyed writing it. He now looked forward to a summer of
quiet repose.

I

*What a pity it is that Yankee Missionaries, the world over, are so very
Kantankerous . . . ! If they were only round, plump, & jolly, instead
of being lean, lank, flabby, & emaciated, I'm sure they would give
infinitely less trouble to others. Were I an arbitrary prince, I would
appoint them all by the simple rule of avoirdupois—weigh body instead of brains!*

CAPTAIN LOUIS M. GOLDSBOROUGH TO MARSH, PIRAEUS, JUNE 5, 1853

Marsh's plans for a restful season on the Bosporus were upset by State Department orders to go to Athens and investigate the tangled affairs of Rev. Jonas King. Regret at leaving Constantinople was mixed with the hope that this assignment might gain him the additional portfolio to Greece. The U.S.S. *San Jacinto* was put at Marsh's disposal, and on August 1, 1852, he reached Athens and went to work.

Jonas King had lived in Athens for more than twenty years, first on a relief mission during the Greek rebellion against Turkey, later with the American Board of Foreign Missions and as acting United States Consul. He was embroiled with the Greek government on two counts. One was a property dispute. In 1829 King had bought a two-acre plot near the Acropolis. City authorities insisted the land would one day be needed for public use, but had refused to buy it back; King could neither use the property nor sell it. The Greek government now ordered him to surrender it for what he considered a small fraction of its real value. The other case involved a charge of proselytism. For years King had been free to hold Protestant services in his home, but in 1850 the government had arrested him, convicted him of "heterodox preaching," and sentenced him to imprisonment, to be followed by banishment.

Marsh was asked to study both these cases, estimate King's losses, and determine how good his claim was. He was also to find out if the missionary's trial had been "fair and legal." Since other religious sects in Greece were not restrained from preaching and expounding doctrine, King's treatment "looks much like persecution," Webster told Marsh; the United States was prepared to protect the missionary.[7]

Athenians were agitated over the case. The local press accused the United States of trying to "terrorize" Greece by sending Marsh with an armed frigate; one paper regretted that the Greek negotiator was Foreign Minister Paikos, "a stupid fellow, who will manage the . . . business wretchedly." The investigation was difficult and tedious; the trial reports were in a state of chaos, Marsh himself had to translate all the "accursed Greek" documents, the crabbed calligraphy of the manuscripts—"totally illegible, and decipherable only inspiration-wise"—left him "purblind as a mole." Every obstacle was put in Marsh's way; witnesses proved intractable, lawyers reticent, judges openly hostile. Jonas King himself was a nuisance— quarrelsome, plaintive, forgetful of facts and dates, impatient of delay, intolerant of compromise. Thin, lank, reedy-voiced, the New England missionary had alienated most of the Americans and English in Athens. Even those who knew he had been wronged were unwilling to aid him, for he was a constant irritant to good relations with the Greeks; they felt the country would be better off without him.[8]

After six weeks of work in hot midsummer Athens, Marsh went in September to Trieste, where the *San Jacinto* had to undergo repairs, to write his reports. Monuments to Marsh's painstaking industry, these voluminous documents showed "most unequivocally" that King was in the right. Marsh concluded that Greece had treated the missionary's property claim with "slavish injustice and bad faith"; it ought "to release his land from the injunction laid upon it, or to pay him its fair value." [9]

As for the trial, Marsh was convinced that King had been prosecuted simply to coerce him to abandon or compromise his claim for property compensation. Amazed "that a government could stoop to the adoption of such base measures to evade a pecuniary liability," Marsh yet had no doubt that "the ministry was acting in concert with a debased and fanatic priesthood throughout the whole affair." The trial had been conducted "unfairly and illegally . . . with a gross departure from the spirit of the law." Witnesses had perjured themselves, judges had turned prosecutor, the Synod had distributed inflammatory placards and gathered hostile crowds at the court. Marsh did not see how the United States "can help interfering" to aid King.[10]

While waiting for further instructions, in October, 1852, Marsh went on a leisurely Alpine jaunt. He might "be censured for this *deviation*," but felt "entitled to some indulgence" after his "severe labors"; Marsh hoped that Webster would let him "rest my old blind eyes and shattered brain." [11] He had plenty of time. Webster died in October; not until February, 1853, did Edward Everett, the new Secretary of State, find time to commend Marsh for his promptness, assiduity, and perseverance in the King case and instruct him to return to Athens.

Everett agreed that King's trial had been unfair, and the decision "unjust and oppressive," but thought that since the *forms* of law had been observed, it would be hard to get redress; and intemperate American action might endanger other missionaries. Marsh should merely express the President's "decided opinion that . . . the sentence of banishment ought immediately to be revoked." However, Everett gave King stronger support in his property dispute. If Greece refused to pay what Marsh thought just, he was to propose arbitration. Marsh should "avoid the tone or language of menace, but let the government of Greece perceive that the President is quite in earnest." [12]

These instructions, Marsh warned the Secretary of State, were not emphatic enough. The government should peremptorily *"demand* a remission of the sentence of banishment," otherwise American prestige would suffer. Marsh feared "a disastrous effect upon our national character and influence abroad . . . if the weak and unprincipled government of Greece be allowed to enforce the illegal and oppressive sentence of its corrupt tribunals against an American citizen." [13]

Back in Athens, Marsh found "evasion and procrastination . . . the cardinal features of Greek diplomacy." Foreign Minister Paikos, "insolent on paper, & creeping, fawning, sycophantic, timid and false in conversation," delayed as long as possible; he hoped that the Russian-Turkish crisis would force Marsh to return to Constantinople, or "that the approach of the sickly season will drive both me and the ships of the squadron from Athens." When it finally came, in mid-June, 1853, Paikos's answer was "framed in the tone of lachrymose sensibility and injured innocence, which the diplomatists of Greece invariably assume, whenever a claim is preferred against her." [14] But he refused to remit the sentence of banishment, on the specious ground that the King of Greece had no power to revoke judgments.

Marsh received this refusal with "severe displeasure." He had no more time for direct negotiations; in July the threat of war required him to go to Constantinople. But Jonas King was never banished. A year later Greece lifted the sentence of exile. In this the missionary saw "the hand of God," although conceding that "a desire to obtain aid from the United States" and, above all, the impression Marsh made on the Greek government had assisted Divine Providence.[15]

The land dispute, negotiated concurrently, was equally tedious and tendentious. Paikos first claimed that the city of Athens was responsible, not the State. He then offered a compromise, proposing to pay for the land at 1835 values. Marsh suggested that Greece instead pay King twelve and a half drachmas an acre, or about $23,000, less than a quarter of the original valuation. Sir Thomas Wyse, the capable and influential British Minister to Greece, offered to arbitrate; but Marsh was reluctant to become involved with a mediator. So the matter stood when he left Athens in July, 1853. It was still unresolved in September, when Marsh was replaced as Minister to Turkey. Confident of success, he would even then have returned to Athens to finish the job, had the State Department deigned to notice any of his dispatches on the subject. Marsh thoroughly briefed his successor, Carroll Spence, on the King case, advising him just to "shut his ears, hold his tongue, and look savage." He had "the devil to deal with, but the devil is thoroughly frightened, and if Mr. Spence fails of reaping the fruit of my labors, it will be his own fault." Several years later the case was settled substantially on the terms Marsh had proposed, enhancing his reputation as "an acute controversialist, a sound lawyer, and . . . a perfect Grecian." [16]

But the King case had given Marsh an abiding contempt for "Hellas without Hellenes." He dismissed Greece caustically as "a

poor country on the north shore of the Mediterranean formerly inhabited by *Graeculi esurientes,* now by vermin and Bulgarians." In
a dispatch full of invective Marsh sketched the causes of Greek decline since King Otho's accession in 1832; he described a land characterized by xenophobia and by "a miserable fanaticism, which
proscribes alike the Catholic and the Protestant, and aims to found
a political state upon no other basis than that of . . . sectarian bigotry." Marsh thought the Greeks "the falsest and most bigoted of
people," led by a self-indulgent priesthood.[17] After all his troubles
with the Rev. Jonas King, it is a wonder that Marsh could find
anything to choose between fat priests and lean missionaries.

2

Marsh had traveled in Europe, during the five months of delay on
the King cases, with as much ardor as in Egypt and the Levant.
But new sights and sounds, people and ideas, came too fast to as-
similate; unlike the orderly journals of his Eastern expedition,
Marsh's European letters were hastily scrawled, kaleidoscopic.

From Trieste Marsh and his family went north through the desolate Karst, which struck him as a strange, sad country; thence over
the Julian Alps into Ljubljana and northeast to the Austrian spa
Bad Gleichenberg. Here the mountainous landscape reminded
Marsh of Vermont: "If our soil were as neatly cultivated, and the
forests as carefully protected, and as judiciously and economically
managed, there would be nothing to distinguish the two countries."
While Marsh completed his second report, Caroline bathed dutifully
in the hot springs and dosed herself with the waters. Evenings
brought walks or drives, followed by tea and talk with the ladies
Wyse, wife and sister-in-law of the British Minister at Athens. Caroline found the Wyses intelligent, charming, vivacious: "Tho they
are Roman Catholics, we find they sympathize with us Americans
in practically all things"; thanks to their Irish birth they lacked "all
British stiffness." Marsh enjoyed them too, though he found them a

bit giddy and was rather relieved when they parted ways, "inasmuch as I have told about all I know, though the rest, for aught I see, talk as glibly as ever." Mrs. Wyse attributed to Marsh "a grand talent *pour le silence.*" [18] He took refuge from idle feminine chatter in the society of Baron Joseph von Hammer-Purgstall, famous Austrian Orientalist, at near-by Hainfeld Castle.

In mid-October the Marshes went on to Vienna, where Marsh acquired reading glasses and was generally patched up "so that I should run a spell longer." Guided by Hammer-Purgstall, Marsh enjoyed the sights and the "cheerful, lively" Viennese, "remarkable for devotion & profanity." With Maria Buell he then made a whirlwind tour of Bohemia, Saxony, Bavaria, and the Tyrol. The high spots were Nürnberg, where Marsh renewed his admiration for "all that belongs to the middle ages, except their infernal spiritual & temporal tyranny"; Rembrandts and Rubens in Munich; gems in Dresden's Grune Gewölbe; and three avalanches at Königsee. Back in Austria in December, he found the physicians had failed Caroline sadly. "What do you think the [Vienna doctors] prescribed for Mrs. M's eyes and limbs? A pair of spectacles and a stick! You should have seen her with London-made glasses and crooked staff, essaying to read large print . . . and to walk like Mother Goose!" [19] She still could not see to read, and even a short walk brought severe pain, diarrhea, and fever. She had lost weight and looked hauntingly fragile.

Nevertheless, the Marshes went on to cross northern Italy in "fog, fog, fog! and cold enough to keep you shivering, and just at the freezing point, day & night." [20] In Florence, early in 1853, Marsh learned of his mother's death; she had long been in poor health, but the shock of bereavement was great. In his grief, Marsh went for lonely walks in the eroded Tuscan hills.

Florence also offered the civilized distractions of art galleries and the company of American sculptors and painters—Hiram Powers, Miner K. Kellogg, Eastman Johnson. Powers took Marsh to meet the Brownings. Afterward Marsh went to see them often, and was deeply moved by Elizabeth Barrett Browning's seriousness and candor. She, in turn, was attracted to Caroline; a semi-invalid herself, Mrs. Browning admired her courage. In their evenings together, sipping tea and eating strawberries, the Marshes and the Brownings talked of poetry and Proudhon, of the revolutions of '48 in Europe and Harriet Beecher Stowe, of Dumas's *La Dame aux camélias* and Fanny Kemble. They also discussed spiritualism, a keen concern of Mrs. Browning, who was unconvinced by the Marshes' skeptical citations of Humboldt and Faraday—"I consider facts to be too strong for either of them." [21] The Brownings promised to come to Constantinople in May and June, but Marsh's extended labors in Athens made the visit impossible.

At the end of March, when State Department instructions came at last, the Marshes sailed to Naples, where they had to wait two weeks for the laggard *Cumberland*. As consolation, Commodore Stringham provided gingerbread and pickled oysters, which must have warded off the Minister's seasickness; the delicacies were all gone by the time the *Cumberland* reached Athens in April, though Lieutenant H. A. Wise thought they ought to have been kept "to fatten the missionaries a bit." "The Piraeus certainly is a horrid hole," exclaimed Captain Louis Goldsborough, explorer and future Civil War naval leader assigned to stay with Marsh, "and I shall be rejoiced to get out of it." [22] But Goldsborough, who became Marsh's close friend, waited stoically while Marsh and Paikos bickered, until the Minister grew so uneasy about Constantinople that he would delay no longer. When the *Cumberland* steamed into the Golden Horn July 5, 1853, Marsh had been out of Turkey three weeks short of a year.

3

Back in Constantinople, Marsh was at once plunged into a problem as exasperating as the one he had left behind in Athens. Like Jonas King, Martin Koszta invoked the protection of the United

States and like King he was a cross to his benefactor. One of the Hungarian exiles who went from Turkey to the United States in 1851, Koszta had declared his intention to become an American citizen, but returned to the Levant. On June 21, 1852, a gang of men seized Koszta on the waterfront at Smyrna and threw him into the harbor. He was picked up by a waiting dinghy from the Austrian brig *Huszar,* where he was put in irons.

The American Consul at Smyrna, Edward S. Offley, protested the kidnaping to the Austrian Consul, Veckbecker, but since Koszta had no American passport, Offley dropped the matter. And in Constantinople the Austrian Internuncio, Baron de Bruck, rejected Chargé John P. Brown's demand for Koszta's release. De Bruck accused the Hungarian of returning to foment revolution, for which he would stand trial in Austria.

The trial was forestalled by Captain D. N. Ingraham, a sharp-spoken South Carolinian, whose corvette, the U.S.S. *St. Louis,* was at Smyrna. Ingraham loaded his guns and brought his ship alongside the *Huszar,* preventing the Austrian brig from leaving the harbor. On July 2 Ingraham delivered an ultimatum from Brown; if Koszta were not released, he would *"take him out of the vessel."* Three other Austrian ships made ready to join the fray, and American merchantmen in the harbor helped swing the *St. Louis* around to give Ingraham effective fire. At the last minute, Veckbecker released Koszta into the custody of the French Consul, stipulating, however, that he was to be freed only at the express plea of himself and Offley.[23] Koszta was taken from the Austrian brig, his chains stricken off, and "as he touched shore, the shout from the assembled thousands was a tremendous 'Viva la republica Americana' . . . with groans and 'a bassos' for Austria." [24]

"Now, you gentlemen of the pen must uphold my act," Captain Ingraham wrote Marsh. Marsh gave Ingraham and Brown his unqualified approval. Koszta's arrest was an act "of illegal and private violence." Ingraham's prompt action would curb Austrian persecu-

tion of other refugees, Marsh believed, and give "new force to the
hourly increasing respect with which the American government is
regarded" in Europe and the Levant. Austria protested, but Secretary of State Marcy upheld Ingraham and Marsh. Authorized to
negotiate with de Bruck, Marsh proposed to send Koszta directly
back to America. To this de Bruck finally agreed, reserving the
right to proceed against Koszta "the moment he is again surprised
on Ottoman territory." [25]

Just when the ticklish matter seemed at an end, Marsh was mortified by Koszta's refusal to accept these terms. Previously anxious
to depart as soon as possible, "Koszta now suddenly became quite
cock-a-hoop, forgot his fears and his 'gratitude' together," as Marsh
put it, "boldly declared, that he would return to Turkey" whenever
he liked, and refused to embark. Meanwhile, Offley accused Marsh
and Brown of disgracing America by ceding Austria the right to
imprison Koszta; he would not authorize Koszta's release from the
French Consulate. In vain did Marsh explain that he had given up
nothing, that Austria's reservation was no part of the agreement
proper. "As the head of the Legation, and as a professional lawyer,"
Marsh could not "consent to be governed by the opinions of Mr.
Koszta" on legal questions, he told Offley. And Marsh warned Secretary Marcy that he could no longer "maintain a position of respect-
ability or usefulness, if ignorant and presumptuous subordinate
officials" could defy him "for the sake of giving themselves a fac-
titious importance, or of gratifying a private malice." By threatening
to withdraw all protection, Marsh finally forced Koszta to embark,
but the Hungarian maintained to the last the right of "going and
coming wherever my business demands." [26]

Marsh's worries did not end with the departure of the ungrateful
Koszta, whose "folly, impertinences and obstinacy" had all but
nullified the efforts made on his behalf. "I suppose," prophesied
Brown, "that both yourself & me will appear in the U.S. [as] Austrian Agents, as in the affair of Dainese!" [27] In fact, Marsh's enemies

combined against him. Dainese prepared Koszta's statement of grievances and Greeley published it; all was shown to President Franklin Pierce.

Marsh was no passive scapegoat. He sent long letters to papers in Vermont, Boston, and New York, criticizing Koszta, as he had Kossuth, in strong terms. A friend remarked that "going among the Turks had not improved [Marsh's] humanity much—else you had not flayed alive those two very notorious *soi-disant* Americans right in the face of the multitude who had been invited to admire them." [28] But, for the time being, Marsh was out of harm's way; the President had just recalled him and appointed his successor.

4

An ancient dame, who sat on a stone at the receipt of customs, put me this question, "Where do you live?" It puzzled me confoundedly, & does yet. Indeed, where do I really live?

MARSH TO LUCY WISLIZENUS, MILAN, JAN. I, 1853

Marsh felt that he was not at home anywhere. After four stimulating years abroad, the prospect of settling down again did not entice him. His dismissal was only one of many misfortunes. He had sought the Ministry to Greece; both that and an expected salary increase were denied him. Disgusted, Marsh suspected that "an enemy has done this"; he felt "cruelly used." Though meager, his ministerial remuneration was still better than nothing. As the 1852 election approached, Marsh was dismayed by the prospect of "being turned out and going home." Financial disaster had overtaken him in Vermont; he wanted to put off "the mortifications & vexations that inevitably await me." He made no plans. "I do not know what I can do at home," he wrote, discouraged. "I cannot return to the law, after so long an interval, and I see no other opening." [29]

For a time Marsh believed that "the undesirableness of my post" would postpone his recall. He half pretended apostasy to Pierce's party. "My wife turned Democrat two years ago because the custom house people at Boston charged duty on some gewgaws she sent home from Egypt. She has been a savage free-trader ever since." Marsh himself felt "mightily inclined to Democracy"; another year or two in the Old World would make him "a desperate Radical." He had "clear given up Tariff (since my factory failed) and most Whig devilry." [30]

Washington friends bolstered Marsh's hope that he might stay on in Constantinople. Painting Pierce's portrait, G. P. A. Healy found the President "a most unaffected agreeable man, so much so, that my wife cannot believe he is a real Democrat." Pierce told Healy that Marsh would be allowed to remain "as long as he [the President] can keep off those who are besieging him for office, he thinks very highly of your excellency." [31] Others thought that state pride in Vermont-born Pierce might help Marsh.

But Marsh's enemies were telling the President that the Minister took long vacations at government expense, that Austria had outwitted him in the Koszta affair, and that when Americans in Constantinople most needed him, he was away wasting time on the trifling concerns of an insignificant Athenian missionary! Marsh's former Chargé, Homes, found the President hostile. "I am surprised," Pierce said sternly, "that Mr. Marsh should remain away from Constantinople at such an important crisis"; he would listen to no explanation that the Minister was in Athens on State Department orders. "I think I can hear the whiz of the axe as it comes down on my neck," Marsh mused. "I pity Gen. Pierce. Don't he wish the Whig office-holders had but one neck so that he could decapitate us all at once?" [32]

5

While Marsh waited for the President to end his mission in Turkey, the Ottoman Empire itself seemed about to expire. In July, 1853, after months of intrigue, 40,000 Russian troops invaded European Turkey; the Crimean War had begun.

The immediate provocation was a dispute over the Holy Places in Palestine, which Russia wanted made available to the Greek Orthodox Church. The real roots lay deep in European power politics, particularly in Russia's age-old desire to control the Straits. Marsh's sympathies were entirely with the Turks. Hating Russia, he feared that the conquest of Turkey would lead to "the establishment of a Russian *suzeraineté* throughout Christian Europe." He regarded Turkey as "the most effectual obstacle to the advance of political barbarism," and considered the integrity of the Ottoman Empire essential to freedom and culture; were Constantinople to fall to Russia, Marsh envisaged the "destruction of existing European civilization," and the revival of "absolutism in politics and obscurantism in religion." [33]

Many Turks favored an immediate declaration of war, but the Sultan and his advisers, under Stratford Canning's thumb, were not ready to fight. Promising protection against attack, England urged Turkey to yield to the Russian demands. Apprehensive lest this enrage Moslems and endanger Christians in Turkey, Marsh ordered Commodore Stringham to stay at Constantinople with the flagship. He condemned British appeasement—not only as "wrong & shameful," but also as a tactical blunder. The Greek Christians were already three times as numerous as the Moslems in European Turkey; after the privileges Russia had gained for them she "will need no war to conquer Turkey." England and France would then be too late, Marsh predicted, to prevent Russia's complete absorption of the Ottoman Empire.[34]

Despite the presence of the British fleet in the Bosporus, six Russian ships invaded the Black Sea port of Sinope on the night of November 30, destroyed a dozen Turkish ships of war, and massacred 4,000 men. Even after this disaster, however, Stratford's influence was strong enough to prevent Turkish retaliation for many weeks. Failure to punish the Sinope atrocity convinced Marsh that England meant "to permit the abject humiliation, if not the final sacrifice, of Turkey." Intending no action, the British forces were unprepared when it finally came; ignorance and delay, Marsh believed, prevented a decisive check to Russian ambitions. The close of the Crimean War left Russia as strong as ever.

Marsh was dismayed that Russian propaganda against England had won over many of his own countrymen. His warnings against Russian wiles have a familiar ring a century later. Even more than the dexterity of Muscovite diplomats, Marsh feared Russia's army of spies and secret agents, "disguised in the forms of travellers for pleasure or the pursuit of science, *couriers de voyage,* servants in great families, political exiles, foreign correspondents of newspapers, Levantine merchants and adventurers, professional gamblers, *chevaliers d'industrie,* and even cripples and beggars." [35]

Marsh's strictures on the land of the czars were typical both of his secular bias and of his partisan view of history. Personifying nations, he condemned or praised them in moral terms, and adhered to a devil theory of history. "For heaven's sake," he exhorted a friend, "don't sympathize with the hellish nonsense of Russia & Rome—the Czar & the Pope. I hope yet to see them both dangle on a gibbet. . . . Till then, there is no hope for liberty on the continent." Only the English—despite the Crimean War—were admirable in Marsh's eyes. "Don't be too hard on poor old England," he wrote; "in spite of the misconduct of her *rulers,* the existence of her *people* is the sole source of light & hope to European civilization and Christianity. All else is devilish." [36]

Marsh's affection for the British was strengthened by the distinguished group he met in Turkey in 1853: Admiral Sir Richard Saunders Dundas, later commander-in-chief of the Baltic fleet; the Earl of Carlisle, parliamentarian, prison reformer, and bellelettrist; the scholarly Rawlinson brothers, George and Henry; and especially Sir Harry Verney, Florence Nightingale's brother-in-law, pioneer in land reclamation and rural housing, an evangelical utopian with whom Marsh kept up a lively correspondence over the next quarter of a century. Marsh enjoyed many evenings at Stratford's house with these men. And he impressed them; Lord Carlisle thought

Marsh "one of the best conditioned and fully informed men it is possible to find anywhere." [37]

6

Marsh received news of his "decease" in September, 1853. "I kiss the firman and put it to my forehead," he wrote flippantly; " 'Tis the will of our Lord the Padishah. The Democracy is great." [38] On Christmas Day the Marshes left Constantinople for good.

Marsh was in no hurry to get back to America. Anticipating nothing but trouble in Burlington, he strung out the homeward trip as long as possible. After six days of seasickness—"we had died," Marsh maintained, "had the voyage been a day longer"—they reached Malta. There Sir Harry Verney entertained them several days before they went on to Sicily. Marsh felt "grievously light-headed and queasy still," but he had seen "nothing fairer in Europe." The desolate Sicilian landscape, the contrasts between jagged peaks and smooth seas, appealed to Marsh both aesthetically and philosophically. At Syracuse he gathered papyrus but grieved to find the famous fountain of Arethusa, the metamorphosed wood nymph of Greek legend, nothing but a conduit for washerwomen. Poking in a ravine near Centuripe in central Sicily, he uncovered a flint arrowhead "just like those of our Indians" which "all the Sicilian antiquaries declared . . . to be altogether unique." But the crowning delight of the trip was Mt. Etna. Marsh, who considered "every bit of lava . . . a sacred thing," fully indulged his "most extravagant passion for volcanoes." Looking across the chasm of the Val de Bove, filled with hot and smoking lava, he saw hundreds of cones dotting the sides of Etna, many of them rising more than five hundred feet. "What is Vesuvius," marveled Marsh, "after this?" [39] He struck up a friendship with the great vulcanologist Gemmallaro and sacrificed his sleep to read about earthquakes in Seneca's *Questiones Naturales*.

Marsh found unexpected pleasures in Sicily. "Since I became an *Ex*," he remarked with delight, "I am a more important person than when I was in full bloom as a diplomat *en fonction.*" The Marshes were "loaded with civilities, and every potentate I meet offers me straightway the half of his kingdom. I should like to accept this of Sicily." [40]

Marsh reached Rome in time for carnival, which he thought "a foolish festival truly, but showy." They stayed two full and happy months. "There is no time," he complained, "to see anybody or anything at Rome. One is daft at once, and driven hither and thither by all manner of whirlwinds." He avoided other tourists, finding "society and sight-seeing . . . incompatible." This interdiction did not extend to the Brownings, who were wintering in Rome, or even to his old *bête noir* Martin Van Buren, whom Marsh saw now and then, and found agreeable. The former President was angry that President Pierce had rebuffed him, but Marsh doubted that "the trials of this present administration keep him awake o' nights." Van Buren talked "pretty coolly of all his enemies old and new." [41] Also in Rome were the Estcourts, with whom the Marshes toured the city, until Estcourt—now a general—left for the Crimean War and his death, a year later, of cholera.

In April the Marshes too departed, and traveled over the Apennines to Ancona, Bologna, Modena, and Milan. Spring was late; at the end of May a thick snowstorm caught them crossing the Alps, and Caroline had to be carried by wheelbarrow across avalanches that blocked the road to Innsbruck. Marsh was fascinated to learn that much of the Alpine region had not long before (geologically speaking) been submarine; he wrote from "the Primeval Ocean" to inform Baird that Switzerland had "emerged from the waters and become dry land. Trees have grown, shed their leaves and perished, and been succeeded by new forests, and a vegetable soil has been formed, and subdued by tillage, and men have built here a city called Bern. . . . All this is recent; the oldest inhabitants inform me that it is not above fifty million years since the highest part of town was upheaved above the sea." [42] With this souvenir of Old World antiquity Marsh turned reluctantly homeward.

❧VIII❧

Makeshifts of a Bankrupt

AFTER FIVE YEARS ABROAD, Marsh was met at home with the honors due a returning notable. The Burlington Cornet Band serenaded him on his arrival, August 23, 1854, and at Town Hall the local citizenry congratulated him "on his safe return to his native State & rejoice to know that he returns rich in experience & honored and respected for his most valuable labors." [1] Marsh unfortunately found himself rich in nothing else. If his fellow townsmen paid him public homage, in private they came thronging to his door to collect what they could on the dollar.

I

There have been Marshes who not only had *money, but actually* kept *it till they died.*

MARSH TO LADY ESTCOURT, BURLINGTON, MARCH 31, 1857

Marsh's financial distress was largely the result of the extraordinary misfortunes of the Vermont Central Railroad, in which he had invested heavily. This railroad was one of several chartered during the 1830s and 1840s in order to connect landlocked Vermont with Boston markets and Canadian forests. Promoted by Marsh's old friend, former Governor Charles Paine, and by the Burlington mercantile firm J. &. J. H. Peck & Son, with which Marsh was associated in banking and other ventures, the Vermont Central had secured a big tax exemption and the best route across the state, from

White River Junction to Montpelier and Burlington; its first train steamed into the Queen City in December, 1849. But its financial structure was shaky from the start. Construction costs were four times the estimated figure. New stock was issued, and at once depreciated; directors voted themselves enormous salaries and commissions; treasurers absconded. Meanwhile the line deteriorated; sleepers rotted, freshets and fires destroyed bridges and roadbeds, and there was no money for repairs. After Paine and the Pecks had milked the Vermont Central, the bondholders took over in December, 1852.

Marsh came back deep in debt for worthless stock. Nor was he the only sufferer; a feud between the Vermont Central and the Rutland & Burlington, its chief competitor, had prostrated Burlington, their joint terminus. With the lake trade gone and the factories at Winooski dead, half of Burlington's business firms—including the Pecks'—failed within a few years.

Marsh lost real estate as well as cash; the Vermont Central's spur line into Burlington cut across his most valuable properties. While Marsh was in Turkey, his brother-in-law, Wyllys Lyman, pocketed a large sum from the Vermont Central in return for persuading other landowners—including Marsh's agent—to sell their preempted land at $1,000 an acre. On his return, Marsh demanded $10,000 redress for this illegal sale, but the Vermont Central was already bankrupt; he recovered nothing.

About $50,000 in debt, Marsh next discovered that his promissory notes were held by the very men who had done most to ruin him: the Pecks. Marsh would have surrendered everything to be released from debt, but the Pecks demanded full payment, hoping to collect his future earnings. They filed suit against him in September, 1856. Marsh feared that if they got "the whole of their monstrous claim established, I shall still be liable to the very villains who have defrauded us in a large sum"; although the bankrupt Peck Company owed Marsh a great deal of money, it could not be applied against what Marsh owed the Pecks individually.[2]

During Marsh's protracted efforts to extricate himself from the difficulties "in which the villainy of the Pecks and Lyman's imbecility and knavery" had involved him, he became utterly dispirited. "The 'old man' is getting 'grumpy,' " grieved his son, "sighs heavily, won't laugh or joke, & is . . . a very stupid companion." Marsh's only consolation was the grim "hope of seeing J. H. Peck on his way to Sing Sing." Caroline tried to comfort her husband; she was quite prepared for the worst, she told him, and "only wish you may have philosophy and faith enough to see all go without too much pain." "You must indeed my dear husband remember," she chided him gently, "that these things . . . assume an apparent magnitude which they really do not possess." It was his moral duty not to give in to morbid self-pity; he had "too much yet to accomplish in this world . . . to allow yourself to think for a moment that you are likely to be broken down by pecuniary *misfortune* or Peck *malice*." [3] When Marsh asked how she liked being married to a pauper, Caroline scolded him for his materialism.

Not until April 27, 1860, did Marsh finally reach an agreement with "the creditors of the rogues who cheated me . . . surrendered all the property I have in the world . . . and now, at the age of fifty-nine, I begin . . . with a debt of $10,000, in good new notes, and not a shilling to pay it." [4] Two months later, a long-standing claim against the government was settled in his favor, enabling Marsh to pay this debt. He faced the future with more courage than he had enjoyed for a decade. If he was poor, he was at least free.

2

The whole opposition arises from the malice of a Levantine renegade.
. . . He can forge lies faster than I can answer them. . . . In fact out
of the pages of Eugene Sue, I have never heard of so accomplished a
villain as this man.   MARSH TO CHARLES D. DRAKE, 1857

Struggles for government compensation had soured Marsh's life as much as the quarrels with Peck and the Vermont Central

Railroad. The amount involved was not great, though important enough to a bankrupt. But his claim was clearly just, his enemies virulently hostile, and the litigation endlessly prolonged—the time and effort Marsh devoted to it almost precluded more useful work. His bitterness, indeed, made all activity seem futile.

Marsh claimed $1,000 a year for special judicial duties at Constantinople. American diplomats in China were compensated for such work, but Congress had accidentally neglected to provide for those in Turkey. Since his predecessor, Dabney Carr, had just been reimbursed, Marsh anticipated no difficulty. He also asked extra compensation for his Greek mission. During his year's absence from Turkey he had had to pay rent for his house there and wages to servants and watchmen, while horses and supplies which could not be kept easily had to be sold at a loss; all in all, Marsh was "a loser to a considerable amount by the performance of the arduous duties imposed upon him." [5]

Jeremiah Mason pushed his cousin Marsh's claims through the Senate Committee on Foreign Relations, and Solomon Foot persuaded the Senate to grant him $13,500. But opposition, instigated by Francis Dainese, developed in the House. Dainese was still assailing Marsh in connection with Kossuth, King, Koszta, Amin Bey, and himself. Pressing a claim of his own, Dainese had secured an anti-Marsh faction that included State Department Chief Clerk William Hunter, Archbishop John Hughes of New York, and several Catholic Congressmen—notably Joseph R. Chandler of Pennsylvania, later United States envoy to the Papal States. These men were persuaded that Marsh persecuted Dainese because he was a Catholic. Chandler and other representatives maintained that Marsh had already received too much money for "trifling" services; and to Marsh's shocked surprise, the House rejected his claims.[6]

When Congress reconvened in December, 1855, Marsh took time off from his misfortunes in Vermont to attend to those in Washington. Alienated from Burlington by bankruptcy, he was glad to be back in the capital. In Turkey he had been "quite homesick

for F Street," and decided that if he could "choose my own habita-
culum for life, it would be just in that good neighborhood." He
stayed with James Gilliss and then with Spencer Baird, but was hap-
piest at the home of David A. Hall, Vermont-born lawyer and agent
for the American Board of Foreign Missions. Hall's household was
thoroughly disorganized, "a regular *Polnische wirtschaft,*" Marsh
called it; but he was made much of by Hall's daughters, nieces,
cousins, and friends. He enjoyed Chinese tea, macaroni, mild flirta-
tions, and destructive games of battledore and shuttlecock with a
youngish lady, Charlotte Bostwick. The provocative Charlotte told
her elderly admirer of her "great dread of being left an old maid";
Marsh supposed "she would not make such a confession to a single
man." Caroline received long, despondent letters from her husband,
but Charlotte Bostwick found his "lurking humor" unquenchable,
and sighed for him when he left. She long remembered the solemn-
looking, bearded gentleman of fifty-five, with "that invincible, respectable, 'Varmonit' look that rode Juggernaut-like over all the
last fashions, defying . . . the Capital's best society." [7]

Meanwhile, Congress played shuttlecock with Marsh's claim.
Foot feared another defeat. In a newspaper article, the "diabolical
Dainese" had ridiculed Marsh's claim for eleven months' service
in Greece, showing that he had spent but twenty-three days in
Athens "and devoted the remainder of his time, as any gentleman
of leisure and taste travelling upon the money and in the time of
Uncle Sam might do, in a minute study of Italy, Germany, &c."
Dainese found a new ally in Senator Richard Brodhead, a Pennsylvania Democrat whom Marsh had antagonized a decade earlier
in the House. Brodhead computed that of four years abroad Marsh
had spent only two and a half at work, for which he had received
a grand total of $53,000—"a pretty large sum for a brief trip to
Europe." [8]

Foot came to Marsh's support. Congress had just admitted the inadequacy of the Turkish Minister's salary by raising it from $6,000
to $9,000. "That he is a man of economical habits, everyone who

knows him will admit," yet Marsh had had to supplement his pay with $5,500 of his own. The Senate again passed Marsh's claim, but Brodhead continued his attacks in the papers, warning the House against abolitionist "sympathy to Mr. Marsh, who is the leader of the niggerites in his native State, & the personal friend of Beecher and company."[9]

Marsh defended himself as best he could against these calumnies. He maintained that he had received not $53,000 for two and a half years, but $34,500 for three years and ten months; that all his travels had been authorized by the State Department; that the delay in reaching Constantinople had been unavoidable; that his mission to Athens had saved $100,000 and the freedom of an American citizen. But fast as Marsh could reply, new charges were leveled at him. Hopes for his Greek claim all but vanished. Even his judicial claim, which he had thought unassailable, had been rejected by the House Foreign Affairs Committee, because Chairman Pennington feared that similar payments to every diplomat in Turkey back to 1830 would come with "a giant's grasp upon the public treasury."[10]

As the oppressive summer wore on, Marsh's spirits dropped lower than ever. He would have left Washington, but Dainese was "concocting some new villainy against me, & I must stay & watch him." The "new villainy" was a "proof" that Marsh had spent most of his expense allowance on "private" presents to the Sultan, "private" use of horses, and the like, and had received five or six dollars a day board in Greece, although rates at the Hotel d'Orient in Athens were "only $2. per day, *everything included except the more costly liquors.*" Dainese succeeded in "completely poisoning . . . the Committee of Foreign Affairs";[11] Marsh's Greek claim no longer had a chance. On August 12, he left Washington for New York and Burlington to contend with Pecks and politics.

The two years since Marsh's return to America had been "years of almost unmixed bitterness—and the next promises to be like unto them." Marsh regarded himself as permanently ruined, feeling that his perplexities were destroying his memory and intellectual powers,

and had paralyzed his hopes of usefulness. Lack of money even prevented him from taking Caroline to Philadelphia for medical treatment. "My claim, my unhappy claim!" he mourned. "Well, I tell
her sometimes she deserves no better, for marry-ing a beggarman." [12]

The Marsh-Dainese feud continued after 1856 with unremitting
bitterness. Dainese persuaded friends in Constantinople to swear that
Marsh had misused funds, and Marsh got the Turkish government
to testify to Dainese's mendacity; the two men hurled charges at
each other in public and private letters; session after session, bills for
Marsh's claims were beaten. One factor in his defeat was a 328-page
Congressional testimonial to Dainese's sterling virtues as consul.
The report reprinted Dainese's accusations against Marsh, "the
skulking assassin of private character" who "disseminates *calumny* in
high quarters under the seal of privacy." Marsh castigated Congress
for placing more credence in the tales of a "perjured swindler"
than in the solemn declarations of a Minister. But slander as usual
found more ears than truth, and Dainese's friends in Congress
were as numerous as ever. Dainese "can defeat y'r bill," warned
Francis Markoe in 1858, "& you can defeat his. Will you combine?"
he asked. Justin Morrill likewise urged Marsh and Dainese not to
attack each other's claims, but Marsh felt he could "only lose by
any coupling of my name with that of so depraved a scoundrel." He
still hoped to succeed "without much of that touching pitch which
cannot fail to defile." [13] He did not succeed.

Not until 1860 did Marsh have another chance. This time he and
Dainese swallowed their pride and agreed not to oppose each other.
It was April before the bill for Marsh's claim was reported out of
committee, but Francis Markoe enlisted the aid of his brother-in-
law, George W. Hughes, railroad magnate, engineer, and a freshman Democratic member of Congress. Hughes "disarmed the
hostility & won the cooperation of his own party," called up Marsh's
bill out of regular order, and got it past the House without opposition. Foot rushed the bill through the Senate committee and

secured the final Senate vote on June 12. The former Minister was at last rewarded with $9,000 for his mission to Greece.[14]

This was small return for six years of misery. The prolonged battle warped Marsh's judgment. Henceforth he tended to see himself as persecuted, vilified, wronged; he suspected enemies everywhere. The struggles of the 1850s cost him faith in justice and the power of truth. "Even when a boy, I used to say that 'Satan is mighty and will prevail.' "[15] Now he had proof of it.

His personal devils remain vague and shadowy figures. It might reveal much about Marsh to know why his partner Lyman deceived and cheated him and why Dainese hated him so passionately he spent six years trying to destroy his reputation. Marsh viewed his enemies as malevolent conspirators, but the facts hardly bear him out. His Vermont associates were the victims of their own cupidity, while Dainese, whose efforts Marsh at first appreciated, resented the Minister's refusal to recommend him as Consul. But we know little of these men's motives or of their later histories. None of his enemies save Peck appear to have suffered any evil consequences. Against the Vermont Central Railroad, however, as we shall see, Marsh was to take a reformer's revenge.

3

Every man has his limit of possibilities. Mine I dare say is a narrow one.   MARSH TO FRANCIS MARKOE, MARCH 29, 1855

The parlous state of his property had made money the overriding consideration in Marsh's life. One single criterion determined everything he did: how much would it pay? The search for a Marsh family fortune in England, which a distant Middle Western kinsman asked him to help finance, intrigued him, but the cost of finding hypothetical Marsh millions would be too great, the chance of reward too small. How could he settle his debts? Should he teach, write, return to politics, go back to the law, enter industry? Hiram Powers

even suggested that Marsh should found a newspaper similar to
the *Times* of London. Truly, the world was his oyster; but the
pearls in it were not large enough. Marsh turned down almost every
opportunity that came his way because nothing paid well enough.
He spent his energies, instead, on tasks that rewarded him still
worse, while waiting for something good to turn up. *"Kommt Zeit,
kommt Rath,"* thought Marsh; "a door will be opened in time." [16]

One open door was the law. Francis Markoe obligingly suggested
to John A. Rockwell, a Connecticut Congressional colleague of
Marsh's who was seeking a Washington partner, that Rockwell and
Marsh "would form a firm so respectable & strong as to carry all
before you!" But Marsh decided against it. Long away from the law,
he would have had hard work to brush up enough for Supreme
Court practice; certainly he had not prosecuted his own claim with
much success.[17] The prospect of legal work was, in fact, as dis-
tasteful as ever.

Marsh gave more serious thought to a Harvard professorship. The
chair of history had been unoccupied since Jared Sparks vacated it
to become president in 1849. Marsh's historical essays were well
known at Harvard; George Ticknor and C. C. Felton, Professor
of Greek soon to be Harvard's president, proposed and the Corporation unanimously agreed on Marsh. The salary was $2,000 a
year; he would find "a noble sphere of usefulness, and very agreeable social relations in the University." Marsh's experiences "in the
actual scenes of history, added to your comprehensive studies, seem
to point you out," Felton added, "as the person who, of all the
country, can make the most of it." [18]

With great reluctance Marsh declined the offer. He had always
wanted such a career—though perhaps it was "rather literary dis-
sipation & scientific dilettantism than scholarly *labour,* that I have
dreamed of as a release from the uncongenial cares & associations
belonging to the life of a country lawyer." He loved history and
thought Cambridge society "an irresistible temptation." But lawsuits

and claims cases took more time than a professor should spare, and "duties . . . oblige me . . . to look for the occupation which promises the largest pecuniary rewards." [19] The loss was both Marsh's and Harvard's.

He turned down many other teaching jobs, among them, in 1859, the provostship of the University of Pennsylvania at a salary of $3,000. "I hate boys, hate tuition, hate forms," Marsh told Baird bluntly; "the objections . . . are infinite." His feelings about schoolboys had changed little in the forty years since he had taught at Norwich Military Academy. His one university position, on the board of trustees of the University of Vermont, paid him nothing. Marsh's most constructive work as trustee concerned the "sadly deficient" university library, for which he drew up a plan of purchases, acquired part of the great collection of bibliographer Henry Stevens, and procured a new building.[20]

The world of science also beckoned. Many friends in scientific Washington thought Marsh might succeed Joseph Henry as Secretary of the Smithsonian Institution. Baird wrote that Henry was "in a condition of apparently irreconcilable warfare" with Assistant Secretary Jewett, who continued to champion publicly the cause of a large library. Jewett, Baird, and others hoped that Henry would resign; Henry "would lead a far happier life," averred J. M. Gilliss, "with equal if not greater usefulness to the world in his old pursuits." If Henry did go, would Marsh allow his friends to secure the appointment for him? Francis Markoe characterized the Smithsonian as "an Augean stable—a disgrace to the country," and wanted Marsh to clean it up. "Many of our leading men," he assured Marsh, "agree with me that you are the fittest man in the U.S. to be at its head." [21]

But Henry stubbornly stayed on. Backed by Bache, the Secretary persuaded the Regents to abandon the library altogether and devote more money to research. Bache was the real power, according to Gilliss; "he winds Henry about his finger and in fact controls the

Smithsonian as well as the Coast Survey." Empowered by the Board, Henry dismissed the stunned Jewett in July, 1854, touching off a public battle. Choate resigned from the Board in protest; others defended Henry; Horace Greeley opposed both and called for a complete overhauling of the Smithsonian.[22]

Marsh kept out of the controversy. Henry invited him to lecture at the Institution, assuring Marsh he was not trying to "purchase his silence"; the $134 Marsh was paid for a talk about camels early in 1855 could hardly be considered a bribe. Indeed, Marsh felt that Henry had administered the compromise "injudiciously & what is worse *unfairly*." He wrote out for the House Select Committee on the Smithsonian a long résumé of the Institution's history. But his restrained and dispassionate comments bore no resemblance to the other attacks against Henry, who was grateful for Marsh's "fairness." [23] Marsh's relations with the Smithsonian Institution remained cordial and intimate. Had he done as his friends wished, he might have pushed Henry out of Washington and become Secretary in his place. Fortunately, Marsh's ambitions did not lie in this direction.

Marsh's Washington friends also hoped he might return as a Senator. In January, 1853, Senator Upham died suddenly of smallpox, and Judge S. S. Phelps was appointed to finish his term. Would Marsh fight for the seat in 1854? Many political leaders in Vermont and Washington would "be rejoiced to see you in the Senate." [24]

Unfortunately, Marsh lived on the same side of the Green Mountains as Senator Solomon Foot. This was a fatal handicap in Vermont politics. Ever since the conflict between Joseph Marsh and the Allen brothers, East and West each had its own Senator, until the introduction of direct primaries and the election of Ralph E. Flanders in 1946 broke the "mountain rule" for the first time. "Why shall I not advertise a place for you at Woodstock," urged the ever helpful Gilliss, "or some other place on the right side of the mountain?" [25] But Marsh feared that the change-of-residence ruse would not work. He did accept the Whig nomination for the Vermont septennial Council of Censors, but was narrowly defeated by a

Know-Nothing ticket which campaigned on a promise to abolish the Council of Censors itself.

The whole Whig party was, in fact, split irrevocably by the Kansas-Nebraska Act of 1854. Most Vermont Whigs switched over to the new Republican party, and in 1856 Marsh enlisted enthusiastically for Frémont. Personal antipathy strengthened Marsh's Republican sympathies. "I have never liked Mr. F[illmore], & have a crow to pick with him when I get home," he had written in 1853. As Vice President, Fillmore had opposed Marsh's appointment to Turkey, and as President had treated him "basely." But Marsh thought James Buchanan, the Democratic candidate, even worse. Emphasizing the danger of a Democratic victory, he pressed his conservative Massachusetts friends to support Frémont. Otherwise, he warned them, Frémont would choose all his advisers from a "dangerous radical cabal." [26] But he gained no votes among the Cotton Whigs, and never quite forgave Winthrop and Choate for their "apostasy." Marsh did not stop to think that it was his views of the South that had changed, not theirs.

Marsh again turned down Congressional opportunities. James Meacham, his 1849 successor in the House, died during the 1856 campaign, but Marsh refused the vacancy. He also rejected Solomon Foot's offer of his Senate seat; he hesitated to bind himself for life "to such slavery as a senatorship now is, and that with so meagre a compensation." Just when Marsh said no, Congress raised its pay. Now he would "gladly accept" it, but correctly supposed that the increase in compensation would "remove Mr. Foot's wish to resign." This put Foot in a most embarrassing position, especially since he was "largely indebted for the place I hold to the generous support of *your friends*." If Frémont were elected, Foot promised to get Marsh "a first class foreign mission"; if the Republicans lost the national election, he was "ready to resign my place in the Senate" in Marsh's behalf. But Marsh could not accept this from his old friend, even after party leaders urged him to run as a candidate who could win *"without struggle* or *opposition."* [27]

Marsh's personal stake in the election was a diplomatic appointment. In July he had "a long and satisfactory private interview" with Frémont; in August he hit the hustings with as much energy as he could muster, and for three months devoted himself entirely to the campaign. But despite Vermont's 29,000 majority for Frémont, the national election went to the Democrats. "Well, exit Pierce, enter Buchanan!" Marsh wrote despairingly. "Which is the poorer creature of the two will soon be known to those who are able to dive low enough for such investigations." [28]

Marsh never again ran for elective office. In 1858 he even turned down the Republican nomination—tantamount to election—for governor; he "could not live on the salary" without social mortification. [29] Small wonder! for the Vermont governor received just $750 a year.

4

When my friends took old iron & files & hammers away from me, & put books in the place of them, they did me & the world a mischief.
MARSH TO FRANCIS J. CHILD, JULY 26, 1862

Judging from this catalogue of refusals, one might imagine that Marsh had succeeded in limiting himself to the narrow path of pecuniary duty. But he was an unregenerate dabbler. "What *will* you undertake next?" asked Gilliss wonderingly, acknowledging some maple seeds Marsh had sent him. "Arboriculture, mathematical Instrument making, Architecture—three professions mentioned in one letter! If you live much longer you will be obliged to *invent* trades, for you will have exhausted the present category." [30]

Of all Marsh's careers, that as instrument-maker was the briefest. Dissatisfied with the crude measuring and surveying instruments he had used abroad, Marsh "Yankee-like set to work to invent" better. The idea of engraving glass rulers on the under side occured to him. He bought a fine diamond point and went to work etching and coloring glass. By the summer of 1855 he had constructed three instruments: a protractor of plate glass leveled on one edge, with a metallic or ivory tongue and engraved parallel lines on the under surface; a similar ruler; and a circular protractor engraved on a square plate. He also had in mind a dioptic vernier.

Marsh took pride in his creations. He had become "quite a dextrous glass worker," drilling through glass plates "holes less than one fortieth of an inch in diameter, and (in one *painful* instance) even polishing the same." He boasted that his instruments possessed beauty, "certainty & celerity of adjustment," and "precision quite unattainable by any other means." [31] Hoping they might "sell if but as an ornament," Marsh turned his "divers cunning inventions" over to his friend J. H. Alexander, surveyor and mathematician. "Are these instruments *new?*" Marsh asked. "Are they good for anything? . . . How can I turn them to account?" Alexander was discouraging. Marsh's idea of transparent visibility was thirty-five years old, and glass instruments in general were no longer popular, for they broke too easily. Only the dioptic vernier, if Marsh could finish it, would be a real improvement; the others were not worth pushing commercially. And so it turned out. Marsh could get no patents; his time had gone for naught but the thrill of invention. "Tho' the rude accoucheurs of the Patent Office suffocated the birth," Alexander comforted him, he had at least had "the sweet spasm of conception & the pleasant pangs of parturition." [32]

5

Marsh did not put his main hopes for solvency in glass etching. Marble quarrying in Burlington, and lecture tours away from it, took up most of his time after he returned from Europe until several years of penury had convinced him that riches lay along neither road.

Fine marble outcroppings had been discovered at Mallett's Bay, six miles north of Burlington, by Marsh's cousin-in-law David Read. With Marsh, Read incorporated the Winooski Marble Company in 1855, for "quarrying marble, slate, & other stones & minerals in the state, and manufacturing & selling same." [33] At this time marble was imported almost exclusively from Italy; Marsh's was one of the earliest American ventures.

He had already begun operations. "Quarrying, which is now the great affair of the nation," wrote Marsh in the fall of 1855, "goes on well. I go down every day." He thoroughly enjoyed scrambling around in the rocks, woods, and dense brush, finding new colors and varieties and checking progress, although he got many bruises and sprains in consequence. Other veins of marble were found near Burlington, but Marsh did not worry about competition, for they were "inferior in quality, and in advantages of quarrying and shipping." [34] At Mallett's Bay the strata were nearly horizontal, and beds of marble up to six feet thick lay directly at the surface. The marble itself was extremely hard, which made it difficult to work, but resistant to corrosion and capable of taking a high polish. Marsh superintended cutting and sawing, a tedious operation done with iron saws, sand, and water. The blocks were then carted to the bay and carried off by steamer.

By the end of September, 1855, they had sent two boatloads— more than 1,200 cubic feet—to market in New York, and Captain Meigs, in charge of construction at the Federal Capitol, ordered 400 cubic feet of Mallett's Bay marble. "Everybody is running marble mad," Marsh wrote, "and I hope we may take advantage of the excitement, and sell out at a fair profit." But demand fell off rapidly. The great expense of washing and polishing the Winooski stone led most buyers to prefer softer, foreign stones for ornamental work, while Meigs at the Capitol found Marsh's marble "too hard and brittle to work well" for mantelpieces and too expensive for plain work.[35] Far from being a bonanza, the Winooski marble never paid its way. Years later Marsh's share of the quarry was sold for a mere $3,600.

6

I shall hang my "lecturing" on the same peg with my other failures and
follies. It must be a long peg and a strong peg to hold them all.

MARSH TO CAROLINE MARSH, FEB. 22, 1857

The last string to Marsh's bow was lecturing. American zeal
for knowledge was insatiable. Engaged by earnest secretaries of
countless civic associations, Marsh tried to eke out a living by bowd-
lerizing and puffing up for popular consumption his experiences in
the not-so-mysterious East. He launched his lecturing career in
Burlington in September, 1854, then went on to Boston, New York,
and Washington, visited upstate New York late in January, 1855,
and made even more extended tours the two following winters,
addressing dull, middle-sized audiences in innumerable dull towns.

Marsh was less adept at lecturing, unfortunately, than at quarrying. Perhaps his impersonal approach made him unsympathetic to
audiences. Certainly he exhibited on lecture platforms none of the
pungency that made him a popular campaigner. Marsh himself was
bored—"The Environs of Constantinople" was nothing a man could
get excited about, when talking on it for the thirtieth time. The
press, to be sure, spoke of "large and appreciative audiences" ("that
is," Marsh interpreted the phrase, "an invisibly small one"), and
commended his "statesman-like views." One paper praised him as
an "easy and vivid narrator," but also mentioned the need for perfect silence in the hall, the slightest sound drowning out Marsh's
voice. "His quiet manner, his rapid utterance, the compact language
. . . the absence of all personal adventure and of all . . . vague
adjectives," commented his wife, were "not likely to draw large
audiences." [36]

The disenchantment was mutual. If Marsh's hearers did not take
to him, he found them, their towns, everything about the lecture
circuit, repugnant. Traveling in Europe had been the keenest pleasure; in America it was a confounded nuisance. Trains were crowded,
dirty, unsafe, usually late for connections; roads were rutted seas

of mud or dust; the countryside was flat, uninteresting; baggage was lost or damaged; mail failed to arrive; accommodations were meager, dark, dirty, often a "miserable old-fashioned country tavern, where I cannot find even a room with a fire, to say nothing of other comforts." [37] On every tour, Marsh suffered from exposure, exhaustion, cold, hunger, or thirst.

His laments make better reading than his lectures. On one chilly trip to New York he was detained two and a half hours "in a miserable hole" and served as captive audience for "a discussion between a Know-nothing and a half drunken German." A few days later, near Elmira, Marsh's train overtook one which had been derailed, "and our engine finished the mischief by running into the train, breaking two cars and carrying away its own smoke pipe, cropping one man's ear, and otherwise maltreating sundry good citizens." But his most serious grievance concerned his fees. Too often he delivered a "thin lecture to a thin audience" for a slender reward. Since money was his only object, it was discouraging not even to cover expenses. One "very large audience" of 1,200 "to their shame, paid me only $30"; his average return was not above fifty dollars.[38] Perhaps he was too diffident to ask for more; others fared better.

Another difficulty was limitation of subject matter. There were many things Marsh could not safely mention. With his claim under critical Congressional scrutiny, he had to build up the image of Marsh the single-minded public servant, the man with no eye for anything but his job, the paragon who never took a vacation. As he explained to Caroline Paine, who was writing a book (*Tent and Harem*) about their experiences in the Orient, "any notice of any *civilities, kindnesses* or *favors of any sort* shewn our party by persons of any rank . . . might very seriously *injure me.*" [39] Marsh's lectures were thus extremely circumspect, abstract, and impersonal.

Most of his speeches were mediocre travelogues, but in a few political, religious, and agricultural discourses he had something important to say. Marsh's discussions of foreign affairs were simple, lucid, and, allowing for his prejudices, able. Perhaps his most penetrating observations concerned the American image abroad. Distinguishing sharply between the "people" of Europe, who regarded Americans as "the great source from which universal liberty is to flow," and the European governments, who considered the United States "a daring unconscientious and unscrupulous nation," Marsh enumerated the factors he thought most responsible for the mixed European views: (1) American expansionism; (2) Southern defense of slavery as a positive good; (3) encouragement of European revolutionary movements; (4) protection of naturalized and intended Americans; (5) the American spoils system, which produced foreign officials distinguished only for their "ignorance, vulgarity, and vice."[40] Marsh wanted to increase his country's prestige abroad; he also sought to use foreign opinion as a lever to change domestic policy. The purpose was not new; but Marsh was one of the first to systematize American self-consciousness and to analyze the ingredients of America's reputation overseas.

Marsh's favorite topics were science and agriculture. "You don't know how scientific I'm getting," he wrote Baird before speaking at Hartford on "The Study of Nature." Generally he talked about European crops and agricultural techniques, housing, ox harnesses; he compared the climate, terrain, public works, and railroads of the Old and New worlds. While remaining "the architects of your own fortunes," American farmers should follow Europe in applying science and purpose to agriculture, should introduce new domestic plants and animals, and should adopt forest conservation in order to prevent floods and soil erosion.[41] Vermont's hilly pastures did become well wooded again, but only because sheep raising ceased to be profitable and not because Vermonters took Marsh's advice. A more novel suggestion of his, however, met with immediate response: the introduction of camels to the American West.

7

Like Franklin, Jefferson, and other statesmen before him, Marsh was enthusiastic about bringing exotic plants and animals to America. In promoting the introduction of camels, Marsh surpassed the fancies of any of his predecessors. As early as 1847 he had suggested that dromedaries "might thrive on the sands of the South or the great prairies of the Southwest"; armed with Egyptian and Palestinian experience, he returned to the subject in his Smithsonian lectures of January, 1855. Descanting on the camel's speed and hardiness, describing its adaptations to desert life, Marsh concluded that properly selected camels could be naturalized in the United States with "ultimate success." [42] Much of the trans-Mississippi West supported neither horses nor mules, but surely camels accustomed to the Sahara and the Arabian desert could find ample water, acacia, and mesquite in the American Southwest.

The camel could serve both as beast of burden and as weapon of war. Marsh had earlier scoffed at the notion of "subduing the Comanches . . . and other Rocky Mt. Bedouins, with corps of dromedary dragoons," but two years of observation persuaded him that military "economy, celerity, and efficiency" would be enhanced by dromedaries. Not only would they enable the Army to keep open supply and mail routes, they would also help check hostile Indians, for the agile camel could haul guns and other matériel up and down steep slopes. "There are few more imposing spectacles," Marsh told his Washington audience, "than a body of armed men, advancing under the quick pace of the trained dromedary"; this sight "would strike with a salutary terror the . . . savage tribes upon our border." [43] He concluded with specific suggestions on how to select and bring camels to the United States.

Marsh was not the only camel enthusiast in America. For three years Secretary of War Jefferson Davis and a few others had also recommended that camels be tried in the United States. But it was Marsh's Smithsonian lecture, above all, that persuaded Congress, in

March, 1855, to send Major Henry C. Wayne and Navy Lieutenant David Dixon Porter with $30,000 and a Navy storeship to buy camels in Tunis, Malta, Smyrna, Salonika, Constantinople, and the Crimea. Wayne and Porter debarked thirty-three camels at Camp Verde, Texas, in May, 1856, and forty-one more the following year. The transport problem was solved, Wayne wrote Marsh; acclimation, breeding, and employment still had to be tested. Difficulties soon arose. Army men disliked the smelly animals, and became "seasick" on them; horses went wild with fright. Some camels were knifed by soldiers, others stolen by Indians. Thanks to Marsh's advice and Wayne's sagacity, the survivors got on well enough, though they chafed under the restraints of civilization, as Marsh had warned. In 1857 Lieutenant E. F. Beale used them to survey a route to the Colorado River. Beale praised the "noble & useful brute" as sure-footed and docile, and Secretary of War Floyd, hailing "the entire adaptation of camels to military operations on the plains," proposed to buy a thousand more. The Civil War interfered, however. Some camels were captured by Confederate troops; the rest were used in the Nevada silver mines or sold to circuses. The last one died at Griffith Park, Los Angeles, in 1934. Enthusiast though he was, Marsh had never supposed that the camel could succeed in a *settled* West. "So essentially nomade [*sic*] indeed is the camel in his habits," he wrote, "that the Arab himself dismisses him as soon as he acquires a fixed habitation." [44]

Marsh had tried meanwhile to capitalize on public interest in the government's camel venture. Adding to his Smithsonian lecture and earlier travel sketch, "The Desert," he wrote a book-length manuscript in ten days; *The Camel* was published the same month the beasts themselves reached Texas. Reviewers praised its "extensive scholarship and acquaintance with many tongues, for which the writer has so enviable a fame," but few realized that the "racy, piquant" extracts "from the unpublished journal of a traveller" [45] were in fact from Marsh's own pen.

The core of the book concerned the species and breeds, anatomy and environmental adaptations, diet, training and treatment, burden and furniture, speed and gait, and geographical range of the camel. Having digested the camel studies by the geographer Carl Ritter, the Orientalist Baron von Hammer-Purgstall, and the French engineer Carbuccia, Marsh estimated his own work as the best and "the fullest account of the animal" in English.[46]

The Camel's thoroughness may explain why it sold so poorly. In July, Marsh complained that it had passed almost unnoticed; a few months later the publishers, Gould & Lincoln, told him it was "very near a total failure." They had done better with Biernatzki's *The Hallig; or, The Sheepfold in the Waters,* a translation, dictated by Caroline to Marsh and other amanuenses, of a pious, romantic novel by a German evangelical pastor about life on a small Danish island in the North Sea. Marsh himself contributed a brief biographical sketch of Biernatzki and translated the author's preface and most of the first chapter, "The Island Home," which is an extraordinary, impressionistic piece of regional description. But *The Camel* and *The Hallig* together brought the Marshes only $125. Marsh concluded that Gould & Lincoln were either "very stupid or very stingy, probably both," and decided to carry his "next grist to another mill." [47]

The fall and winter of 1856 marked the nadir of Marsh's career. The marble quarry was a failure, *The Camel* had no sale, Dainese had defeated his Greek claim again; creditors importuned while new debts materialized every day. "Everything goes wrong with me," Marsh deplored; "I am *d'une humeur de dogue.*" Then came the long, hard campaign—and the Republican defeat. Marsh tried to see Frémont in New York, "but got entangled in that vile vulgar labyrinth of squares and places about 8th & 9th streets" and blistered his feet so badly that he could not walk for several days. Back in Burlington, marble business and new Peck charges brought on a headache that drove Marsh "nearly crazy." He spent a bitterly cold Christmas in Woodstock and planned a trip to combine recuperation and remuneration. "If ever an old vessel wanted mending," he wrote despondently, "it is I." [48] On January 29, 1857, he set out for the Middle West on his longest—and last—lecture tour.

8

This minute and faithful record of my travels . . . is composed with no view of magnifying my perils and mine adventures, but solely to the intent that a curious and enlightened posterity may have authentic information on the modes and facilities of locomotion practiced and enjoyed in this century.

MARSH TO CAROLINE MARSH, DAVENPORT, IOWA, FEB. 18, 1857

Veteran traveler in the Levant, Marsh considered his Middle Western expedition of 1857 the worst journey he ever made—a fitting climax to this chapter of disappointments. At Niagara his hotel "was so filthy . . . that even the cataract could not wash it clean"; by Cleveland he already repented his undertaking. Leaving Cincinnati at 5:00 A.M. Marsh *"failed to connect* at Richmond, the train having been purposely delayed for some rascal reason growing out of a Railroad quarrel, and so *lost* Lafayette. We were put into an extra train at Richmond, with orders to keep *behind* a freight train," and reached Indianapolis, sixty miles away, six hours later. Marsh was then to start for Chicago, "but while I was expecting the train *in*side, it went by on the *out,* carrying my trunks with it . . . so that my Chicago appointment is lost also. . . . The natives I meet in the cars don't know so much as a yellow dog. I am much inclined to return directly home." The next day, beyond the Wabash, Marsh's train "met a freight train that had run off and broken down the tracks. We then walked a quarter of a mile, in Indiana mud, and sat eight hours in the cars, waiting for a messenger to go nine miles on foot, and get a locomotive to supply ours, which broke down just after we got started again." He reached Chicago after twenty-five hours, "making four nights out of seven in the cars, and to make it pleasanter, I had nothing to eat from 7 yesterday morning until $1\frac{1}{2}$ P.M. today, all our stoppages being in deep cuts, where there was no provender for man or beast. . . . The only pleasant thing I have enjoyed thus far is the anticipation, that a woman in the Nursery Car where I was, who promised each of her six children a sound whipping, will be as good as her word." [49]

In Chicago Marsh found some solace in visiting his old friend William B. Ogden, now one of the wealthiest men in the Middle West, and the lively painter G. P. A. Healy, who had settled there under Ogden's patronage. For Chicago itself, Marsh reserved his most caustic remarks. Though the inhabitants had done "everything possible to combat the natural disadvantages of the locality," it was not enough. Marsh compared Chicago unfavorably with the Levantine swamp where he and Caroline had been so ill, "only Migdol has no city, which is one advantage, and has mountains in sight, which is another. As for the inhabitants . . . I think them somewhat alike, though the stray Bedouins are more *picturesque* than Chicago travellers." [50]

From Chicago to Galena on the Mississippi, 150 miles away, took Marsh's train twenty-nine hours:

We were obliged to cross on the ice, or temporary foot bridges, or ferries, five streams where the bridges had been carried away by the freshet, or broken down by trains; were two hours in freight cars without light, fire, or seats . . . and at one time stood on the ice two hours waiting for a ferry boat to take over 200 passengers, at 8 or 9 a trip. The weather has been excessively cold, and many of the passengers froze their ears, and some their fingers and feet, while on the ice. On the whole, it was the most laborious and disagreeable journey I ever made.

Marsh neither ate nor slept during the entire trip. Only "virtuous indignation at my own stupidity, in coming out here," kept him going.

He reached St. Louis at three in the morning on February 15, after a week in which he had *"two nights in bed,* rest in cars or at depots, *travel* 600 miles, *receipts* $65, which does not leave a large balance in my favor, deducting wear and tear and expenses." Happy to see his sister- and brother-in-law, Lucy and Fred Wislizenus, he talked steadily for two days, refreshing them all "like some radiant comet lighting up for a space our . . . gloom." Marsh also saw his

old friend Charles D. Drake, who had returned to private law
practice. In St. Louis too were the Reverend Biewend, Marsh's
Lutheran pastor from Washington, now a professor at Concordia
College, and Dr. Seyffarth, of Leipzig, a famous Orientalist and
"ein feiner mann." Marsh was elected Fellow of the Archaeological
Society of St. Louis, "an easy & honourable position, duties nix,
emoluments ditto, and . . . nothing to pay but my postage. Truly,
I am a Hans in Glück!" But the lecture circuit soon reclaimed him.
Marsh found "the mud of Bloomington . . . deeper and blacker
than any East of it, but far behind that of Davenport in profundity":

We reached Mendota at 4 in the morning, waited 4 hours, and were then
treated to a ride of 30 miles in a freight car. After this, was a hiatus of a
mile, and no conveyance between. I could not hire anyone to carry my
trunk, so I passed my hand through the handles, and swung it over my
shoulders and commenced to march. I lost my india rubbers at the first
plunge, but recovered them, and waded to the other depot. I then went
twenty miles on a locomotive, then 35 in a freight car.

But he was too late for his lecture. "If I were to go directly home
now, I should reach Burlington with less money than I started, but
have I not seen the Great West?" [51]

The return trip was no better. "Another month of squalling
babies," Marsh told his wife, "would extinguish me effectually."
The "fine generous people" of Kalamazoo gave him twenty-two
dollars for a lecture, "& even their fair words won't tempt me among
them again. In fact I have made up my mind after this trip, to
give up the thankless task of enlightening the world, & I shall let
wisdom die with me, an it will."

It the trip had contributed nothing to Marsh's pocket, it added fuel
to two of his pet hates—the railroads and the West. Lucy Wislizenus
feared that her brother-in-law had taken "such a *disgust* at the
entire West that he will never venture out among us again." Her
fears were completely confirmed. "Not all the gophers in Illinois,"
Marsh wrote Baird, "would tempt me to dwell in this famed West,
even were I as desperate a naturalist as you." [52]

❧ IX ❧

Vermont Public Servant

AFTER HIS GRUELING Western journey, Marsh returned to
Burlington to be "grievously tormented of Satan incarnate in Pecks."
Family problems also taxed him. His son, George, now a student
at Harvard Law School, came down again with typhoid fever at
Woodstock. Near death for a month, he never fully recovered; he
had delusions that his parents were persecuting him, and began to
drink heavily. His worried father wished that George were "well
married to some wise & prudent woman, who would govern &
direct him." [1]

In the hours away from his son's bedside in July and August,
Marsh climbed and measured Mt. Tom and other Woodstock hills
with his brother Charles, using a barometric method taught him
by the geographer Arnold Guyot. But the winter's trip and the summer's crisis had exhausted him. In November he caught a severe
cold; neuralgia recurred, and for two months he was seriously ill.
Dr. Leonard Marsh prescribed a change of air, so Marsh went for
several weeks to Boston and New York. In the congenial society of
old friends, away from Pecks and Daineses, he gradually recovered
health and spirits.

I

I had in my boyhood a good fishhook *acquaintance with the piscatory
population.*   MARSH TO SPENCER BAIRD, OCT. 12, 1881

Just when all his private projects had failed, opportunity came to
Marsh from a new quarter. In November, 1857, he was appointed
Vermont Railroad Commissioner at a salary of $1,000 a year.
"Among my many blanks I have drawn one small prize," he wrote.
"Nothing could come in better time, and I am by no means dis-
posed to look this gift horse in the mouth." [2] In fact, Governor
Ryland Fletcher had already made Marsh Fish Commissioner, State
House Commissioner, and head of the Ethan Allen Monument
Committee.

The most unusual of these odd jobs was the fish commissionership. Fishing in Vermont was not what it once had been. Vermonters
bemoaned the disappearance of salmon and the extermination of
trout by voracious pickerel the early settlers had introduced into
ponds. Every year the state legislature passed dozens of acts to protect fish in specific lakes and streams. But preservation was not
enough; Marsh was asked to find means of replenishment.

His forty-five page report was characteristically thorough. After
summarizing the history of fish breeding from Roman times, Marsh
described recent experiments in artificial propagation. He approved
fish ponds in general, but warned that damming lakes and reservoirs
indiscriminately often "seriously impeded the drainage of the soil."
He had seen large tracts of land in Europe thus made "barren and
pestilential wastes." But he considered prospects good locally, both for
breeding indigenous varieties and for introducing new species of fish.
Marsh hoped to restock Lake Champlain with shad, salmon, and
trout, "which formerly furnished so acceptable a luxury to the rich,
and so cheap a nutrient to the poor of Western Vermont, but which
now are become almost as . . . extinct as the game that once enlivened our forests." [3]

The most important aspect of Marsh's report was his inquiry into the causes of this decline. He attributed it to the following man-induced changes: (1) the practice of taking fish in the spawning season; (2) the pollution of waters by industrial and urban development; (3) the clearing of forests, which increased runoff and caused stream flow to fluctuate violently; (4) the destruction, along with the forests, of insects—a major food source for fish larvae.

The fish report, like his agricultural lectures, showed that Marsh was sensitive to the complex nature of the interrelationships and adjustments between species, and to the active role man played in transforming the environment. Marsh knew that it would be difficult to check the abuses he catalogued; one could not prevent the discharge of all industrial wastes, or renew stream flow entirely in the dry seasons. Nor could the most restrictive fish and game laws, however efficiently enforced, "restore the ancient abundance of our public fisheries." But if *some* regulations were not imposed, Marsh warned, Vermont would lose her forests and topsoil as well as her fish.[4]

The legislature thanked Marsh for his "noteworthy" report, but found it inexpedient "in the present state of information" to act upon it. Action finally came at the national level, as a result of extensive research in the 1870s promoted by the United States Commissioner of Fish and Fisheries. It was more than coincidence that this commissioner was Marsh's protégé, Spencer Baird. Baird's monumental reports credit Marsh with the first important contribution toward the restoration of salmon in the United States.[5] In this, as in many other aspects of conservation, Marsh had pioneered.

Marsh's ichthyological researches, which netted him only a hundred dollars, inspired him to build an aquarium; he sat by the hour watching his pets "chaw one another up most catawampously."[6] Intellectually, the investigation proved extremely rewarding. It provoked Marsh to ponder on the economy of nature. Perhaps nothing that he did during this decade was of greater import for his future work.

2

Marsh owed his State House commissionership to a catastrophe. One January evening in 1857, with furnaces stoked for a meeting of the Constitutional Convention, the twenty-year-old granite State House caught fire; before the Montpelier fire engine could reach it, the building was gutted. Nothing was left but a bleak granite shell. After a five-week battle, the legislature decided to keep Montpelier as the capital, and Governor Fletcher asked Marsh to draw up a plan for a new State House. Marsh thought the sum the legislature had allowed—$40,000—was too small, the time too short, but reluctantly took on the job. He met his fellow commissioners, Norman Williams, of Woodstock, and John Porter, of Hartford, on March 17, "with just two weeks," he grumbled, "to build a State-house." [7]

Marsh was responsible for the final plan. He alone understood architecture; he alone had definite preferences. "Both Judge Porter and myself," wrote Williams, "desire you to exercise your own taste & judgment. . . . We shall adopt what you propose." The new State House is generally credited to Ammi B. Young, who had designed the previous building, but Marsh departed from the old plan in several important respects. The Capitol he designed was a three-story granite structure, steamheated, gas-lighted, and as fireproof as possible, with no wood in the first floor, staircases, or partitions. For lack of time, the commission had to leave details of finish and decoration to construction superintendent Dr. Thomas E. Powers, of Woodstock, and to the architect Marsh selected, Thomas W. Silloway, of Boston.[8] But Marsh worked closely with Silloway in drawing up specifications. The architect prevailed over Marsh's desire for an iron dome, and for square instead of lozenge-shaped lights in the windows; but on one point Marsh was adamant: he refused to countenance any ornamentation in the pediments and portico.

No sooner had construction begun, in the spring of 1858, than a bitter feud developed between Silloway and superintendent Powers. The energetic Powers was obstinate, proud—and ignorant of architecture. To economize, he used the cheapest materials he could get, including burnt stones from the old building; he flattened the dome, built staircases of wood instead of iron; he ignored Silloway, and finally replaced him with a more subservient architect. Silloway remained in Montpelier to write Marsh frantic notes about the superintendent's departures from the plan. Marsh could not dismiss Powers, but corrected some of his mistakes and made him promise to produce *"exactly* what the commissioners desired." Despite the imbroglio, the building cost less than $150,000 and was ready for occupancy in October, 1859. Without Marsh's constant support, Silloway testified, the result would have been dreadful; "nothing but devotion to the cause on your part has arrested the evil." Marsh had "rendered the state a good service." The Vermont State House still stands, perhaps not "the finest specimen of Greek architecture" in the country, as the architect Stanford White termed it,[9] but a worthy example of the classic style and a handsome monument to Marsh's taste.

3

The decay of commercial morality . . . is to be ascribed more to the influence of joint-stock banks and manufacturing and railway companies . . . than to any other one cause of demoralization. . . . Private corporations . . . may become most dangerous enemies to rational liberty, to the moral interests of the commonwealth, to the purity of legislation and of judicial action, and to the sacredness of private rights.
MARSH, *Man and Nature* (1864)

First fish, then architecture, now railroads; Marsh prided himself on being master of all trades. In fact, his reports as railroad commissioner were significant essays on political economy.

As elsewhere in New England, Vermont railroads were no unmixed blessing. The Vermont Central–Rutland & Burlington quarrel, followed by bankruptcy, strengthened feeling that the state should curb the railroads. Private responsibility had been found wanting, Jacob Collamer told the Assembly in 1855; reckless railroad rivalries and frauds "imperatively require that some efficient power of constant inspection and control should be provided for the public safety." A railroad commissioner should be appointed to examine records, regulate rates, and report whether "any railroad corporation has exceeded its legal powers or . . . incurred a forfeiture of its franchises." [10]

The railroad interests protested against this proposal. These "extraordinary powers [might] be executed with most summary despotism, to the detriment and even destruction" of Vermont's railroads. "Capitalists would view . . . such extreme and odious legislation . . . as evidence of a deep-seated and inveterate hostility on the part of the people, to any further investments in railroads," and would thereafter shun Vermont.[11]

The commission was established despite the railroad lobby, but the reform candidate, Marsh's old crony George W. Benedict, did not get the commissionership. The Supreme Court instead gave the job to Charles Linsley, a tool of the railroads. In his annual report, Linsley stated that the corporations were so poverty-stricken it would be unfair to ask them to make any improvements in service.

The railroad men were consequently dismayed when in 1857 the legislature stripped the Supreme Court of its appointive power and replaced the benign Linsley with that inveterate foe of railroad corporations, George P. Marsh! They were certain Marsh had it in for them. The Vermont Central had ruined his real estate, bankrupted him and his associates, and prostrated Burlington. For years Marsh had traveled about the state finding fault with the railroads, even recommending government ownership! [12] And he had recently returned from the Middle West, where closer familiarity with the iron horse left him with still greater contempt.

Commissioner Marsh was as critical as the railroads feared. He was also extremely thorough. In the summer and early fall of 1858 he covered every mile of track in Vermont at least twice. He asked the corporations embarrassing questions: How much were their legal advisers paid? Did any officers or employees have a personal interest in contracts? What were the contract prices? Why were repairs delayed? To whom were passes given? Which stopovers and transfers were necessary and why? Though managers were "dilatory" in replying, by October Marsh had finished. He expected his report to "bring a hornet's nest about my ears," [13] but had no disposition to draw the stings.

Marsh's railroad report was a devastating condemnation of corporate irresponsibility—a situation few understood until Charles Francis Adams, Jr., wrote "A Chapter of Erie" in 1869. The misfortunes of Vermont's railroads Marsh considered the good luck of her citizens. It was too bad the corporations had lost money, but the absence of wealthy stockholders was "eminently favorable to the independence, the impartiality, and the purity" of the state legislature. Vermont's railroad managers had sufficient funds "to serve as a temptation to private fraud and peculation," but not enough to corrupt public officials.

Even the stockholders, Marsh maintained, were fortunate that their shares were practically worthless. Observing "that a still further decline [in the value of their securities] was at all times probable," those who had bought before would not be fooled again, and their losses were a drastic warning to the uninitiated. Since there was no temptation to speculate, Vermont's commercial virtue remained untarnished. As a result, concluded Marsh, "we . . . have thus far escaped the enormous moral, political, and financial evils to which the almost universal corruption of great private corporations has elsewhere given birth."

Even in Vermont, Marsh pointed out, viewing the Vermont Central with baleful eye, shareholders sometimes got or gave well-remunerated offices and lucrative contracts at public expense. But now the railroads were bankrupt, "waifs and strays . . . subject to absolute disposal and control" for the public good. Marsh set forth the proper aims of railroad reorganization. The bankrupt roads should not be run for the benefit of their managers; the legislature had "the right and duty" to take them over. Private franchises were not sacred when they became "nuisances or abuses." Marsh recommended a complete revision of Vermont railroad law and offered to draw it up.[14]

Turning from the general to the specific, he entered a long list of grievances. The Vermont railroads were "all imperfect in construction"; tracks were badly built and unsafe, routes poorly planned. Freight trains were appallingly slow—why should goods require seventy or eighty hours to reach New York or Boston when passengers got there in one seventh of the time? Marsh demanded specific bridge and roadbed repairs and safety devices. Many of the passengers' complaints were well-founded, he felt. The railroads charged extra fare for tickets bought on board, but opened ticket offices only five or ten minutes before trains left. People were often carried beyond their stations because conductors failed to announce stops.[15]

The worst annoyances were changes and waits between trains. Marsh knew that some railroads deliberately harassed passengers to coerce their choice of route. The most flagrant offender was the Vermont Central; originally chartered between Burlington and Windsor, it no longer operated through trains to either terminus. Instead, the railroad compelled travelers to and from Burlington to change trains at Essex Junction, seven miles to the northeast, where the Vermont Central connected with its subsidiary, the Vermont & Canada. From this desolate spot a spur line squirmed perilously along steep grades to meet the Burlington & Rutland line in Burlington. The Vermont Central meant to wreck the Rutland road by denying it a decent rail outlet north and west; the Burlington bypass, as has been seen, proved disastrous for the town and for Marsh himself.

The Vermont Central trustees now explained to Marsh that "a change of cars at Essex is deemed necessary for the proper accommodation of the travelling public." Marsh snorted at this excuse.

"Whatever advantage may accrue to the Railroads from the arrangement, the 'travelling public' is in no respect 'accommodated' by submitting to [this] annoyance." [16] The Vermont Central had rigged its schedule so as to make northbound Rutland Railroad passengers wait at Essex nine hours or more. Essex Junction was infamous; Senator S. S. Phelps never spoke more truly for his constituents than in his "Lay of the Lost Traveller":

> With saddened face and battered hat
> And eye that told of black despair,
> On wooden bench the traveler sat,
> Cursing the fate that brought him there.
> "Nine hours," he cried, "we've lingered here,
> With thought intent on distant homes,
> Waiting for that elusive train
> Which, always coming, never comes,
> Till, weary, worn,
> Distressed, forlorn,
> And paralyzed in every function,
> I hope in Hell
> His soul may dwell
> Who first invented Essex Junction." [17]

Essex Junction, Marsh charged, failed to meet the charter obligation of a good connection at Burlington. The Vermont Central ought not embarrass and annoy those who preferred the Rutland or the steamboat route to Burlington. If it did not make a proper junction with the Rutland & Burlington, the Vermont Central's franchise should be forfeited. In the next session, the legislature gave the railroad another two years to rectify this "gross case of abuse" and complete the extension to Burlington. In use by May, 1861, the extension was abandoned that fall and never reopened.[18]

Marsh underestimated corporate pressure on the Vermont legislature. "There has never been a time," wrote an assemblyman, "that rail road influences were brought to bear so directly on members" as after Marsh's report appeared in 1858. A bill embodying Marsh's proposals and giving him additional powers was shunted into the

Committee on Roads, made up of "creatures of the Rail Roads," which killed it. Meanwhile the railroad lobby tried to get rid of Marsh, and almost prevented his reelection; not until the third ballot did Marsh garner a majority. They then tried to abolish the office entirely; this failing, they slashed Marsh's salary from $1,000 to $500, hoping that he would resign.[19]

But fighting the corporations was for Marsh a labor of love. "My anathema on the scoundrel railroaders," he later wrote, "& on all railroaders, whom I loathe with all my soul." In his second annual report he deplored the legislature's failure to carry out his suggestions, and reemphasized the need for effective control over the railroads. Government supervision would benefit everyone "except peculators and speculators, the furtherance of whose private interests is not one of the appropriate functions of the legislature of Vermont." But the legislature still took no action. All hope of reform vanished with the end of Marsh's extraordinary railroad commissionership in 1859. His immediate successor, subservient to the railroad lobby that put him in office, discovered "a community of interest between the public and the railroad companies" and considered "faultfinding" no part of his job.[20]

The gigantic frauds of the post-Civil War era, when powerful companies corrupted every branch of government, strengthened Marsh's conviction that private corporations were evil, railroads particularly reprehensible. "Joint-stock companies have no souls; their managers . . . no consciences. . . . In their public statements falsehood is the rule, truth the exception." American fear of being overgoverned—and overtaxed—had become a political shibboleth. Marsh believed that all transport and communications facilities should be government owned and operated. He was well aware of the perils of bureaucracy, but argued that "the corruption thus engendered, foul as it is, does not strike so deep as the rottenness of private corporations."[21] Replace individual selfishness with public responsibility, Marsh urged, or all will suffer. His attitude toward corporations was entirely consistent with his philosophy of resource conservation. In both fields he saw private interests endangering public welfare; in each instance he advocated public control rather than private reformation. Since men were not saints, the state must serve as custodian of the common weal.

⚘ X ⚘

The English Language

It is a rash thing for a Yankee man to attempt to teach English, but we are a bold people, and I am resolved to venture it.

MARSH TO LADY ESTCOURT, JUNE 3, 1859

EARLY IN 1858, Marsh had accepted an offer to teach English language and literature the following winter at Columbia University. Unlike all the academic jobs he had turned down, this was a short-term appointment in a special postgraduate program; the base pay was $1,500; and the course "can hardly fail," according to Columbia trustee Samuel B. Ruggles, "to yield the Professor a considerable amount in fees." [1]

Throughout the summer and fall Marsh snatched moments from his commission tasks and private perplexities to work up lectures. By October he had reviewed enough English, German, Catalan, and Italian folk literature to keep him a jump or two ahead of his students. Cleaning out his disordered study, making "a holocaust of all the old medicines, old papers, old shoes and other rubbish I could find," [2] he settled down comfortably in a boarding house at 22 University Place, near Ninth Street, and started lecturing.

I

Marsh's course began with "An Apology for the Study of English," a defense of postgraduate work in what was usually thought a topic for the nursery. Addressed "to the many, not to the few," his lectures were a grab bag of miscellaneous essays on language and literature. Writing without source materials was "making bricks without straw"; Marsh confessed that he was ignorant of linguistics and "evolving my facts out of the depths of my own consciousness."[3] But what he lacked in documentation he made up for in liveliness. He discussed speech origins, the practical uses of etymology, the structure and vocabulary of English. He lectured on inflections, on the impact of the printing press, on rhyme, on the King James Bible —which he considered the supreme English masterpiece—and on linguistic corruption. Finally, he talked about the American language, explaining how dialects developed and defending change as essential to any living tongue.

The course went well, but the class was smaller and the remuneration far less than Marsh had hoped. Marsh's colleague, the German-born political scientist Francis Lieber, who had come to Columbia after many years at the University of South Carolina, had the same problem. "My dear Fellow-Lecturer to many benches and few hearers," Lieber addressed Marsh, "had we not better turn Buddhists at once and lecture, in deep meditation, to ourselves, on ourselves, and by ourselves?" Marsh made up his mind not to stay a second year. "The course does not *pay*," he wrote flatly; "a business which yields no profit, ought to be given up."[4]

The winter was a therapeutic and social if not a financial success. Caroline was better; she could walk a quarter of a mile without pain, and Marsh envisioned waltzing with her "to the admiration of the beholders." New York society was stimulating. Marsh enjoyed the company of the geographer Arnold Guyot and the geologist James Dwight Dana, both at Columbia that winter. Henry J. Raymond, of the *Times,* introduced Marsh to notable New Yorkers, among others William Cullen Bryant, the essayist Richard Grant White, and Vincenzo Botta, Italian refugee scholar at New York University. Marsh renewed old friendships with Caroline Paine—now living in New York—and Charlotte Bostwick, who had found a husband after all, a Brooklyn clergyman. He also saw much of a Swedish pioneer in comparative philology, Maximilian Schele de Vere, who "listened very well to what I said, though a capital talker himself"; [5] and the fiery Polish exile Adam Gurowski.

More than anyone else, the ebullient Francis Lieber made his New York stay pleasant. Marsh found the political scientist "so *subjective* in conversation, that he doesn't give one a fair chance to understand him," but the two shared many passions and prejudices: love of German literature, sympathy toward nationalism, a similar wry turn of humor, and wide-ranging interests in various fields. Lieber begged Marsh to stay on as Columbia librarian "so that we might 'Beaumont & Fletcher' it," but Marsh felt the previous incumbent had "set a bad example, worked too hard and too cheap." [6]

In pursuit of "small duties & large pay," Marsh took on a strenuous task in the spring of 1859. He had decided to publish his Columbia lectures, and spent months running from library to library for notes and references. For Marsh, who loved to be thorough, the Boston and New York libraries were discouragingly full of material. In July he returned to Burlington "like an escaped convict to his cell," grateful only that he had "too much work to do, to dwell on the *Widerwärtigkeiten* of our position there." Besides coping with lectures and legal problems, Marsh turned out his second railroad report, some "slovenly and bitter" articles for Hale's *Christian Examiner,* and two brief poems for Abby Hemenway's Vermont anthology. The lectures kept him "a writing and a writing, with all my might, for fear the printer's devil, now full 300 pp. behind me, will *emporte* me." Gone were the carefree days when he and Baird used to "scribble about nothing . . . before we came to be a couple of such sapless dry old sticks as time, trouble, and Satan have made us." Working day and night, Marsh did not "exchange a reasonable word with anybody once a month. . . . Whereas I used to be a conversable and . . . witty person, I am grown the dullest old owl in Christendom." [7]

Printing was completed by October, both on Marsh's *Lectures on the English Language* and on Caroline's new volume, *Wolfe of the Knoll,* a collection of poems inspired by German literature and her travels in the Levant. But it was too late for the fall season; their new publisher, Scribner, held both books over until spring. Marsh was furious at the delay, which he claimed "defeats one of the principal motives I had in publishing. . . . If I were to hear tomorrow that the plates of my volume were destroyed, I should be rather glad than sorry." But he eventually calmed down, concluding that the world "has already waited 60 centuries for us and will probably hold out a couple of months yet." [8]

"The appearance of Marsh's book," Lieber exclaimed, "big, substantial, wholly excellent—together with his wife's poetry—small, aethereal, wholly charming—is one of the finest literary phenomena." Up in ice-bound Vermont, the Marshes were warmed by the reviews. *Wolfe of the Knoll* received universal praise; even the London *Athenaeum* noted benignly that this was no ordinary transatlantic drivel, "a third-rate Germanism, served up by silly people," but superior stuff, comparable to that of "our own romantic poetesses." Marsh fared almost as well. Acclaiming him as "a man of profound and varied scholarship" and "a philologist neither perversely wrongheaded nor the victim of preconceived theory," American periodicals characterized the *Lectures* as "the best guide we know of" and "one of the most valuable contributions to American literature which has at any time been made." But Anglophiles condemned Marsh's "heroic attempt to defend American pronunciation." One trenchant critic found Marsh "Teutonic enough in theory, [but] he Latinizes terribly in practice . . . and is carried away in a mass of long and hardly intelligible words." [9] This was perceptive and just; Marsh had not always followed his own principles.

Marsh considered his book overpraised. He was amazed he had ever written it. Had he suspected eighteen months before that he would be "the author of an actual, printed book . . . the 'English Language' would have been one of the last things that would have occurred to me as the probable subject." [10]

2

*That wild man up in Vermont is writing seven books, each in seven
quarto volumes, all to be finished seven weeks from this date.*

MARSH TO S. F. BAIRD, MAY 10, 1860

Marsh's English studies were not quite so fortuitous as he claimed.
The subject was much in the air in the late 1850s; widespread interest
had been aroused by the linguistic work of Dean Richard Trench,
by R. G. Latham's and W. C. Fowler's texts, and by William Dwight
Whitney's research in comparative philology. Marsh's lectures established him as an authority in the field, and he was overwhelmed by
requests for literary and philological advice. At long last released
from his creditors, Marsh had boundless energy. He planned to edit
a new edition of *Appleton's Cyclopaedia.* He helped Philadelphia
librarian Samuel A. Allibone with his *Critical Dictionary of English
Literature and British and American Authors.* He corresponded
with W. D. Whitney and Josiah W. Gibbs at Yale and with H. Cop-
pée at the University of Pennsylvania.

Perhaps the most impressive project with which Marsh was connected was the *New English Dictionary.* Readers and editors were
enlisted throughout the English-speaking world, and the London
Philological Society chose Marsh as its American secretary. It was his
job to promote the dictionary and to guide American scholars, who
were to work on American and eighteenth-century English literature. Marsh instructed readers to take complete notes on all words,
phrases, and idioms not in published concordances to the Bible or
Shakespeare, and to send etymologies to him. The Vermonter expected these efforts to result in "a more complete thesaurus of the
English tongue than now exists of any language, living or dead."
He was mortified, therefore, by the "utter neglect" with which most
Americans treated his invitation, and saw little reason to hope that
acceptable readers could be found even for American authors. After
the death of editor-in-chief Herbert Coleridge in 1861, the whole
project was put aside for decades.[11] Marsh's work on the *New Eng-*

lish Dictionary, while largely fruitless, did bring him into friendly contact with English philologists and with a few cooperative American scholars like Charles Eliot Norton.

Marsh also became involved in the famous "Battle of the Dictionaries." Since 1828, when Noah Webster published his *American Dictionary,* a feud had raged between him and Joseph E. Worcester, whose edition of Samuel Johnson's *Dictionary* appeared the same year. Worcester charged Webster with corrupting the English language; Webster accused Worcester of plagiarism. The controversy embroiled important literary figures; Bryant, for example, promised to attack relentlessly "until every trace of Websterian spelling disappears from the land."[12]

Early in 1860 Worcester's new *Dictionary of the English Language* was published and the Merriam brothers brought out a revision of Webster's. The support of Marsh, as a recognized expert, was eagerly sought by Websterians and Worcesterians alike. In an important comparative review in the New York *World,* Marsh judged both dictionaries "far from perfect." Of the two, however, he much preferred Worcester's. Worcester had a better selected vocabulary, simpler and more accurate etymologies; Webster relied too much on "internal" evidence instead of "reading and excerpting real live English books." Marsh also awarded Worcester the laurels for pronunciation and spelling. Webster confounded such different sounds as the *a* in *fate* and *fare;* Marsh denounced Webster's spelling reforms as "stereotyped cacography." The Merriams took Marsh's criticisms in good part; they even offered him an editorship to rectify their mistakes. In the next edition of Webster's Marsh is thanked for "some valuable suggestions in respect to the principles which should be followed in the preparation of a popular English Dictionary." [13]

Marsh was already editing another dictionary: the *Christian Review* had asked him to prepare an American edition of Hensleigh Wedgwood's *Dictionary of English Etymology.* Nothing interested the historically minded Marsh more than the origin of words, so he accepted with alacrity.

Only the first volume of Wedgwood's *Dictionary, A* through *D,* had been published; this 500-page octavo tome detailed the origins and histories of 2,000 selected words. Marsh considered it "the ablest work that had appeared on . . . the derivation . . . of English words," but felt that Wedgwood depended too much on dictionaries and not enough on literature. Marsh had no faith in the etymologies of scholars "who know languages only by vocabularies and paradigms"; only through the widest reading could word origins be traced accurately. He set to work to correct Wedgwood's errors, and hounded his friends for help. What Turkish words could H. A. Homes provide? What about *bosh* and *derrick?* Would James Russell Lowell please check in the *Laws of Oleron* for the word *buoy?* Harvard professor E. A. Sophocles, whose *Glossary of Later and Byzantine Greek* "hugely delighted" Marsh, certified his derivation of *carboy* from the Turkish and Arabic *qaraba.* H. S. Dana, of Woodstock, helped with *oss, stoupla, dromond, parpine.* By September Wedgwood was in press, and the weary Marsh was finding etymologies "poor intellectual food" and regretting that he had "foolishly spent . . . too much time" over "a sour task." [14]

Marsh's additions consisted "almost wholly of historical illustrations of the etymology of some 200 words," using Old Catalan, Hispano-Latin, Old Dutch, and Old Scandinavian sources "in great part new to English etymology." His contributions were gems of erudition, capsule histories of such words as *average, awning, baggage, ballast, canoe,* and *ceiling.* Marsh's *cheese* is a good specimen of his work. He contradicted Wedgwood's derivation from the Finnish, and cited Grimm to show that Gothic names for *butter* and *cheese* had a Roman origin. Pointing out that real cheese—as opposed to dried curds—apparently appeared only in well-developed civilizations, he went on to derive the word *ost* and related expressions for *cheese* in Scandinavian tongues from the Swedish *ysta,* "coagulate," and discussed methods of coagulation used by various pastoral peoples. Then he dealt with other words for preparing and using soured milk, such as the New England *lobbered* milk, connected with the Persian *labwah,* rennet, and *leben,* to suck, and the Latin *labium,* lip; and finally discussed the relationship of words in various languages for *run* and *coagulate.*[15]

Reviewers acclaimed the beautifully printed volume. "The acute mind of Marsh, the peer of etymologists," had produced "one of the most fascinating books of the time . . . to be read through both for delight and instruction." But Marsh was paid only $400 for his labors, less than the cost of his reference materials. He decided not to carry on with the remaining volumes.[16]

3

English is emphatically the language of commerce, of civilization, of social and religious freedom.

MARSH, *Origin and History of the English Language*

Not all Marsh's labors were linguistic. He wrote essays on Italian independence. He began work on what was to become *Man and Nature.* He furnished the *North American Cyclopaedia* with a biography of James Marsh and a sketch of Norse languages and literature. He agreed to help his friend Markoe publish a "funny book," and consulted with the humorist J. G. Saxe, temporarily editor of the Burlington *Sentinel,* whose "Proud Miss McBride" Marsh considered the funniest poem in English. Marsh himself was addicted to punning, when he was in a good humor: "When I tried in vain to turn a screw with a shilling piece, I said, 'This won't do it. There's no *purchase* in money.' Another time. When my sister-in-law ripped her dress in travelling I said 'Lucy, you rip where you didn't sew!' Pretty good, aren't they?" [17]

But linguistic work dominated his days. Marsh agreed to lecture on the origin and history of English at the Lowell Institute in Boston the winter of 1860-61. By midsummer 1860 he was "cabbaged, cribbed, confined by erysipelas," but he kept on working fourteen hours a day, and opened his lecture series November 14. Cambridge had never seemed more enticing; there were Atlantic Club dinners, evenings with Everett and Ticknor, sessions with Bancroft, Lowell, and such new friends as Charles Eliot Norton and Francis J. Child, the noted compiler of ballads. But Marsh's eyes began to fail again. On December 19 he lectured against his doctor's advice, and inflammation set in that night.[18] He holed up in desolate Burlington for the rest of the winter, grumbling at the world and working through amanuenses to finish Wedgwood and begin preparation of the Lowell Institute lectures for the press.

Published in 1862 as *The Origin and History of the English Language and of the Early Literature It Embodies,* the Lowell Institute series was more learned but less readable than Marsh's previous volume. Tracing English from Anglo-Saxon times through the Elizabethan era, Marsh studied changes in structure and vocabulary by means of detailed analyses of *Piers Ploughman* and the writings of Wycliffe, Chaucer, and Gower. The book embodied the philological theories of Jacob Grimm, Franz Bopp, and Rasmus Rask, together with Marsh's own ideas on such diverse topics as translations, dictionaries, slang, and Ruskin. Though it had many defects, *The Origin and History* was probably the best history of English yet published; Max Müller himself frequently quoted Marsh with approval. But while Marsh's *Lectures* went through four printings in two years, was used as a text by F. J. Child at Harvard, and was pirated in England,[19] the general public found *The Origin and History* forbiddingly technical; only scholars appreciated it.

Marsh gained greatest renown in his own day as a philologist, and even now is listed as such in most biographical dictionaries. More of his published work deals with language than with any other subject. So far as he confessed to being a professional in anything, he felt most at home in this field. Marsh's geographical work is today more significant to the world, yet in linguistics too he was an innovator.

Rarely was Marsh neutral about any topic. The subjective, tangential discursiveness of his philological and other books is at once their

weakness and their special charm. He tells us, for example, that printing has cheapened not only the cost of making books but also the
quality of literature:

None seek the audience "fit though few," that contented the ambition of
Milton. . . . Popular literature is . . . in the ascendant. . . . The dialect of personal vituperation, the rhetoric of malice . . . the art of damn-
ing with faint praise, the sneer of contemptuous irony, the billingsgate of
vulgar hate, all of these have been sedulously cultivated . . . they are
enough to make the fortune of any sharp, shallow, unprincipled journalist,
who is content with the fame and the pelf, which the unscrupulous use
of such accomplishments can hardly fail to secure.

And it is amusing to learn that the slang word *lovely* was "the one
epithet of commendation in young ladies' seminaries and similar
circles, where it . . . is applied indiscriminately to all pleasing material objects, from a piece of plumcake to a Gothic cathedral." [20]

Marsh viewed language as an integral part of culture, affected by
and modifying all other aspects. Consequently, he clothed it with his
prejudices about peoples. English, for example, he described as "the
reflection of the waking life of an earnest, active nation, not, like so
much of the contemporary expression of Continental genius, a magic
mirror showing forth the unsubstantial dreams of an idle, luxurious,
and fantastic people." Grammar and vocabulary, Marsh believed,
bore the marks of national history and character. Thus, in Italy, oppressive tyranny had stamped a base and hypocritical tone on the
language; Italian was by turn abject and pompous, its strength destroyed and its meaning perverted by cloying superlatives and dimin-
utives. After demonstrating the superiority of Gothic to Latin
tongues, Marsh calculated the proportions of Germanic and Romance words used by various writers and rated them accordingly. [21]

Was language static or dynamic? This question engrossed mid-
nineteenth-century philologists. Marsh realized that language, like
all culture, was always in flux; new ideas, processes, and environ-
ments demanded new vocabulary and syntax. But this relativist approach to language by no means submerged his personal preferences.

Just because change was inevitable did not mean, Marsh cautioned, that it was desirable. There was good change and bad; just as races may deteriorate, so do languages become corrupt. Marsh wanted to conserve English more or less as it was. It had improved little in the past two and a half centuries; further progress seemed to him unlikely. And any profound change would make the great English literature of the past unintelligible. Marsh never specified, however, how such changes could be prevented.

His most original observations concerned American speech. Just as the democratic character of American development called for a history of everyday life, so Americans required a more practical knowledge of their own language. "This falls in," Marsh remarked, "with the present tendency of the American mind. We demand, in all things, an appreciable, tangible result." As jacks of all trades, Americans must master all vocabularies. "Every man is a dabbler . . . in every knowledge. Every man is a divine, a statesman, a physician, and a lawyer to himself." Hence we need "an encyclopaedic training, a wide command over the resources of our native tongue, and . . . a knowledge of all its special nomenclatures." [22]

Marsh was one of the first scholars to compare "American" favorably with "pure" English. Most American philologists were, in H. L. Mencken's phrase, "uncompromising advocates of conformity to English precept and example [who] combated every indication of a national independence in speech with the utmost vigilance." A patriotic nonconformist, Marsh decided that "in point of naked syntactical accuracy, the English of America is not at all inferior to that of England," and that many so-called American "vulgarisms" were as correct as the pallid English versions. Marsh also noticed that Americans articulated separate syllables more carefully. This he ascribed to the effect the dry American climate had on vocal membranes and—a novel idea at the time—to the fact that Americans in general read more than the English, and learned to pronounce words as they were spelled. The reading habit and the American tendency to move about accounted, Marsh believed, for the striking uniformity of speech in the United States, in contrast to the diversity of dialect in England.[23] Much of Marsh's analysis is still valid. It anticipates to a remarkable degree the opinions of later professional philologists.

4

I cannot conceive of anything finer than to be sent to wish Italy joy on the fulfillment of her dream of many centuries. Truly, it is like being the first ambassador to the Sleeping Beauty after her awakening!
JAMES RUSSELL LOWELL TO MARSH, MARCH 20, 1861

Never had Marsh known Burlington to be so unpleasant and unhealthy as in the winter of 1860–61; diphtheria was epidemic, and he saw "no house without a very sick patient." His own ill-health kept him from going to Washington in search of a diplomatic post—not that Marsh had done much to merit such a reward. He had rejoiced in Lincoln's nomination as "probably the strongest that could have been made," but had taken little part in the campaign. Nevertheless, as an old standard-bearer of the victorious Republicans, Marsh congratulated Vermont on "the bright prospect of a return" to virtue,[24] and sought service under the new Administration.

"George P. Marsh of Vermont and Jay Morris," commented Carl Schurz, who was himself seeking appointment as Minister to Sardinia, "are pushing for the same position." In love with Italy, Marsh had long thought of Rome as "a very desirable diplomatic residence," and hoped Frémont would appoint a "fit person" in place of "the poor creature [Lewis Cass, Jr.] who now disgraces us there." Tuscany he found still more charming. "I commend Florence to you," he wrote Markoe. "It is . . . the cheapest large town in Europe. . . . As a residence the city is delightful, & all the advantages very great." Above all, Marsh admired the Piedmontese; "no Europeans," he wrote in 1851, "have more sympathies with us, or . . . more truly deserve the respect of Americans." Deeply impressed by Piedmont's rapid progress under the liberal Sardinian government, he now thought Italy "better prepared for free institutions than any other country on the continent." [25]

After Garibaldi's triumphs in 1859 Marsh's Italophilism became still more ardent; he longed to destroy Austria's "hell-born tyrannies." "My red republicanism, which is always hard to keep down," he wrote Lieber, "is at present more rampant than Mrs. Marsh makes my Calvinism. I wish I was 30 years younger, and *kugelfest,* & had a *Heckethaler.* I would do fine things for liberty; but old, poor, & above all not shot-proof, really I can't afford it." [26]

Political sentiment thus reinforced Marsh's preference for the people, climate, and art of Italy. He now tried to secure the mission to the new kingdom of Sardinia, which included Nice, Savoy, and Piedmont, with its capital at Turin. "From much study of the language, history, and especially the present political relations of Italy," Marsh claimed, "I could be more useful there than elsewhere." William Cullen Bryant had been expected to get the post, but withdrew and sent Lincoln a warm note recommending Marsh as "a person of an immense fund of information and . . . of great personal merit." Vermont's Congressmen supported Marsh as "among the first scholars, politicians & statesmen in the nation"; Vincenzo Botta knew no one else "who would be so acceptable to both countries"; [27] Caroline Marsh's nephew Alexander B. Crane (a friend of influential Judge David Davis, of Illinois), Henry J. Raymond, and many others urged a mission for him, preferably in Italy.

Of the other contenders for the Sardinian plum, Carl Schurz, who had fled from Germany after the abortive revolution of 1848, was Marsh's most formidable rival. As February drew to a close, and illness still kept Marsh from Washington, he began to despair of getting "anything but a chance to decline an unwelcome offer." And on March 7 the papers reported that Schurz would be appointed to Sardinia. Marsh had little further hope. "Indeed," he wrote, "I should hesitate about accepting Spain, and I would certainly not go to St. Petersburg, Berlin, Paris, or any part of Spanish America." France was too expensive, Prussia and Russia unendurably cold, and "of course any second class mission would be entirely out of the question with me." Solomon Foot repeated his earlier generous offer: "You shall have the mission to Sardinia or my place in the Senate. The minute Carl Shurtz [*sic*] is nominated I shall resign my seat and telegraph Governor Fairbanks to give it to you." [28]

Marsh's despair was premature. Although Schurz stood high in the President's favor and Lincoln wanted to give him the post, his German birth militated against him. "The *national* feeling of the Germans is so intense," Marsh warned, and his Italian friends agreed, that Schurz "could hardly be acceptable to an Italian government." Other Italians opposed him as a "revolutionary, socialist follower of Mazzini." On March 16 the Italian Minister in Washington wrote Secretary of State Seward that Schurz would be *persona non grata* in Turin. On March 17 Marsh finally arrived in the capital, and the next day Lincoln appointed him Minister of Italy, "because of the intense pressure of [his] State, and [his] fitness also." [29]

"Beate!" exclaimed Lieber, on hearing Marsh had been "excellencified." "To be in the midst of a forming Italia, and a scholar like you! Now then for the collection of memoires, by you and Mrs. Marsh—historical and social, instructive, bright and salient memoires!" Except for Greeley's *Tribune,* which had favored Schurz and denounced Marsh as an aristocrat unsympathetic to Italian republicanism, the press approved Marsh as "exactly the best man for the place . . . one of our few able & experienced diplomatists." [30]

Marsh was surprised by his success and quite unprepared. "Nobody thought Mr. Marsh would get it," wrote Caroline. "Nothing but the feeling that Mr. Marsh was breaking down under his bookmaking induced us to [try] for this appointment," she confessed to her sister, "and even then both he and I felt so drawn in different directions that we scarcely knew what we wished." Marsh had books to finish at home, he was anxious to help his son, he was uneasy about leaving the country when the Union seemed in imminent danger. But the facts "stared us in the face, we were earning the barest living with the hardest work, Mr. Marsh's eyes were failing, and two years had made his shoulders stoop, and changed him almost to an old man." Aside from his small stipends at Columbia and as Lowell Lecturer, Marsh had earned less than $400 for the literary toil of the past three years. Health was an even greater consideration. Marsh knew he was "fast wearing out," but not until the day he was appointed did Caroline discover "how strong the impression was in town" that he "could not long endure his present mode of life." [31]

The decision made, Seward was anxious for Marsh to reach Turin as soon as possible. The days passed in a fever of preparation. There were clothes and books to pack, the house to rent, property to dispose of, publishers to make arrangements with, friends to say good-by to, luggage to send off, passages to book. Neighbors, relatives, and total strangers pressed Marsh for help in getting post-masterships, clerkships, consulships.

He was besieged too by applicants for jobs in his own legation. "I dare say you take your son as Secretary of Legation," inquired Lieber. "If not, take mine." Lowell recommended their mutual friend Charles Eliot Norton, who had spent several years in Italy; Marsh himself wanted Norton, but the appointment was the President's, not his.[32] If Marsh could not pick his assistant, Caroline at least could select hers, and chose the daughter of her brother Thomas, twelve-year-old Carrie Marsh Crane, from Terre Haute, as companion and amanuensis. Carrie was the first of a flock of nieces and nephews the Marshes brought to live with them in Italy.

As Marsh got ready to leave, tension mounted between North and South; all hope of compromise was extinguished at Fort Sumter on April 12. Five days later Marsh delivered a farewell address to a thousand fellow townsmen dazed by the news of civil war. "I shall never forget that eloquent, earnest, patriotic, statesman-like speech," declared one hearer twenty years later. "It had the true ring, nothing could have been more timely." Marsh reminded his audience he had foretold that the Italians would burst their fetters; his prediction was now fulfilled. Never in world history had there been so great a revolution with so little bloodshed. *To* such a people Marsh should delight to go, and *"from* such a people as ours *once was,* he should also delight to go." But now the North must expiate the Southern crime of slavery on the field of war. Amid cheers, Marsh asked Vermonters to pledge half a million dollars and twenty-four regiments to the Union cause.[33]

Half an hour later he was on his way to New York, and on April 27, 1861, he set sail for Europe with his family and with William Dayton, Anson Burlingame, and James S. Pike, Ministers to France, Austria, and the Netherlands. Marsh thus left his homeland for the second and last time, and at the age of sixty began a new life of more than two productive decades in Italy.

☙XI☙

Risorgimento and Civil War

IT WAS SEVEN YEARS since Marsh had left Europe for America to battle his creditors, Congress, and other countrymen who seemed to him determined to defeat his efforts to earn a living. They had been seven lean years, dominated by despair. Now Marsh again sought his fortune abroad. The new Minister to Italy was by upbringing and temperament a New England optimist—a man who is sure that things are better than they are going to be. He was delighted and surprised to find himself happy, if not wealthy. In the Italy to which he came, drought and hail, war and revolution, impoverished the land and the people; but the Old World was generous to Marsh, and he reaped a rich personal harvest. He served America for twenty-one years in Italy—a term unequaled by any other United States chief of mission.[1] With the passage of time, Marsh fulfilled his best destiny.

I

I never felt half the interest in a political question I do in the liberazione dell' Italia dai Goti.

MARSH TO FRANCIS LIEBER, JUNE 3, 1859

Marsh had left a land newly torn by secession and armed strife for a nation recently unified and temporarily at peace. The arms of Garibaldi and the diplomacy of Cavour had overcome Austrian rule; the Two Sicilies, Lombardy, Tuscany, and Emilio threw in their lot with Sardinia, and Victor Emmanuel II of the House of Savoy became first King of Italy. Only Venetia, under Austria, and Rome, under the Pope, still resisted the Risorgimento; but with Cavour's firm and temperate guidance the final unification of Italy seemed assured.

In Paris Marsh learned, however, that Cavour was ill; as he neared Turin the statesman's death was announced. The Piedmontese capital was draped in black; Italian patriots were overcome by the loss of their leader. But Cavour's death was greeted, Marsh reported, with "ill-suppressed exultation among the advocates of temporal and spiritual despotism throughout Europe." No one dared predict what would become of Italy. "You have arrived," Cavour's lieutenants told Marsh, "at a sad moment." [2] The heroic phase of the Risorgimento was over; Italy entered a new era.

The early years had fired liberal imaginations everywhere. Dormant since the time of Dante and Petrarch, Italian national consciousness was reawakened by Napoleon, only to be suppressed by the Holy Alliance, which doomed Italy to remain, in Metternich's contemptuous phrase, "a mere geographical expression." After the abortive uprisings of 1848 only the kingdom of Sardinia was free from Austrian or papal suzerainty. Mazzini fled to England; leadership of the Risorgimento centered thenceforth in Piedmont. The more moderate Cavour, head of Victor Emmanuel's government, invited exiles from other provinces to join him in building a liberal, independent state, and sought an ally to help expel Austria from Italy. An ally of sorts materialized in 1859 in the person of Napoleon III of France. Garibaldi and the French trounced Austria at Magenta and Solferino, and only Napoleon's fear that too strong an Italy might require no French protector prevented unification of the entire peninsula.

Marsh had long been dedicated to the cause of Italian liberty. European travel had reversed his notions about the relative merits of Teutons and Latins. "Stupidity, churlishness, and rudeness," he

MARSH, 1861. PHOTOGRAPH BY BRADY
Courtesy of Frederick H. Meserve

CAROLINE CRANE MARSH, 1866

had found, were "as rare among the Italian peasantry, as they are general among the German." Italians were sympathetic, cosmopolitan, "inherently and collectively a civilized people." [3] Not only was Italy "intellectually and esthetically . . . the most finely endowed nation of Europe," but Italians were "the only race, whose character holds out any encouragement for . . . the political regeneration of the continent." Italy, declared Marsh, required only freedom to assume her place as a first-class power. Let America, Marsh urged, give her "but the tithe of the million of muskets she asks for her unarmed militia." The United States ought in every possible way aid "a noble people who have groaned for a thousand years under the direst of curses—the tyranny of the soldier and the tyranny of the priest." [4]

Marsh managed to squeeze his new opinion of Italy into the collar of environmentalism; he still made a virtue of adversity. He thought Italy's fertile soil, salubrious climate, and beautiful landscapes exposed her people to the seductions of a luxurious and indolent life, but fortunately these natural advantages were compensated by physical difficulties requiring extreme ingenuity to surmount. Few countries, he wrote, "task more highly the thinking and constructive faculties of the people, in order to bring out their utmost productiveness." In engineering, for example—bridging torrents, tunneling the Alps, irrigating the Po plain—the resourceful Italians accomplished "the most stupendous achievement with a very moderate amount of mechanical aid." [5]

Politically, too, Marsh saw Italians in the forefront. In 1859–60 they provided "the sublime spectacle of radical revolutions . . . accompanied not with riotous license and wild disorder, but with an almost absolute cessation of private crime." Marsh contrasted this success with German failures. Italians were *realistic;* German nationalism was "one of those unsubstantial, shadowy phantoms, half metaphysical conception, half poetic figment." He predicted that any German union would endanger European freedom: history had shown the Teutonic race to be "grasping, unjust, aggressive, and disorganizing . . . arbitrary, unassimilative, unprogressive, and anti-democratic." [6] It was fifteen years since Marsh had praised the Goths in New England.

Marsh's political philosophy had not changed fundamentally; inherent national differences still served as his chief props. But new heroes and villains peopled his stage. Nor was he alone in rejecting the earlier stereotype of Italians as shallow, immoral, decadent, irresponsible. Many Americans shared Marsh's new view of Italy. Sympathy for the downtrodden, admiration for Garibaldi, a renascent classicism, commercial self-interest, and anti-Catholicism all contributed to pro-Italian feeling.[7] And Americans were proud that Italians had elected to follow their revolutionary example.

2

I have for many years hoped to live to see James Buchanan and Pius IX hanged. . . . I shall never have full faith in the people of either country until it does justice on its great betrayer.

MARSH TO J. S. PIKE, NOV. 21, 1861

Of all the problems confronting Italy, the Roman question cried out most urgently for solution. How long must Italy remain deprived of her ancient capital? How soon could Napoleon III be persuaded to withdraw his troops from Rome? How could Pope Pius IX be made to yield his temporal power? These queries were uppermost in every mind, Marsh reported.

Other nations and institutions were sometimes rehabilitated in Marsh's eyes, but the Papacy remained a fixture of his demonology. The evils he saw in the Catholic Church were personified by Pope Pius IX. In the first years of his rule, Pio Nono had inaugurated a program of liberal reform, proclaimed a political amnesty, and supported the revolutionary Roman Republic of 1848. Encouraged by these signs, the United States Congress voted to send a chargé to the Papal States. Marsh was one of a small minority who opposed this move. "Do not, for heaven's sake," he wrote, "commit yourself to the belief in a *liberal Pope!* It is a contradiction in terms—an impossibility in the very nature of things. Whatever Pius IX may think now, he will find that he can't be both Pope and patriot." [8]

History, Marsh felt, had justified his warning. Pius IX soon turned reactionary. Having "set the ball of revolution in motion . . . the treacherous and malignant pontiff," as Marsh put it, was "the first to sacrifice those who had been deceived by his professions." He thought no pope "more aggressive in his aspirations . . . or more obstinately wedded to all the traditional abuses of the Vatican" than Pius IX.[9]

Marsh was delighted to find apparent Italian unanimity about the Roman question. "A large majority of the leading minds of Italy," he reported happily, "regard the temporal power of the Pope as a source of enormous and uncompensated political and social evils." Almost everyone the Minister talked with hoped and expected that Italy would soon recover Rome. Indeed, the Pope's conduct, thought Marsh, was undermining the "hereditary veneration" felt for the papacy; and he looked for nothing less than a formal schism. Meanwhile, various seminary scandals, together with tales of clerical intrigue in France, aggravated the public against the priesthood. The warmest adherents of Catholicism, Marsh judged, "join in the contempt"—even "execration—in which the clergy is held by the middle classes." [10]

Marsh's prophecies were mainly wishful thinking. His anti-Catholic bias prevented him from learning what public opinion really was. From his Puritan perspective, holding faith, morals, and reason in a single nexus, Marsh was unable fully to comprehend Catholic, pluralistic, irrational Italy.

The American Minister's high regard for the Italian government had a sounder basis. On June 23 he was presented to King Victor Emmanuel, a rough, ugly man of forty-one, interested in hunting, women, and cigars, loved by his subjects for his simplicity, his vigor, and his passion for black bread and onions. Marsh considered the King a man of courage and common sense who accepted without demur whatever policies Parliament chose.

The Ministry, made up of men of talent and patriotism, pleased Marsh even more. "Few such cabinets," he commented admiringly, "have surrounded an American president." [11] Finest of all was the premier, Baron Bettino Ricasoli, a wealthy Florentine aristocrat who had persuaded Tuscany to cede sovereignty to Victor Emmanuel. A commanding figure with piercing, humorless eyes, a spade beard, and a jutting chin, Ricasoli was legendary for his obstinacy. Calm, able, self-reliant, he was adamant both against the plots of extremists and the carpings of reactionaries. He and Marsh soon became very close, sharing not only political sympathies—Ricasoli was the firmest Unionist in Italy—but also interests in agriculture and forestry.

Though nominally a Catholic, Ricasoli advocated separation of Church and State and determined to make Rome part of the Italian kingdom. His confidence in an early settlement was strong at first; meeting Marsh at the Foreign Office in September, 1861, Ricasoli said, "I invite you, Mr. Minister, to Rome. I invite you there *this year, this very year.*" The most serious obstacle was France, whose troops protected the Papal States. Rumors circulated that Napoleon wanted to replace Ricasoli with an Italian premier less anxious to "settle" the Roman question. In August, 1861, a new French ambassador arrived in Turin, Corsica-born Vincente Benedetti, intimate of Napoleon; as Marsh suspected, his appointment portended heavy French pressure.[12] Pleasing neither the pro-French party nor the Garibaldians who wished to march directly on Rome, Ricasoli's position soon became untenable; he resigned in March, 1862.

The new prime minister, Urbano Rattazzi, a cautious Piedmontese lawyer, impressed Marsh as a man of "pleasing address" but little more. If the uncompromising Ricasoli could not break the Roman impasse, timid, hesitant Rattazzi, who tried to please everyone, had no more success. Demonstrations broke out all over Italy for a march on Rome. When Rattazzi suspended the liberal journal

L'Opinione, Marsh wrote in disgust that the government was "far behind the people." [13]

Risorgimento united again behind Garibaldi, who left his island retreat at Caprera to organize riflemen in Piedmont and Lombardy. His popularity and influence, reported Marsh, were "greater than ever, and no man doubts that he could overthrow the government, and make himself dictator, in an hour, if he chose to give the signal." After several hours' talk with the general, Marsh came away feeling that Garibaldi, "in spite of his apparently uncontrollable impetuosity, is a man of consummate prudence." Garibaldi's courage, dignity, and singleness of purpose impressed him. "Even at this giddy height of popular exaltation," he noted, "Garibaldi retains his simplicity of manner and habits." [14] Marsh's usual suspicion of popular heroes seems to have deserted him in this instance.

Put off time and again by the government, in August, 1862, Garibaldi marched on the papal capital with the cry *"Roma o morte!"* But he suffered a shameful defeat at Aspromonte, and was himself wounded and imprisoned by the government. Fearful that the "feeble and slippery" Rattazzi would execute Garibaldi or allow him to die of his wound, Marsh offered the general a haven in the United States. The King grudgingly offered Garibaldi amnesty, the general threatened to emigrate, the Ministry backed and filled; at last Garibaldi was released and allowed to return to Caprera.[15]

Confidence in the King and Ministry had fallen far. Many expected Victor Emmanuel to abdicate, and Rattazzi resigned at the end of 1862. His eventual successor, the conservative General Luigi Menabrea, was no more to Marsh's taste. Intrigue was rife; there was talk of war with Austria, of a treaty with Austria against France, of many fantastic designs. Marsh gradually came to believe that, however talented in debate, Italians were unable to commit themselves to determined action. His view of Italian politics grew more objective and critical.

Henceforth Marsh dwelt increasingly upon general European affairs in his dispatches. As an Italophile and a linguist, he was well placed to gather confidential information about trends and events throughout the Continent. Transmitted privately to Seward, Marsh's lengthy comments were regarded with special interest by the Secretary of State. His thousand-odd dispatches—detailed, pithy, colorful —comprise an analysis of contemporary Continental affairs of remarkable scope, continuity, and insight. Marsh's nephew did not exaggerate when he told him that "you can in half a page compress more real matter and give a better statement of . . . affairs than others could do in ten pages." [16]

3

Marsh found his fellow diplomats an agreeable, distinguished lot. Most were friends of the new Italy; most were also pro-Northern in American matters. Fully half of them had served in Turkey; "we are a very heathen Oriental set," Marsh commented.[17] The turnover through death and dismissal was rapid, however; in 1863, when Sir James Hudson returned to England, Marsh became dean of the diplomatic corps.

The Marshes liked the frank and cheerful Hudson better than any of his successors. Long devoted to Italy, Sir James introduced Marsh to many Italian scientists and scholars. The Marshes were shocked when Hudson was replaced by Henry George Elliott, brother-in-law of Earl John Russell; the reason was not nepotism, as they first thought, but "the grossly immoral life led by Sir James and his suite." "Alas, alas, alas, for appearances," lamented Caroline Marsh, "and whom can one believe and trust in this so-called high life!" Elliott, an early supporter of Garibaldi in Sicily, was agreeable enough, though limited intellectually. But the Marshes found most British diplomats cold, reserved, arrogant, supercilious, and condescending. "If you want an Englishman to be civil," Caroline concluded after an encounter in which young Herries, the British Secretary of Legation, came off second best, "treat him haughtily."

Marsh got along well with Benedetti, of France, an old colleague from Constantinople. But Italians resented French interference; the overbearing, choleric French Minister was not popular in Turin. Benedetti's successor, Sartiges, soon gave way as French Minister to Baron Joseph Malaret, who helped the Italian government put down Garibaldi at Aspromonte and for six years wielded great influence over Victor Emmanuel. The Prussian Minister, Count Brassier de St. Simon, was a liberal lover of Italy and of women; he gave bachelor dinners at Turin, maintained a wife at Nice, kept a mistress at Piobesi castle, where the Marshes later lived, and intrigued with Ricasoli to ally Italy and Prussia against Austria. Marsh was more intimate with the scholarly Swiss Minister, Tourte; and with the Turkish Minister, Rustum Bey, accomplished linguist and gourmet. Baron Rosenkranz, the Danish Chargé, was Rustum's linguistic antithesis. When he came to Turin, he announced that he would learn Italian at once, as "he did not wish to be as ignorant as an American Minister of every language but his own." [18] After a talk with Marsh—in Danish—Rosencranz had to retract his remark.

4

The character of the United States Foreign Service has been declining ever since the days of John Quincy Adams.
MARSH TO CHARLES ELIOT NORTON, JUNE 12, 1862

Marsh was outstanding in this diplomatic circle. Like most American Ministers, however, he bore a "legacy of disgrace" bequeathed by predecessors who drank to excess, failed to pay their bills, engaged in street brawls, or lived in attics and did their own cooking.

Turin had fared better than many capitals in its American diplomats. The first was Vermonter Nathaniel Niles, a Harvard-educated physician, who had written Secretary of State Forsyth in 1838 that Sardinia had "by far the most enlightened, active and wealthy population" in Italy; Niles was forthwith sent to sign a treaty of commerce, and later leased the port of Spezia as a United States naval depot. His successor, New Jersey editor William B. Kinney, was a liberal humanitarian often consulted by Cavour. But he was followed as Chargé in 1853 by John Moncure Daniel, editor of the Richmond *Examiner*. The biting tongue and highhanded insolence of this Southern aristocrat, his wild parties, and his homosexual amours offended Turin society; his open hostility to the Risorgimento made him most unpopular with the government. Reviling the Piedmontese as *"lazzaroni"* who "stank of garlic and onions," [19] Daniel hurried home at the outbreak of the Civil War.

Lewis Cass, Jr., at Rome, and Joseph Chandler at Naples had been little better than Daniel at Turin, and Marsh felt he had to "make amends for the discredit thrown on both countries by their last representative[s]." Thanks to his knowledge of Italian and his diplomatic experience, this was not hard. Reports against him, to be sure, were spread by Catholics and Greeleyites. The American sculptor W. W. Story heard in Rome that Marsh was pro-Austrian and unsympathetic to Italy; on the basis of other tales "showing Mr. Marsh's want of tact," Story decided that "as a minister he is null." [20] These rumors, as Story later discovered, were baseless. Marsh was successful from the start in winning Italian confidence and friendship.

Marsh's labors were multiplied and often seriously embarrassed by the absence of a good secretary—or rather, the presence of a very bad one. Daniel had left behind young Romaine Dillon, who stayed on as Marsh's Secretary of Legation until the new Secretary, William Fry, should arrive. Where was Fry? This question haunted Marsh's dispatches; and Seward replied vaguely: Fry will soon sail; Fry is ill in Paris; Fry has been granted a leave of absence; Fry is missing; Fry has returned to America. Meanwhile Dillon remained in Turin.

The opinions expressed by Dillon, a keen-witted, brash young man, put him outside the pale. One evening he told Caroline Marsh that " 'no . . . statesman can suppose that Christianity would exist a single century if the *Papacy* were broken down.' Some difference of opinion certainly," she commented, "between him and his *chef!"*

Dillon was both a Southerner and a Catholic. As Marsh asked, "how could I—an American-Puritan-Liberal-Union-Republican—be expected to go on with an Irish-Papist-Bourbon-Secession-Democrat?" But his apprehensions of Catholic conspiracy were so strong that he felt powerless to take action. Marsh suspected that Dillon was "kept here by Archbishop Hughes in order to counter-act any mischief I might do by my anti-Popish sentiments. . . . I dare not ask to have him recalled, because I have already suffered too much from Catholic malice at Washington [e.g., in connection with Dainese and his claims] to venture to provoke the hostility of Chandler and Hughes and the rest of that gang, by new offenses." [21]

Meanwhile, Dillon publicly and repeatedly criticized Northern conduct of the Civil War. Marsh finally warned him that Italians were astounded that "a person so habitually unreserved in his condemnation of the course of his government . . . should be retained in its service." [22] Vexed at this rebuke, Dillon accused Marsh of hastening his recall; apparently Seward had written to Horace Greeley about the situation.

Marsh was furious with Seward for this heedless disclosure; for no secret was safe with Greeley. The Minister had submitted to many indignities to avoid open conflict, only to have the Secretary of State "prejudice the usefulness of this legation, by still further embittering Mr. Dillon." This "well-merited" complaint, together with criticism by the New York *Times* Italian correspondent, at last brought Dillon's recall. Fry resigned the post he had never filled, and in 1862 Green Clay, of Kentucky, went out as Marsh's new Secretary of Legation—a boy of twenty-one, complained the Minister, with "no taste, and not a single qualification, for the duties of his position." [23] Marsh came to like Clay, however, and was sorry when he resigned six years later.

Marsh had had no official secretarial help for the first year, because he would not entrust Dillon even with copying dispatches. Instead, he hired Joseph Artoni, an exile who returned to Italy in 1861 after twenty years in Philadelphia. A neat, trim, serious little man, "a dear good soul, as sincere as the light," Caroline described him; [24] Artoni served faithfully for two decades as Marsh's private secretary.

The consular situation seemed to Marsh as bad as the secretarial. He urged that all Democratic incumbents be replaced at once by loyal Republicans. "I do not believe," he wrote Seward a month after reaching Turin, "there is an American consular agent in Europe, appointed by Presidents Pierce and Buchanan, against whom there is not grave cause of suspicion." At the strategic Leghorn consulate, for example, Southerner Robert M. Walsh was "clamorously hostile to the policy of the Italian Government and a partisan of . . . papal misrule." Over Marsh's protest Seward gave the consulship to a personal friend, Andrew J. Stevens, an insubordinate schoolmaster who proved hard to get along with. At Genoa, Marsh had Southerner W. L. Patterson replaced by the Rev. David Hilton Wheeler, "a plain, sensible, thoughtful and scholarly man." Later editor of the New York *Methodist* and president of Allegheny College, Wheeler wrote a book, *Brigandage in Northern Italy,* for which Marsh did much of the research, editing, and proofreading. At Palermo, former Harvard professor Luigi Monti was so helpful to American travelers in Sicily that Marsh had to explain to him that "it is not the business of Consuls to suggest to American citizens methods of evading" customs duties.[25] At Florence, the Consul-General, Col. T. Bigelow Lawrence, son of the textile manufacturer Abbott Lawrence, was more interested in Italian society than in Italo-American commerce.

Marsh preferred William James Stillman, the artist-journalist who was Consul at Rome. "We have never had a better agent, diplomatic or consular," he wrote Seward, urging Stillman's promotion, "who was more acceptable to the Americans who visit that city, or more creditable to the government." But the anti-Catholic Stillman was in continual conflict with American Ministers to the Papal Court. As a result, he was demoted to Crete in 1865. At various times Marsh lent Stillman money, and in his newspaper and periodical articles Stillman praised Marsh extravagantly. Stillman stood out in contrast to other American diplomats in Rome, for most of them were (owing to the efforts of Archbishop Hughes, Marsh believed) "ultramontanists in politics and obscurantists in religion." Marsh warned Seward that to send another Minister to the Papal Court would be "almost an act of discourtesy to the Italian government." [26]

There were few occasions, however, when the State Department took Marsh's advice on personnel in or affecting his mission. During most of his diplomatic career, legation and consular assistants proved more of a hindrance than a help. Marsh himself was partly to blame. He inspired devotion and loyalty in many individuals, but he was unable to conceal his dislike of, or contempt for, second-rate subordinates. Only when he picked his own staff was he able to achieve smooth, efficient administration.

5

Secretary of State Seward had a villainous scheme, charged an anonymous critic, to spread antislavery propaganda through his envoys in Europe. If Dayton in France failed to follow instructions, "the Secretary had instruments elsewhere, suited to his purpose. They were Mr. Cassius Clay in Russia, Mr. Fogg and Mr. Fay in Switzerland, Mr. Pike at the Hague, and, we regret to say, Mr. Marsh at Turin." [27]

Marsh certainly considered molding European opinion in support of the Northern cause his most important task. For a time it seemed that European intervention might be a decisive factor. The success of the American Revolution had depended, in the last analysis, upon the force of European arms; Union victory in the Civil War might depend upon keeping Europe out of it. Marsh and his fellow envoys had no easy task. Europeans disliked slavery, but had no other reason to favor the North; and to many the slavery question seemed utterly submerged. Indeed, Marsh was convinced that without assurances of British and French sympathy and aid, the South would have succumbed at once.

To counteract pro-Southern sentiment, Marsh arranged, with Seward's approval, "to furnish facts and arguments to be employed in disabusing the English people on the legal and moral aspects of the question of the right of the Southern States to secede from the Union." His writings were widely circulated, but he was too biased against Britain to pen anything persuasive for the English press. In his private correspondence Marsh labeled the British government "that most wicked and malignant of modern political societies," and in an official dispatch wrote that "England . . . is generally regarded . . . as the most selfish, unprincipled and perfidious Power of modern Christendom." He had long suspected just how perfidious Albion was. The success of the Puseyite and High Church movements twenty years before "revealed to me . . . such a degree of intellectual decrepitude and of moral degradation [in Church and State] that no iniquity or folly on their part has since seemed incredible to me." He only regretted that his official position kept him from writing "freely" about the "decay" of England.[28]

In Italy Marsh did not have to cope with such problems. "Our Italian friends are unanimous in favor of the North," he wrote Edmunds in the discouraging days of 1863; no country in Europe backed the Union cause more warmly. Repugnance to slavery, the articles of Vincenzo Botta and other Italo-Americans, and Marsh's own prodigious influence kept Italy stanchly on the Union side throughout the war. This stand, as Marsh pointed out in his dispatches, involved material sacrifices; stoppage of the Southern cotton supply forced several large Genoese factories to close and entailed severe hardship. Nevertheless, only the Papacy and Bourbonites gave comfort to the South. "All tyrannies sympathize," Marsh concluded; "the slave-driver and the priest are twin-brothers." [29]

Italian friendship enabled the Minister to deal promptly with Confederate privateers in the Mediterranean. When Marsh heard rumors that Southern ships were loading supplies and arms at Genoa, in June, 1861, Ricasoli alerted police to the danger. Late in October, Consul F. W. Behn wired that a three-masted schooner, which he mistook for the Confederate privateer *Sumter,* had been sighted off Messina. Marsh at once asked that all harbors be closed to rebel ships, and Italy agreed to forbid them entry except in stress of weather. In fact, the *Sumter* did not reach Gibraltar until January, 1862, and, completely disabled, never ventured out of harbor. This was not known, however, and her presumed presence in the Mediterranean excited a "tremendous panic" among United States merchantmen. No one would ship goods in the face of such a danger. Marsh repeatedly urged Seward to send out a ship and "clear the situation up," but months passed before he dispatched a frigate, which was considered impotent against the heavy fire of the *Sumter.* Not until June, 1862—two months after the *Sumter* had been abandoned—did the arrival of the U.S. *Constellation* restore Northern confidence.[30] Other Confederate vessels appeared occasionally, but from then on the Mediterranean was safe for Union shipping.

Union sympathizers in Europe waxed increasingly critical, however, over the prosecution of the war. Marsh feared that the defeat at Bull Run "stamped us as cowards," the battle of Manassas destroyed confidence in early Northern victory, and the government's failure to free the slaves "forfeited the confidence of European philanthropists, who had hoped we would show some signs of a national conscience." Southern claims that the contest was simply one between free trade and protection carried more conviction. As long as men believed the war was about freedom "we had the world with us, but at present," Marsh lamented, "the current seems to be setting in favor of the South." Italians already knew the Confederacy was evil; it was "only necessary to demonstrate to them" that Lincoln and Seward were "honestly against slavery." [31]

How sincere *was* the North? Torn with doubt himself, Marsh found it the more difficult to convince others. Initially sanguine, he grew impatient, discouraged, and despairing. At the start Marsh had seen "men and money . . . offered without stint, millionaires . . . serving in the ranks as privates"; Yankee enthusiasm was unanimous. Within a few months idealism had evaporated. Congress

failed to vote "the infamous Dred Scott supreme court" out of existence, it passed Crittenden's "vile resolution" asking for a "shameful" peace, it neglected to punish Pierce and Buchanan. The North
had "abandoned every principle" for which the Republicans had
fought. Grieved, Marsh wrote Republican leaders "to ask what all
this backing and filling of the party means," but he got no answer. "I
know the Northern *people* are right enough," he fretted, "but why
are those who should lead them lagging in the rear?" [32]

As the months passed and McClellan's errors multiplied, Marsh's
jeremiads grew more violent. He called the general a "pro-slavery
politician and imbecile nincompoop," and gloomily predicted a final
Southern triumph "unless we are rescued by the strong arm of a
military dictator." "Nothing but a reign of terror will serve us." [33]

The long-delayed Emancipation Proclamation hardly raised the
President in Marsh's estimation. The Minister considered it "foolish
in form" and "technically speaking, unconstitutional." He grudgingly conceded that Lincoln was honest and good-natured, but
thought him feeble when right, obstinate when wrong, and utterly
unfit to be President. He agreed that Lincoln's renomination was
"expedient," but condemned the President's leniency to Southern
traitors.[34] To Marsh, remote from American realities, the dilemmas
of the Administration appeared inexplicable, the proper path clearly
marked, the errors unforgivable.

6

While frustrating Confederate forays for Italian arms, Marsh
sought to purchase matériel for the North. Through his efforts,
tens of thousands of muskets, pistols, and swords found their way
from Genoa and other Italian cities to the Union armies—though
the Southern competition doubled the prewar prices.

Men were to be had more easily than muskets. Marsh received
thousands of applications for army service from "men who have
tried in vain to get knocked on the head in Italy, and now want a

chance in America." All wanted to be officers, however, and most were penniless; one layman offered to serve as a hospital surgeon on condition that his whole family receive passage to America and a life income. Since the least ray of encouragement would have multiplied the number of applicants tenfold, Marsh was careful to offer no inducements. But the Italians refused to believe that Uncle Sam could be "stingy," and they continued to throng the legation. "They threaten to worry us out of our lives," Marsh complained. Finally he had to publish announcements that the United States would not pay anyone's way to America. Ordinary immigrants, on the other hand, were welcomed; personally, Marsh was always pleased at the prospect of an infusion of Latin blood into the melting pot, as an "antidote against the Celtic." [35]

One Italian soldier whose way the North would gladly have paid was the great Garibaldi himself. The notion of enlisting the general in the Union forces was no mere pipe dream, but a serious proposal which came close to succeeding. Told that Garibaldi "might be induced to take part in the contest for preserving the Unity and Liberty of the American people, and the institution of Freedom and Self-Government," in July, 1861, Seward instructed Henry S. Sanford, American Minister to Belgium, to go to Italy and, with Marsh, offer Garibaldi a major-generalship in the United States Army.[36]

Marsh was deeply disturbed by "this worse than *old-woman* scheme, calculated to prove our weakness and the imbecility of our leaders . . . and at the same time to excite against us the hostility of every power in Europe which does not sympathize with the Italian hero." But Marsh's opinion had not been asked. Late in August he and Sanford secretly sent Artoni to Garibaldi's retreat on the island of Caprera to find out if he was "at liberty to entertain propositions on the subject." In Garibaldi's presence, the flustered Artoni threw caution and instructions to the winds, and told him that Lincoln intended to make him commander-in-chief of the Union forces! When they learned what had happened, Marsh and Sanford were staggered; the news of "this *undreamed*-of offer" might have dire effects. And Garibaldi replied that he was "immediately at your disposal, provided that the conditions . . . are those which your messenger has verbally indicated to me." [37]

The American proposition also enabled Garibaldi to exert pressure on Italian policy. He now wrote Victor Emmanuel that unless His Majesty allowed him to march on Rome or Venice, he would go to the United States. He put the King in a difficult situation: to attack Rome or Venice would bring all Europe down upon him; to allow Garibaldi to leave the country would be unpopular, perhaps disastrous, at home. Finally, he told the general to follow the dictates of his conscience. This was tantamount to rejection; Garibaldi now seemed certain to accept the American offer.

It was vital to correct immediately Garibaldi's misapprehension about his promised rank, and Marsh chartered a small steamer to take Sanford to Caprera on September 8. But Garibaldi's expectations were so high that no compromise was possible. He felt he could be serviceable only as commander-in-chief, with power to declare the abolition of slavery. This, of course, was out of the question. Marsh assured the Secretary of State it was all for the best; Garibaldi's "constitutional independence of character and action, his long habit of exercising uncontrolled and irresponsible authority," and his natural pride all made it impossible for him to accept any rank the President could constitutionally offer him.[38] Unfortunately, word of the affair leaked out; for months, Southern agents made the most of this evidence of Northern military weakness.

A year later, after Garibaldi's defeat at Aspromonte, in 1862, he asked and Marsh confidentially offered him asylum in the United States. The need for a competent Union general appeared as urgent as ever, and Garibaldi, imprisoned and in trouble, was less demanding than before. "It might possibly relieve the government of Italy . . . from embarrassment," Marsh wrote Italian leaders, and "offer the prisoners an opportunity of usefulness to us without prejudice to the interests of Italy." While dickering with the Italian government, Garibaldi agreed to go to America and "appeal to all the democrats of Europe to join us in fighting this holy battle." [39] But first the North would have to proclaim the enfranchisement of the slaves.

A few days later Marsh sent Garibaldi a copy of Lincoln's Emancipation Proclamation with the confident hope that "we shall soon have the aid both of your strong arm and of your immense moral power in the maintenance of our most righteous cause." Seward confirmed this offer; Marsh should "inform the General that he and his friends will be welcomed with enthusiasm . . . and that a proper command will be assigned him." Garibaldi sent an aide to Marsh to discuss raising and arming 2,000 men. [40] Before negotiations started, however, Garibaldi made his peace with the King and Ministry, and declined the American offer once and for all.

❧XII❧

Turin

THE PIEDMONTESE were proud of Turin as a diplomatic center. For eight centuries the seat of the House of Savoy, this Alpencircled city of 100,000 came into its own with the Risorgimento. The ducal court was now imperial, the consuls-general and chargés-d'affaires of foreign states were now accredited as ministers and ambassadors. But Turin itself remained matter-of-fact. A town of gray buildings arranged in monotonous rectangles, it was remarkable among the cities of Italy for its lack of the medieval and picturesque. From the balcony of the Hotel de l'Europe the Marshes looked across the Piazza Castello to the massive Palazzo Madamma, the residence of the royal family. Evenings they drove along the broad Corso Massimo d'Azeglio, a miniature Bois de Boulogne, Turin's social rendezvous; "but oh the caprices of the monde!" exclaimed Caroline:

It does not do to drive beyond the limits of the Corso, unless one would at the same time put himself out of the pale of the *best society*. At the end of a short half mile everybody turns round and goes back again and so to and fro till twilight . . . it must soon become the greatest of bores. After a few turns you recognize every carriage, every toilette, and every face.[1]

I

Comfortable, conservative, clannish, Turinese society centered about the court. Victor Emmanuel's German-born sister-in-law, the

Duchess of Genoa, prescribed strict etiquette for the widower king and strict education for his children, Amadeo, Umberto, Maria Pia, and her own daughter, Margherita. In addition to the royal family, society comprised the Turinese *codini*—Carignanos, Cisternas, Alfieris, Dorias, and other ancient families, with palazzi in town and villas in the Piedmontese hills; foreign diplomats; and Italian statesmen from the aristocracy of other provinces.

To name the statesmen and scholars Marsh came to know would be to sound a roll call of the Risorgimento. Among them were the noted Lombard economist Conte Giovanni Arrivabene, the venerable Conte Gaetano de Castillia of Milan, Garibaldi's supporter Marchese Giorgio Pallavicino-Trivulzio, and Giuseppe Arconati-Visconti of Milan. All four had been young revolutionaries, sentenced to death and then exiled; all were now senators. Other frequent visitors at the Marshes' were quiet, white-haired Baron Carlo Poerio of Naples; ninety-year-old Prince Cisterna, father-in-law of the future King of Spain; Piedmontese patriot and artist Marchese Massimo d'Azeglio, Cavour's predecessor; and the folklorist Conte Constantino Nigra, whose influence with the Empress Eugénie served him well when he became Italian Ambassador to France. Aristocratic, brilliant, idealistic, yet sophisticated, these men contrasted sharply with Washington officials; democrat though he was, Marsh was in many ways more at home in the Italian capital.

Marsh enjoyed superb relations with all the ministers of foreign affairs. With Ricasoli (Foreign Minister in his own cabinet) Marsh was on terms of frank intimacy. Rattazzi's Foreign Minister, Giacomo Durando, founder of the influential liberal journal *L'Opinione,* was likewise eager to please Marsh. His successor, the gentle but effective Conte Giuseppe Pasolini, became one of Marsh's closest Italian associates, although he was also an old friend of Pius IX. The short, smiling, dignified Pasolini had gained universal popularity as Prefect of Turin, and kept it as Foreign Minister despite his conservative, clerical bias. With Pasolini, Marsh discussed agricultural and engineering schemes which were to transform the

Italian landscape. Pasolini's secretary, young Chevalier Emilio Visconti-Venosta, succeeded him in 1864. In charge of the Foreign Office for most of Marsh's term as American Minister, Visconti-Venosta was prudent and helpful.

Other important officials Marsh admired were Senate President Conte Federigo Sclopis, Italy's premier jurist and a renowned *littérateur;* Marco Minghetti, a Bolognese mathematician and economist who became premier in 1863; and—especially congenial to Marsh—solemn, sagacious Quintino Sella, mineralogist, Alpinist, and indispensable Finance Minister in a long series of conservative cabinets. Radicals also regularly visited Marsh, notably the eloquent Angelo Brofferio, a popular romantic dramatist and editor of the republican *Voce della Libertà,* whom Marsh thought the best speaker in Parliament.

Once a land her own patriots had fled, Italy was now a refuge for exiles from other countries, and Turin the residence of many disappointed revolutionaries. Most famous was Kossuth, grown worn and sad in the decade since Marsh had seen him. Ferenc Pulszky, who had directed foreign affairs in the short-lived Hungarian Republic, was a cheerful, many-sided man, who made Marsh his confidant. In 1862 Pulszky was arrested with Garibaldi at Aspromonte, but Marsh promptly got him released. Traditional American sympathy for suppressed minorities and Marsh's personal friendship for many of the exiles made him a natural recipient of their hopes, plans, and fears. Desirous of European emancipation, Marsh was, however, a political realist; he often dissuaded his hot-headed friends from desperate steps.

Kossuth was not the only old acquaintance rediscovered. Old Baron Tecco, former Minister to Constantinople, and the poet and historian Regaldi, a traveling companion on the Nile, also welcomed Marsh to Turin. The bellelettrist Abbé Giuseppe Filippo Baruffi, friend of their New York well-wisher Vincenzo Botta, superintended the Marshes' introduction to Turin society. No week passed without several visits from Baruffi, raconteur and gossip *par excellence.* An opponent of papal temporal power, he was, decided the careful Caroline Marsh, "a priest that even a Protestant can respect." [2]

Through Baruffi the Marshes met the astronomer Giovanni Plana, famous for his study of the moon. Though aged and half deaf, Plana was an iconoclastic liberal, full of fire and humor. A nominal Catholic, Plana enjoyed ridiculing papal pretensions, but no religion escaped his barbs. "I came to see you a few days ago," he once told the Marshes, "but I forgot you were superstitious Protestants and came on Sunday—I did not see you of course." [3]

Another well-known scholar Baruffi brought to Marsh was poet Cesare Cantù, author of the immense *Storia Universale.* A striking, sardonic figure, with hawklike nose jutting out over great walrus mustache, Cantù had recanted his youthful radicalism and become official Vatican historian. But Marsh found it impossible not to like him, though he later stigmatized Cantù as "bigoted, sectarian, obscurantist in religion and retrograde in politics." [4]

Marsh also knew the physicist Carlo Matteucci, the Genoese economist Girolamo Boccardo, the Orientalist Michele Amari, the Bolognese geologist Giovanni Capellini, the Sanskrit scholar Gaspare Gorresio, director of the Biblioteca Nazionale in Turin, the well-known Italo-Swiss sculptor Vicenzo Vela, and the landscape painter Angelo Beccaria.

2

Marsh regretted that he could not see more than he did of such artists and scientists. It was not time but social opportunity that was lacking; untitled literary men were not admitted to aristocratic and diplomatic circles, and the *codino* code made class lines difficult to cross. Turin society was, to be sure, superior to any Marsh had ever seen "in culture, refinement, and manner"; he was "constantly surrounded by very agreeable people." [5] But the gentility was excessive, conversation stilted, formal, empty.

Women set the social atmosphere. "I don't know how it is," sighed
Caroline after a stream of crinolined callers had departed, "all these
Piedmontese ladies bewitch me with their indescribable grace and
delicacy." There were brilliant women who kept famous salons: the
dark-haired Marchesa Arconati-Visconti and Emilia Toscanelli
Peruzzi, friend of Napoleon III and patroness of art; heroines of
the Risorgimento, among them the Contessas Balbo, Confalonieri,
Margherita Provana di Collegno, and Marchesa Pallavicino-Trivulzio, the Florence Nightingale of Garibaldi's campaigns; the stun-
ning young Contessa di Castiglione and the energetic, determined
Marchesa Doria, rival leaders of Turin society; and the benevolent
Baroness Spinola of Genoa, who demanded of Marsh when they
first met, "Did you bring any parrots from America?" [6]

One of the Marshes' intimates was young Rosa Arbesser, Princess
Margherita's governess, who at once made Caroline Marsh her con-
fidante. Rosa chattered for hours on end—tales about court personalities, gossip about the King, tirades against the Duchess. Caroline hardly knew "at which most to wonder—at the things related,
or at the imprudence of the narrator." But Marsh could not abide
"our talkative German friend." He preferred hearty Contessa Clara
Gigliucci, renowned as the soprano Clara Novello. Clearheaded,
witty, frank to the point of bluntness, Clara Gigliucci was "a real
live woman," Marsh declared,[7] a welcome contrast to the ladies of
Piedmont, who with all their sweet charm were mostly inconsequential, empty-headed creatures.

Gossip, slander, and struggles for power were as fierce in the social as in the political arena. There were many tales of flagrant moral
misconduct. Caroline could hardly believe "that the persons I meet
here in society are guilty of the sins laid to their charge. But . . .
if there are no evildoers, there is a prodigious number of liars."
Stories of illicit liaisons, adultery, poisoning, crimes of passion, even
incest, came readily to the lips of well-bred Piedmontese ladies. After
hearing of one lovely marchesa's lurid misdeeds, Marsh exclaimed
to Caroline, "Well! well! I thank God we are not like these publi-

cans!" Caroline was more broad-minded. Under Mediterranean skies "the soft twilight of my charity" had deepened. Contrasting New England and Italian education and matrimony—"the teachings of a Puritan preacher and a popish priest, the marriage of choice and the marriage of *convenance"*—she had to conclude that *"these publicans* were not worse than *we Pharisees* might have been under the same circumstances." [8]

Caroline herself throve in Turin. Thanks to the mild climate she felt stronger than for fifteen years past. She gave receptions and formal dinners three times a week, received callers continually, and even went occasionally to the theater (mostly French and "highly immoral"). Her unfailing cheerfulness, her willingness to listen to people and sympathize with their troubles, endeared her to Italians.

But the endless round of empty conversation, the pointless rituals of cards and calls, the other frivolities of court life, were more than the Marshes could bear. "I grow very tired, sometimes," Caroline wrote after a year in Turin, "of the everlasting sameness of this *high* society." Note-writing took half her time, "and all this work leaves nothing to show for it." [9] Marsh himself was by no means exempt from these vexing duties. He had to return calls; there were ministerial dinners and court balls almost every night; and at home incessant interruptions made both work and relaxation impossible.

3

Turin social life occupied Sundays as well as weekdays. "How rational people live without one day in the week wherein to feed their own interior life," Caroline could not understand. Occasionally, Marsh managed to preserve a quiet New England Sunday for rest, reflection, and reading aloud—Robertson's sermons, Monod's *Les Adieux à ses amis et à l'église,* Wycliffe, Stanley's *History of the Jewish Church,* Franchi's *Religion of the Nineteenth Century,* Samuel Vincent's *Méditations religieuses.* He also went—reluctantly —to church, because he thought it good policy for a Protestant diplomat in Italy; too many Catholics equated Protestantism with atheism.[10]

Pleasanter diversions were the royal hunts, to which the King invited the diplomatic corps. On the first outing, at Stupinigi Forest, Marsh found himself with half a dozen chiefs of legation, "all professed sportsmen . . . with their own guns." Weaponless for twenty-five years, Marsh "did not think of shooting . . . but they put a double-barrelled gun into my hands . . . & I marched forth with the rest." Peasants drove the game toward the Ministers, who fired, and "nine times out of ten at the very least—missed." Not so Marsh. "When my attendant shouted, *la lepre,* a hare! and pointed out the animal, I 'winked and held out my cold iron,' not really meaning the poor beast any harm, but, to my astonishment and that of my man, he fell dead. . . . Notwithstanding the practice & self-complaisance of my fellow diplomates, I did as well as the average of them, but . . . any other Vermont boy . . . would have killed more than the whole nine of us." Marsh's proficiency with firearms made him *persona grata* with Victor Emmanuel, who longed to hunt buffalo in the Wild West.[11] The American Minister regaled the King with descriptions of Western roundups.

American and English visitors brought occasional respite from the inanities of Turin society. Hiram Powers came often from Florence; in the spring of 1862 he did a bust of Caroline, grave and classical. Lady Estcourt came twice to Turin; so did Dr. Humphrey Sandwith, blithe and humorous as ever, returning with his bride from a Mediterranean honeymoon. Marsh's younger brother, Charles, a kindly, shy man of forty-four, broken in health by years of toil on the Woodstock farm, visited for several months in 1864.

Many American envoys to other European countries called on Marsh for business or pleasure. Marsh considered Sanford at Brussels able but overzealous and vain. The Minister to Switzerland was the knowledgeable New Hampshire editor George G. Fogg, whom Marsh liked. Bradford R. Wood at Copenhagen was an old Congressional crony; Marsh renewed his enjoyment of Wood's witticisms.

With James S. Pike, Minister at The Hague, Marsh became intimate on the voyage out, and the two corresponded frequently about their trials as overworked officials. Among the American travelers who stayed with the Marshes were Robert J. Walker, Marsh's tariff and expansionist enemy of the 1840s, who came to sell Union bonds in 1864; Alexander Dallas Bache of Smithsonian memory, now sadly aged; and Dr. Elizabeth Blackwell and her sister Dr. Emily, pioneer physicians whom the Marshes had known in Vermont.

The most illustrious European visitors were the poet Richard Monckton Milnes; Matthew Arnold, who was much taken with Marsh and his "handsome" wife; Ferdinand de Lesseps, builder of the Suez Canal, who overwhelmed them with eloquence; and the great philologist Max Müller, with whom Marsh talked grammar for hours. On an Alpine excursion at Simplon in 1862 Marsh encountered an admirer, the ethnographer Rev. Isaac Taylor; the aspects of nature were soon forgotten in the charms of philology. The next edition of Taylor's *Words and Places* credited Marsh with help throughout and with virtual authorship of a chapter on Teutonic place names in the Italian Alps.

4

At the start of his Italian mission Marsh was a tall, homely man with a full beard and sideburns. Sixty, he looked forty-five, his face unlined and his hair ungrizzled. He had been gaining steadily, and now weighed 230 pounds. But his square, solid physique had held up remarkably well; he could without difficulty work fourteen hours in his office and library, or climb hills all day for weeks.

Although somewhat reserved and cold with strangers, Marsh was completely unpretentious, and left an impression of vigor, honesty, and erudition. To Consul D. H. Wheeler he "looked like a Vermont farmer, and talked with the trenchant force of a business man in New York." Matthew Arnold considered Marsh "that *rara avis,* a

really well-bred and trained American . . . a savant . . . redeemed
from Yankeeism by his European residence & culture." To his colleague Pike, however, Marsh seemed too bookish; Pike thought he
lacked breadth and political acuteness despite "great knowledge on a
vast variety of subjects." [12]

Marsh had come to Italy expecting "little work and big pay."
"We shall have a fine, lazy time of it," he wrote a month after reaching Turin. He was wrong. "I have been entirely disappointed," he
declared half a year later, "as to the rest and relaxation I looked for,
and have, at few periods of my life, been obliged to work so hard." [13]
Marsh was not a good judge of this; every period of his life seemed
the most arduous at the time. Official diplomatic duties were not
too taxing—relations between Italy and the United States, while
friendly, were so undeveloped that little high-level negotiation, save
that concerning the Civil War, was required. But minutiae and
what Marsh called "suits of fools" did consume endless hours.

European travel was becoming ever more popular, and the im-
pudence of American tourists increased in proportion to their numbers. They treated their Ministers as glorified bankers, hotelkeepers,
and personal servants; and they were furious if these factotums took
any time off. Marsh told Seward he was called upon "to look up
inheritances and investigate genealogical records; to search after the
lost baggage of travellers; to act as mail agent [at his own expense]
for reception and forwarding of letters; to aid in introducing patent
medicines for man and beast"; to purchase and forward merchandise; to obtain "a private audience for some applicant for royal
charity; . . . to replenish the purses of travellers whose 'expected
remittances' have failed to arrive"; to collect postage stamps and
autographs; and to procure a lock of Victor Emmanuel's hair. This
seemed to him the ultimate indignity; "I should as soon think of
making a museum of the nail-parings or old shoe-heels of European
sovereigns." [14]

For such causes as these Marsh sat daily from ten till three in
the legation office, in addition to attending the dinners and evening

receptions where the significant diplomatic work was accomplished. The rest of the day he devoted to writing. Between diplomacy, scholarship, and social life, he was incessantly busy.

Marsh was engrossed with public affairs and transacted business with zest and thoroughness. Yet he was able to spend half his life in study. He arose before five and did a day's work in the library before the legation opened. Back from the office, he attended to a voluminous correspondence before dinner, then went calling, received guests, or read to Caroline till bedtime at ten, unless there was an evening function. The mild climate of Turin was as good for him as for Caroline. His eye ailment and neuritis disappeared. Rheumatism sometimes bothered him, but this was not unusual for a man of his age and build; occasional sciatica and stomach trouble were a small price to pay for living in Italy instead of hibernating in Vermont.

He longed for his own library. Not until August did the 600 books he had shipped from America reach Turin; then he regretted he had not sent "six times six thousand." "How endless are the wants of a scholar! Every time I cast a glance at my shelves, I say to myself, why did I bring *this* book, and why didn't I bring *that?*" [15] Meanwhile he kept buying books for himself and his Cambridge friends: Italian works for the Harvard library; lyric poetry and dialect materials for Child; classics for Felton; science for Baird.

Marsh's work habits had not changed. Surrounded by dozens of books lying open on his desk and on the floor, he swiftly collated materials on a wide variety of subjects. He worked without stopping; to relax he had only to turn from one book to another in a different language or on a different topic.

Completing work on the *Origin and History of the English Language* was tedious and tiresome. "Isn't it hard," Marsh exclaimed, "that I should be shut up in a closet 9 by 10, working over old lectures, instead of revelling in Italian literature and Italian nature?" He ignored the protests of his nephew Edmunds, who warned him that it was "just as sinful to commit suicide" by overwork as any other way; [16] in the spring of 1862 Marsh sent the manuscript to the printer. But the royalty of thirty cents per volume barely paid for his postage.

Though he spoke of writing as little better than slave labor, Marsh nevertheless decided to go on with it; his reputation might eventually earn him more. Even while he was preparing his next volume —*Man and Nature*—Scribner urged new literary efforts. "You are so accustomed to hard work that you cannot be idle," the publisher told Marsh. Scribner recommended a textbook "in the department of English languages and literature of which you are the acknowledged head"; Marsh planned a manual comparing American and European political and religious institutions, and did considerable research for a history of Mediterranean commerce.[17] But nothing came of these envisaged volumes.

Weary of checking sources and reading proof, Marsh took more interest in the literary labors of his friends Child and Norton than in his own. Child did not know "another man in America to whom I could go with a difficulty"; Marsh was helping him with Chaucer. "You are the editor for [Chaucer]," Child told Marsh, "if you had your eyes—and I should be satisfied to do small chores for you." Marsh was a Chaucer enthusiast: "I have formally proclaimed him to be (chronologically) the first, and all but the greatest dramatist of modern Europe." He advised Child on word meanings, style, and other points, including the delicate one of the poet's ribaldry. "In publishing in America," he warned, "one must tread gingerly, you *can't* print his naughtinesses entire, and yet one hates sadly to mangle him." Marsh's suggestions left Child "blazing like a rapt seraph with gratitude." [18] Norton, whose work on Dante Marsh took pains to further, was also deeply indebted to the American Minister.

To Norton and Child, Marsh confided his "heretical" ideas about language. He was fascinated by Italian dialects, including that "bastard patois" Piedmontese, and at length concluded that Latin, instead of being the parent tongue, was but a brother of no greater antiquity. But this was work for the future.[19] For the present, Marsh was less interested in studying the languages than in enjoying the landscape of Italy.

5

Why did not Providence give us Alps and a good climate?
MARSH TO DONALD G. MITCHELL, JUNE, 1865

For complete respite from care Marsh turned to the Alps. The view from Turin, half-surrounded by rugged, snowy summits— Monte Viso, Monte Rosa, Monte Cervin, the Matterhorn—made Marsh "half mad with admiration." "I did not know there was on earth any such beauty as that of . . . the Piedmontese Alps, and the air is as refreshing as the scenery is exquisite." [20]

To admire the Alps was one thing; to get to them, quite another. American Ministers had to be constantly at their posts, unless given specific leave of absence. Although the court deserted Turin all summer, Marsh could not quit the capital for more than ten days without having his salary cut off. The jaunts of certain American diplomats received so much unfavorable publicity that Seward later sent out "anti-vagabond" circulars, which threatened to abrogate even the ten-day privilege. "I detest that rule," Marsh wrote bitterly to Pike at The Hague. Perhaps the vagabonds appointed by Pierce and Buchanan had been "too peripatetic," but surely Republican envoys could be trusted with some liberty. For Marsh the problem was serious: "Mrs. Marsh must go into the country, and I don't want to be divorced." [21]

No foolish scruples detained Pike; he went where and when he pleased, and advised Marsh to do likewise. Marsh took this advice. Legation business frequently kept him in Turin—he grumbled that he was summoned back from the Alps three times in one month to furnish passports—but conscience alone never confined him. Legation subordinates postdated his departures and predated his returns; when out of town he often headed his letters "Turin." He swore his friends to secrecy, fearing that if the press got wind of his trips "Greeley will have me sent to the penitentiary for absenteeism." [22] Marsh's official morality had begun to decay, it will be recalled, as early as 1850, when he left for Egypt before receiving Webster's *congé*.

The short trips Marsh took, that first Italian summer, renewed his joy in mountaineering. In July he went to Monte Rosa and Lago Maggiore; in August the whole family drove north through the luxuriant valleys of Piedmont to the foot of the Matterhorn. Marsh scrambled up the moraine and across the glacier, wound around crevasses and crossed snow bridges to the 11,000-foot summit of Théodule Pass, then zigzagged down between Gorner and Zermatt. Carried by porters, Caroline fared so well on this trip that Marsh vowed her next adventure should be a balloon flight from the top of Mt. Blanc.

Thereafter, Marsh went to the Alps every summer. Some of his trips were to the near-by valleys of Aosta and Alagna, the Vaudois country. Others were to places more remote; in the fall of 1863, for example, he went to the Alps of Dauphiné and down the tempestuous Durance to Embrun, then west to the Rhone, seeing Aigues Mortes, which "ought to be kept under glass," Marsh felt, "for the benefit of those who love to pry into the life of the Middle Ages." [23]

But Marsh liked the high Alps best. He climbed the Becca di Nona and saw Alpine pastures so inaccessible that goats were pulled up to them by ropes. He scaled the Schilthorn in Switzerland and the Faulhorn in the Bernese Alps. He crawled through the Col de la Traversette in the Alpine crest north of Monte Viso. He was fascinated by glaciers—Zermatt, Aletsch, Grindelwald—and was almost crushed to death studying ice structure and flow. Given a choice, Marsh would have perched his summer home "on the brink of a glacier." [24]

Sometimes the Marshes took friends with them, but most of the expeditions were family affairs. Caroline found peaks and passes easier to bear than cities and dressing for dinner, though Marsh believed that she "feigned pleasure, to gratify her foolish husband who is ice-mad"; young Carrie kept up with her uncle on his most hair-raising exploits. Marsh's enthusiasm, sturdy constitution, and early training in the Green Mountains enabled him to perform wonders of endurance. "Considering my age and inches (circumferentially), I am not a bad climber," he bragged, "going up and down many thousand feet in a day, without overmuch puffing and panting." He compared his Alpine exploits with the trifling efforts of most tourists. "Did you go to the Lake [Fiorenza]?" (the usual tourist goal), some travelers asked him. "No," replied Marsh, "but we went a thousand yards above it." He walked ten or twelve miles a day without fatigue, and had more stamina than at forty. Sometimes he wondered whether a man in his grand climacteric, fifty pounds overweight, should indulge in such exercise, but he always returned from his summer climbs refreshed, ready to tackle "brain work" with renewed vigor. "As I am getting so strong at 63," he boasted, "I suppose I shall climb the Himalayas at 100." [25]

Even when rheumatism and old age made climbing impossible, Marsh's love of the Alps never waned; he could always look at them. Nothing in nature ever gave him so much enjoyment; he regretted only that life was too short to visit all the mountains in the world.

Marsh's summer excursions were also excellent opportunities to study the people of Italy. His initial infatuation with the Italians had sustained some severe shocks; the best Italian intentions seemed to him crippled by a lack of energy and decision. His country trips helped him understand why political unification was not enough. Each of Italy's six or seven major provinces had its own dialect, laws, and personality. Except in Piedmont, the population was two-thirds illiterate, stanchly Catholic, conservative and particularistic, as hostile to rule from Turin as from Vienna; progress would be slow and difficult. The mistakes of her leaders, Marsh discerned, were not the sole causes of Italy's distress. In certain Alpine valleys, however, Marsh met people who were sturdy and self-reliant despite their poverty and isolation. They renewed his faith in the simple rural virtues and strengthened his belief that human nature throve best where nature was harshest.

All things considered, Marsh had never been happier than during these years in Italy. Equable Turin, the beautiful mountains, even the social life, when there was not too much of it—Marsh saw everything *couleur de rose*. His doubts about the wisdom of returning to Europe soon vanished. Homesickness and the wish to take a more active part in the war almost impelled him at times to return to America, but as the years passed he found more and more reason to stay where he was. The thought of an Atlantic voyage was unendurable; he had no way of earning a living at home; his family was scattered or gone; Vermont winters were too severe; finally, "giving up the Alps seems to me like giving up all the material world." He had "such a passion for the *nature* of Italy," he wrote after four years there, "that I do not see how I can ever live under another sky." [26]

The perennial flaw was lack of money. Marsh had not yet found any remuneration adequate; his salary of $12,000 a year in Italy was no exception. Like most American diplomats, he considered his pay miserably insufficient; his complaints of governmental niggardliness were as numerous and bitter as during his previous mission. Staid old Turin was mushrooming like a Western frontier town; the cost of living had more than doubled in five years. Marsh was paying $2,000 a year for a half-furnished apartment in the Casa d'Angennes. The Turinese, he suspected, "know everybody's salary, and take the whole, generously letting us run into debt for any trifle we may want beyond our income." [27]

As in Turkey, the disparity between the poverty-stricken American Minister and his affluent European colleagues was glaring and painful. The ten-day rule made matters worse, for it would have been cheaper to travel in the Alps than to summer in Turin. Marsh thought his requests for leave of absence "would draw tears from the eye of a Cyclops," [28] but the Secretary of State remained dry-eyed and stingy.

Marsh's pecuniary embarrassments increased at the end of 1861, when the owner of the Casa d'Angennes turned him out, Marsh related angrily, "because we would not submit to a small addition of $400 to the rent we already paid for an apartment hardly large enough to swing a cat in." Marsh had not been happy in this palace; thick, cold, stone walls and floors made it difficult and expensive to heat.[29] He did not realize its virtues until he tried to find another house. Weeks of hunting turned up nothing. In despair, Marsh finally took rooms in a hotel at Pegli, a Riviera suburb of Genoa, four hours by train from Turin. In this remote place, in the winter of 1862–63, he returned in earnest to his most significant work: *Man and Nature; or, Physical Geography as Modified by Human Action.*

☙XIII☙

Man and Nature

MAN AND NATURE was the most important and original American geographical work of the nineteenth century. The climax of a lifetime's study by an acute observer and profound scholar, it has had a far-reaching effect on American thought and action. Though its importance was acknowledged from the first, after the turn of the century Marsh's work was for some time neglected. It was perhaps the easier to overlook because his conclusions had come to be taken for granted. Since about 1930, however, Marsh's pioneer scholarship has begun to receive proper recognition. *Man and Nature* was indeed, as Mumford called it a generation ago, "the fountain-head of the conservation movement." [1] Marsh had disciples who furthered one or another proposal for the conservation of forests, for the preservation of watersheds, for the regulation of rivers. But until the twentieth century, no one except Marsh perceived the problem of conservation as one of interdependent social and environmental relationships.

Man and Nature also ushered in, as Marsh intended, a revolution in geographical thought. It made men aware of the ways their own behavior, unconscious as well as conscious, transformed the lands in which they lived. Others before Marsh had explored aspects of man's impact on nature. The vivid clarity of Marsh's presentation, the remarkable organization of his material, and the irrefragable moral of his conclusion were his signal contributions. Marsh had conducted "triumphantly," his memorialists at the American Academy of Arts and Sciences proclaimed, "the investigation of a subject so abstruse, so vast, and so complex, that it is fair to say he had no rival in the work." [2]

I

Ever since we were married, my wife has been pestering me about making a book. . . . After fifteen years' punching, I made one about camels which took so surprisingly that the publishers actually sold not far from 300 copies in little more than three years. This I didn't find very encouraging, but Mrs. Marsh told me about Herschel, who tried 279 times before he was able to make a speculum . . . Jean Paul, who wrote 40 books before he sold one, &c, &c. So I made another book which did pretty well . . . I hoped she would be satisfied. But no! she insisted I had not told all I knew, & said she would give me no peace till I had. I quarrelled with her as long as I could, compared her to the late Mrs. Albert Dürer of Nuremberg, of Xantippean memory, & the like, but the more I begged her to leave me alone, the more she wouldn't . . . and I have been enforced to begin another great volume, the object of which is to tell everything I know & have not told in the others, after which I am to have peace. I think I shall name it "Legion."

MARSH TO LADY ESTCOURT, FEB. 18, 1863

Marsh viewed the work in prospect in no grandiose terms. He belittled it, made fun of himself, and gave out that he was an idle fellow who set pen to paper only because of Caroline's incessant scolding. *Man and Nature,* as Marsh saw it, would be a "burly volume" on a "dreary subject" and "ruin the printers" as well as himself. Yet there was some basis for Marsh's self-deprecation. Like many scholars, he was inclined to gather materials endlessly and put off the task of synthesis and composition. Caroline urged him on, fearing "that the accumulating process would be going on until the brightness of your intellect and memory would be dulled by age and the world would lose the results of so many years of study." [3]

Marsh had started *Man and Nature* in Burlington, the spring of 1860, in the creative expansiveness following his release from debt. "I began another book this morning," he wrote Spencer Baird with an air of mystery; "I won't tell you what the book is about, because you'll call me an ass (it's none of your *ologies*)." But two months later he explained that "it's a little volume showing that whereas Ritter and Guyot think that the earth made man, man in fact made the earth." Concerned lest his friends think he was going too far afield, Marsh forestalled criticism:

Now, don't roll up the whites of your eyes, and quote that foolish old saw about the cobbler and his last. I am not going into the scientific, but the historicals, in which I am as good as any of you. What I put in of scientific speculations, I shall steal, pretty much, but I do know some things myself. For instance, my father had a piece of thick woodland where the ground was always damp. Wild turnips grew there and ginseng, and wild pepper sometimes. Well, sir, he cleared up that lot, and drained and cultivated it, and it became a good deal drier, and he raised good corn and grass on it. Now I am going to state this as a *fact* and I defy all you speculators about cause and effect to deny it.[4]

Any farmer, in other words, knew that agriculture altered the environment.

Other tasks intervened, however; Marsh had to put *Man and Nature* aside. In 1862, on a wintry April afternoon in Turin, he finished and sent off the manuscript of the *Origin and History of the English Language*. An hour later Caroline went to his library to see how he was enjoying his newly recovered leisure. She found him "with a heap of manuscripts, loose notes, etc., about him":

"What are you doing now?" I asked. "At work on my next book," he said in the quietest way in the world—and sure enough the projected *"Physical Geography"* was already in the forge. "Well," I said, "it cost me fifteen years of hard work to *wind* you up to the writing point, and now I believe you are likely to run on without stopping for the next fifteen." "Perhaps so," he answered, but did not look up.[5]

In the peaceful isolation of the Riviera Marsh set to work in earnest. At his desk in the hotel, or striding along the Pegli beach, he watched the ever-varied splendors of the Mediterranean coast; the joy of those days and the love of nature permeated his pages. But the sea was not always still, nor the face of the land genial. Penetrating cold northern winds and hot, rain-laden siroccos from the south reminded Marsh that nature could also be destructively violent. The rains turned to torrents in narrow valleys to the north, and the turbulent waters of the Varenna and other streams tore away chunks of rock and soil, even wrenching trees from their footholds, while the slopes melted into landslides. Often the wind-worked sea churned up the shore, overcoming hastily erected bulwarks, splintering fishing smacks, and threatening to engulf Pegli itself.

If nature distracted Marsh from his labors, man and his works did not. There was little to attract sight-seers in the small fishing village, or in the hotel, a great stone building on the beach. Marsh spent every other week in Turin, leaving Pegli Monday night and returning Friday afternoon. At Pegli he wrote all morning, and afternoons walked along the beach, wandered in the famous Pallavicini gardens, read aloud to the family, or listened to Carrie's lessons. The book took shape. Marsh worked all the harder for fear that, like Darwin, he might be anticipated; this "would be rather hard," reflected Caroline, "when he has been studying the subject for so many years, and only been prevented by adverse circumstances from giving his thoughts upon it to the world long before." [6]

Marsh had been studying the interrelations between man and nature since the age of five, when his father drove with him in the Green Mountains, taught him to recognize the various trees, and showed him what a watershed looked like. The significance of watersheds and their vegetation had early been clear to him: forests retained moisture and prevented soil from washing off the hills; cutting and burning increased runoff and erosion, led to flooding and drought. These changes Marsh saw himself, substantiating the observations of such naturalists and travelers as André Michaux,

Isaac Weld, Jr., Samuel Williams, and Timothy Dwight. Indeed, many in Woodstock and towns near by remarked upon the change in the landscape and shook their heads sadly over it. Nor could Marsh fail to observe what Benjamin Silliman had seen near Burlington: fields littered with innumerable stumps, and trees "girdled, dry, and blasted, by the summer's heat, and winter's cold—scorched and blackened, by fire." As landowner and mill operator, Marsh witnessed the rapid depletion of virgin forests in the Green Mountains; once a great timber export center, twenty years later Burlington was the country's second largest importer. As a sheep raiser, Marsh knew well how flocks cropped the scanty vegetation and bared steep slopes to sun and rain. As farmer, manufacturer, and lumber dealer, Marsh "had occasion both to observe and to feel the evils resulting from an injudicious system of managing woodlands and the products of the forest." [7] Nowhere in North America, not even in the tobacco and cotton lands of the South, were forests removed and soils exhausted faster than on the flanks of the Green Mountains. Born only forty years after Vermont was settled, Marsh witnessed most of the process of deterioration.

His experience thus differed profoundly from that of the previous generation of American naturalists. Jefferson, Franklin, Benjamin Rush, and their contemporaries were absorbed by man's impact upon the environment, but regarded the transformation of nature as beneficent and desirable. The Jeffersonians thought almost every change an improvement: clearing the forests ameliorated winter cold and summer heat; draining swamps banished disease; and cultivating the wilderness transformed the countryside from primitive chaos to order and civilized beauty. The characteristic attitude toward man and nature was well expressed by Vermonter Ira Allen; he praised the settler who "sees the effect of his own powers, aided by the goodness of Providence; he sees that man can embellish the most rude spot, the stagnant air vanishes with the woods, the rank vegetation feels the purifying influence of the sun; he drains the swamp, putrid exhalations flit off on lazy wing, and fevers and

agues accompany them." Most Americans before Marsh believed
in the plenitude of nature and the inexhaustibility of natural resources, and had serene confidence in their ability to master the
environment; indeed, they considered this conquest the American
destiny. Only a few worried about dwindling timber supplies, or
heeded Franklin's warning that "whenever we attempt to amend
the scheme of Providence, and to interfere with the government of
the world, we had need be very circumspect, lest we do more harm
than good." [8] Marsh acknowledged man's power to transform the
environment, but assessed the results more realistically than did his
predecessors.

Marsh first broached in 1847 what was to be the central theme of
Man and Nature. In a lecture to a local Vermont agricultural society, he depicted the changes that a single generation had wrought
on the face of the land—"the signs of artificial improvement are
mingled with the tokens of improvident waste." He blamed the
greed and thoughtlessness of Vermont farmers for the removal of
the forest cover, and warned them that their fertile valleys might
"soon be converted from smiling meadows into broad wastes of
shingle and gravel and pebbles, deserts in summer, and seas in
autumn and spring." Could man redress the balance of nature? Yes;
a solution was at hand. In Europe forests were cut for timber and
fuel only at stated intervals; governments safeguarded them from
depredation and exhaustion. It was "quite time," Marsh stated
firmly, "that this practice should be introduced among us." He did
not then suggest public ownership of forests, but appealed "to an
enlightened self-interest to introduce the reforms, check the abuses,
and preserve us from an increase of [the] evils" he had described.[9]

Over the next two years Marsh's interest in forestry matured.
Confiding to the botanist Asa Gray that he had long planned to
write "an essay or a volume on the . . . economy of the forest," he
diffidently sent Gray an outline of his scheme. Marsh had already
developed a multiple-purpose approach to conservation. In this
prospectus he discussed the manifold influences of tree cover—amel-

ioration of the local climate; modification of the environment of smaller plants; replenishment of mold and humus; and, notably, the forest's "uses in checking the rapid flow of rain-water and melting snows, thereby diminishing the frequency and violence of freshets, preventing the degradation of highlands and the consequent wash of gravel from above upon cultivated lands, and at the same time acting as a reservoir, which gives out in summer the moisture accumulated in the wet seasons." In addition, the forest was a place of recreation and natural beauty, a refuge for animals and plants "against parching winds and the heat of the sun," and a breeding place for useful insect-eating birds. These values, Marsh realized, had to be weighed carefully against man's need for fuel and timber. He called for a detailed study of the proper balance between wooded and arable acreage and recommended a national program of experimental forestry.[10]

Four years in Turkey and along the Mediterranean enlarged his view of the subject. In those lands man had everywhere left so conspicuous an imprint, that to Marsh the soil itself seemed historic; the record was painfully clear. The same patterns of destruction—extirpation of forests and wild life, overgrazing, a heedless or too ambitious agriculture—recurred wherever civilizations had flourished and fallen. For Marsh each area pointed a moral: the sterile sands of the Sahara, the desolate pock-marked Adriatic Karst, the malarial Roman Campagna, the rock-strewn valleys of Provence and Dauphiné. Long ago fertile and populous, these regions now stood barren and deserted, monuments to human improvidence.

Only gradually did Marsh acquire these insights. His years in Europe were too full of bewildering variety to be reduced immediately to coherent order. Continually traveling through strange lands, Marsh was overwhelmed by a multitude of new experiences, and felt inadequately prepared to cope with them all. "Seriously it is a shame," he wrote, "that I have not the knowledge of *nature* that every traveller . . . ought to have. I see strange stones, plants, animals, geographical formations, and gaze vacantly at them, but what availeth it?" He would "write a book some day," but only a collection of curiosities, designed to "show that one ignoramus is as good a traveller as any body." [11]

Such a book was *The Camel*. Into it Marsh dumped an assortment of out-of-the-way facts, curious statistics, bits of learned lore, legends, jokes, and anecdotes. Yet it was more than frivolous exuberance of knowledge; it was a solid study of domestication and adaptation, directed toward a practical goal. The special purpose of the book was to promote the introduction of camels into America; and Marsh viewed this effort as an instance of man's conquest of the "widely dissimilar, remote, and refractory products of creative nature." [12]

Utility also animated Marsh's next study of the environment. His 1857 *Report on the Artificial Propagation of Fish* was a searching inquiry into the economic agencies, pastoral and industrial, agricultural and forestal, responsible for the increasing irregularity of river flow. Clearly foreshadowing his later geographical work, the fish report was an exercise in miniature for *Man and Nature*. And shortly thereafter Marsh wrote his "Study of Nature," a brilliant essay on the study of landscape, art, and science.

2

Man is everywhere a disturbing agent. Wherever he plants his foot, the harmonies of nature are turned to discords.

MARSH, *Man and Nature*

Marsh had more time for his scientific interests once he reached Italy. As he had done previously in Turkey, he established exchange relations for the Smithsonian. He equipped himself with scientific instruments, but used them less diligently than in Egypt and Palestine, and sent home few plants, no pickled fish. He concentrated instead on transplanting to Italy some American flora and fauna, including conifers, maize, agave, okra, turkeys, hummingbirds, and flying squirrels. Alpine excursions gave Marsh new insights into natural processes. He studied the movements of glaciers and the structure of moraines, measured the extent and character of avalanches. He took copious notes on agricultural techniques, crop diseases, diet, and other aspects of rural life. Large-scale designs to change the environment fascinated him—the irrigation of the Piedmont plain, the digging of the Suez Canal, the construction of Alpine tunnels, the drainage of the Maremma and other swamps; and he visited such engineering projects as he could.

As usual, though, creation impressed Marsh less than destruction —the erosive force of wind and water in the Alps and the Apennines, avalanches at Eismeer and Grindelwald, landslides along the Riviera, Dauphiné mountain streams yellow with soil stripped from their valleys. Some of this was natural and inevitable; but much of the destruction had been amplified by man. Normal erosion was balanced by new growth; but where man interfered the soil was carried off faster than it could be regenerated, fields were gullied, stream channels deepened, dams and harbors silted up. A soil initially barren might evoke courage and resolution; but unremitting deterioration seemed to erode human will, and sped the common doom of land and people. Marsh wondered whether man was destined to destroy himself.

The general problem of survival worried few. But governments had long been troubled by the threatened extinction of timber resources. For centuries the forests of Europe had succumbed to the settler's ax, the rapacity of his livestock, the demands of industry, and the needs of a growing population for fuel and shelter. However, as feudal lords gave way in the later Middle Ages to powerful monarchs, control over the land became more centralized and absolute. Dwindling state forests were rigorously guarded against depredations; private woodlands were kept inviolate as game preserves, parks, and sources of revenue. The penalties for theft, illegal foraging, even pasturing in the forests, were severe. A partial balance was struck between man and nature.

Not for long, however, did the woods hold their own. In the age of world discovery and of great navies, need for timber again increased. Spurred by scarcity, the science of silviculture developed; by the mid-nineteenth century European schools of forestry were teaching how and when to cut trees so as to derive the maximum yields without reducing reserves, how to replenish, and what species to plant. Even in improvident America, some woodlands had been managed—first by agents of the Crown, later by New England communities which had exhausted local fuel resources—so as to assure a steady and dependable supply of timber. In the 1820s the United States government established in Florida a live oak reservation for the Navy. But in America forest legislation was rare, and such laws were seldom observed, almost never enforced. There was no forestry research or education; Americans were too busy getting rid of trees to think about improving them. "Of course," wrote Marsh in 1879, apropos the new Arnold Arboretum in Massachusetts, "the *improvement* of forest trees is the work of centuries. So much the more reason for beginning *now*." [13]

Most forest legislation before the nineteenth century was designed simply to save wood, not to conserve soil or water or anything else; the idea of watershed protection was absent even in Germany, where scientific forestry had developed furthest. Some localities in the French Alps had, to be sure, recognized the protective value of forest cover as early as the sixteenth century, and passed ordinances which prohibited clearing. But the French Revolution swept aside these local laws along with the punitive national forest code; wholesale depredations slaked popular resentment against noble proprietors who had hitherto reserved the forests for themselves. Within a decade, overcutting brought disaster. Brooks became torrents, tearing away fertile lands or burying them in silt; fire, overpasturing, and the ax swiftly completed the destruction of a million arable acres. In the upper Durance and the denuded limestone tributary valleys of the Rhone, Marsh saw catastrophe that made the deforestation and erosion in his native Vermont seem benign by comparison.

About the time Marsh began to consider the consequences of deforestation, a few French scientists and engineers turned their attention to erosion in the Vosges and the Jura Alps. During the 1850s Moreau de Jonnès, Jean Baptiste Boussingault, Antoine Becquerel, and François de Vallès studied the ways in which plant cover affected runoff, stream flow, and soil temperatures. Thanks to their advice and to the warnings of such noted foresters as Lorentz and Clavé, the French government in 1860 inaugurated a program of watershed control and afforestation. By the time Marsh's *Man and Nature* appeared, France had begun to regulate the worst torrents—though not all the damage has yet been repaired; while in Italy, foresters like Salvagnoli, di Bérenger, and Siemoni were urging national control of timber resources.

Thus in Alpine Europe Marsh found a spirit in accord with the warnings he had expressed in America. Just as the scenes of desolation he observed in Piedmont and Dauphiné reinforced his gloomy prognostications about the hills of Vermont, so did the theories of Boussingault, Becquerel, Vallès, and Salvagnoli bear out his ideas of causation. History demonstrated that man was the architect of his own misfortunes; what the Old World had suffered, Marsh believed, might well become the fate of the New. At Pegli he wrote ominously:

Man has too long forgotten that the earth was given to him for usufruct alone, not for consumption, still less for profligate waste. . . . There are parts of Asia Minor, of Northern Africa, of Greece, and even of Alpine Europe, where the operation of causes set in action by man has brought the face of the earth to a desolation almost as complete as that of the moon. . . . The earth is fast becoming an unfit home for its noblest inhabitant, and another era of equal human crime and human improvidence . . . would reduce it to such a condition of impoverished productiveness, of shattered surface, of climatic excess, as to threaten the depravation, barbarism, and perhaps even extinction of the species.[14]

To repair past ravages and buttress future hopes, America must follow the example of Europe, and submit to state control of natural resources. Marsh urged his countrymen to replace their profligate habits with a program of public responsibility.

3

After the deluge comes the history of the deluge.
REVIEW OF *Man and Nature* IN *Scribner's Monthly*, NOV., 1874

Heterogeneous as Marsh's materials were, the broad outlines of *Man and Nature* are straightforward enough. A brief Preface explains the purpose of the book. A Bibliography of more than two hundred items follows. Then comes a lengthy introductory chapter, which opens with a physical description of the Roman Empire 2,000 years ago. Comparing its previous well-wooded, well-watered condition with the existing arid deserts around the Mediterranean, Marsh ascribes the decay to oppression and impoverishment of the peasantry, who were forced to abandon their lands. The soil was thus "exposed to all the destructive forces which act with such energy on the surface of the earth when it is deprived of those protections by which nature originally guarded it, and for which, in well-ordered husbandry, human ingenuity has contrived more or less efficient substitutes." Once man has conquered nature, he cannot relax his care of it.

This lesson led Marsh to consider the quality and extent of human influence. In their natural state, terrain and soils, flora and fauna, generally change slowly. But man, especially civilized man, "guided by a self-conscious and intelligent will aiming as often at secondary and remote as at immediate objects," transforms the environment rapidly. The evidence convinced Marsh that human impact—by contrast with that of animals—was unique in scope and intensity.

No natural force balances man's influence over the material world. Species he extirpates are gone forever; animals he domesticates seldom revert to a wild state; "when the forest is gone, the great reservoir of moisture stored up in its vegetable mould is evaporated, and returns only in deluges of rain to wash away the parched dust into which that mould has been converted." In some countries man has planted new forests, checked inundations, drained swamps, fixed sand dunes with grass and trees; but such precautions are rare, Marsh notes. Through ignorance, carelessness, or greed, mankind lays waste the world at a rate which increases with his power to subjugate the environment. Marsh shows that arid or semiarid lands of steep relief are most subject to destruction, but no areas are wholly immune; in America, Africa, and Australia, industrial man is already taking toll. To arrest such evils and restore a balance of nature both morality and science are needed: a feeling of responsibility toward future generations and a thorough knowledge of the terrain, soils, climate, and vegetation of the continents. But geological, topographical, and hydrographical surveys will require decades; "we are, even now, breaking up the floor and wainscoting and doors and window frames of our dwelling, for fuel to warm our bodies and seethe our pottage. . . . The world cannot afford to wait until the slow and sure progress of exact science has taught it a better economy." Hence Marsh proposes to derive from "the history of man's effort to replenish the earth and subdue it" some practical and immediate countermeasures.[15]

Chapter II, "Transfer, Modification, and Extirpation of Vegetable and of Animal Species," deals with perhaps the most complicated aspect of the entire subject. Few naturalists today would have the temerity to discuss the dispersal of flora, the economic role of plants, the origin of domesticated species, the results of transplanting in various soils, the interaction of plant and animal life, the numbers of birds and insects, the effects of introducing Old World animal species into the New World and into islands, the utility of the earthworm, the breeding of fish, the role of birds in the distribution of seeds, and the place of diatoms in the economy of nature—all within the space of seventy pages. At the time Marsh wrote, however, it was novel to consider these ecological relationships as a part of science at all. What he had to say was new and important:

"Whenever man has transplanted a plant from its native habitat to a new soil, he has introduced a new geographical force to act upon it. . . . The new and the old plants are rarely the equivalents of each other, and the substitution of an exotic for a native tree, shrub, or grass, increases or diminishes the relative importance" of plant cover generally. Plants grown for food are seldom returned as waste to the same soils. Man revolutionizes nature by moving or killing plants and animals, and by consciously and unconsciously influencing their predators, habitats, and food supplies. Marsh's classic example of ecological chain reaction concerned beavers:

So long as the fur of the beaver was extensively employed as a material for fine hats, it bore a very high price, and the chase of this quadruped was so keen that naturalists feared its speedy extinction. When a Parisian manufacturer invented the silk hat, which soon came into almost universal use, the demand for beavers' fur fell off, and this animal—whose habits, as we have seen, are an important agency in the formation of bogs and other modifications of forest nature—immediately began to increase, reappeared in haunts which he had long abandoned, and can no longer be regarded as rare enough to be in immediate danger of extirpation. Thus the convenience or the caprice of Parisian fashion . . . may sensibly affect the physical geography of a distant continent.[16]

Marsh next turns to the woods. Though only one phase of organic life, forests occupy a chapter of 200 pages, more than one third of *Man and Nature*. "As man and boy," Marsh explained, "I knew more of trees than of anything else." Before man came on the scene, most of the habitable globe was wooded; and "forests would soon cover many parts of the Arabian and African deserts," Marsh believed, "if man and domestic animals, especially the goat and the camel, were banished from them." [17] Marsh's chief concern was to examine the effects of forest destruction, first on climate, then on vegetation and surface.

The connection between forests and climate had long interested both Americans and Europeans. Much propaganda had been written to prove that trees did, or did not, ameliorate temperature extremes, increase or reduce humidity, precipitation, and wind. No conclusive studies existed, as Marsh carefully pointed out; but he gathered together research done by French, Swiss, Austrian, Italian, and German engineers and hydrographers and summarized their findings. Marsh has sometimes been blamed for promoting the notion that trees increase rainfall, and hence that the arid West can be watered by afforestation. He believed nothing of the sort. Most of the evidence showed him that "more rain falls in wooded than in open country," but "we cannot positively affirm that the total annual quantity of rain is diminished or increased by the destruction of the woods." Marsh was certain that forests "maintain a more uniform degree of humidity in the atmosphere than is observed in cleared grounds . . . promote the frequency of showers, and . . . equalize [the] distribution [of precipitation] through the different seasons." [18] But much more important, and less disputable, was the influence of forests on vegetation, soils, and water. To this Marsh devotes the bulk of the chapter—the most influential part of his book.

Where forests are present, Marsh concludes, "tree, bird, beast, and fish, alike, find a constant uniformity of condition most favorable to the regular and harmonious coexistence of them all." But "with the disappearance of the forest, all is changed":

The soil is alternately parched by the fervors of summer, and seared by the rigors of winter. Bleak winds sweep unresisted over its surface, drift away the snow that sheltered it from the frost, and dry up its scanty moisture. The precipitation becomes [ir]regular as the temperature; the melting snows and vernal rains, no longer absorbed by a loose and bibulous vegetable mould, rush over the frozen surface, and pour down the valleys seaward, instead of filling a retentive bed of absorbent earth, and storing up a supply of moisture to feed perennial springs. The soil is bared of its covering of leaves, broken and loosened by the plough, deprived of the fibrous rootlets which held it together, dried and pulverized by sun and wind. . . . The face of the earth is no longer a sponge, but a dust heap. . . . Stripped of its vegetable glebe, [the soil] grows less and less productive, and consequently, less able to protect itself by weaving a new network of roots to bind its particles together, a new carpeting of turf to shield it from wind and sun and scouring rain. Gradually it becomes altogether barren. . . . The too general felling of woods [is] the most destructive among the many causes of the physical deterioration of the earth.[19]

Marsh documents these statements thoroughly. Reviewing the history of deforestation throughout Europe, he examines in detail the resulting changes in landscape and soil fertility. He surveys the literature of forest regulations, discusses forestry practices current in Western Europe, and considers how far they might be adopted in the United States.

Avaricious logging and careless fires had already wasted America's finest virgin timber, leaving behind a depleted soil, denuded, or covered by a scrubby inferior second growth. Considering the increasing demand for wood for fuel and construction, both industry and nature would benefit, Marsh believed, by regulated cutting of seasoned timber only, and by the substitution of artificial for natural forests. Man could improve upon nature even in this realm; European foresters had demonstrated that planted woods, with well-pruned, even-aged stands and a smaller number of species, yielded faster-growing and healthier trees than the natural forest.

Where trees were essential to preserve soil moisture and plant cover, however, Marsh felt cutting should be prohibited entirely. "We have now felled forest enough everywhere, in many districts far too much." Most farmers, he realized, found tree-planting unprofitable because "the growth of arboreal vegetation is so slow that . . . the longest life hardly embraces the seedtime and the harvest of a forest. . . . The value of its timber will not return the capital expended and the interest accrued" for several generations. But "the planter of a wood must be actuated by higher motives than those of an investment. . . . Both the preservation of existing woods, and the far more costly extension of them where they have been unduly reduced, are among the most obvious of the duties which this age owes" to the next. Moreover, Marsh believed that "the establishment of an approximately fixed ratio" between woodland, pasture, and arable would reduce the "restlessness" and "instability" which he had criticized as major defects of the American character.[20]

In Chapter V, "The Waters," Marsh views man's activities more benignly. In one long section he shows how drains and dikes reclaim land from the sea in England and Holland. Another section describes aqueducts, reservoirs, canals, and irrigation, and their effects, intentional and accidental. A third concerns flood control by dams and embankments, and methods used to prevent silting; another discusses river and harbor improvements. Marsh ends the chapter with a survey of underground water supplies and ways of tapping them. He concludes that "the cost of one year's warfare, if judiciously expended" in reforestation and the construction of conduits and covered reservoirs, "would secure, to almost every country that man has exhausted, an amelioration of climate, a renovated fertility of soil, and a general physical improvement, which might almost be characterized as a new creation." [21]

The penultimate chapter, "The Sands," first discusses the origin, structure, and distribution of sand dunes, and briefly assesses their use against encroachments of the sea. But no matter how effective dunes may be as barriers, "when their drifts are not checked by natural processes, or by the industry of man, they become a cause of as certain, if not of as sudden, destruction as the ocean itself." The bulk of the chapter is a study of the damage caused by drifting dunes in Europe, and of methods of stabilizing them with grass and trees, notably in the Landes of Gascony, where hundreds of square miles were being ruined by sand until the French government arrested the devastation with plantations of maritime pine.[22]

In the final—and shortest—chapter, "Projected or Possible Geographical Changes by Man," Marsh considers the probable effects of great canals—Suez, Panama, Cape Cod, Mediterranean–Dead Sea, and Caspian–Sea of Azov. He speculates about watering the deserts of Arabia, diminishing the destructiveness of earthquakes by sinking deep wells, and diverting the course of lava flows. But unconscious and secondary effects engage Marsh's attention most of all. Every human action, he emphasizes, leaves an imprint. The rubbish hills of the Nile are almost as conspicuous as the Pyramids; the waste of centuries buries cities hundreds of feet; the long lines of iron railways may influence the "distribution and action" of electricity; accelerated erosion caused by clearing and cultivating river valleys has displaced masses of matter, thickened the crust of the earth beneath deltas and estuaries, and shifted the center of gravity and consequently the motions of the globe. The legal maxim that "the law concerneth not itself with trifles" certainly did not apply to man's impact on nature, Marsh added. Although the extent of these effects could hardly be measured and their consequences might be obscure, "we are never justified in assuming a force to be insignificant because its measure is unknown, or even because no physical effect can now be traced to it." Knowledge would accumulate, and each new observation of the relations between the human race and the world around it would help to answer "the great question, whether man is of nature or above her." [23]

4

Man and Nature was almost half completed when Marsh left the Riviera in the spring of 1863 for a medieval castle nine miles southwest of Turin. Pleasant as Pegli had been, the long trips to and from the capital were tiring and expensive, and Marsh was glad to find a place closer by. This too, however, had certain inconveniences. The castle overlooked the village of Piobesi, which contained "3500 peasants, and nothing else," wrote Marsh. "It furnishes neither meat drink nor clothing, and we are as badly off as Sydney Smith when he lived '12 miles from a lemon.'" [24] There was no adequate road; to go by train to the capital one had to walk to Candiolo, two miles away. The castle itself, a massive, gray-walled stone pile, was damp and chill, the rooms dark and small. But these drawbacks proved temporary. Fires banished the damp, sunlight dispelled the gloom, and the romance of living in a medieval castle made up for small inconveniences.

The compensations were many. Marsh's study opened out on a broad, sunny terrace and faced a great tower inhabited by countless starlings; on another side the castle overlooked cloisters festooned with climbing roses and wisteria; there was even the promise of a treasure trove, for the previous tenant, Brassier de St. Simon, had found 80,000 lire in gold in a hole in the castle wall. Best of all was the unobstructed view of the Alps, whose snow-covered peaks seemed so near that Marsh amused himself "knocking the icicles off the eaves of that respectable hillock, Mt. Rosa, by shying pebbles at 'em. Nay, when it is *very* clear, I can reach the walls of the mountain with my pipe-stem." [25]

Piobesi besieged the castle with offers of service and produce; Marsh had to hire a regular army to work in the small garden. The Piobesans learned that in America all the poor were free and happy except the slaves, who would be equally well off when the war was over. They sympathized with the national cause of the munificent American who spoke with them in Italian and as equals. When Vicksburg fell, Marsh was greeted by a display of red, white, and blue rockets on the meadow below the castle, where the villagers cheered for the Northern victory. Marsh provided wine and money, and singing and dancing went on in the castle garden until midnight.

Marsh was moved by the courtesy and dignity of the destitute, illiterate villagers. Shocked at the hardships they endured, he gave more money than he could spare, provided meat at the annual *festa* of Santa Anna, and made a parting gift of new beds and other equipment to the local hospital. He won such gratitude that twenty years later the castle was still known by his name; visiting Piobesi, James Jackson Jarves reported that Marsh was "worshipped even now like a god." [26]

"The quiet here," wrote Caroline after three months in Piobesi, "is more complete than anything I ever hoped for. . . . I sometimes think that Mr. Marsh would never have got through this immense work on which he is now engaged if Providence had not kindly put us here for a few months." [27] Many days Marsh did not have to go to Turin at all, and the work went rapidly. As always, Marsh arose early and wrote steadily through the morning, putting down his pen occasionally to watch the birds sweep around the tower or alight at his low open window. The first nightingale sang on the evening of April 27; two days later Marsh finished the first draft of his manuscript. These spring weeks were the least interrupted, the best period for work in Marsh's life.

Fast as Marsh progressed, new source material continually appeared and had to be incorporated; the job seemed unending. Wading wearily through piles of papers, Marsh grew so despondent that Caroline feared he might commit a "libricide" in some moment of exasperated fatigue. Other factors conspired to drag out the task. Marsh had to go more often to Turin, partly on diplomacy, partly to negotiate another lease of Casa d'Angennes with the Contessa Ghirardi, "as formidable a business as the taking of Vicksburg." [28] The hard winter's work had left him tired, nervous, and depressed; his health failed in minor ways, and an old complaint in his side caused him much pain and many sleepless nights. Even the weather turned against him. From cool spring Piobesi passed to scalding summer; one could hardly walk on the sun-baked terrace flagstones. Summer also brought an intolerable plague of flies. They were everywhere—on Marsh's eyelids, on his inkstand, on the very point of his pen. He could not write half so much in a day as before.

Despite these tribulations, Marsh revised the manuscript for the last time early in July. On the same day, he signed the contract for the Casa d'Angennes, and went off to the Alps happily secure in the thought that he would have a roof over his head in the fall. But the Casa d'Angennes—promised for September 1—was not even ready when the Marshes, having lingered on in wet, wintry Dauphiné, finally moved in on November 9. It was an unpleasant homecoming.

Furniture had been ruined, knicknacks broken or lost; damp walls and smoking chimneys made life miserable. It was as dark and glum within as without. A year of quiet and peace was over; in busy Turin Marsh could hope for little repose. Nor could city society compensate for the bright calm of Pegli and Piobesi.

In addition to these vexations, Marsh had unhappy experiences with the publication of *Man and Nature*. First, Marsh's English publisher, John Murray, refused to bring out the book at all. Murray criticized *Man and Nature* for its "want of definite purpose." "It is too general," he told the author; "it will be difficult to make the public understand what it is about." [29] This was a shock, particularly since Marsh had only switched to Murray from his previous English publisher at Scribner's insistence.

With Scribner, Marsh also had differences. The New York publisher deleted a number of sharp partisan comments about the Civil War as both irrelevant and insulting; this dismemberment grieved Marsh deeply. Even so, for every provocative or extraneous remark Scribner caught, a dozen slipped through. Pungent asides on the evils of nicotine, the iniquities of railroads, the dangers of Catholicism, and a hundred other topics make the book interesting though discursive. Marsh had no compunction about digressing. "It is hard to 'get the floor' in the world's great debating society," he explained to his readers; "when a speaker who has anything to say once finds access to the public ear, he must make the most of his opportunity, without inquiring too nicely whether his observations are 'in order.' " [30]

Publication delays annoyed Marsh. Scribner had promised to bring the book out in November, 1863, but the necessity of finding a new English publisher and the loss of two shipments of proof held it up in the press. Marsh grumbled that his facts would be out of date before the public saw them and fretted lest someone anticipate him. Spring came, but *Man and Nature* still hibernated in the publisher's burrow. Were it not too late, remarked the disgusted author, "I should be strongly tempted to suppress the book altogether, as it will not now subserve some of the leading purposes for which it was designed, and I have almost entirely lost my interest in it." [31]

In May of 1864, *Man and Nature* finally appeared. No eager public stormed the shops; sales were poor, Scribner explained, because times were bad. Doubtful that the book would earn anything, Marsh gave the copyright to the United States Sanitary Commission, a Civil War charity. But farsighted friends purchased it for $500 and presented it to the author.[32]

5

More than a thousand copies of *Man and Nature* were sold within a few months, and Scribner had to prepare a new printing. "The demand continues," he told Marsh; "I must confess I have been favorably disappointed." Reviewers found the book "a mine filled with attractive treasure"; "delightful" in method, style, and content, it inspired hope, directed intelligence, invigorated virtue. James Russell Lowell welcomed as a public benefaction a book "so interesting and instructive, which will lure the young to observe and take delight in Nature, and the mature to respect her rights as essential to their own well-being." Some reviewers thanked Marsh for pointing out the path of duty in resource husbandry; others, for refuting materialism by his demonstration of the superiority of mind over matter. Critics praised his memory—"he forgets nothing that he has ever read or observed"—his powers of observation, his sympathy for nature, his industry. One discerned in Marsh "the eye of a traveler, the heart of a poet, the intelligence of a philosopher, and the soul of a philanthropist." [33]

Some readers wished for "fewer facts and more philosophy," or objected to Marsh's "pessimism," but all agreed that "our American Evelyn" had made a unique and invaluable contribution. Favorably received by scientists as well as by the general public, *Man and Nature* went through several editions and sparked the national forestry movement. Within a decade it was an American classic with an international reputation. "One of the most useful . . . works ever published," declared a reviewer ten years later, *Man and Nature* had "come with the force of a revelation." [34]

Paradoxically, the effect of *Man and Nature* in some quarters was not to restrain but to rekindle optimism about resources. Misapplying Marsh's thesis, railroad promoters, speculators, and even some scientists claimed that afforestation would permanently increase precipitation in the Great Plains, and that rain would follow the plow.[35] The droughts of the 1880s and 1890s finally dispelled this illusion.

Marsh's major influence was far different. His warnings reinforced other portents of a timber famine. Together with the enthusiasm for tree-planting which swept the country in the Arbor Day movement, *Man and Nature* inaugurated a revolutionary reversal of American attitudes toward resources. It stimulated the American Association for the Advancement of Science to submit a memorial on forests to Congress in 1873; the outcome was a national forestry commission, the establishment of forest reserves and the national forest system in 1891, then watershed protection, eventually a government program for the conservation of all natural resources. A quarter of a century after Marsh's death, *Man and Nature* was still the only work in its field. It was last reprinted in 1907 (1885 edition), on the eve of the momentous White House Governors' Conference and Theodore Roosevelt's creation of a national conservation commission.

In Marsh's day every important figure in American forestry testified to the fundamental importance of *Man and Nature,* and sought out its author for advice. Franklin B. Hough, first United States Forestry Commissioner, boned up on *Man and Nature* before writing the significant A.A.A.S. 1873 memorial, credited Marsh with being the first to combat indiscriminate clearing of woods, and called upon him to direct the American forestry movement.[36] N. H. Egleston, Hough's successor as Forestry Commissioner, was outspoken in praise of Marsh's pioneer work, "to which, to more than any other source, perhaps, we are indebted for the awakening of our attention here to our destructive treatment of the forests, and the necessity of adopting a different course." Others spoke similarly: George B. Emerson, who thought *Man and Nature* "the best volume on its subject that has ever appeared"; Bernhard Fernow, the German-trained forester who succeeded Egleston; John A. Warder, president of the American Forestry Association; Charles Sprague Sargent, director of the Arnold Arboretum; I. A. Lapham and J. G. Knapp, of Wisconsin, who initiated one of the first state forestry movements. Geographers, too, paid homage to Marsh's work. The explorer Ferdinand V. Hayden considered Marsh "one of my ideal American scholars of the highest type" and carried "his splendid book . . . with me all over the Rocky Mountains." [37] Arnold Guyot, whose *Earth and Man* had inspired Marsh to fundamental disagreement, thanked Marsh for having taught him so much and hoped for "more of that kind of instruction which you know so well how to impart." Early in the twentieth century, William Morris Davis, dean of American geographers, praised the extraordinary breadth and quality of his endeavors.[38]

Marsh's influence was not limited to his home country. Even more rapidly than Americans, Europeans put his ideas to use. In France, Élisée Reclus gained insights from *Man and Nature* for his own great geographical work, *La Terre,* and corresponded with Marsh for years. In Italy, Boccardo, Bérenger, and other foresters found Marsh's work of inestimable value. From England, Charles Lyell wrote that Marsh had disproved his own theory that man's geological impact was one of the same order as that of brute animals. *Man and Nature* strengthened Brandis and other foresters who were trying to stem forest destruction in India. "I have carried your book with me along the slope of the Northern Himalaya, and into Kashmir and Tibet," wrote forest conservator Hugh Cleghorn.[39]

In the light of these testimonials, it is extraordinary that Gifford Pinchot, self-styled "father of conservation," who recognized *Man and Nature* as an "epoch-making" work, should have doubted that it had much influence. Even the modest Marsh thought it had had some effect. "Though it has taught little," he said of the book in 1881, "it has accomplished its end, which was to draw the attention of better-prepared observers to the several questions discussed in it." [40]

6

The first command addressed to man by his Creator . . . predicted and prescribed the subjugation of the entire organic and inorganic world to human control and use.

MARSH, The Camel (1856)

Marsh's geographical insight came from a divided mind. He conceived of nature as a unity; but his religious and philosophical outlook, a combination of Calvinism and romanticism, predisposed him to exalt the role of man in nature. Donne's famous words perfectly mirror Marsh's creed: "No man is an Iland, intire of it selfe; every man is a peece of the Continent, a part of the maine; if a Clod bee washed away by the Sea, Europe is the lesse, as well as if a Promontorie were." The reverberating intricacies of cause and effect obsessed Marsh; he was overwhelmed by the moral consequences of the realization that every action, even every thought, left an indelible mark in nature and in the mind of God. "Not a sod has been turned," he wrote, "not a mattock struck into the ground, without leaving its enduring record of the human toils and aspirations that accompanied the act. . . . Every turf is the monument of a hundred lives, and to our eye . . . the very earth of Europe seems decrepit and hoary." [41]

Geography he defined as "the science of the absolute and relative conditions of the earth's surface and of the ambient atmosphere [and] the investigation of the relations of action and re-action between man and the medium he inhabits." Alexander von Humboldt was his master. "As taught by [Humboldt] and his school," Marsh wrote, geography "is no longer a fortuitous assemblage of independent facts and quantities . . . its dry details have assumed an organic form and a human interest, and it has become at once a poetry and a philosophy." [42] Like many scientists of his day, Marsh abhorred the mechanistic rationalism of the preceding era. His own intellectual heritage—Vermont Transcendentalism—came from the seventeenth-century Cambridge Platonists, the German idealists, Coleridge, and Marsh's cousin, the philosopher James Marsh.

He nevertheless eschewed the teleology so characteristic of the new geography. Ritter's notion that the earth had been planned as the nursery of the human species, and Guyot's variations on this theme, displeased Marsh as science and offended him as religion. He sensed in their approach an environmental determinism that would ultimately reinforce the materialism of Buckle and Montesquieu. To account for God through the evidence of the material world seemed to him both imprudent and impious, the one because such proof was questionable, the other because God should be felt, not understood, by man. Science and religion were neither antagonistic nor complementary. "It is a poor Divinity," Marsh contended, "which rests its claims to godhead on the instincts of the beaver or the sagacity of the ant. . . . Spiritual religion must look elsewhere than to the natural world for its evidences; its authority is endangered, not by the revelations of science, but by that weakness of its advocates which appeals to lower and feebler grounds." [43] This passage was written a few months after the appearance of Darwin's *Origin of Species.*

Marsh's recognition of man's unique powers was based on philosophy as well as on observation. In 1829, James Marsh had argued that only their "peculiar powers"—not possessed by inferior, irrational animals—gave human beings free will. In like manner, a generation later, George Marsh affirmed that one of his principal aims was to show "that man is, in both kind and degree, a power of a higher order than any of the other forms of animated life." Objecting to "Man the Disturber of Nature's Harmonies," the title Marsh had first proposed for *Man and Nature,* Scribner asked:

"*Is* it true? Does not man act in harmony with nature? with her laws? is he not a part of nature?" "No," replied Marsh, "nothing is further from my belief that man is a 'part of nature' or that his action is controlled by what are called the laws of nature; in fact a leading object of the book is to enforce the opposite opinion, and to illustrate that man, so far from being, as Buckle supposes, a soulless, will-less automaton, is a free moral agent working independently of nature." [44] If man dug his own grave, it was not because fate willed it so.

Marsh's awareness that man transformed nature unconsciously as well as consciously did not lead him to believe, like some later conservationists and neo-Malthusians, that in the long run man's efforts to improve upon nature will boomerang. Marsh neither disdained nor despaired of civilization; he warned that its perpetuation depended upon continued human dominion over nature. This, in turn, required careful control and intelligent planning. Nature did not care whether man succeeded or failed.

Marsh had been infected with some romanticist follies—notably nationalism and racism—but he never became a primitivist, an admirer of the simple life. Unlike Thoreau, who loved nature but wished it kept wild, Marsh wanted it tamed; Thoreau appealed chiefly to aesthetic sensibility, Marsh to practicality. More at home in the woods than Rousseau or most of the Transcendentalists, Marsh had too keen an understanding of nature to see any ethical virtue in the wilderness or to make a fetish of forests. He rejected the primitivist plaint that "the progress of physical knowledge [had] promoted a materialistic and sensuous philosophy . . . tamed the imagination of the bard, vulgarized the phenomena of nature, and dispelled the poetry of common life." On the contrary, better knowledge of, and increased command over, nature had stimulated philosophical insight, ennobled landscape painting, and revived poetic imagery. "Wherever modern Science has exploded a superstitious fable or a picturesque error, she has replaced it with a grander and even more poetical truth." The poet Goethe and the traveler Forster had inspired the geographical studies of Humboldt, "the clearest exemplification of the connection between the progress of science and that of the fine arts." [45]

Marsh likewise refuted the charge that scholars engaged in "detecting the hidden powers and exploring the secret paths of Nature, in binding and loosing her mighty energies, and developing the inexhaustible resources she offers for improving the physical condition of man," were sensuous materialists. To be sure, "unlimited power and boundless knowledge do not necessarily imply moral perfection." But Marsh never supposed harnessing nature the ultimate goal; "our victories over the external world" were only "a vantage-ground to the conquest of the yet more formidable and not less hostile world that lies within." Could one contribute to the other? Indeed it could: "If our race is ever generally released from the restraints which physical necessities now impose upon it, and allowed the leisure and the repose which the mastering of the most exalted themes and the climbing of the loftiest summits of human thought require," it will be through mastery of the forces of nature. Science had "already virtually doubled the span of human life by multiplying our powers and abridging that portion of our days which the supply of our natural wants imperiously claims as its tribute." [46]

Toward the environmentalism of Buckle and Guyot, Marsh was as antagonistic as he was toward the romanticism of Rousseau and Ruskin. *Man and Nature* emphasized the catastrophic effects of man's efforts to bend nature to his will, but Marsh pointed out that human impact was sometimes unintentionally benign. For example, songbirds were rare in the virgin forest, but "find the most abundant nutriment, and the surest retreat . . . in the fields tilled by human husbandry." Even where the effects were less fortunate, Marsh did not conclude that man had better stop meddling entirely. He should make his meddling conscious and rational rather than thoughtless and destructive. Man turns the harmonies of nature to discords, the more so the more civilized he becomes; he must therefore create new harmonies! Like the Transcendentalists, Marsh emancipated man from the bonds of determinism; unlike them he asserted man's free will with respect to nature in unsentimental terms: "The life of man is a perpetual struggle with external Nature," he wrote; "it is by rebellion against her commands and the final subjugation of her forces alone that man can achieve the nobler ends of his creation. . . . Wherever he fails to make himself her master, he can but be her slave." If Marsh did not share Emerson's faith in nature's ultimate beneficence to man, neither did he accept the fatalism of those who later thought the close of the frontier doomed further progress. "The multiplying population and the impoverished resources of the globe," wrote Marsh, "demand new triumphs of mind over matter." [47]

To contrast Marsh's common-sense approach with the closed-space doctrines of some of his followers is to measure a real loss of understanding. A few have joined Marsh's belief in man's ability to transcend the environment with something of his concern about waste and improvidence. But most have entered the camps of extreme optimism or pessimism, where they have found emotion more serviceable than reason.[48]

How valid is *Man and Nature* today? An extraordinary testimonial to Marsh's pioneer work was offered in an international symposium on "Man's Role in Changing the Face of the Earth" held at Princeton in 1956, in which eighty scholars from a score of sciences engaged in a "Marsh Festival." After paying tribute to Marsh, the participants went on to discuss subjects Marsh had dealt with—each now a field in itself—as well as many others, such as man's impact on grasslands, man's role in the evolution of plants, the nature of culture and its relationship to environment, atomic energy, mineral depletion, and world population growth. In the field of conservation, Marsh's analysis of watershed problems remains essentially sound. Much more is known today, however, about the nature and distribution of the world's soils; ecology has also become more sophisticated since Marsh's day, notably through the study of biotic communities.[49] In the realm of ideas there has been less progress. War, depression, the advance of science, and the accelerated use of resources have made us conscious of the problems Marsh posed; but if we see more clearly than ever that man can destroy himself, we do not yet know how to forestall the destruction. Man's conquest of nature seems certain to continue, but Marsh recognized earlier than others that the triumph would be futile if man could not learn to control himself.

Marsh's constant attention to the interrelationships of all aspects of nature, his ability to deal with one problem without losing sight of others, and his skill in interweaving the most diverse testimony into clear and meaningful description and explanation—these qualities are in the great geographical tradition. He will be remembered for his masterful expositions of the round-robin character of natural resources, his comprehensive delineations of the symbiotic relations between man and his habitat, and his balanced consideration of social aims and physical needs, resources and responsibilities. Without neglecting details, he viewed problems in the large, which is the way they are posed in reality.

Some scientists who followed Marsh took his own word that he was not truly learned, merely a dabbler. Some who regard good writing as the sign of a popularizer and eclectic interests as the mark of a dilettante have underrated his contributions to knowledge. Far from invalidating his work, Marsh's conception of nature as a quasi-organic unity added a new dimension to scientific insight. He excelled in synthesis because he believed in it; the totality of nature rather than its constituent parts remained for him the fundamental reality.

This all-embracing perspective is difficult for scientists to work with even today. "The traditions of natural science," a modern geographer has pointed out, "are tied to instruments that yield elementary measurements"; scientists are apt to view with distrust or skepticism attempts to deal with diverse aspects of nature in combination. But the "difficulty of direct observation" of such matters as "the proportions between precipitation, superficial drainage, absorption, and evaporation" did not deter Marsh from studying their implications for humanity.[50] Whatever the gaps in our knowledge, synthesis is always essential; someone must undertake it. Marsh did.

❧XIV❧

Florence

WHEN *MAN AND NATURE* was finished, Marsh searched for something quite different to do. He quipped that he was taking refuge from Man and Nature in Woman and Artifice; without doubt, he had undergone a great catharsis. It was many years before he again undertook serious geographical work.

The social and political changes he observed at the close of the Civil War seemed to Marsh as alarming as the physical transformations he had described in his book. From the America of peace and Reconstruction he held ever more aloof, and began to look upon Italy as his permanent home. But home was no longer the solid Piedmontese capital to which Marsh had grown accustomed. Even in Italy time did not stand still; the sudden shift of the court from Turin to Florence presaged historic events.

I

Florence . . . is not to be compared to Turin. The climate is bad, the habits and morals of society detestable.

MARSH TO C. D. DRAKE, SEPT. 30, 1865

The change of capital was a part of the secret September Convention of 1864 between Italy and France. Napoleon III agreed to withdraw his garrison from Rome within two years; Italy guaranteed, in return, to protect papal territory from invasion and re-

volt. Napoleon tried to convince the Pope that if Italians transferred their capital to Florence they would not want to move it
again; but most Italians considered Florence a face-saving step toward Rome. France encouraged this belief. "You will eventually
go to Rome," wrote the French Minister in Turin, "but a sufficient
interval must elapse to save us from responsibility." [1]

Turin was shocked, however, that Victor Emmanuel had con-
sented to quit the ancient seat of the House of Savoy. Angry edi-
torials filled the Turin press, mass meetings protested the move and
threatened King and Ministry. Fearing a riot, royal troops fired on
the crowd: "the consequence of this weak and wicked mismanagement," Marsh reported, "was that between fifty and sixty unarmed
and peaceable citizens . . . were shot dead in the streets." The next
day the Minghetti cabinet resigned, and General Alphonso La Mar-
mora took over the shaky government. Formerly the mainstay
of the monarchy, the Piedmontese were bitterly alienated. "When it
leaves Piedmont," Marsh predicted, "the dynasty of Savoy slips the
cable of its sheet anchor." [2]

It was not the fate of the monarchy, however, that most concerned Marsh. Even if the 1864 Convention did presage acquisition of Rome, he feared Italy might lose more in concessions
than she would gain from unity. "The fascination of the King and
his leading advisors by the magic of the Empire is so complete,"
Marsh wrote Seward, that they would "submit to any humiliation
which Napoleon III may choose to inflict upon them." [3]

Meanwhile, Florence was invaded by government officials, fortune seekers, pickpockets and other riffraff. "The Florentines were
quite wild with joy" when they first heard their city was to have
the capital, Marsh reported, "but they are now pretty well sobered
down, and I think the wisest of them wish they had been spared the
honor which is vouchsafed to them." [4] Apartments were dear, food
cost thrice what it had before. For Marsh himself the move to
Florence was troublesome, and the State Department did not defray the heavy cost. Marsh found no house he could afford; for a

year he commuted uncomfortably between Turin and Florence. Eventually he rented the Villa Forini, a commodious dwelling outside the Porta alla Croce. This was to be his home, year-round at first, then summer, for the next seventeen years.

2

You have been uncharitable and unchristian like in condemning my motives to your poor unfortunate son that seemed cast off by yourself and the world.

MRS. M. BRAKELEY TO MARSH, MAY 14, 1865

Marsh had hoped to tide over the capital transfer by spending a few months in the United States. Lincoln's assassination left Washington in crisis, however, and Seward thought it unwise to grant the Minister's request for leave. But Marsh had just learned news so terrible "that the receipt of the secretary's letter was a relief to me." [5]

His son George had not done well in the Boston law office he entered after his recovery from typhoid in 1857. He drank more and more, and in fits of depression bitterly complained that his parents had neglected him. In May, 1862, he was drafted into the Union Army, but was discharged in August for "chronic hepatitis and general debility." Far gone in alcoholism (and perhaps tuberculosis), George lived in New York on a trust fund which his father doled out to him weekly. In his boarding house he was befriended by a Mrs. Brakeley. He told her "all his misfortunes from his early childhood," as she later wrote Marsh, "commencing at the death of his mother. He had longed for the affection that only a mother could feel but that great blessing had been denied him, as a child he was deformed and sickly and very unattractive and as a man he was no better." Early in February, 1865, he had a hemorrhage, and died on the seventeenth. "After severe invectives against yourself and all his friends," Marsh's lawyer wrote him, "he leaves all his property to a Mrs. *Brakeley*." [6]

Was Marsh to blame for his son's tragic life? "We all know the ardent love he cherished for his poor boy," wrote his sister-in-law, "and the affection with which he followed him under the most discouraging circumstances." Friends assured Marsh that they knew George's "unnatural exhibitions of ill-feeling towards yourself and Mrs. Marsh [to be] the misfortunes of a mind diseased." Marsh could never convince himself, however, that he was entirely guiltless, that there was no germ of truth in George's monomania, that he could not have helped him at some crucial point. George did have some cause to feel neglected. After his early childhood with grandparents in Woodstock, he had been brought up by a busy and demanding father and a kind but invalid stepmother. Most of Marsh's solicitude was for Caroline and her health; George was more or less ignored. Emotionally the situation was not an easy one, and Marsh's high expectations for his son made it no easier. With Caroline, George at first had a warmer relationship. But after his typhoid attack she felt that his outbursts were too much for Marsh to bear; she was glad when George left home. "Till he has more reason and more self-control," she explained, "we can do him no good, and he can be no comfort to us." [7] There were some better times; George occasionally showed affection for his father and offered to help him in political or literary work, and Marsh wrote his son frequently, in a pleasant tone though usually not about personal matters. But he never found anything for George to do, nor trusted him with any business affairs. The two had drifted apart even before Marsh left for Europe and George for the Army, his eventual collapse, and his final illness.

George's vindictive will was an added blow. Marsh expressed his grief in rage against Mrs. Brakeley; he insisted on contesting the will. Hurt by Marsh's accusations, she rejected the bequest and wrote him a long letter describing how his son had died. If George had been wrong "in believing that he had been unjustly dealt with," she told him, "it was not the fault of the heart but the head." [8]

For weeks after George's death, Marsh could hardly eat or sleep;

his eyes again failed him, and for a long time he could do no work. Small wonder that he no longer wanted to go home. "The scenes I should be obliged to revisit," he confessed, "are too full of the graves of disappointed hopes, for me to feel strength enough to return among them." Friends repeatedly urged him to return, but he always had some excuse—ill-health, lack of time, fear of the ocean voyage. Caroline went back once, alone, in 1869; but her easy trip did not diminish Marsh's reluctance. "The accomplishing of a voyage to America and back, and then of a final return to the U S, seems to me to require the performance of 3 miracles." He really did not want ever to leave Italy. "In this climate," he explained, "my chances of life are double what they would be at home. . . . For an old man and a solitary, life is more enjoyable and fruitful here than in America." Marsh shunned the social as well as the physical climate of New England; "in Vermont I should never retain the elasticity that is as necessary to usefulness as to enjoyment." [9]

Having decided not to go, Marsh wanted to make sure that he would not be *sent* home. Many were clamoring for diplomatic appointments; Lincoln had to be convinced all over again that Marsh was the best man for the job. Energetic on his uncle's behalf even before the 1864 election, George F. Edmunds assured Marsh the following spring that his post was still secure.

This assurance vanished with Lincoln's assassination. Marsh had known President Johnson in Congress, thought him sincere and honest even when they had disagreed. But there were many political demands on the President, and Marsh would not have been "thunderstruck" had he been supplanted. However, by July, 1866, Edmunds was able to tell Marsh that his post was safe until the next election. [10] Of Lincoln's other original diplomatic appointees, only four remained in office.

Marsh was so firmly established in the legation in Italy that Grant's accession to the Presidency in 1869 caused him little worry. Vermont's Congressional delegation again insisted upon his continuance as Minister, "as much for the honor of the whole country

. . . as for that of our State." Three days after his inaugural Grant told Charles Sumner that "I do not propose to make any change in Italy, though the pressure for the place by half a dozen people is awful." [11] He replaced every other envoy in Europe save Bancroft, who stayed on in Berlin until 1874. In eight years Marsh had become a diplomatic fixture. As long as Edmunds remained in the Senate and a Republican in the White House, it seemed that Marsh might remain in Italy.

3

The great statesmen who brought about Italian independence have per-ished untimely, and their survivors have been displaying in these latter days enthusiasm rather than judgment, zeal rather than knowledge, the virtues of agitators and dreamers rather than those of soldiers and politicians.

E. L. GODKIN, "THE POPE AND CATHOLIC NATIONS," *Nation,* NOV. 7, 1867

The Italy in which Marsh had elected to stay confronted difficult tasks and grave vicissitudes. Piedmont had progressed, but else-where, especially in the south, industry was lacking, agriculture primitive, disease rampant, isolation crippling. Most of the country was still held by great landlords, lay and ecclesiastic. When the gov-ernment confiscated the monastic estates Marsh predicted that "aris-tocratic privilege and priestly power will [soon] fall to the ground together." He was too sanguine. The Church deterred tenants from buying land, and most small farmers lacked the necessary cash. Marsh blamed the failure of land reform both on "apathy in the Italian public, and want of moral courage and sense of duty in Italian statesmen." [12]

Bedeviled by domestic embarrassments, French interference, and Austrian and papal threats, Italian statesmen had little opportunity to be firm or sensible. Ministries changed "as often as the moon"; there were thirteen cabinets in the first ten years, all, Marsh re-ported, "so entirely occupied with keeping themselves and their seats well balanced, that they have no time to think of anything else." The government assumed all provincial debts and spent huge sums on a modern navy and a large army, befitting Italy's role as a modern nation; large loans were floated to meet these extravagances. By 1866 the financial situation was so desperate that a ruthless tax program had to be adopted, increasing the government's unpopularity. Worst was the *macinato,* a "highly impolitic, unjust and offensive" impost on flour and meal, "its object being," Marsh remarked sarcastically, "to spare the rich by extorting a contribution from those who have no property to tax." [13]

The domestic scene was depressing in other respects. With poverty went lawlessness. Marsh witnessed murder, theft, and other violence during a week of carnival in Milan which left hundreds in the hospitals. Italians were "the gentlest, kindest, most sympathetic nation in Europe," but, he commented, "they have a way of trifling with knives and sticking each other in tender places, which might seem odd to a stranger." Domestic law and order were no more popular than foreign tyranny had been. The tax collector and the policeman were universally hated; the public regarded even confessed murderers as victims of state coercion. The problem of crime, Marsh discerned, was less one of law than of social attitudes. The Italian people "practically regard robbery and assassination as natural calamities, acts of God, which no more concern the public, or call for preventive or punitive action on its part, than the death of a citizen from a stroke of lightning." [14]

These defects notwithstanding, after a decade Marsh still retained faith in Italy's future. Commerce was growing, manufactures reviving, education increasing. If the government would move as rapidly as Marsh thought the people were ready to, all would be well. To be sure, under the highly restricted suffrage parliament neither represented nor responded to public opinion. But Marsh still saw the people, like the landscape, through rose-colored glasses.

Incompetence in foreign affairs paralleled Italian domestic deficiencies. After the 1864 Convention came an alliance with Prussia, war against Austria, defeats at Custozza and Lissa. Nevertheless,

Austria, beaten by Prussia, ceded Venetia to Napoleon III, who turned it over to Italy.

No sooner was Venice acquired than Italians began to dream again of their main goal; the date set for French evacuation of Rome was drawing near. Excitement mounted; late in 1867 Garibaldi again marched on Rome. The Italian government stood aside, but papal troops defeated Garibaldi at Mentana. Arrested finally by the government, he called on the American Legation for protection; and Marsh hurried back from a Swiss sanatorium, where he had been trying to cure his rheumatism, to intercede with Menabrea and Rattazzi. Marsh prudently refused to accept Garibaldi's claim to American citizenship, and thus prevented the aging general from renouncing Italy, which might have had serious consequences. But thanks in part to Marsh's pleading, Garibaldi was released to return to Caprera. "I shall remember all my life, with gratitude," wrote Garibaldi, "your generous and courteous solicitude for me in troubled times." [15]

Incensed by Garibaldi's violation of the September Convention, Napoleon garrisoned Rome anew. As in the case of Venice, however, luck was with Italy. The Franco-Prussian war broke out in 1870, the French army withdrew from Rome, and in September Napoleon was overthrown. The fall of France resolved the Roman question at last. Italian troops marched into Rome; the Risorgimento was complete. If Italy could only "free herself," Marsh wrote, "from the Old Man of the Sea, who had ridden her for so many centuries, there is no reason why she may not be strong and prosperous." But the government offered the Pope what Marsh considered "humiliating" concessions, including Vatican City, which preserved the principle of Catholic temporal power. The only obstacles to secular autonomy, Marsh decided, were those "the weakness of the Italian government has created." [16] He still supposed that the people were more anticlerical than the government.

Rome was finally to be the capital, but there was plenty of attendant confusion. "We Italians have got Rome at last," wrote

Marsh, "but 'tis a large elephant, and a hungry. What shall we do with it?" [17]

4

Once the Civil War was over, Italo-American relations took a more prosaic tack. Problems of trade, tariffs, and tourism were uppermost, though a few echoes of the conflict still sounded. Marsh demanded the extradition of John H. Surratt, implicated in Lincoln's assassination. Surratt had fled America, enlisted in the papal Zouaves, been recognized, escaped, and was caught in the Alps. The humane Italians refused to yield him, however, unless Marsh guaranteed that Surratt would not be executed. While the Minister was arguing the point, Surratt escaped again.[18] Marsh was more successful in other matters. He squelched Italian support for French imperialism in Mexico. And he helped select Senate President Sclopis as an arbiter to determine how much Britain owed the United States in the *Alabama* claims case. Sclopis became president of the tribunal—a good choice from the American point of view.

Marsh's ordinary diplomatic work remained unexciting, even humdrum. The most tedious negotiation he ever carried on was for a treaty of commerce and navigation with Italy. In May, 1864, he called Seward's attention to the need for such a treaty. "Your known sagacity and your familiarity with the subject," replied Seward, "afford a sufficient guaranty that the conduct of the negotiation . . . may safely be left to your discretion." Difficulties proved endless, delays paralyzing. Italian duties were low and most American goods entered almost free. But United States duties changed suddenly and capriciously; many Italian goods were virtually excluded by high tariffs. Menabrea felt that the new treaty should compensate Italy for this discrimination; Marsh proposed various modifications. Not until 1871 did he and Sella work out a compromise. The treaty was ratified seven years after it had been proposed.[19]

Trade between the two countries nevertheless remained insignificant. In 1881 it amounted to $11 million worth of Italian goods —chiefly oranges and lemons, sulfur, marble, and straw hats—and $12 million from the United States—largely petroleum, cotton, and tobacco. The United States took only 8 percent of Italy's foreign commerce; Italy, less than 2 percent of America's. In a late dispatch, Marsh explained why trade remained stagnant. "The United States and Italy are, in most respects, geographical parallels to each other"; hence neither country needed the other's wares. Furthermore, "the financial systems of the two countries"—internal taxes in Italy and high tariffs in America—"oppose still more formidable obstacles to any considerable extension of trade between them." Marsh judged that trade was more likely to decrease than increase. His efforts to encourage investments in Italy likewise met disappointment. "Italy offers a wide field for American enterprise," he wrote a prospective investor, quoting an eminent stateman who hoped that Italy would be "invaded by Americans and Englishmen." [20] But Americans found more profitable fields to exploit elsewhere, and Italo-American commerce continued to stagnate.

More important than the trade agreement were the immigration and naturalization arrangements Marsh made in 1868. The United States regularized immigration with all European countries in the late 1860s, but Italy posed special problems. When Italians who returned after some years in America were conscripted by Italy, they often turned for help to Marsh, who was required by law to "make a peremptory demand for the release of any American citizen unlawfully detained abroad." To avoid conflict Marsh usually tried to effect "the *quiet withdrawal of the party into a foreign jurisdiction.*" Marsh also had to cope with bogus passports issued to Italians after the uprisings of 1848–49 and with fraudulent naturalizations. Thousands reaped the benefits of citizenship in both countries, without obeying the laws or paying the taxes of either.[21] After Marsh's work, however, such nuisances decreased considerably.

The number of bona fide Italian immigrants mounted meanwhile, owing to the demand for cheap labor on transcontinental railroads.

From around a thousand a year before 1860, the number of migrants approached three thousand annually soon after the Civil War. Some complained of their treatment in America, but immigration rose to almost nine thousand in the year 1873. The New York Emigration Commission at length objected that too many Italians were dependent on public charity. Importuned from both sides of the Atlantic, Marsh had a warning published in Italian papers in 1873: "The severity of the winter climate," he wrote, "causes the suspension of . . . out-door labor for a considerable period." Immigrants might not immediately find work; "the representations of Emigration Agents are not implicitly to be depended upon," stated the Minister with characteristic irony.[22] Italians then accounted for only .4 percent of all foreign-born in the United States. After 1879, however, departures to America increased steeply; in 1896 more Italian immigrants arrived than any other.

Marsh also carried on scores of minor negotiations. He concluded consular, postal, and telegraphic conventions. Between 1864 and 1870, when Italy took back Spezia for her own naval base, he vainly sought a substitute anchorage for the U. S. Navy. He wangled permission for the Smithsonian Institution to send its publications to Italy duty free—no easy job, for "your Italian is ticklish in the purse": Italy wanted the Smithsonian to pay freight both ways and "give everybody a small present . . . besides."[23]

Far more disagreeable to handle were the complaints of American travelers. As the number of Americans in Italy increased—in 1873 Marsh estimated there were a hundred permanent residents and four thousand transients who spent from a week to a month in Rome—irritating incidents multiplied. Those that concerned religious freedom Marsh took seriously, though even on this subject the Minister was careful not to offend Italy. But he considered most of the faultfinding either groundless or malicious. There were indigent American ladies who floated into Florence and Rome with unfounded tales of Italian police tortures; Marsh had to ship these eccentrics back home, sometimes at his own expense. Italian widows, wives, and mistresses of Americans haunted the legation, each one believing "American officials to be bound to support her if her husband fails to do so." Spirited American girls who would "have the Romans know that a Yankee girl can do anything she pleases, walk alone, ride her horse alone, and laugh at their rules" created infinite problems; Henry James's portrayal of their "foolish simplicity" in *Daisy Miller* reminded Marsh of the scrapes he had had to rescue them from. Young Preston Powers, Hiram's son, wanted Marsh to protect his fiancée from her father's whippings, and could not understand why the "somewhat rigid rules of official propriety" prevented Marsh from interfering in Italian family affairs. And one American woman appealed for revenge after she was arrested for publicly insulting the King and declaring her loyalty to the Pope; the State Department agreed with Marsh that she deserved no support.[24]

Marsh did not always find Italy blameless. Her customs service, for example, was notoriously corrupt. On one occasion, customs officers confiscated all tobacco on an American brig—including the plugs the sailors were chewing. Marsh forced Italy to back down in "a vague and grudging" way—"one of the very few cases," he noted, "in which the Government of Italy is known to have disapproved of wrongs or abuses committed by its subordinates against foreigners." His usual role, however, was to defend Italy against his importunate fellow citizens. Disappointed petitioners often criticized the Minister roundly when they returned home. They did not understand his solicitude for young Italy, or share his lively "interest in her emancipation from spiritual thraldom as well as in her moral and material progress." [25]

Such solicitude so endeared Marsh to Italy that he survived without discredit the most embarrassing episode of his diplomatic career: one of his most confidential dispatches was published in the 1870 volume of U. S. *Foreign Relations*. In this dispatch Marsh had charged the Italian Ministry with being "so constantly in the habit

of blindly following the dictation of the Emperor of France" that
it had only been "forced by the fear of popular violence" to occupy
Rome. "Its future course in this matter," he predicted, "will be
characterized by vacillation, tergiversation and duplicity, as it has
always been since 1864." The State Department later claimed that
the disclosure was "accidental," but this section of the dispatch was
in cipher. Marsh suspected that it had been published "with the
malicious object of making the Legation in Italy untenable any
longer by its writer." He was dressing to dine with the Minister of
Foreign Affairs when a servant gave him the newspaper with his
dispatch in it. "He almost fainted," recalled an aide, "on reading
this indiscreet divulgation and in the thought that in a few minutes
he would have to face and receive the hospitality of the very men
he had so severely handled." But instead of snubbing him, the
Italians took pains to make Marsh feel at ease; Foreign Minister
Visconti-Venosta was "more gracious than ever"; Ricasoli crossed
the room "to salute Mr. M. in a marked manner." [26] No one bore
him resentment.

Only the high personal regard in which the Foreign Office and
the court held Marsh, other observers confirmed, prevented his recall. Marsh's fellow diplomats, whom he served as dean and spokesman for so many years, also valued him highly. "It is truly consol-
ing," wrote Garibaldi, "to hear an authoritative voice rising from
the very midst of that Diplomacy which seems to busy itself with
the affairs of nations only to involve them in a labyrinth of decep-
tion and despair." Comparing Marsh with other American diplomats of his time, a colleague judged that "as a representative of our
country abroad, no one, not even Lowell, has stood for it so nobly
and unselfishly; Charles Francis Adams alone rivalling him in the
seriousness with which he gave himself to the Republic. Lowell
was not less patriotic, but he loved society . . . Marsh in those days
of trial loved nothing but his country, and with an intensity that
was as ill-requited as it was immeasurable." [27]

5

I have never feared the war, *but from the beginning, I have dreaded a* peace *which should involve the sacrifice of what it has cost in so many lives, so much treasure, to win.*

MARSH TO CHARLES SUMNER, APRIL 15, 1865

Reconstruction in America brought as many problems as unification in Italy, and Marsh was no less critical of his own government. While "the determination of the President and the administration to maintain slavery at all hazards" had marred Northern conduct of the Civil War, "the constant assertion . . . of the doctrine of the imperishability of State rights" was responsible, in Marsh's view, for most of the evils of the Reconstruction era. To combat the idea of state sovereignty he wrote a series of articles in 1865 for E. L. Godkin's new weekly, the *Nation*. Marsh maintained that since the "people," not the states, had created the Union, the states had no sovereignty whatever; when they rebelled, they ceased to exist as states, and became Federal territory.[28] Thus the Union had legal authority to do whatever it wished with the South.

Marsh's severity against the South brought him close to Radical Republicans of the most vindictive stamp; Charles Sumner was his *beau ideal*. Marsh regretted that the chief Confederate leaders had not been hanged. "If such wretches as Davis and Toombs & Wise & Lee & Forrest & Mosby are to be pardoned and welcomed back with open arms," he wrote his colleague, John Bigelow, "I am for opening all our penitentiary doors and pensioning & promoting the inmates. All this is an exhibition of that weak sympathy with criminals, which is one of the strongest proofs of the demoralization of the age." Marsh advocated Negro suffrage, since "we must come to that at last, and it is quite as well to come to it gracefully, and at once."[29] He wanted, above all, to make sure that former Southern slaveholders never would be able to take power again.

As the years passed, however, Marsh took less and less interest in

American affairs. Disappointed by Johnson's softness toward the South, he acquiesced in Grant's nomination as a political necessity, but thought ill of him. The scandals and corruption of the Grant Administration left Marsh with little hope for his homeland, which seemed to him mired in materialism. High diplomatic posts went more and more to moneyed men. "The effect of this narrow policy," Marsh predicted, "will soon be to confine the diplomatic service to the rich, and thus to strengthen the aristocracy of wealth . . . which is so fast becoming a threatening evil in our American life." [30]

Marsh's state sovereignty articles began a long and valuable association with the *Nation,* for which he wrote extensively on scores of subjects. (To protect his diplomatic position he frequently used the pen name "Viator.") He felt well fitted for this sort of work, "not to teach—I disclaim that—but to stir up people to teach themselves more than I know, and in that way, I do *some* good." Sharing Godkin's liberal political and social outlook, he thought the *Nation* the most promising new feature of American life. When Godkin considered accepting a history professorship at Harvard, Marsh wrote him that he was indispensable as editor: "History can afford to wait, the policy and political morality of our day cannot." [31]

Marsh's weightiest contribution to the *Nation* was a series of "Notes on the New Edition of Webster's Dictionary." This did "not interest the multitude as much as it ought," wrote Godkin, "but I know the best of our readers follow it with great satisfaction." One reader, James Russell Lowell, complained that Marsh "does not get under way quite rapidly enough for a newspaper," and objected to Marsh's "Congregational" style. "But all he says," added Lowell, "is worth reading for its matter." [32]

Most of Marsh's other *Nation* articles were brief and pithy. He discussed "The Proposed Revision of the English Bible" (a "very valuable . . . widely read" article, according to Godkin); promoted the Early English Text Society of London; reviewed "Boccardo's *Dictionary of Political Economy"*; wrote on "Pruning Forest Trees,"

"The Education of Women," "Agriculture in Italy," "The Aqueducts of Ancient Rome," "'Protection of Naturalized Citizens,'" "The Catholic Church and Modern Civilization," "The Excommunication of Noxious Animals by the Catholic Church," and "Monumental Honors," a satire against pro-Southern statesmen. In another satirical piece, "A Cheap and Easy Way to Fame," Marsh poked fun at biographical dictionaries which offered immortality at stiff prices. "If I can't go down to posterity on cheaper terms than these," wrote Marsh, "I'll stay here!" [33]

In "Physical Science in Italy," an extended review of Boccardo's *Fisica del Globo,* Marsh discussed the proliferation of the sciences and pleaded for breadth of learning. Specialization was necessary, but not all should specialize. Marsh thought it better "to taste a variety of scientific and literary viands than to confine ourselves to a single dish of stronger meat." [34] The *Nation* articles are good evidence that Marsh practiced what he preached.

As always, Marsh concerned himself with his friends' projects. "The hardest work in the world is *our* work," he explained; "the easiest, other people's." He contributed notes on a few words to the revived *New English Dictionary.* He furthered the research of the Columbus scholar Henry Harrisse. The Senate commissioned him to "report on the practicability of the substitution of the Phonetic for the Latin alphabet." He supported the cause of the historian John Lothrop Motley, who had been summarily dismissed as envoy to Holland. For American educators he collected statistics on deaf-mutes in Italy. He advised Henry C. Lea on his *History of the Inquisition*—a subject which greatly interested Marsh—and arranged for a young Harvard-trained scholar, Franklin P. Nash, to do the necessary archival research in Italy. [35]

Through *Man and Nature* Marsh became acquainted with the British geographer Henry Yule, who lived in Sicily from 1863 to 1875 while preparing his definitive edition of Marco Polo. Marsh and Yule exchanged scores of letters, discussing word origins, Eurasian culture contacts, forestry in India, international politics, and the health of their invalid wives. Yule once expressed concern that this generous correspondence was taking time from Marsh's official duties. "I am grown too lazy to work," the American Minister replied, "or to follow any consecutive study, & I would rather spend three hours in running down a word or looking up an idle question than in writing the best despatch ever penned by diplomate." [36] Marsh's own "scientific" interest at this time was right-handedness among American Indians. Settled and happy in Florence, he could afford to be frivolous for a change.

6

Florence is a mighty fine museum and a mighty poor residence. Vile climate, detestably corrupt society, infinite frivolity, servant's hall of Tophet. MARSH TO SPENCER BAIRD, AUG. 2, 1865

In his own home the Minister was well equipped to cope with the demands of Florentine life. The Marshes lived in a roomy, comfortable, odd-angled fifteenth-century villa in the open plain of the Arno. Surrounded by hedges of laurel and bay, gardens of wide-spreading magnolias, and thickets of laburnum and acacia, the Villa Forini boasted massive portals, long, narrow passageways, slippery scagliola, great stone staircases, and bulky furniture in the irregularly shaped rooms. In the largest of these the Minister installed his books. He had sent for the volumes stored in Vermont, so that most of his library was at last together in one place.

At the Villa Forini the Marshes gathered around them an Anglo-American circle of distinction: Hiram Powers, Isaac E. Craig, Joel T. Hart, John Adams Jackson, and other well-known artists; T. Adolphus Trollope, James Lorimer Graham (who became U. S. Consul-General in 1869), journalist Jesse White Mario, and many more. The permanent residents in Rome were no problem compared to the press of visitors from America. Caroline gave weekly receptions and innumerable formal dinners, but there was not nearly enough time or energy to take care of everyone. Many old friends came to see them: Admiral Goldsborough, William Cullen Bryant, Caroline Paine in 1866; Justin Morrill and Bayard Taylor in 1867; Bancroft, Motley, and Taylor all together in the spring of 1868, along with Willard Fiske and G. P. A. Healy; Asa Gray, Charles Eliot Norton, and Manning Force, the following year. Admiral Farragut left an excellent impression, McClellan a poor one; Seward, alas, arrived in Florence in July, and found "no one" in town. Marsh made new British friends: Matthew Arnold introduced the journalist Grant Duff, who was delighted with the American Minister; he met Augustus Hare, writer of travel guides, and the historian Lord Acton. Introduced to George Eliot and G. H. Lewes, he was not at all prejudiced by Trollope's warning that their relationship was not "normal." [37]

Court festivities were virtually continuous; the marriage of Prince Umberto to his cousin Princess Margherita at Turin in 1868 was the most strenuous merrymaking of all. When Marsh returned to the villa, the flying squirrels he had asked Baird to send for the royal couple had arrived. "What a foolish habit they have," remarked the Minister, "of sleeping all day and capering all night. Well, that's the way princes do." [38]

The Marshes could never have borne all these social demands but for Caroline's improved health. On the advice of Dr. Elizabeth Blackwell, Marsh took her to Paris in 1865 to consult the famous gynecologist Dr. J. Marion Sims. Sims found that Caroline had a noncancerous tumor of the womb and operated successfully. "If she could or would hold still two months," wrote Marsh, "she would be as good as cured." [39] Caroline never regained full strength, but did get about from then on without difficulty.

Marsh himself was less well. "The sorrows of the past year," he wrote after his son's death, "have made me suddenly an old man." Rheumatic attacks forced him to spend every summer at spas— Lucca, Monsummano, Divonne-les-Bains, Bad Gastein, Wildbad,

Aix-les-Bains. Warm salt baths, vapors, drugs, exercise, rest—all had
no effect; Marsh regarded himself as a hopeless case. "My medical
advisors are trying to cheer me with fair words," he wrote, "but I
know, from their prescriptions, that they think me an ugly cus-
tomer. Think of swallowing strychnine in heroic doses, and friction
—*hard* friction, with bella-donna!" [40] What was sadder, he was
kept from his beloved Alps, and almost died of boredom in dull
resort towns.

The most serious bout came in 1871 in Strasbourg. "The Dr. has
prevented me from rushing, or rather tumbling into the street,"
scrawled Marsh with his rheumatic hand, "and running amuck
among the Strassburgers, only by keeping me constantly stupefied
by subcutaneous injections of morphine." To make matters worse,
a vein had burst in his right eye; his oculist tabooed "all reading
and writing, now and hereafter." But Marsh committed *"felo de
me,* or at least *oculis,"* by reading and writing as much as ever. His
disgust with these "scarecrows," who "begin all their counsels with:
Fee, faw, fum! To blindness you'll come! [and] wouldn't even let
me revile the wicked, for fear of bursting a blood vessel inside the
eye," was apparently justified. A new oculist, Dr. Meurer, of Co-
blenz, restored his vision in 1873. "Since I have seen Dr. Meurer,"
Marsh wrote in glee, "I do nothing but curse bankers . . . and
booksellers all day long, and am neither sick nor sorry afterwards." [41]

Though he was much improved, Marsh rallied slowly from a
typhoid attack in 1872. Deprived of exercise, he put on weight rapidly; dieting was of no avail, and he feared that he would "soon
outweigh the colossal Bohemian girl now on exhibition with a
singing fish." [42] His hair and beard had become white; in his early
seventies, he was well on the way to old age. But he still had reserves of strength, and his mind and memory were unimpaired.

7

I do not like Rome the better for becoming the capital of Italy. It is to me materially as detestable as it is morally, and I think a cataclysm, which should sweep it into the abyss, would be no evil!

MARSH TO C. D. DRAKE, MAY 8, 1871

Marsh's objections to Rome as a residence were more severe than his first strictures against Florence had been. The vexations of moving made him see new residences in the worst possible light, and he rarely realized how much he liked a place until he had to leave it. With Rome, "a capital in the center of a desert 50 miles square," he had grounds for dissatisfaction. The physical disadvantages were serious; it was hot, crowded, "filthy, fetid, infectious," and the government remedied these conditions but slowly. Like the earlier transfer of the capital to Florence, the new move was unsettling for the local population. Into Rome poured many thousands of northern Italians—speculators, contractors, demagogues, merchants, beggars. And all the difficulties of the government were magnified in this new Italian melting pot.[43]

For Marsh the move was financially ruinous. "The change from Turin to Florence," he recalled, "cost us a sacrifice equal to a quarter's salary." The removal to Rome cost still more. Not until 1872 could Marsh find a "tolerable apartment" in the Casa Lovatti, Via San Basilio, but it cost him $1,000 a quarter. A Congressional grant of $6,000 "to defray the extraordinary expenses" of the two capital moves was lost in the bank failure of 1873 before Marsh ever laid hands on it.[44]

As the years passed, Marsh's fears of penury intensified. He was not miserly, but all his letters proclaim his need for parsimony. Rome was his last stand; with old age staring him in the face, he felt more keenly his inability to provide for retirement and for Caroline after his death.

❧ X V ❧

Rome

THE YEARS PASSED tranquilly under Roman skies. Changes were no longer abrupt, exciting, militant. In America, Republican President followed Republican President; in Italy, Victor Emmanuel and Pius IX gave way to new kings and popes. But the aging American Minister to Italy stayed on, by now an almost legendary figure.

With the material Rome, Marsh made peace; with the spiritual, never. Dwelling in the bastion of Catholicism, he became once more the iconoclast assailant of ecclesiastical authority. In these last years of strength he turned again to nature, revising his greatest work, guiding the efforts of others, rekindling his pleasure in mountain and forest, stream and sky. Nature helped compensate for the disappointments Marsh felt he had endured—disappointments which obscured and corroded pride in jobs well done, praise well merited, and peace well won.

I

The Europeans don't really understand how a government purely of law can operate. A government which is never arbitrary or violent, is in their view not really a government but only a quaker committee.
MARSH TO WILLIAM T. SHERMAN, MARCH 22, 1877

There was little cheer to be found in Italian affairs. Marsh's dispatches reflected his pessimism. Venice and Rome gained, Italy was at last independent; yet poverty and lawlessness proliferated. Natural calamities were partly to blame. Torrents ravaged the Po plain in 1872; in other years frost, hail, drought, floods, volcanic eruptions, grape disease, and silkworm blight left Italian peasants "more abjectly wretched" than any others in Europe. Debts, large standing armies, and other extraordinary expenses gave rise to oppressive taxes, eliciting ominous mutterings of revolt.

Mainly responsible for Italy's impoverishment, Marsh decided, were the conservative ministries, now indecisive, now arbitrary, that had so long controlled Parliament. When the liberals came to power in 1876 promising lower taxes, broader suffrage, and state aid to education, Marsh hailed their victory and anticipated early relief for the poor. The deaths in 1878 of both Victor Emmanuel and Pio Nono marked the end of an era. Marsh judged that the new king, Umberto, had "all his father's good qualities and appears to be free from all his bad ones." [1]

The period of hope was brief, however. Umberto celebrated his inauguration with a general amnesty "which turned loose upon society a large number of the most depraved and dangerous inmates of the prisons" and further undermined law and order. The Liberal ministry proved weak and vacillating. Marsh despised the opportunistic premier, Depretis, as a man of "habitual indecision, procrastination and inaction." [2] The government's economic and social programs were ineffective. Abolition of the *macinato* did not lower the price of bread, but simply swelled the profits of millers and bakers. State monopolies and high tariffs made it harder than ever for the poor to obtain the necessities of life.

To be sure, electoral reforms added several hundred thousand new voters to the rolls, and the cabinet did its best to make schooling available to all. But Marsh no longer believed education was a panacea. "The most demoralized and dangerous of the lower classes," he observed, "are not to be found among the totally uninstructed so often as among those who have received that half-education which is all that those classes can aspire to." [3]

The root of the problem, Marsh supposed, was the inequalities of

Italian society, the gulf between rich and poor. Italy was still remote
from rational capitalism. Instead of being invested in industry and
commerce, "the superfluous means of the rich are often absorbed by
a horde of undeserving retainers." Sloth and superstition were
widespread. The government restored *festas*, "days of idleness and
vice," Marsh called them; the Roman carnival of 1881 was "more
costly and more brutal than any for the last 30 years." He was
dismayed to find many Italians "weary of self-government," and
even suspected a plot to return Rome to the papacy "and plunge
Europe again into the miseries attending the Religious Wars." [4]

Not Italy alone, but all Europe, Marsh feared, was "relapsing into
Medieval barbarism." War threatened in 1876 in the Balkans and
Constantinople. This time Marsh found little to choose between the
belligerents; "Satan's house is divided against itself." "The Turks
ought to be driven out of Europe," he wrote, "but when we ask:
what better have we to put in their place? it is *not* easy to find a
satisfactory answer." (Apprehensive lest riots "endanger the lives
and properties of all foreign residents in Turkey," he urged Secretary of State Hamilton Fish to make "a display of at least moral
force"; Fish took the necessary steps.) [5]

World history had reached its nadir, Marsh thought. "In the
worst periods of the French Revolution & Bonapartean Wars, men
may have seen a sky as lurid as ours of today, but there were then
some bright spots," he wrote in 1878. "Now . . . there are only degrees of darkness in the general pitchiness." The early 1880s seemed
to him "to threaten more serious evils to the cause of modern
civilization" than any previous crisis. In one of his last dispatches,
the aged Minister wrote that he had "never seen the political horizon of Europe in so disturbed and so menacing a state." [6]

2

In view of his morose outlook on international affairs, it was
perhaps fortunate that Marsh's regular diplomatic duties had become lighter. Consular and commercial treaties still had to be tidied

up, but few matters of moment called for much labor by the Minister, and Italian-American relations remained friendly and undisturbed. Petty duties he delegated more and more to subordinates. Consequently, Marsh could leave Rome in the oppressive heat of summer, using the Villa Forini at Florence as a retreat or as a base for mountain excursions. Even in the winter he rarely spent over two hours a day in the legation. When there was more work, he did it at home, or in evening conferences with Italian officials.

This degree of leisure was made possible principally by George Washington Wurts, of Philadelphia, who arrived in Florence in 1865 highly recommended as "a young gentleman of fortune" and ambition. Appointed unpaid attaché, Wurts promptly became indispensable. A dapper bachelor, Wurts was snobbish and elegant— he had two dozen pairs of gloves and a dinner service of solid gold. But he was cultivated, hard-working, intensely loyal, and he idolized the Marshes.

In 1868 President Johnson appointed as Secretary of Legation the Rev. Henry P. Hay, "DD., LL.D., and M.D.," of Tennessee. The gauche, bumptious Hay was *"in every subject* one of the most objectionable persons" Marsh had ever known; the Minister feared that Wurts and Artoni would be driven away, leaving him dragoman to his own secretary.[7] Fortunately, Hay, dissatisfied with his salary and his reception, departed instead. Wurts finally became Secretary of Legation, a post he held to the end of Marsh's term. Handling most of the legation routine, Wurts was invaluable to Marsh. It was an ideal arrangement for the old Minister, and enabled him to carry on diplomatic work (except for social duties) as well in 1881 as he had twenty years earlier.

With his consuls Marsh was less fortunate. Consul-General T. Bigelow Lawrence and his "charming and noble-minded" wife guided the Marshes through the intricacies of Florentine society, but Lawrence was no diplomat, and Marsh could not trust him with important work. At Rome, Marsh had to dismiss Consul-General Charles McMillan for appearing at one of Caroline's re-

ceptions in a state of "palpable intoxication." McMillan was succeeded in 1879 by the brilliant but unstable Eugene Schuyler. Better
known as a translator of Tolstoi and Turgenev, Schuyler had been
Secretary of Legation at Constantinople, where his denunciations
of Turkish rule got him into considerable trouble. Marsh's initial
distrust of his new consul-general turned into dislike when Schuyler
asked to be formally introduced to the diplomatic corps. Marsh refused, on the ground that the consulate-general was a commercial,
not a diplomatic position.[8] The ambitious Schuyler, who transferred
to Bucharest in 1881, never forgave the slight.

One novel diplomatic task gave Marsh more enjoyment than any
other in his later years. In the summer of 1874 he was asked to arbitrate a boundary controversy between Italy and Switzerland, and in
September he set out for the disputed area, the Alp of Cravairola,
northwest of Locarno midway between Lago Maggiore and St. Gotthard. The territory in question was seven square miles of steeply
sloping rock with a patch of pasture and a stand of evergreens. It
contained a few summer huts for herdsmen, no permanent dwellings.
Climbing more than seven thousand feet by mule and on foot,
Marsh spent fourteen hours in the open, in a heavy rain, and passed
through the debated land, "but saw little of it except the entrance and
the exit." Despite this wet, strenuous hike, Marsh was "neither stiff
nor sorry the next day, which for an old cripple is pretty well." The
legal part of the question was "certainly as thorny as the physical."
Marsh spent a week in Milan, examining six centuries of documents
and charters, and at length produced a twenty-two-page decision.
Geographically, the valley was certainly Swiss; it belonged to the
watershed of the Val Maggia, and its forests and waters were indispensable for the protection of soils in the lower Rovana. No one
understood better than Marsh the merits of undivided watersheds.
But it was equally clear to him that the area was by historic right
Italian. Although "the ultimate best interests of both parties would
be most effectually promoted by assigning the territory . . . to Switzerland," he had to rule in favor of Italy. Both countries acclaimed

Marsh's report, and Congress grudgingly allowed him to keep their gifts—from Switzerland, a plain gold watch; from Italy, a small marble-topped table inlaid with Florentine roses.[9]

3

A Marsh was burned for heresy; that has confirmed our obstinacy. The whole race of us are desperate heretics to this day.

MARSH, AT THE NEW ENGLAND SOCIETY OF NEW YORK, DEC. 21, 1844

That the heretical Marsh should be stationed in Rome, the seat of the Papacy, was an ironic conclusion to the life of this New England Puritan. It reanimated him, however, to a final assault against his old enemy. His first years in Italy had convinced Marsh that the spiritual as well as the temporal power of the Church was waning; his comments on religious affairs reflected his confidence in the triumph of "reason." He dismissed the Syllabus of Errors of 1864 as "but the cooing of the dove" compared with previous "wolfish howl[s] against . . . scientific and social progress." Nor was Marsh alarmed by the Vatican Council of 1869–70, which made papal infallibility a dogma. Marsh hoped the Council would "stop nowhere . . . elevate Joseph to the rank of Mary, in short declare Catholicism to be avowedly what it has always been practically, a polytheism, and finally gratify the pet wish of the drivelling old idiot who calls it together by proclaiming the pope personally infallible, God's alter ego." [10] The more arrogant the Church became, Marsh believed, the sooner it would collapse.

He could not have been more mistaken. Far from hastening its demise, Pius IX restored the papacy to greater influence than it had held for 400 years. Papal infallibility, which Marsh had expected to weaken the Church, had in fact unified it and redoubled its energy. By the early 1870s he saw that he had been wrong. Italy's failure to subjugate the Pope, Protestant complacency, the upsurge of Catholic immigration, and the increasing acceptance of that religion in America convinced Marsh that only intense efforts could overcome the Church.

To warn Americans about the dangers of Catholicism, Marsh wrote in 1874 a tract called *Medieval and Modern Saints and Miracles*. He anticipated bitter opposition; his *Nation* article on the papal encyclical had received "a torrent of abuse from the Catholic press." But because Marsh's diplomatic position made anonymity essential, he had great difficulty finding a publisher. Not until 1876 did Harper's agree to bring out the book. Few copies were sold, and it had little impact. "The public has looked in vain," the publisher wrote Marsh, "for the authority of a name to substantiate the startling statements made in the book." Even reviewers who shared his prejudices agreed that concealment of Marsh's name "will not only render him liable to severe criticism at the hands of the Church, but will also weaken the authority of his somewhat surprising statements with skeptical Protestants." [11]

Saints and Miracles was written in haste and anger. Marsh's worst literary effort, the book is a badly organized potpourri of diatribes against Catholicism—excerpts from the lives of saints and descriptions of miracles, interlarded with homilies on Mariolatry, the confessional, the Inquisition, the martyrdom of Hus, the character of Pius IX, Jesuits, papal infallibility, bookburning, forged documents, feminism, medieval architecture, Cardinal Newman, and religious persecution in general.

Marsh had outgrown some of his earlier biases, however. He abjured the "materialist" doctrines he had once professed, that race and place determine religion and national character. He had a few good words to say for Catholics. Marsh had met as fine human beings in Catholic Italy as in Congregational New England; "even the priesthood [displays] examples of piety, truth, honor, charity, benevolence." Italian servants and shopkeepers were more honest, he thought, than their English and American counterparts. Marsh found Catholics superior to Protestants in "the minor morals—the urban-

ities and amenities of mutual intercourse . . . the courteous regard
for the sensibilities and the self-respect of others, so characteristic of
the Latin nations, and which contrast so strongly with the bluff, if
not brutal address of the Englishman, the offensive self-sufficiency
of the German, and the rude self-assertion of the American." [12]

So much for Catholics as individuals. But predominantly Catholic
countries had, Marsh believed, low moral standards, and the few
really enlightened citizens lacked the *esprit de corps* which they
possessed in places like New England. Reason alone, Marsh had
come to suspect, could never free Italy from Catholicism. Traditional
social patterns, complex ties between Church and State hierarchies,
would hinder ecclesiastical disestablishment. Among the masses,
Catholicism was a way of life. People seemed to hate priests; yet
this hardly weakened their attachment to their faith. Even an
"emancipated" scientist told Marsh that he could not "overcome the
prejudices of my education, which prompt me to sustain a church
in which I do not believe." [13] The Church's monopoly of education
insured its continued supremacy in the minds and hearts of the
people.

The Church itself, Marsh condemned wholly. Far from growing
more enlightened, humane, and progressive, Catholicism was, he
maintained, as tyrannical, cruel, and corrupt as during the darkest
ages. The dogma of the Immaculate Conception made Christ "an
altogether superfluous personage," Marsh charged, and divided the
domain of grace "between Mary in heaven and the pope on earth."
The new devotion to the Sacred Heart of Jesus, Marsh considered
"the grossest case of purely material worship in modern times, [and
one] surpassed in folly, vulgarity and indecency by few chapters in
the history of . . . religious aberrations." [14]

This movement had nevertheless done the most, Marsh believed,
"to revive the flagging zeal of indifferent Catholics, and to secure
perverts [*sic*] from Protestantism" in the United States. Marsh was
appalled by the gullibility and ignorance of his fellow countrymen;
they took nothing seriously. "A settled moral conviction of any sort

is [considered] a weakness or provincialism," Marsh complained; "and any attempt at an exposure of the policy of Rome is triumphantly put down by classing it with the old vulgar mob-watchword of 'No Popery.' " Yet the Papacy had "openly proclaimed itself the enemy of all human liberty," and was "assiduously laboring to sap" the foundations of freedom. "The danger of papal aggression on American liberties," Marsh declared firmly, "is as real, as obvious, and . . . almost as imminent" as the threat of Civil War in 1860.[15]

Marsh's fear of Catholic expansion and his strictures against the Church did not abate in later years. He undertook special studies of the Inquisition and of bookburning and suppression of anti-Catholic literature. He expressed alarm lest the Vatican foment revolution in the United States. "Our Popish friends are growing more and more bellicose," he wrote; "nothing short of blood will satisfy them." Marsh made it a rule, whenever "Catholic Popality comes within my reach, to give him a rap on the back of the head with a sharp stone, or a poke in the eye with a stout stick, and always feel the better for it."[16] He reveled in his own combativeness. For him the Church was an enemy made to order; had there been none he would have been obliged to invent one.

4

The best advice that can be offered to farmers impatient to rush into costly canalling and grading for the introduction of irrigation, is that often given with respect to new medicinal remedies: "Let a friend try it first."   MARSH, *Irrigation, Its Evils, the Remedies and the Compensations* (1874)

Far more realistic and effective than Marsh's fulminations against Catholicism were his renewed warnings about environmental damage. In 1874 he published a revised and enlarged edition of *Man and Nature*. He also ventured further into a related field, in a paper on irrigation prepared at the request of the United States Commissioner of Agriculture. Irrigation was just then a subject of much hopeful speculation. Optimists viewed it as a panacea for the arid West, which might transform the Great American Desert into a garden of Eden. In areas of scanty or unreliable rainfall, irrigation could, they thought, insure year-round supplies of fresh water and increase crop yields tenfold. Irrigation was said to be simple and cheap; all the settler had to do was dig a ditch and let the water flow.

Drawing upon millennia of Mediterranean history, Marsh exploded these myths and cautioned against hasty or excessive irrigation in the United States; "cautions which," he added privately, "our headlong pioneers seem much to need." Irrigation could be of "great economical advantage" provided we "protect ourselves and our posterity by . . . *prophylactic* measures," but Marsh feared that "our characteristic impetuosity and love of novelty" might do much damage. Irrigation was not cheap and easy, but costly and difficult; and it posed grave and enduring problems. Irrigation required reservoirs and artificial lakes, which sometimes burst their barriers and flooded the country below. Irrigation often exhausted the soil, produced hardpan, or concentrated lethal salts at the surface. Irrigation might multiply yields at the expense of nutritive value and flavor. Finally, in such areas as the humid East "simple and less expensive methods" like terracing were just as effective.

Marsh was mainly interested, however, in the dry regions of the West. Knowledge of Western climates and soils was virtually non-existent. No one knew how much land was irrigable, or whether enough water was available to make irrigation profitable. Water used for irrigation deprived adjacent lands of their normal supply, thus disturbing the balance of nature. Before embarking on major irrigation works, the country required a comprehensive hydrographical survey, which would show how much water each river basin received from rain, melting snow, and ground water; how much would be needed in each basin for agricultural, industrial, and domestic purposes; how much the supply could be augmented by water diverted from other areas; and the probable effects of such diversions. After the survey should come irrigation experiments "in each geographical section of the country having marked peculiarities of climate, soil, and adaptability to special culture." [17]

The social effects of irrigation concerned Marsh as much as the physical. "Acquisition of the control of abundant sources of water by private individuals," he warned, "may often result in the establishment of vested rights and monopolies liable to great abuse." Because irrigation required large capital outlays and skillful management it tended "to promote the accumulation of large tracts of land in the hands of single proprietors, and consequently to dispossess the smaller land-holders." In Europe the latter had become hired laborers with "no proprietary interest in the land they till." The rural middle class, "which ought to constitute the true moral as well as physical power of the land," would soon vanish.[18]

Irrigation therefore required new social insights along with technological skills. "We must look to our rulers," Marsh insisted, "for such legislation as shall prevent the greatest amount of evil and secure the greatest amount of good, from the introduction of a system so new to us. . . . Like all attempts to appropriate to the use of individuals gifts of nature which have long been common to all, [irrigation] must clash with many rooted prejudices, many established customs, and many supposed indefeasible rights." One such right was the ownership of all water within the bounds of one's property. This common law riparian principle worked well enough where rainfall was ample. But a farmer in the arid West might be forced out if deprived of water by upstream neighbors. A new water code, Marsh insisted, was necessary to protect the rights of all.

Only public ownership, he believed, could solve Western water problems. "The first article of the water-code should be a declaration that all lakes, rivers, and natural water-courses are the inalienable property of the State, and that no diversion of water from its natural channels is lawful without the permission of the public authorities." The law should forbid perpetual or long-term "concessions of water-rights to individuals or to corporations . . . because, in consequence of the change in volume in water-courses from the destruction of forests and from other causes, and of the varying numbers and wants of the population, a grant, which at a given period was unobjectionable, may become highly injurious to the public interests ten years later." All irrigation should be "under Government supervision, from Government sources of supply." [19] Each state should regulate the time, manner, and amount of water used on the basis of local conditions and needs.

Marsh thus envisaged government control of irrigation as an instrument of social improvement. The state should not merely protect small landholders, it should "promote the division of the soil into . . . farms of relatively narrow extent" by giving small farmers a larger proportion of water and at lower rates than to great proprietors. "Further encouragement might advantageously be given to poorer occupants who build and inhabit houses upon these lands." [20]

Marsh's broad policy, especially his advocacy of public ownership, "made considerable breeze in Congress." Although his report aroused much indignation among promoters of Western lands, Baird predicted that "it will doubtless have a decided effect in influencing national and state action." Within a few years, Marsh's warnings on irrigation found a powerful champion in John Wesley Powell. In his influential *Report on the Lands of the Arid Region of the United States* (1878), Powell cited Marsh to support his thesis that Western settlement ought not follow Eastern models. A decade later, as chief of the United States Geological Survey, Powell inaugurated just such an irrigation survey as Marsh had proposed, and meanwhile forbade the sale or lease of potentially irrigable public lands.[21] Western landowners and speculators aborted Powell's program, but the government control of irrigable waters envisaged by Marsh was partly reestablished by the Newlands Act of 1902, which created the Bureau of Reclamation. With water, as with forests, Marsh's insights became the guiding principles behind na-

GEORGE PERKINS MARSH IN HIS LIBRARY AT THE VILLA FORINI,
FLORENCE, ITALY

tional conservation policy. Subsequent pressures on Western water resources attest to his foresight in urging timely planning.

In his last years Marsh renewed his passion for forests and forestry. An epistolary friendship with Charles Sprague Sargent, director of Harvard's Arnold Arboretum, was mainly responsible for his resurgence of interest. "I have long been a student of *Man and Nature,*" Sargent wrote in 1879, noting a few minor botanical errors, "and have derived great pleasure and profit from your pages." For three and a half years the elderly diplomat and the youthful botanist exchanged observations on such topics as forest conservation, the acclimation of olives in Massachusetts, the uses of pine cones, anastomosis of beeches in the Black Forest, the sex of cypresses, the grafting of figs and pomegranates, Ruskin's essays (which Marsh despised), the girdling of trees by squirrels, the vegetation of the Dolomites, the artificial regeneration of trees, experimental work in the Arboretum, historical botany in colonial America, and the supposed sanitary effects of eucalyptus in California. As enthusiastic as a youngster, the octogenarian Minister strolled through forest groves, magnifying glass and measuring tape in hand. Sargent later testified that Marsh's acuity of observation and "knowledge of the literature of the forest and forestry was unexcelled even by that of the few specialists who devote themselves exclusively to the study of this subject." [22]

To Sargent and other friendly critics Marsh owed much for the revisions of *Man and Nature* that occupied him until the day of his death. Changes between the 1864 and the 1874 and 1885 editions, while numerous, were mostly minor. The author corrected errors, added fresh evidence, cited new works and illustrations of natural and man-made processes; but the book's central theme and spirit remained the same. Marsh recorded new instances of waste: since *Man and Nature* first appeared, "the forests of the Adirondacks have continued to be the scene of ever more and more rapidly encroaching inroads from the woodman's axe"; only "a wiser legislation or

a sounder public opinion" could avert imminent "total destruction."
But he also noted that science had prevented waste; the successful
shipment of refrigerated mutton from New Zealand to Britain in
1882 might signal the end of indiscriminate slaughter of animals.[23]
If Marsh found disturbing evidence of man's unconscious impact on
his environment—in the subsidence of coal-mining areas in Pennsylvania and Belgium; in the interchange of marine life between
the Mediterranean and Rea Sea along the Suez Canal; and above
all in the climatic effects of great urban agglomerations [24]—he also
predicted that man's conscious control over nature would increase.
The advent of electricity, in particular, opened "a prospect of vast
addition to the powers formerly wielded by man" and presaged
"new and more brilliant victories of mind over matter." [25]

With power would come greater knowledge. Marsh speculated
on the ways man might influence even the rotation and orbit of the
earth. "The immediate effects now elude human understanding,"
he concluded, "but who shall say that the mathematics of the future
may not . . . calculate even these smallest cosmical results of human action?" [26] Though pessimistic about social and political progress, Marsh foresaw unlimited scientific advance.

5

*What does any mortal want an Encyclopaedia . . . for, and where does
any mortal find the money to pay for it? An alphabetical work,
whereof A. shall be obsolete and forgotten before the litera longa, the
thieves' letter, is arrived at!*

MARSH TO HENRY YULE, FEB. 15, 1875

Religion and nature were not the only topics that engaged Marsh's
attention. As in earlier years, he reflected and wrote on a wide
variety of subjects. In 1874 he became an associate editor of *Johnson's Universal Cyclopaedia,* for which—at the rate of twenty dollars
a page—he prepared many literary, linguistic, and geographical
articles. He wrote about Genoa, Girgenti, the Po, the Pontine
Marshes, Sicily, and the Tiber; he sketched the lives of half a dozen

Iberian poets and chroniclers; he discussed Catalan and Italian language and literature, Romansch, Index, Lexicon, and Improvisation; he contributed the Index (Papal), the Sicilian Vespers, and Legend, "wherein I must tread gingerly," he noted, "in regard to my position." He also wrote historical bagatelles on the Olive, Mulberry tree, Straw manufacture, and Velvet; and geographical pieces on Watershed, Well, and other topics. It was these that Marsh most enjoyed. "As men please themselves more in their dilettantisms than in what really belongs to them," he explained, "I have taken more pleasure in writing on Irrigation, Inundations, Fireproof constructions, the Mt. Cenis and Mt. Gotthard Tunnels, the draining of Lake Fucino, etc. etc. than in literary articles."[27] A dozen years after the first appearance of *Man and Nature* Marsh still insisted he was an amateur in geography.

Sometimes the job was irksome, especially when he was at Rome with a deadline to meet and all his books in Florence. Then Marsh had to dive "into the limbo of material elaborated in my inner man by 'unconscious cerebration' [to] fetch up enough brain dribble to fill some pages." "Needs must whom the devil drives," he explained, "and Auld Sootie . . . is now after me with a sharp stick and howling: write! write!" Yet when the *Cyclopaedia* was finished—it had earned him $2,300—he sought other remunerative work, "which . . . the greatly increased expenses of living in Italy make a necessity for us."[28] A sad admission for an eminent scholar and honored diplomat, at the age of seventy-five!

Old age and infirmity did, in fact, prevent Marsh from preparing much for publication after this, although up to the end of his life he continued to revise his books—and to lose his temper with critics. When one scholar claimed Marsh had underestimated Milton's vocabulary by more than half, the Minister retorted: "He must have counted *fool, fool's, fools,* as three words, and (if Milton had used it) *blunder, blunderest, blunders, blundered, blunderedest, blundering,* as six." Marsh's reputation as a thorough and accurate word counter was later rehabilitated.[29]

Marsh kept on with other linguistic research. He enjoyed finding words which had no cognates in other tongues (on his Italo-Swiss boundary expedition, he picked up *inalpare* and *disalpare,* to drive the cattle to and from the Alpine pastures in the spring and fall). He investigated the origins of Italian dialects, and promoted a forestry dictionary, an Italian grammar, and a Bible translation. Ever impressed by the mutability of language, Marsh amused himself "watching the changing pronunciation . . . made *without the consciousness of the individual*—in persons whom I have observed during our residences at . . . Turin, Florence, and Rome." [30] His next to last published article, "The Biography of a Word," delightfully illustrated the flux of language through the rise and decline of one made-up word (for a donkey's bray) in his own family.

Art and architecture also continued to claim Marsh's attention. Time did not fog his connoisseur's eye; on the contrary, as he had said many years before, old age was "gilded with the most exalted pleasures of the world of sense. . . . Perception of beauty . . . attains not its ripeness, save under the rays of an autumnal sun." Marsh feasted his eyes everywhere in Rome. He helped the New York Metropolitan Museum of Art acquire some valuable paintings. He acted as agent between American artists and Italian marble workers, selected the sculptor for the Rhode Island State Memorial, procured a cast of a bust of Mercury for the University of Vermont, engaged W. W. Story to do a statue of Joseph Henry for the Smithsonian Institution, commissioned Preston Powers to make a marble bust of Jacob Collamer for Vermont's contribution to the Hall of Statuary in the Capitol, and advised New England's governors on the Bennington Battle Monument. The Carrara marble statue of Ethan Allen—Marsh's choice—was considered "the most elegant monument in New England." [31]

Perhaps the most enduring example of Marsh's taste and persuasiveness is the Washington Monument. Its completion long delayed by war and lack of funds, the unfinished obelisk stood, forlornly truncated, on the Mall in Washington, D.C. In 1879 Marsh learned with horror that it was to be surmounted by a colossal statue. This was heresy. Marsh had "sketched every existing genuine . . . obelisk," he wrote his old friend Robert C. Winthrop, president of the Washington National Monument Society. It was an "esthetical crime" to depart from forms and proportions "fixed by the usage of thousands of years," which satisfied "every cultivated eye." Marsh found "the notion of spitting a statue on the sharp point of the pyramidon . . . supremely absurd." No ledge, molding, or other ornament must disfigure the face. The height of the pyramid must be ten times the width. The proposed truncated apex was "quite out of harmony with the *soaring* character of the structure." Marsh's criticisms were effective; the Society abandoned the statue, adopted most of his other suggestions, and proudly announced that the monument would "make no pretensions to illustrate the arts of 1880." [32]

In recognition of his contributions to science and art Marsh was honored by many learned societies. Harvard, Dartmouth, and Delaware had conferred LL.D.'s, but no honor pleased him more than his election in 1876 to the Reale Accademia dei Lincei, the ancient Italian scientific society.

6

Rome has been everything to all men. For the American Minister in the 1870s it was a city of incongruous disharmonies. There was the moral Rome, which in Marsh's eyes the Vatican made the capital of evil. There were several material Romes: one an aggregation of monuments and works of art; another a sprawling malarial slum, steaming in summer and bitter in winter. The government gradually began to clean up the slums, sometimes at the expense of the monuments. Applauding the erection of new apartments, the drainage of swamps, the installation of sanitation, and the reconstruction of aqueducts, Marsh predicted that Rome would be "a grand city to live in"—by 1900. [33]

Social Rome loomed largest in Marsh's life. People from all over
the world congregated there—aristocrats, diplomats, politicians,
priests, and, most visibly, tourists. Throughout the winter, Rome
rang with English voices; the city was "a monstrous mixture of the
watering place and the curiosity shop." Sight-seers Baedekered
through palaces and churches, bothered Marsh for introductions to
the Quirinal, and presented themselves to the Pope, "as they would
to the Devil," Marsh grumbled, "if he were to give audiences above
ground." "I shall be truly thankful," sighed the harassed Minister,
"when we come to sackcloth and ashes, and get rid of some of the
gaping idiots who come all the way from America to see such
things." [34]

Quite apart from this common throng, the Marshes' social duties
increased enormously; they gave dinners for twenty, receptions for
fifty, two or three times a week. Life for the Anglo-American colony
in Rome in those days has been described as a continuous picnic,
but it was not one for the American Minister, who had to furnish
the setting and foot the bills.

Everyone made the Grand Tour. Ralph Waldo Emerson stayed
for a week and "was quite a lion," Caroline reported; but his senile
garrulity irked the tough-minded Marsh. Bigelow, Bancroft, Lowell,
R. H. Dana, Fanny Kemble, Willard Fiske, Bayard Taylor, and
other American diplomats visited at various times. Matthew Arnold
returned in 1873, found Marsh ill and "sate a long time with him,
because he liked it." [35] Marsh also enjoyed meeting the British
historian Lecky and the Germans Mommsen and Moltke.

Then there were the artists—Story, Cushman, Harriet Hosmer,
Mrs. Terry, and the rest. The majority were women, the "white,
marmoreal flock" described by Henry James. Marsh found "the
female persuasion . . . slightly redundant" even among the transients. It created social problems. "Ladies come in trios and quar-
tettes, with no male attendant. What can one do with such at a
dinner table?" At one reception appeared "a *he* accompanied by
eight *shes*. How despairing!" [36]

Worst were the visits of "royal tramps," as Marsh called touring nobility. "We are bound to believe that such entities have their uses," he assumed charitably, but they were "a grievous trial to poor innocent diplomates, and . . . they ought never to be allowed to go abroad." In general, aristocrats bored him. "Gentlemen in swallow-tails and ladies with trains are wonderfully alike all over the world," he complained. The longer Marsh lived abroad, the more he asserted his native republicanism. He hoped to "live to see the playing at foot-ball with coronets and mitres, crowns and tiaras." [37]

As Minister, however, he had to consort with crowns, tiaras, and mitres. In 1877, to do proper honor to General Grant's imminent visit (which wore them out with problems of protocol), the Marshes moved into the forty-room Palazzo Pandolfi, a most expensive place "with more tinsel than gold in its fitting up," Marsh noted. But the sun poured in through great bay windows, and there was a good furnace. These were important considerations, for Marsh was subject to painful attacks of sciatica. The winter of 1880 was Rome's severest on record, "almost fatal to all old people, myself included," wrote Marsh; he had bronchitis for months. "I have aged more in the last six months," he observed sadly, "than in any previous six years of my life." [38]

In 1879 the Marshes moved again, to the Palazzo Rospigliosi, just opposite the Colosseum. Their apartment was 126 steps up, but Marsh was tempted by splendid rooms and furniture, a private gallery, a fine library, and "the most magnificent view of Rome and its environs I know." [39] What if the stairs were many and steep! When he could not climb them, Marsh was carried up and down in a sedan chair, but it was not easy for two men to hoist his 200-pound frame up a narrow staircase.

Marsh in his late seventies was active and cheerful, but tired rapidly; always low-pitched, his voice became less distinct. He disliked idle chatter, and talked freely only when closeted with such intimates as Henry Yule, George Bancroft, Humphrey Sandwith, Frank Nash. Then he became communicative and witty; a flow of dry humor and piquant learning delighted his listeners. In his later years, such flashes of humor were less frequent, but memory, judgment, and power of invective stayed with him to the last.

He was always finding new friends and excitements. The Marshes "are so very kind and considerate and are so fatherly and motherly to us young people who are striving to do something," wrote Lucy Wright Mitchell; she dedicated her *History of Ancient Sculpture* "gratefully and reverently" to Marsh. Many echoed her feeling, from Mrs. Owen Wister to Oliver Wendell Holmes, Jr., who thought himself fortunate to be remembered by such a great and busy man. What drew them was less Marsh's erudition than what Charles Eliot Norton called "his moral qualities. His modesty, his simplicity, his generosity, his patience . . . won and held my deepest admiration and respect." Young friends often stayed with them; Marsh enjoyed their visits. "There is nothing in my expectations of life," he wrote, "to which I look forward with so much pleasure as the prospect of being able to do good to our young people." [40]

Marsh's letters were "glorious and mirth-provoking, and soul-inspiring, and greatly refreshing," wrote Baird, who received more of them than anyone else. Even when the Minister's "quaint original handwriting, once seen never to be forgotten," became crabbed with rheumatism, it was well worth deciphering. Unlike his prolix published work, Marsh's private communications were pithy, colorful, explicit; letters written in anger against some folly still seem warm and wrathful. In formal writing Marsh sometimes effaced himself with endless revision, but his personal notes were vigorous and sparkling. Had Marsh "put his personality into literature," remarked one associate, "he must have been the most popular writer of his age." [41]

Other proclivities developed with the years. One was his taste for food and drink. Marsh had become a true gourmet, a man learned in the preparation of *risotto* à la Milanese and Roman punch ("add rum or whiskey . . . to any common ice-cream"). He thought dry champagne (then fashionable) "a nauseous and poisonous tipple adulterated with some nasty drug," and condemned "the craze about dry wines":

Fruit which would have been neglected thirty years ago, as immature or diseased, is now subjected to the press without scruple, and the acid and corrosive juice obtained from it is doubly brandied and recommended to purchasers as dry wine. . . . People who habitually imbibe this caustic fluid will find in the long run that they have put an enemy into their mouths, if not to steal their brains, at least to ruin their digestion.[42]

Marsh's own digestion remained excellent.

The Marshes' social burdens were lightened by numerous relatives. Carrie Marsh Crane, Caroline's niece and namesake, stayed with them from 1861 until 1865. Not beautiful, she was "a very nice good girl," bright, eager to learn; by the time she went home, Carrie spoke Italian more fluently than Marsh himself. Several young cousins followed her as Caroline's amanuenses. Other relations paid shorter visits: young Dr. Edward Crane, private physician to the Empress Eugénie and later editor of the Paris *American Register;* Senator Edmunds and his family in the summer of 1873.

Marsh arranged in 1874 to bring back his favorite, Carrie, who had failed to enter college, as Marsh had planned for her, and finally had a nervous breakdown. All these years Carrie had dreamed of returning to Italy. "I love you more than I can ever tell you dear uncle," she wrote Marsh, "and think of you almost all the time. Sometimes I want you so much that it seems as if I could not wait another hour." Marsh looked forward eagerly to her arrival, but on the way to Italy Carrie was lost in a shipwreck off the Scilly Islands. The calamity overwhelmed him; "she was the comfort, the hope, the stay of my declining years, and the world has nothing which can supply her place," Marsh mourned. "A childless old man needs some such support as this affectionate and strong and heroic girl was to me, some green and growing thing on which to fix his pride and earthly hopes."[43] It was in many ways a harder blow than the death of his son.

Other nieces and nephews arrived: Marsh's "little Dutch niece" Carrie Wislizenus, "a perfect model of industry"; Alexander B. Crane, a "half worn-out New York lawyer," whose septuagenarian uncle chased him up and down the Alps; the Edmundses again. The summer of 1881 brought the Marshes Alexander Crane's six children, ranging in age from two to twelve. Far from resenting this incursion, Marsh was delighted, took a keen interest in their progress in school, and spent hours chatting with them. "Every night after tea Uncle asks us what we have been studying all day," wrote the eldest girl, "and then he tells us lots of funny and serious things." [44]

Love of children—with the exception of stupid schoolboys, perhaps—was, Marsh stated, his "strongest passion, next to selfishness." He claimed the feeling was reciprocal. "Till I grew a beard, all babies would come to me, even from nurses' arms." By a curious accident, Marsh was able to adopt, in 1877, a two-year-old Swedish boy. A wealthy American, Mary Gilpin, had bribed the guardians of a young Swedish orphan, Carlo Rände, to give him up to her. Miss Gilpin, whom Marsh described as "a monomaniac, if not altogether insane," arrived in Rome, and complaints about her maltreatment of Carlo came to Marsh's attention. Marsh eventually found him and brought him to the Swedish Minister. Soon afterward the child was taken to the Marshes' home, "where it could more conveniently be cared for," Marsh explained to the Secretary of State, "and still remains with us." [45]

Young King Karl, as they called him, stayed with the Marshes permanently. Although Carlo was a slow learner, Marsh adored him. He spoiled him inordinately, and left cross words to Caroline. The stocky, golden-haired boy remained "a constant source of amusement" to the aging Minister, who termed his "affection for him [a] great blessing . . . because it tends to keep our moral nature from sinking into the torpor which so often accompanies old age." [46]

Old age was rendered more painful by the death of old friends. Of Marsh's immediate family none was left. Lyndon died in 1872;

Charles, of tuberculosis, in 1873. The old Marsh homestead was
bought by railroad magnate Frederick A. Billings, who had returned a millionaire to his native Woodstock. Billings rebuilt the
house in the gilt-and-gingerbread fashion of the times; fortunately,
Marsh never saw the result. In Burlington, too, the old order had
passed away. The town had recovered from its mid-century depression, but few of Marsh's Vermont associates were left to see the new
prosperity. Only old John Pomeroy lived on, spry and hearty in
his late eighties. The years had taken toll of other colleagues. Bache,
Henry, Gilliss, Alexander, Choate, Sumner, Foot, Powers, all were
dead. Though Marsh had many younger friends, his own generation was spent. The same was true in Italy; all the men who held
power when Marsh first came were gone but Garibaldi. "We feel the
loneliness of survivorship," wrote Marsh in 1880, "and have comparatively few ties except those of duty." [47]

7

I have waited for leisure until it is too late. Ach, mein verfehltes Leben!
MARSH TO F. P. NASH, JUNE 5, 1879

The ties of duty sometimes galled Marsh sorely. He occasionally
wondered whether he could bear his burdens; "they are very heavy,"
he wrote, the winter of his bronchitis, "and I feel I may at any time
sink under them." "To be a 'free man' for a little before I go hence,
is my most earnest aspiration." He thought of retiring, but was deterred by his nephew Alexander Crane: "Do not resign! . . . You
cannot leave so good a reputation or do your country so much good
as by holding on and bravely performing your duties at your post
until the chord of life is snapped." Caroline had all she could do
to cheer him, and "at the same time to conceal . . . his condition
from outsiders who were *gaping* for his place and eagle-eyed to see
shortcomings." She herself would have liked to return to the United
States, but she knew that he could not. Packing and shipping the
library would take many months, and deprive him of the use of

his books for still longer; and he would lose his feeling of financial independence. Money and weather were the chief determinants. "The *official* position I could well spare," he wrote a British friend, "but I do not look forward with pleasure to a return to our climate, of which it is enough to say that . . . it is a good deal worse than yours." [48]

Marsh's imminent retirement was periodically rumored, however —especially when he was too busy or too feeble to carry out his social obligations. One visitor complained that Marsh used his scholarly reputation to excuse him from performing "the ordinary courtesies or even duties of resident Ministers. . . . Our legation at Rome is . . . inaccessible to the ordinary American traveller, as the Minister generally pleads ill-health for not receiving." This was promptly denied by a friend; whenever Marsh was too ill to go to the office he received visitors at home. It would disgrace the United States, continued Marsh's defender, if "through political intrigues or the petty spite of conceited travelers, he be removed from the responsible position which he has filled so long and so nobly." [49]

The Hayes election in 1877 again imperiled Marsh's position. As a Republican, Marsh had supported Hayes, but the new Administration promised civil service and other reforms; Marsh anticipated that he would be replaced, "even if on no other principle than that a new broom sweeps clean." The Minister knew he had enemies; "I have offended many, because I could not or would not aid them in the accomplishment of special objects." But friends assured the President that Marsh was as fit as ever, and, to Marsh's amazed pleasure, Italy officially requested his retention. This appeal, together with pressure by the indefatigable Edmunds, who as a member of the Electoral Commission of 1877 had been influential in electing Hayes, saved the post for Marsh, although new envoys were appointed in Britain, France, Germany, Russia, Spain and most of the smaller countries. But Edmunds warned his uncle that "if I should fail to see things exactly with Administration eyes hereafter, your merits might not seem to be quite so clear." [50]

Marsh hung on, however, mainly owing to Edmunds's extraordinary prestige in Washington. A scrupulously honest man in an
era of political corruption, the Senate majority leader wielded tremendous power. When Edmunds quarreled with Hayes in 1880
he warned Marsh to "be prepared for the axe," but its fall was prevented by the protests of the entire Vermont delegation and the
Secretary of State. Marsh had another narrow escape when Garfield was elected a year later; Secretary of State Blaine, who "wants
all the places for his friends," Edmunds wrote, planned to recall the
Vermonter. But Garfield was assassinated, and succeeded by Arthur,
over whom Edmunds had more influence. Working through Grant,
whom Arthur admired, Edmunds convinced the new President that
Marsh was still fully capable and that it would be most injurious
to take him from Rome. [51] Garfield and Arthur replaced the incumbents in all the other European legations save for Marsh's friend
Lowell in London and John L. Stevens in Stockholm. After twenty
years in office, Marsh seemed likely to go on indefinitely.

In truth, Marsh was much better in 1881 than for years past. He
was "once more taking an interest in everything that ought to interest rational beings, ready to perform all official duties . . . and
writing now and then an article for a periodical." On his eightieth
birthday Marsh scrawled with stiff rheumatic fingers that despite
"many discouraging symptoms" he was "free from pain and in
tolerable spirits tho most annoyed by all sorts of demands upon my
time." [52]

Still more formidable were the demands upon his purse. Marsh
did not spend quite double his salary, but, he said, "I have *needed* it,
and I have avoided many expenses which for the credit of my position and the country I should have incurred." Were it not for a
$7,300 legacy from his brother Charles, Marsh estimated that after
twenty years of service he would "be returning home a poorer man
than when I left it." [53]

Lack of money and his increasing inability to write prompted
Marsh to try to sell his 13,000-volume library. Harvard, Brown, and

the New York and Boston public libraries nibbled at his rare Catalan and Old Norse volumes, but bought nothing. Marsh then turned to the University of Vermont. He was willing to "sacrifice" his books for $10,000, but President Matthew H. Buckham and the trustees thought this price high. Their hesitation was confirmed by Marsh's stipulations on storage: "How the Trustees can consider an apartment *over* the Museum of Natural History *containing objects preserved in spirits* and connected by *framed* walls and *wooden* staircases with other apartments . . . as 'practically safe from fire,'" the indignant Minister could not understand.[54] Not until after his death did Frederick Billings buy the library for $15,000 and present it to the University of Vermont, with H. H. Richardson's Romanesque building to house the volumes. There the collection is still intact.

8

I am not discouraged by the comparison of what all must admit to be a bad present with what I hold to have been a worse past.
                                    MARSH TO HENRY YULE, JULY 10, 1876

In his later years Marsh's view of life became increasingly somber. This perspective stemmed, in part, from the disabilities of his own old age and from the complexities of the age in which he lived. Human blindness and selfishness seemed to him unending; man would go on and on misusing his world, his resources, himself. Of justice and reward, Marsh expected little. The small triumphs that once had meant much to him were unavailing against the general decay of human affairs.

Pessimism seemed apropos not only in Italy, where long-sought union brought apathy and poverty in its wake, but also in America. Slavery was no more, the South was utterly vanquished; but to what end? That corruption and debauchery should flourish as never before? To Marsh, as to other survivors of a more heroic and hopeful era, the age lacked form, purpose, morality, conviction, courage;

every victory entailed new discouragements. Thus in each election it seemed vital to Marsh that the Democrats be defeated, but no cause for rejoicing when the Republicans won. In 1876 he was not pro-Hayes, only anti-Tilden; he considered Tilden "the embodiment of all that is worst and most dangerous in American politics," and congratulated Edmunds on saving America from this incubus.[55]

But if America could be saved, was it worth saving? In Marsh's eyes it had become a morass of materialism, where greed for gold and the reign of robber barons portended "the most pernicious of aristocracies." Marsh favored civil service, but doubted that it could prevail over dollar worship and political patronage. From America came such an "uninterrupted succession of mortifying and dis- couraging moral & political news" that he wondered whether "any- body believes in anybody's honesty these sad days." [56]

For this state of affairs Marsh held unprincipled corporations responsible. The shenanigans of Vanderbilt and Jay Gould justified his animadversions against "the great companies of transportation [which] defy all control, but that of the purse." When Edmunds fought in the Senate for the Interstate Commerce Act,[57] he was echoing railroad commissioner Marsh's old denunciations of the practice of pooling and the tyranny of corporate combination.

Along with industrial concentration went engrossment of land by the few, especially in the West. Marsh deplored this trend. "Small tenements have always been the salvation, large farms often the ruin, of European countries," he cautioned. Similarly, he attacked the growth of cities. His ideal society was Jeffersonian; a pre- dominantly rural population, with many "small villages just large enough to support a blacksmith, a carpenter, a schoolmaster . . . would afford far stronger evidence of solid and stable growth, than . . . the new suburbs . . . and the increasing numbers of heterogen- eous municipalities, which are doing so much to un-Americanize our people." Distrust of bigness provoked Marsh to condemn territorial expansion. "What have Texas and Florida and New Mexico and

even California profited us?" he asked. "Cuba would be still worse
and it will be long before the $7,000,000 Seward threw away on
Alaska come back into our wallet." [58]

But Marsh's *bête noire* was still immigration; "there *I* find the
root of all evil." The social fabric of the country was shredding, he
felt, under the impact of alien peoples. "When our fathers passed the
naturalization laws," Marsh held, "they administered to the commonwealth a fatal poison, slow indeed, but sure." Marsh no longer
sought to extend democracy. Increased immigration made universal
suffrage highly dangerous. The country already had too much democracy, he thought; echoing his father's characterization of Vermont's
lower house, he termed the federal House of Representatives "a
disorderly mob." [59]

Marsh denied that he was a pessimist, but he saw "no intellectual
general gain within . . . two generations. . . . *Some* better scholars
are now trained indeed, but the hoi polloi are below the standard of
60 years since." Despite the growth of the school system, strides in
literacy, and advances in publishing, reason did *not* rule human
affairs: "You cannot convert a savage who worships a serpent, by
proving to him that his fetish is venomous." Similarly, ignorance
was not "a mere vacuous defect of knowledge, [but] a positive
quantity . . . laboriously acquired, a darkness that can be felt."
And the ignorant were legion, Marsh thought. Most men who knew
how to read and write could not "form a legitimate judgment on
any abstract moral proposition," or figure out any logical problem;
many so-called "cultivated" people were totally unable to "weigh
evidence, whether direct or circumstantial, and determine which
way the balance inclines." The semiliterate were more ignorant, because more self-confident, than the illiterate.[60] Mistrusting education as a lever for change, Marsh renounced faith in progress.

The only gain Marsh saw during his lifetime was the progress
of women; the best hope for the future was their release—through
"mechanical improvements—from a large share of those petty cares,
that ceaseless round of household labors, which have hitherto so

injuriously affected the health, the temper, and the intellectual life
of the female sex . . . and made them the drudges, not the help-
mates" of men. He and Caroline were avowed feminists; friends of
the Blackwells and other women who pioneered in medicine, education, and the arts, the Marshes devoted considerable time, effort, and
money to the cause of equal rights. Marsh had early been "particularly solicitous of the approbation of intelligent women, because,"
he believed, "female influence [is] one of the most important conserv-
ing principles of American society." If Caroline appeared to be a
typical delicate Victorian wife, she was in reality strong-minded and
independent. Marsh blamed men who shut their wives indoors for
the "sickly sensibility . . . often developed in women." But men as
well as women were damaged; by ignoring matters connected with
hearth and home, "the heart of men becomes hardened and their
sensibilities deadened." Marsh did not insist that men and women
were the same; in fact, he wrote, "we know next to nothing at all
about the relative powers and capacities of the two sexes." Nor
would they be known until we "make woman legally and socially
the peer of man, afford her equal if not identical means of education,
give free scope to the natural laws." [61]

Italian residence confirmed Marsh's feminism. In Italy, men ruled
absolute; public opinion made it "disreputable for a woman to
bring into active exercise the qualities which command respect &
ensure success in a man." The Marshes founded an orphan asylum
in Florence to "raise up teachers for the schools" and promote "the
better education of women, which may teach Italian females to
respect themselves by compelling men to respect them." [62]

Marsh's feminism should be viewed in the context of his own
relations with women, with whom he was humorously flirtatious
and consistently gentle. "I have passed my 80th birthday," he told
Mrs. Mark Pattison, "and am free to kiss any pretty woman I like."
Demanding equality for women, he alleged that they had a "higher
and more generous moral nature" than men; "women are stronger
than we," he wrote, "partly no doubt because they are less selfish."

He viewed most men in his own image, as self-centered; and most women, like Caroline, as altruistic, forgiving, pliant. In his own apothegm, "men yield to temptation; women to importunity. Men are swayed by their prejudices, women by their partialities." [63]

His relationship with Caroline was an enduring source of emotional strength; he derived satisfaction from taking care of her, comfort from her love and faith. His niece never "knew a husband who depended more entirely upon a wife." Because he was seventeen years her senior, Marsh was always her mentor; because he was strong and she an invalid, he was literally her supporter.[64] Marsh gloried in both roles.

Few of his other roles pleased him. Marsh was as severe with himself as he was with civilization; he saw no prospect of improvement in either. Abhorring vanity, he indulged in self-abasement. He had inherited, he thought, none of his parents' virtues, and feared that the sufferings he had endured had neither cleansed his soul nor improved his character. As it was "an impeachment of the Divine justice to suppose . . . forgiveness possible," Marsh never prayed to be forgiven. But he bemoaned his misspent years. "I have given nine-tenths of my long years to sin, one tenth to remorse, nothing to repentance," he wrote—"a dreary condition for a man of 76!" [65] He accused himself also of lack of patience, prudence, and faith.

Faith he did lack. Marsh's self-condemnation stemmed in part from a lifetime of religious doubt. Brought up as a Congregational Calvinist, he never professed that creed, but held it a "duty to adhere to the religion of one's cradle until one finds a less objectionable one, which I have not." In fact, Marsh distrusted all organized religion. "I have never connected myself with any church," he explained, "partly because my recollection of the past & my consciousness of the present assure me that I am not fit for membership of the Church of Christ, & partly because I know no church which does not disgust me as inspired by anti-christian sectarianism. Miserable fragments are they all." Yet he rejected the catholic churches,

Roman and Episcopal, as authoritarian, anti-intellectual, and oligarchic. Instead he adopted the evangelical idea that "we serve God most acceptably when we are at the same time serving our brother-man." Though he believed in the Trinity, Marsh's favorite writers were Unitarians, especially James Martineau and Edmund Sears. "A living faith in a philosophically erroneous divinity," he rationalized his heresy, "is better than a dead conformity to confessions which, if even abstractly true, have lost their power over the hearts of men." He himself could not achieve this "living faith." Although Marsh thought all would be "explained & compensated in a world to come," the God he served was an impersonal justice, without emotion or charity. He could not even be certain of this deity's existence; if he were, "life would be only a passive waiting, not a discipline." [66]

Marsh's creed was a moral strait jacket: "A weak character may be generous," he wrote; "only a strong one can be just." Fortunately, he was frequently weak. Otherwise he must have denied free will; for he accorded the virtuous little choice of action. "Our means," he asserted, "moral as well as material, are so meted out to us that we never have more than enough to fulfil our obligations." [67] Life was a treadmill driven by the conscience.

Marsh reduced his articles of faith to one, "the first clause of which I hope, the second I know, to be true: Christ Jesus came into the world to save sinners, of whom I am chief." Confronted by this mixture of skeptical egotism and stern humility, Caroline Marsh termed her husband, in his later years, "the last of the Puritans." [68]

9

Leaving the faithful Wurts in charge of the legation in Rome, Marsh departed for Florence and his young grand-nieces and nephews early in June, 1882. A month later the whole family left Florence to summer at Vallombrosa, on the Tuscan slopes of the Apennines. The mountains remained Marsh's favorite recreation; he had had two wonderful excursions in his beloved Dolomites, another in the hill towns of Tuscany, others in Bavaria, Auvergne, and Switzerland. Too ill to leave the Villa Forini, Marsh had spent the entire summer of 1881 in Florence. But the past winter his health had much improved. He had been engrossed by European affairs, corresponded with Baird about the warm-water fish of the Gulf Stream, arranged to have part of *Man and Nature* reprinted in India, written Norton about Italian grammar and American civil service reform, and revised *Lectures on the English Language*.

Now he was glad to be going to the mountains again. Once an ancient monastery, Vallombrosa had been transformed, by Marsh's friend Adolfo di Bérenger, into a school of forestry, which Marsh had long wished to visit. The ascent from the Arno was full of interest; he marveled at how like Vermont the hillsides were, and delighted in seeing the great chestnut stands. The hotel, not far from the *foresteria,* afforded a magnificent view of hills dark with fir and brilliant with chestnut, forests of smooth beeches on the mountains above, olive-covered slopes and vineyards below, with the towers and domes of Florence in the distance. The thick-walled convent near by, gray and massive amid murmurous green, lent an air of "solemn sweetness." [69] On the mountain, as soon as the sun burned off the cold morning mists, Marsh took long walks through the avenues of firs, talked with forestry students, and visited Berenger, W. W. Story, and other intimates.

In mid-July word came from Wurts that Congress had merged the post of Consul-General with that of Secretary of Legation. Consul-General Lewis Richmond was appointed to both posts; Wurts was out of a job. Ostensibly a measure of economy, this move had been instigated by former Consul Eugene Schuyler in revenge for Marsh's treatment of him in 1879. For the Minister it was decisive. "I hardly know how I could get on without him," Marsh had said of Wurts some years before; now, at the age of eighty-one, he was certain he could not. He had too little strength to carry on the legation work himself or to train a new secretary; "by putting it out of my power to perform the duties of my office," the government forced him to resign. Wurts urged him to reconsider, to wait for explanations; [70] and though the Minister's mind was made up, he did not yet send in his resignation.

Instead he spent his days sitting in front of the *foresteria,* watching Carlo and his nieces and nephews at play, being read to, dictating letters, correcting *Man and Nature.* Walking in the pine groves, Marsh measured the high boles of the trees and speculated on the history of the forest. Not even in old age did he outgrow his insatiate greed for knowing things. Noting rates of growth, Marsh was "more than ever impressed with the superiority of the timber of the artificial forest, both in quantity and quality, as compared with the natural and spontaneous growth." Man was of a higher order than nature, and, certainly, a more purposeful creator. Vallombrosa's firs grew fast; Marsh believed that "the famous ridge-pole of a barn in Waterbury, Vermont, which squared six inches, with a length of sixty-five feet, might easily be matched here." The American Minister was disappointed, however, to find "not a single *compatriot* among the forest growths" of Vallombrosa; he asked C. S. Sargent to send him seeds of American trees, "particularly the *sugarmaple,* the American *ash* and *elm* . . . and the *black birch.*" [71]

Three days later, on July 23, 1882, Marsh rose early, dictated a few letters, added some notes to *Man and Nature,* and went outside with his family. The day was fine; the sun over the valley below bathed every detail in light, and hundreds of village spires stood out along the banks of the Sieve and the Arno. Thunderheads piled up to the west and south; Marsh described the various cloud forms to the children, explained how they had been named and how they changed with the weather. He turned to the papers, condemned the English bombardment of Alexandria, but commented on Egypt, as he had thirty years before, "I wish the English had complete possession of that wretchedly misgoverned country" [72]—a wish that was soon fulfilled.

About six, Marsh suddenly felt tired, and went in to lie down and drink a cup of beef tea. A few minutes later Caroline found him propped up, breathing with effort; she gave him sal volatile, then chloric ether, but without effect. Distressed, he asked to be raised up, to have the window opened, to be fanned. "Courage, dear husband," said Caroline, "you will be better soon." But when a doctor came from the *foresteria,* it was too late. Marsh was dead. "Ecco," said the doctor, "ecco la morte del giusto." [73] A just man: it was a felicitous epitaph.

At dawn two days later Marsh's body was brought from the great hall of the old convent, wrapped in an American flag, placed on a catafalque with wreaths of yellow immortelle, and carried down the mountain by the foresters. They thus honored the scholar whose work had awakened the minds of men to the significance of their task. The procession wound through the dark woods and was met at sunrise by Italian authorities at Pontassieve. Marsh was buried in the Protestant cemetery in Rome, not far from the graves of Keats and Shelley. Vallombrosa was a fitting end to his long and distinguished life. "Could he himself have selected the manner, time and place of his departure," wrote Caroline, "he would have desired nothing different." [74]

❧XVI❧

A Retrospective View

MARSH LED AN ACTIVE, full, and, on the whole, a happy life. Though not wealthy, he never suffered actual want. He had ample opportunity to gratify interests in the arts, in travel, and in scholarship. He enjoyed friendships with many of the most eminent and entertaining men of his time. He often had to work hard but seldom over a prolonged period. While his diplomatic and other duties were at times taxing, they were varied and generally not oppressive.

Although Marsh had many legitimate causes for complaint, his letters perhaps exaggerated his grievances: he was never given a large enough salary; the State Department did not appreciate him; fools and rogues made his life difficult; he never had enough time for his own work; he no sooner settled in a place than he had to leave it, at great expense and inconvenience.

These complaints were not altogether misanthropic. Marsh clearly enjoyed dramatizing his troubles; indeed, his misadventures are the most colorful parts of his letters. Sometimes Marsh complained for effect; to get any action from Washington he had to cry long and loud about the inadequacy of his remuneration and accommodations. But even when something pleased him, Marsh was often chary about saying so, lest he be thought self-satisfied. Only on his travels in Egypt and in the Alps, when his pleasures came from the outside world rather than from any personal achievement, was Marsh fully able to express delight in life.

Marsh also felt overwhelmed by family tragedies. He endured many, to be sure: the death of his first wife and child, the misfortunes of his second son, the drowning of his niece. But as one reader of his letters put it, Marsh's suffering was "so acute and so frequent as to make one feel as though woe were always impending." [1]

Marsh's personal life was far more felicitous than his accounts of it suggest. He was particularly fortunate in his second wife, Caroline. Intimate details of their relationship seldom appear in their letters and diaries, for they were both reticent New England Victorians; but a picture emerges from the known facts. During most of their married life, Caroline was an invalid who required much care from Marsh. Yet she does not seem to have been a drag on him. Her ailments seldom prevented either of them from doing what they wanted to; together they crossed deserts, climbed Alps, wrote books, gave huge dinners, and assiduously kept up diaries and extensive correspondence. At the same time, Marsh often used Caroline's infirmity as an excuse for avoiding disagreeable jobs, places, and people.

Caroline's physical weakness masked great strength of character and other qualities which gave Marsh support and confidence. She appreciated and fostered his work, but also carried on projects of her own, and had strong views which she was not afraid to express. She made friends more readily than he did; her easy way with people enhanced Marsh's own friendships.

Other members of Marsh's family helped make life agreeable. The Marsh heritage in Vermont gave him a sense of identity both with his birthplace and with Puritan values. His father's and grandfather's influence facilitated Marsh's start in affairs. In Burlington, cousin James Marsh was a constant intellectual stimulus, cousin Dr. Leonard Marsh an invaluable adviser. His first marriage advanced Marsh in the Burlington business community; Harriet Buell's family continued to promote his business and political interests, while his niece Maria Buell was an indispensable com-

panion in Turkey. Only his son George and his brother-in-law
Wyllys Lyman were disappointments to him. But Marsh relied on
the help of Lyman's son-in-law, Senator Edmunds. Whatever the
Minister's virtues as a diplomat, he could hardly have stayed in his
Italian post twenty-one years without Edmunds's support. Caroline's
family was also devoted to Marsh. Her sister, Lucy, supplied much
needed assistance in Washington and Turkey; half a dozen nieces
and nephews relieved social and household burdens in Italy.

Marsh had many reverses and took them hard. But even during
the worst period, after his 1855 bankruptcy, he was happy at times.
Though Marsh was essentially serious about life, he was never
without humor, sometimes frivolous and bantering, more often
ironic and self-deprecating.

The best years were those Marsh was abroad. Congressional service
in Washington had some compensations. But Vermont—which he
had thought of leaving as early as 1835—appealed to him less and
less with the passage of time. When he returned from Turkey in
1854 he had not really lived at home for a decade; he found Burlington provincial, isolated, and too cold in winter.

It was not merely the stimulus of travel that made Marsh more
contented with life across the Atlantic. Despite his complaints about
inadequate pay, he was able to live more comfortably in Europe and
the Levant than in Burlington or Washington; still more important,
his livelihood was assured. Diplomatic salaries were doubtless too
low, but they were regular and gave Marsh a sense of security essential to his scholarly work. Marsh was ill-adapted to private
enterprise. He disliked the tensions accompanying litigation and
competition. His desperate financial needs came into conflict with
his abhorrence for money-making as an end in itself. This dilemma
sapped his business judgment, and partly accounts for his lack of
success.

He was also more competent as a public servant than as an entre-
preneur. In the House of Representatives and its committees, in
legations, and with foreign diplomats, Marsh was controlled, ef-

fective, quick to note change—everything he was not in his own affairs. And once a piece of public work was done, Marsh was finished with it, free to turn to other things. In business, on the other hand, strain was never absent; Marsh would spend all day, sometimes all night, fretting over his problems. As a diplomat, he spent little time in the conduct of official affairs, though of course much was accomplished at social and informal gatherings. But he worked with concentration and efficiency, and his achievements were impressive, as may be seen from the content of his dispatches and the comments of his colleagues.

Marsh was not ambitious in a conventional sense. He hoped to make enough money to provide a comfortable life for himself and his family, but wealth as such did not appeal to him. Still less did Marsh crave position. He turned down the highest political posts offered him, and viewed his diplomatic appointments not as honors, but as means to an end—assured employment in congenial surroundings. Finally, Marsh sought no fame from his scholarly work and did not think he deserved any. He wrote because he had something interesting and useful to say, not to gain acclaim.

Marsh was no sedate scholar, secluded from the outside world. Not content to be a passive spectator, he felt deeply about many of his experiences, and was moved by new sights, new sounds, new impressions of every kind. His accounts of Middle Eastern desert camps and Middle Western railroads are fresh and vivid; his descriptions of Alpine climbing, medieval architecture, rare books and prints, are almost ecstatic.

His friendships were profound and lasting. For a man so much in public life, Marsh had few casual acquaintances. He devoted himself to people he knew well. Strong feeling animates his letters to Choate, Estcourt, Baird, Child, Sumner, Sherman, and others. With men he disliked or who had injured him, Marsh's enmity was unremitting: he saw them so much in terms of their vices that they seem caricatures of perversity.

Marsh tended to identify causes and institutions with people who favored or opposed them, and thus oversimplified many public issues. He expressed opinions about slavery, tariffs, Lincoln, the railroads, and so on, with passionate certainty; when he did change his mind, he held as firmly to the new as he had to the old conviction and was just as impatient with those who did not share his views. That his ideas about national and world affairs were often self-contradictory, Marsh was unaware. Many of his views depended less on facts than on moral convictions; in that realm Marsh never doubted his consistency.

Marsh's notion of democratic behavior emphasizes the contradictions in his character. He considered himself a man of the people; his early orations are full of contempt for Old World aristocracy, and the longer he stayed in Europe, the more confirmed a democrat he became. In times of crisis, he habitually blamed governments and praised the common man. This was a convenient prop, but Marsh scarcely knew the folk he exalted. He had little contact with ordinary people, and was far more at ease with men of cultivation, both abroad and at home. Aloof by upbringing and by temperament, Marsh always disdained the stupid and the vulgar.

Unhesitatingly confident in his views on contemporary affairs, Marsh was modest about his own accomplishments and diffident about his capabilities. He was pleased when people praised his books, but he never regarded them as masterpieces or took credit for his undoubted achievements. He regarded himself as a professional scholar in no field, and as semicompetent only in linguistics. By modern standards Marsh was indeed untrained and amateur; if professional at anything, it was diplomacy, though there too he was self-taught. What was truly professional about Marsh was not his work, but his life; he balanced avocation with occupation, work with pleasure, scholarship with experience, theory with practice, and activity with contemplation, in a fashion remarkable even in his own age.

Marsh's virtue as a scholar was his ability to see scientific and social problems from fresh viewpoints. All of his work—linguistic, geographical, diplomatic—shows his ability to integrate scholar-ship and personal observation. Marsh seldom tried to hide bias, and at times his work was fiercely partisan, as in his writings on religion and on corporations. Yet at heart he was no crusader. Although al-most all his studies were ostensibly undertaken to further his country's welfare or mankind's good, one often has the impression that Marsh paid only lip service to utility; he was chiefly interested in the subject for its own sake. For instance, the idea of introducing camels into America concerned Marsh very little when he was work-ing on *The Camel* and occupies only a few pages in the book, al-though Marsh claimed that was why he wrote it. Zest for etymo-logical detection stimulated his linguistic work more than did zeal for proving the superiority of American English, or of English in general.

Even where social or physical reforms were clearly central to his theme, as in *Man and Nature,* the *Report on the Artificial Propagation of Fish,* and many of his diplomatic dispatches, his tone and content were only occasionally didactic. Fascination for the subject matter itself overcame the pedagogue in Marsh; he digressed to describe, explain, or speculate on some phenomenon which bore little relation to his stated purpose. In one respect this discursive quality improved his work. Preconceived theories and goals did not limit his observations. Though committed on major issues, he was able to examine objectively many disputed hypotheses. He admitted his own inability to decide, for lack of evidence, such questions as the influence of forests upon rainfall.

Marsh rarely fell captive to the programs that he espoused. They seldom dominated his letters or, one may assume, his thought, even when he was working on them most intensively. When a book or an article was finished, he put the subject aside for a time, and pro-fessed lack of interest as well as lack of competence. This is particu-larly evident in his geographical studies. Marsh made effective pleas for forest preservation, for resource husbandry, for flood control, for other conservation measures, but after *Man and Nature* was published, he went on to other things. While he kept up a lively correspondence in forestry and related fields, his letters to C. S. Sargent and Henry Yule show that research excited him more than reform.

Marsh cannot properly be called a conservationist, any more than he can be considered a professional Americanist for his historical and literary essays, or a professional reformer for his advocacy of public regulation and ownership of utilities and railroads. He promoted all these causes, but did not wholly dedicate himself to any of them. While Marsh never devoted himself to a single program or philosophy, his eclecticism did not result in superficiality, as he himself feared. Although he spent most of his time and energy in gathering facts and setting them forth, he did organize them into new syntheses. Had he had fewer interests and diversions, or been less involved in earning a living and seeing the world, reflection might have added new dimensions to his work, though possibly at the expense of breadth. Considering the prejudices of his age and his circle, versatility was a source of strength. If conservation, patriotism, or reform had been a dominating force in his life, his scholarship might have been too narrow and biased to be of value.

Marsh was concerned with facts as such, but the chronology of his work arouses the suspicion that the process of research, even more than the subject matter, was a passion with him. There is no pattern to his work as a whole. His English language studies resulted from his professorship at Columbia. His book on the camel is the outgrowth of travel articles which he wrote because he happened to be in the Levant. His dozen or more scholarly essays of the 1840s and 1850s were on a dozen or more topics. So were his later articles for the *Nation* and Johnson's *Cyclopaedia*. Had he become a professor of history at Harvard, he would doubtless have written histories. *Man and Nature* partly derives from insights Marsh gained as Vermont farmer, businessman, and state official.

Marsh's scholarship must be viewed in relation to his public career and private life. The pattern was this: he would take on a job and prepare a public report, which would go beyond the immediate issue. He would then do further research, write several articles or a book. Meanwhile some other task would have engaged his attention. He used to complain that because his writing did not pay, he was forced to accept other assignments. Some of them were onerous, but he enjoyed many, even the onerous ones. This combination of public and private research on a wide variety of subjects was probably more to his taste than prolonged research in one field. Marsh started each new job with mixed feelings, but once begun he became intensely concerned with it.

To understand why Marsh distributed his energies and spread his talents in this way, it is useful to recall the circumstances of American life and of Marsh's own upbringing. Omnicompetence has been a marked trait of the American from the start,[2] and was surely characteristic of nineteenth-century Vermont, which required and fostered talents as diverse as those of any Western frontier community. As Marsh himself pointed out, Americans needed large vocabularies on practical subjects because they were all preachers, teachers, doctors, lawyers, merchants, farmers; everyone had to become familiar with every calling.

In Marsh's case the virtues of versatility were reinforced by family values. Labor and effort were highly regarded in the Marsh household, and habits of work ingrained at an early age. Marsh enjoyed his encyclopedic reading partly because it was interesting and absorbing, but chiefly because it was inherently good to master a wide range of subject matter, and he did it well. As an adult Marsh had limitless curiosity and a truly inquiring mind. But the mainspring of his scholarly—and of much of his other—work was a passion for acquiring facts, not for the sake of wisdom or morality, but because in the community in which he grew up this was meritorious, even necessary.

Marsh's upbringing and way of life provide the key to *Man and Nature*. How did an untrained nineteenth-century Vermonter, caught up in the practical and political life of his time, happen to seize upon and set forth the first sophisticated analysis of man's relation to his environment—an analysis that must be considered the origin of a revolution in American thought? Every phase of his life was involved: the early semiblindness which took Marsh away from books and impelled him to observe and study the environment; the faith of the Vermont Transcendentalists in man's free will and unique powers; Marsh's awareness of the rapid transformation of the Vermont landscape; the contrasts that suggested themselves to him in the barren and deforested lands around the Mediterranean; his interests in technology; his search for origins and his efforts to foster social history; his distrust of business motives and private selfishness; his desire to promote a better national economy; not least his love of nature.

A retrospective view of Marsh's career illuminates the fundamental source of his insights in the realm of conservation and human history. Marsh lived so much in the world and was so thoroughly committed to everyday affairs that he was, more than any of his scholarly contemporaries, both realistic and pragmatic. Others had written that the earth made man. Look around, said Marsh, and see what man does. He cuts down trees, clears and tills the soil, dams rivers; all these things Marsh had done himself. Was the landscape the same afterward, did streams flow as before, were plants, fish, birds, animals, alike or as abundant? Assuredly not. Where these and other human activities had gone on for a long time, the changes were profound and—since many lands lay abandoned and empty—often ruinous. Anyone with a hoe or an ax knows what he is doing, but before Marsh no one had seen the total effects of all axes and hoes. Once Marsh made this general observation, the conclusion was, for him, inescapable. Man depends upon soil, water, plants, and animals. But in securing his livelihood he may unwittingly destroy the fabric of nature which supports him. Therefore, said Marsh, men must learn to understand their environment and how they affect it. And they must take action, individual and collective, to restore and maintain a more viable milieu.

Marsh preached no panacea; still less did he profess despair, though he believed that selfishness motivated most human action. Deeply engaged in his own life, for all his misanthropy Marsh was more concerned with mankind than with the cosmos. It was not for nature's sake that he wanted to protect it against man, but for man's. Nature was neutral, man had conscious and moral force. That Marsh always believed man's powers superior is a reflection of his own active career and a measure of his commitment to humanity.

Abbreviations in Notes and Bibliography

AAAG	*Annals of the Association of American Geographers*
AAAS	American Association for the Advancement of Science
AAA&S	American Academy of Arts and Sciences
AH	*Agricultural History*
AHR	*American Historical Review*
AP	C. C. Andrews Papers
BDFP	Burlington *Daily Free Press*
BFP	Burlington *Free Press*
BNS	Burlington *Northern Sentinel*
BS	Burlington *Sentinel*
BSI	Spencer F. Baird Correspondence, Smithsonian Institution
Burl.	Burlington
CCM	Caroline Crane Marsh
CE	*Christian Examiner*
CG	*Congressional Globe*
Cj	Caroline C. Marsh, Journal, 1861–65, MS
CM	Charles Marsh
DC	Dartmouth College
DCA	Dartmouth College Archives
DD	Diplomatic Despatches, National Archives
DI	Diplomatic Instructions, National Archives
E	Estcourt
FC	Ford Collection, New York Public Library
FM	Francis Markoe
FW	Frederick Wislizenus
GFE	George Franklin Edmunds
GOM	George Ozias Marsh

GPM	George Perkins Marsh
GR	*Geographical Review*
HM	Henry E. Huntington Library Manuscript
HP	Rush C. Hawkins Papers
HPH	Henry P. Hickok
HUL	Harvard University Library
HVG	A. M. Hemenway, ed., *Vermont Historical Gazetteer*
JCP	Jacob Collamer Papers
JHI	*Journal of the History of Ideas*
LC	Library of Congress
LL	C. C. Marsh, *Life and Letters of George Perkins Marsh*
LW	Lucy Wislizenus
MHS	Massachusetts Historical Society
MLC	Francis Markoe Collection, Library of Congress
M & N	G. P. Marsh, *Man and Nature* (1864)
MV	Marsh MSS, Vermont Historical Society
NAR	*North American Review*
NASBM	National Academy of Sciences, *Biographical Memoirs*
NEQ	*New England Quarterly*
NES	G. P. Marsh, *Address, Delivered before the New England Soc. . . . of New-York . . . 1844*
NYHS	New York Historical Society
OHSI	W. J. Rhees, ed., *Smithsonian Institution: . . . Origin and History*
PR	Post Records, Department of State, National Archives
SFB	Spencer Fullerton Baird
SI	Smithsonian Institution
SIJ	W. J. Rhees, ed., *Smithsonian Institution: Journals of the Board of Regents*
SM	Susan Marsh
SS	*Scandinavian Studies*
UV	University of Vermont
VC	Vermont Central (Railroad)
VGC	Vermont. Supreme Executive Council, *Records of . . . Governor and Council,* ed. E. P. Walton
VHS	Vermont Historical Society
VSA	Vermont State Archives
VSP	Vermont State Papers
WP	Wislizenus Papers
YUL	Yale University Library

Notes

Where several citations occur in a paragraph, they are frequently combined in one note. Unless otherwise identified, all letters and manuscript citations are from the Marsh Collection, UV.

I: WOODSTOCK

1. Perkins, *Narrative of a Tour*, p. 26.
2. John Orvis, "Letter from Vermont, June 14, 1847," in the *Harbinger*, July, 1847, quoted in Ludlum, *Social Ferment*, p. 16; Dwight, *Travels*, II, 334.
3. Roswell Marsh to E. P. Walton, July 23, 1873, in *VGC*, I, 236–38. On Joseph Marsh's career, see Tucker, *Hartford*, especially pp. 10, 34, 113–14, 338–40; D. W. Marsh, ed., *Marsh Genealogy*, pp. 116, 130; *Conn. Hist. Soc. Colls.* (1903) IX, 249; Connecticut, *Public Records . . . 1757–62*, IX, 513, and X, 140; Kane, "Revolutionary History of a Vermont Town," *Vermont Antiquarian*, I (1902), 18; Rice, "Dartmouth College and the State of New Connecticut," Conn. Valley Hist. Soc., *Papers and Proc.* (1876–81), I, 152–206.
4. Mason, *Memoir*, pp. 17, 20–22.
5. Tyler, *Grandmother Tyler's Book*, p. 151; Barrett, *Charles Marsh*, pp. 24–29. See D. W. Marsh, *Marsh Genealogy*, p. 133.
6. Charles Marsh, *Essay on the Amendments;* D. B. Carroll, "Unicameral Legislature of Vermont," MS, pp. 46–56; *Spooner's Vermont Journal*, Nov. 29, 1813; *Annals of Cong.*, 14 Cong., especially 2 Sess., 1816–17, pp. 609–10, 637–38, 714; Fuess, *Webster*, I, 184–88.
7. According to the Rev. John Wheeler, then president of the UV, Charles Marsh "but for his singular modesty could have been for years

our Governor" (to J. H. Green, Feb. 16, 1843, in Lindsay, *Tradition Looks Forward,* p. 145).

8. CM to Francis Brown, in *LL,* p. 16. See Sherman, "Meet Charles Marsh," Kimball Union Acad., *Alumni Bull.* (March, 1947), p. 8.

9. *LL,* p. 8.

10. Perrin, *Fessenden,* pp. 50–70; Larned, *Windham County,* II, 325–26.

11. P. H. White, "Early Poets of Vermont," VHS *Proc.,* 1917–18, pp. 105–7. See also Fairbanks, *Town of St. Johnsbury,* pp. 72–75.

12. H. S. Dana, *Woodstock,* pp. 143–52, 248–57.

13. "A Friend to Real Order," in Woodstock *Northern Memento,* July 4, 1805. See Ludlum, *Social Ferment,* p. 20.

14. T. S. Brown to CCM, 188?; J. L. D., *Woodstock, Vt.,* pp. 16–17; H. S. Dana, *Woodstock,* pp. 23, 42–46, 82, 174–76, 286–301, 459–75. On Paine, see Taft, "Supreme Court of Vermont," *Green Bag,* VI (1894), 31–32.

15. On soils, see McDill, "The Billings Farm"; Kerr *et al.,* "Soil Survey of Windsor County"; Pierce, *Surface Waters of Vermont,* pp. 111, 192; interviews with S. E. Wilson, U.S.D.A. Soil Conservation Service, and John McDill, Woodstock, Vt., summer, 1951. On mills, see H. S. Dana, *Woodstock,* pp. 181–82, 306–17. On the Connecticut River, see Wilgus, *Role of Transportation,* pp. 42–53; L. S. Hayes, *Connecticut River Valley,* pp. 37–38, 160.

16. To "Tom," Nov. 11, 1847.

17. *LL,* p. 11.

18. Very, *Essays and Poems,* p. 161; GPM to C. E. Norton, May 24, 1871, Norton Pap.; GPM to Joseph Neilson, June–July, 1882, in Neilson, *Choate,* pp. 376–77.

19. *LL,* p. 11.

20. H. S. Dana, *Woodstock,* pp. 449–51.

21. CM to Francis Brown, April, 1812.

22. Quincy, quoted in Fuess, *An Old New England School,* pp. 157, 173; GPM, "England Old and New," MS, p. 5 (address at Middlebury, Vt., Dec. 1859). On Andover, see Andover *Catalogue . . . 1816,* and *Biographical Catalogue,* pp. 18–19, 63; Cuningham, *Dwight,* p. 230.

23. CM to Brown, in Richardson, *Dartmouth,* I, 347–48; Shirley, *Dartmouth . . . Causes,* pp. 81–115. See Feuer, "James Marsh and the Conservative Transcendentalist Philosophy," *NEQ,* XXXI (1958), 6–10.

24. G. W. Nesmith to B. F. Prescott, Feb. 17, 1885, DCA. See DC, *General Catalogue.*

25. Ball, *Autobiography*, pp. 19–20, 28; Silliman, *Remarks Made on a Short Tour*, pp. 416–18; DC Treasurer's accounts, Ledger F (1810–29), p. 80, DCA.

26. Richardson, *Dartmouth*, I, 249–50, 272–78. See also H. Wood, *Life of President Brown*, pp. 12–16.

27. *LL*, p. 17. See Cuningham, *Dwight*, pp. 22–26.

28. G. W. Nesmith to S. G. Brown, Nov. 16, 1882. See Ball, *Autobiography*, p. 25; Dartmouth, Course of Instruction, DCA; Fulton and Thomson, *Silliman*, p. 158.

29. James Barrett to S. G. Brown, n.d., in *LL*, p. 17; Rufus Choate to David Choate, Nov. 5, 1816, DCA.

30. Rufus Choate to David Choate, Dec. 16, 1816, DCA; *Dartmouth Gazette*, March 5, 1817, in J. K. Lord, *Dartmouth*, pp. 120–21. On Shurtleff, see Long, *Serving God with the Mind*, pp. 22–48.

31. J. K. Lord, *Dartmouth*, pp. 104–8; Marshall, in Shirley, *Dartmouth . . . Causes*, pp. 201, 302–3, 411, 423.

32. GPM to S. G. Brown, in S. G. Brown, *Works of Rufus Choate*, I, 11; GPM, *Earth as Modified by Human Action* (1874), p. 54n (not in first [1864] ed. of *Man and Nature*).

33. Faculty Records, May, 1820, DCA.

34. Woodstock *Observer*, Sept. 4, 1820.

35. Ellis, *Norwich University*, I, 1–11. See Flint, "Alden Partridge," in Crockett, ed., *Vermonters*, pp. 165–68.

36. GPM to Arnold Guyot, Oct. 27, 1857; "Journal of an Excursion," in VHS, *Essays*, p. 195.

37. GPM, [Report on the Education of the Deaf and Dumb]. See Vermont *Gen. Assembly Journal*, 1823, p. 11; 1824, pp. 16, 61, 67; 1825, pp. 35–38; 1826, pp. 54–55; Ludlum, *Social Ferment*, p. 220.

38. Windsor County Court Records, XIV, 53; H. S. Dana in *Vermont Standard* (Woodstock), July 27, 1882.

II: BURLINGTON

1. *BNS*, July 4, 1829, Feb. 2, 1832.

2. *BFP*, Aug. 25, Oct. 1830, May 27, July 1, 8, Dec. 2, 1831. On Bailey, see G. F. Houghton, "Benjamin Franklin Bailey," in *HVG*, I, 645–46; on Van Ness, T. D. S. Bassett, "Rise of Cornelius Peter Van Ness," VHS *Proc.*, n.s. X (1942), 3–20; *Proceedings and Address of the Vermont Republican Convention . . . 1828*, p. 3; D. A. Smalley, "C. P. Van Ness," in *HVG*, I, 608–14.

3. To CCM, 1839, in *LL,* pp. 30–31.

4. To LW, Feb. 14, 1875.

5. James Barrett to S. G. Brown, n.d.; Mrs. Levi Underwood to Gen. Rush C. Hawkins, Dec. 26, 1896, HP; GPM to LW, Feb. 14, 1875. For Marsh's legal career, see Chittenden County Court Records, Vols. XII ff; Vt. Repts. and Vt. Supreme Court Records, Vols. II ff.

6. GPM to FW and LW, Oct. 13, 1862, WP.

7. *Ibid.; LL,* p. 25. For Buell, see HPH, "Ozias Buell," in *HVG,* I, 592–93.

8. Henry James, "From Lake George to Burlington," *Nation,* XI (1870), 135–36; GPM, "Marsh, James," in Ripley and Dana, eds., *New American Cyclopaedia,* XI, 216.

9. Rufus Choate to James Marsh, Aug. 21, 1821, in S. G. Brown, ed., *Choate,* I, 16; James Marsh to Henry J. Raymond, March 1, 1841, in Cheever, *Characteristics of the Christian Philosopher,* pp. 68–69; GPM, "Marsh, James," p. 217. See also Torrey, "James Marsh," in *HVG,* I, 529; Lindsay, *Tradition Looks Forward,* pp. 129–49; Miller, ed., *Transcendentalists,* pp. 33–38; Torrey, *Remains;* Dewey, "James Marsh and American Philosophy," *JHI,* II (1941), 131–50; Wells, *Three Christian Transcendentalists,* pp. 14–48; Feuer, "James Marsh and the Conservative Transcendentalist Philosophy," pp. 20–24.

10. GPM to Prof. Parke, Oct. 16, 1844, Boston Public Lib.

11. Wheeler to J. H. Green, in Lindsay, *Tradition Looks Forward,* p. 145. For Marsh's friends, see R. F. Taft, "Burlington," in *HVG,* I, 487–519; Siebert, *Vermont's Anti-Slavery,* pp. 19–21, 62–63; G. F. Houghton, "Benjamin Lincoln," in *HVG,* I, 648–49; B. Lincoln, *An Exposition; LL,* pp. 21–22; Buckham, "George Wyllys Benedict," pp. 44–52; Tracy, *John Wheeler,* pp. 10–23; Byington, *John Wheeler,* pp. 16–18; A. Young, *Natural History of . . . Vermont,* pp. 37–43; *BFP,* Nov. 20, 1829.

12. Ozias Buell, will probate, Aug. 20, 1835, and other papers, Oct. 12, 1836, Probate Office, Chittenden Co.; Burl. Grand List, 1825–32, 1837; Burl. Land List and Real Estate Assessment, 1837.

13. *BS,* March 7, 1834; GPM, Oct. 10, 1834, VSP, LXIV, 19. See U.S. Circuit Court, 20 Vt. 666.

14. *VGC,* Oct. 16, 1835, VIII, 229; *LL,* p. 29; *BFP,* Dec. 21, 1838; *BS,* Jan. 22, 1836. For Marsh's woolen interests, see Burl. Land Records, XI, 331–36, 361; Stowell, "Merino Sheep Industry," pp. 213–14; *LL,* p. 28; Auld, *Picturesque Burlington,* p. 166; *BFP,* Dec. 28, 1838; Carman, "Sheep Industry." For Winooski River, see Pierce, *Surface Waters,*

pp. 55, 215; Hill, *The Winooski,* p. 83; *BFP,* July 30, 1830; Z. Thompson, *Natural History,* p. 20.

15. *A Description of the State Houses,* p. 8.

16. Eldridge, "Journal of a Tour," pp. 65–66; Edmunds, quoted in Bailey, "Vermont's State Houses," *Vermont Quart.,* XII (1944), 143. See Vermont, *Directory and Rules of the House,* p. 5; *HVG,* II, 262, 493–94.

17. *BNS,* Oct. 30, 1829; GPM in *BFP,* Sept. 13, 1830.

18. GPM in *VGC,* Nov. 10, 1835, VIII, 261. See Whipple, "Imprisonment for Debt in Vermont," *Vermonter,* XLII (1937), 24; Conant, "Imprisonment for Debt in Vermont," *Vermont Quart.,* XIX (1951), 67–80.

19. Montpelier *Watchman & State Gazette,* Nov. 17, 1835. See D. B. Carroll, "Unicameral Legislature," pp. 96, 113, 152–58.

20. Crane, *Caroline Crane Marsh,* pp. 1–6; *BFP,* Oct. 4, 1839.

21. CCM in *LL,* p. 29.

22. GPM in *LL,* p. 35.

23. *LL,* pp. 36–47.

III: PURITANS AND GOTHS

1. *LL,* pp. 30–31.

2. To F. P. Nash, Feb. 6, 1875; to CCM, in *LL,* p. 33.

3. To CCM, in *LL,* pp. 38; 25.

4. GPM to Charles Lanman, April 21, 1847, in Lanman, *Haphazard Personalities,* pp. 100–101; to Jewett, May 24, 1849. For Marsh's ideas on art, see GPM to William Coleman, Aug. 13, 1840, FC; to S. F. B. Morse, Feb. 14, 1844, Morse Papers; GPM, "Study of Nature," *CE,* LXVII (1860), 43–54.

5. SI, *Fifth Ann. Rept.* (1850), pp. 29–30; *Nation,* XXXV (1882), 95. Fire destroyed Marsh's collection in 1865.

6. Oct. 21, 1833, in Grøndal, *Rafn,* pp. 293–94. See Lowenthal, "G. P. Marsh and Scandinavian Studies," *SS,* XXIX (1957), 41–52, for a fuller account.

7. GPM to CCM, in *LL,* p. 32; to Rafn, Dec. 17, 1834; Richard Beck, "George P. Marsh and Old Icelandic Studies," *SS,* XVII (1943), 202.

8. Rafn to GPM, June 25, Nov. 29, 1834, Nov. 19, 1835. For the background, see Falnes, "New England Interest in Scandinavian Culture and the Norsemen," *NEQ,* X (1937), 211–36; Benson, "Beginning of American Interest in Scandinavian Literature," *SS,* VIII (1925), 133–41;

Einarsson, *History of Icelandic Prose Writers,* pp. 16–21; GPM to Rafn, Dec. 17, 1834; Bancroft to Rafn, Dec. 27, 1836, in Grøndal, *Rafn,* pp. 181–82; *ibid.,* pp. 47–51.

9. GPM to Rafn, Aug. 20, 1839. The evidence on pre-Columbian Scandinavian settlement is summarized in Godfrey, "Vikings in America," and Mallery, "Pre-Columbian Discovery of America," *Amer. Anthropologist,* LVII (1955), 35–43, and LX (1958), 141–50, respectively.

10. GPM, *Compendious Grammar,* pp. iii–iv, ix–xi, 140–42; GPM to CCM, Feb. 28, 1838. See Rafn to GPM, Nov. 29, 1834, in Grøndal, *Rafn,* pp. 295–99; GPM, "Origin, Progress, and Decline of Icelandic Historical Literature," *Amer. Eclectic,* I (1841), 449–60; Auden, "Njal's Saga," *New Statesman and Nation,* LII (1956), 551–52.

11. GPM, "Old Northern Literature," *Amer. Whig Rev.,* I (1845), 256; GPM in *LL,* p. 34. See GPM, "Summary of the Statistics of Sweden," *Hunt's Merchants' Mag.,* XXIV (1851), 194–99; "Origin and History of the Danish Sound and Belt-Tolls," *Hunt's Merchants' Mag.,* X (1844), 218–32, 303–8.

12. GPM, "Swedish Literature: Olof Rudbeck," *Amer. Eclectic,* I (1841), 68–74, 81; "Translations from the German," *Amer. Whig Rev.,* II (1845), 256–58.

13. GPM, "The River, by Tegnér," *loc. cit.,* p. 357; CCM, "Axel," in *Wolfe of the Knoll,* pp. 261–307; Hilen, Longfellow and Scandinavia, pp. 57–58; Sturtevant, "An American Appreciation of Esaias Tegnér," *SS,* XVI (1941), 158; Leighly, "Inaccuracies in Longfellow's Translation of Tegnér's 'Nattvardsbarnen,' " *SS,* XXI (1949), 171–73; John Leighly, personal communication, Aug. 4, 1951.

14. N. H. Julis, May 23, 1838, in Longfellow, *Longfellow,* I, 288; Ole Munch Raeder to Caroline, Dec. 28, 1847, in Raeder, *America in the Forties,* p. 163; GPM to Rafn, Jan. 1, 1864 [translation courtesy of Einar Haugen]; GPM to Andrews, July 5, 1875, AP.

15. Richard Beck calls Marsh "the pioneer American scholar in that field" ("Marsh and Old Icelandic," p. 199). Fiske introduced himself to Marsh in the 1850s, had the run of his library, visited him in Italy, and after Marsh's death took his villa in Florence. See Fiske to GPM, March 13, 1851; GPM to Rafn, Dec. 5, 1851; H. S. White, *Fiske,* p. 12; Hermannsson, "Willard Fiske and Icelandic Bibliography," Bibliographical Soc. of Amer., *Papers,* XII (1918), 197; *Nation,* XXXV (1882), 95; Anderson, "Autobiography," MS; Bayard Taylor to GPM, Jan. 7, 1861.

16. *Goths in New-England*, pp. 10, 14.

17. Mitchell, *American Lands and Letters*, p. 37; Kliger, "George Perkins Marsh and the Gothic Tradition in America," *NEQ*, XIX (1946), 524–31; Saveth, *American Historians*, Chs. I, II, VIII; Ekirch, *Idea of Progress*, pp. 40–95; Curti, *Growth of American Thought*, pp. 247–53; Gooch, *History and Historians*, Ch. IV.

18. *NES*, pp. 48–49; *Goths*, pp. 33, 7, 38–39. For the growth of this kind of patriotism, see Curti, *Roots of American Loyalty*, pp. 122–30.

19. Herodotus, *Persian Wars*, Bk. IV, pp. 285–86; J. White, *Planters Plea*, p. 18.

20. Montesquieu, *Spirit of Laws*, p. 126.

21. GPM, *NES*, pp. 17–27. For connections between environmentalism and Gothicism see Kliger, *Goths in England*, pp. 241–52; T. J. Beck, *Northern Antiquities*, I, 20–21; Vann, "The Free Anglo-Saxons," *JHI*, XIX (1958), 259–72.

22. GPM, *Goths*, pp. 11–13, 19; "Old Northern Literature," *Amer. Whig Rev.*, I (1845), 250–51. See Mierow, ed., *Gothic History of Jordanes*, p. 551.

23. *NES*, p. 34.

24. *NES*, p. 48.

25. Hone, *Diary*, II, 334; GPM, *NES*, p. 48. See *HVG*, II, 334–38, 367.

26. *Goths*, p. 37; *CG*, 28 Cong. 1 Sess., p. 674. For the Irish, see Stilwell, *Migration from Vermont*, pp. 184–85; Handlin, *Boston's Immigrants*, pp. 191–99.

27. *New Englander*, II (1844), 490; Episcopus, *Remarks on an Address*, pp. 10–11.

28. Allen to GPM, June 19, 1844. See *LL*, p. 44n.

29. GPM, *Goths*, p. 14. See James Marsh, "Preliminary Essay," in his edition of Coleridge, *Aids to Reflection*, pp. xiii–xlvi; Nicolson, "James Marsh and the Vermont Transcendentalists," *Philosophical Rev.*, XXXIV (1925), 35–37; Pochmann, *German Culture in America*, pp. 88–95, 132–42.

30. *Goths*, pp. 15–16.

31. *Goths*, pp. 18; 6. See GPM, "Study of Nature," *CE*, LXVIII (1860), 57–58. Marsh used the word *Puritan* in its religious sense "as embracing all those sects, which hold, that the Bible is the *only* rule of Christian faith and practice, and reject the authority of tradition in rites, doctrine, and church government" (*NES*, p. 22n). On Paley's popularity, and the fear among American divines of the corrosive effect of his doctrine of moral expediency, see Glick, "Bishop Paley in America," *NEQ*,

XXVII (1954), 347–54. On the reaction against Locke, see Curti, "The Great Mr. Locke, America's Philosopher," in his *Probing Our Past*, pp. 85–93; Feuer, "James Marsh and the Conservative Transcendentalist Philosophy," pp. 12–19.

IV: CONGRESS AND THE SMITHSONIAN

1. GPM in *BFP*, Jan. 10, 1840.
2. Crockett, *Vermont*, III, 307–12; *BFP*, June 16, 1843, Dec. 2, 1831.
3. GPM in *BFP*, June 16, 1843; *Vermont Patriot* (Montpelier), June 17, 1843; *BFP*, Aug. 11, Sept. 8, 1843.
4. GPM letter of Dec. 5, 1843; to Mrs. HPH, Dec., 1843, in *LL*, pp. 59–60.
5. Adams, *Memoirs*, XII, 57.
6. *Dobbs Family in America*, p. 193; Foot to GPM, April 4, 1860. See Edmunds, *Foot*, pp. 7–14; Kelly, *Woodstock's U.S. Senator;* Hamilton, *Zachary Taylor*, p. 165.
7. GPM in *LL*, pp. 31, 94n.
8. Atwater, *Mysteries of Washington City*, pp. 19–20. See *LL*, p. 67; Bryan, *National Capital*, II, 294–95, 317; Busey, *Pictures of the City of Washington*, p. 143.
9. GPM to J. N. Pomeroy, March 30, 1844.
10. GPM to Mrs. HPH, June, 1844; Collamer to Frances Collamer, Feb. 4, 1844, JCP.
11. *LL*, p. 72.
12. To Pomeroy, Jan. 15, 1844.
13. GPM, *Speech on the Tariff Bill*, pp. 3, 9.
14. *Ibid.*, pp. 5; 13; 4.
15. *BFP*, June 7, 1844; George Allen to GPM, June 19, 1844; GPM, June 30, 1846, *CG*, 29 Cong. 1 Sess., App., pp. 1009–11.
16. GPM to Pomeroy, March 30, 1844; *LL*, pp. 70–71.
17. GPM to Pomeroy, Dec. 16, 1844, Jan. 13, 1845; GPM in the House, Jan. 20, 1845, *CG*, 28 Cong. 2 Sess., App., pp. 316–19.
18. GPM to Pomeroy, March 30, 1844.
19. GPM, *Report on Petition of E. H. Holmes and W. Pedrick*, 28 Cong. 1 Sess., H. Rep. 389, pp. 1–2.
20. GPM, *Report on Spirit Ration*, pp. 1–2. The Senate had killed a similar bill the previous year, Senator McDuffie observing caustically that they "might as well abolish the navy" as give up grog (*CG*, 28

Cong. 1 Sess., pp. 681–82). For later legislation, see *CG,* 29 Cong. 2 Sess., p. 291; 12 *Stat. at Large* 565 (1862); for GPM on corporal punishment, June 15, 1844, *H. Journal,* 28 Cong. 1 Sess., pp. 1135–36; GPM to CM, Sept. 4, 1852.

21. To Edward C. Lester, Aug. 26, 1844, FC. See GPM, *Report on Durazzo Library.*

22. Goode, "Genesis of the U.S. National Museum," in SI, *Ann. Rept. 1897,* II, 83–192, espec. GPM to FM, April 4, 1844, p. 133; GPM, *Report on Memorial of the National Institute for the Promotion of Science,* p. 3. See Henderson, *Hidden Coasts,* pp. 201–18; Pickard, "Government and Science," *Journal of the History of Medicine and Allied Sciences,* I (1946), 65–89; Tappan, Senate Journal, MS, Jan. 23, 1844, p. 6.

23. To CCM, in *LL,* p. 93.

24. *OHSI,* pp. 2, 164, 218, 432–33, 447–48; Adams, *Memoirs,* XII, 236; Oehser, *Sons of Science;* Dupree, *Science in the Federal Government,* pp. 66–90; Pickard, "Government and Science," pp. 446–81.

25. To N. S. Moore, April 22, 1848, FC.

26. Owen, April 22, 1846, *OHSI,* pp. 277–78. See Leopold, *Owen,* pp. 220–26; Adams, *Memoirs,* XII, 177, 235–36.

27. GPM, *Speech on the Bill for . . . the Smithsonian,* pp. 4, 12–13 (also in *CG,* 29 Cong. 1 Sess., App., pp. 850–55; *OHSI,* pp. 410–28).

28. Owen, *CG,* 29 Cong. 1 Sess., p. 712.

29. GPM, *Speech on the Bill for . . . the Smithsonian,* pp. 7–11.

30. Adams, *Memoirs,* XII, 259; *New Englander,* IV (1846), 607; Morse, *CG,* 29 Cong. 1 Sess., pp. 718–19. Morse was no unlettered backwoodsman, however, but a Harvard graduate.

31. Leopold, *Owen,* p. 227; Adams and Johnson, April 28, 1846, *CG,* 29 Cong. 1 Sess., pp. 738, 741.

32. Hough and Marsh, *CG,* 29 Cong. 1 Sess., p. 749; *OHSI,* pp. 469–72.

33. *SIJ,* pp. 11–13.

34. Bache to Henry, Dec. 4, 1846, in Odgers, *Bache,* pp. 165–66; Leopold, *Owen,* pp. 244–45; *SIJ,* Dec. 23, 1847, pp. 27–47. See Borome, *Jewett,* p. 23; Coulson, *Joseph Henry,* pp. 176–77.

35. GPM, SI Affairs, draft of letter to C. W. Upham, Feb. 1855. See Coulson, *Henry,* pp. 189, 211–12; Choate to GPM, Dec. 23, 1846; *SIJ,* pp. 25–26.

36. *SIJ,* pp. 448–51, 724–27.

37. GPM in the House, Dec. 11, 1848, *CG,* 30 Cong. 2 Sess., p. 24.

38. Journal Exec. Comm., *SIJ*, pp. 464–65.

39. GPM, June 9, 1847, in SI, *First Ann. Report* (1847), p. 22, and in Squier and Davis, *Ancient Monuments,* p. x.

40. GPM to Squier, June 6, 16, 1848 (see also Feb. 23, March 6, 1847), Squier Coll.

41. GPM to Mary Baird, Feb. 10, 1847, BSI; Henry to SFB, March 3, 1847, in Dall, *Baird,* pp. 163–64; GPM to SFB, June 19, 14, 1848, April 25, 1849. See J. W. Powell, "Personal Characteristics of Professor Baird," SI, *Ann. Rept. 1888,* pp. 739–44; Oehser, *Sons of Science,* pp. 60, 89, 92.

42. GPM to SFB, Oct. 6, 10, 1848, BSI.

43. GPM to SFB, April 25, 1849; Dall, *Baird,* pp. 184–85.

44. July 9, 1850. See Goode, "The Three Secretaries," pp. 166–67.

V: AMERICAN HISTORY AND MANIFEST DESTINY

1. CCM to Mrs. HPH, Nov. 29, 1845.

2. GPM, "The Late General Estcourt," *National Intelligencer,* Feb. 7, 1856 (also in *LL,* pp. 474–79); *Speech on the Bill for . . . the Smithsonian,* p. 10; *LL,* pp. 100, 103.

3. *LL,* p. 116; GPM, *Report on Memorial of P. J. Farnham and Jed Frye;* GPM to SFB, April 4, 18, 1848, BSI, June 22, 1848. See F. A. Wislizenus, Jr., "Sketch of the Life of Dr. Wislizenus," in FW, *Journey to the Rocky Mountains,* p. 11; Wittke, *Refugees of Revolution.*

4. Collamer to Mary Collamer, Dec. 25, 1847, JCP; Mitchell to Mary Goddard, Jan. 2, 28, 1847, in Dunn, *Mitchell,* pp. 167–70.

5. Mitchell, *American Lands and Letters,* p. 38.

6. GFE to CCM, May 13, 1888; *LL,* p. 73.

7. GPM to Mrs. HPH, June, 1844, in *LL,* pp. 68–69; to GOM, Sept. 30, June 5, 1848.

8. GOM to GPM, dated only 1848; B. Sears to GPM, March 29, 1848; J. V. C. Smith to GPM, June 27, 1848.

9. GPM to GOM, May 13, 1848; GOM to CCM, June 4, 1848; GPM to SFB, June 9, 1848.

10. GOM to GPM, June 12, 1848; GPM to SFB, June 19, 1848; C. S. Richards to GPM, July 4, 1849.

11. Letter of 1848.

12. GPM to Henry Yule, Jan. 10, 1877; to Mrs. E, July 28, 1847, in *LL,* p. 108.

13. Sumner to GPM, May 5, 1847; Everett Journal, Everett Papers,

CLXVI, 161; Ticknor to GPM, Sept. 6, 1847; Choate to GPM, 1847; Boston *Daily Advertiser*, Aug. 27, 1847. See Hayes to Mrs. W. A. Platt, Aug. 30, 1847, in Rutherford B. Hayes, *Diaries and Letters*, I, 215–16.

14. *New Englander*, VI (1848), 312; GPM, *Address . . . Agric. Soc. Rutland Co.*

15. June 9, 1847, Knollenberg Coll.

16. *Goths*, p. 33; *American Historical School*, p. 10. On Marsh's idea of history, see Beard and Beard, *American Spirit*, pp. 264–73, and Curti, *Roots of American Loyalty*, pp. 50–51.

17. *American Historical School*, p. 10.

18. Eggleston, quoted in Ausubel, *Historians and Their Craft*, p. 314; Dunne, *Observations by Mr. Dooley*, p. 271. See E. Eggleston, "Formative Influences," *Forum*, X (1890), 286–87; Kraus, *History of American History*, pp. 187–90, and *Writing of American History*, pp. 127–29; Curti, "The Democratic Theme in American Historical Literature," in his *Probing Our Past*, pp. 5–11, 16–18; Beard and Vagts, "Currents of Thought in Historiography," *AHR*, XLII (1937), 482; Robinson, *The New History*, Chs. I, V.

19. *Address Agric. Soc. Rutland Co.*, pp. 6, 8, 10–11, 17–19.

20. GPM to Gallatin, Dec. 15, 1847, Jan. 3, 1848, Gallatin Papers. The pamphlet Marsh helped distribute was probably "Peace with Mexico" (1847), in Gallatin, *Writings*, III, 555–91; the one he helped write was "War Expenses" (1848), referred to in Gallatin, *Writings*, II, 666.

21. GPM, *Speech on the Mexican War*, pp. 7; 11; 4; 12.

22. Brown of Mississippi, *CG*, 30 Cong. 1 Sess., p. 333.

23. GPM, *Remarks on Slavery*, pp. 9, 8.

24. *Speech on the Mexican War*, pp. 8–11.

25. *Remarks on Slavery*, p. 12; Curti, *Roots of American Loyalty*, p. 45.

26. Churchill to GPM, Dec. 16, 1846; GPM, *Speech on the Mexican War*, p. 11. See GPM to Pomeroy, Dec. 30, 1845; GPM to Gallatin, Nov. 6, 1847, and W. H. Emory to GPM, Dec. 25, 30, 1847, Gallatin Pap.

27. GPM to SFB, June 15, 1848.

28. GPM to Mrs. E, June 10, 1848, in *LL*, p. 124; to SFB, Sept. 15, 1848; to Collamer, Sept. 11, 14, 1848.

29. GPM to SFB, Oct. 6, 1848; *Remarks on Slavery*, p. 9; undated MS.

30. James Barrett to CCM, in *LL*, p. 129n; *Remarks on Slavery*,

p. 11. See Merrill Ober, Oct. 28, 1848, in Clough, "A Journal of Village Life in Vermont," *NEQ,* I (1928), 39.

31. *BDFP,* Nov. 9, 1848; GPM to Mrs. E, Feb. 3, 1849. In Vermont Van Buren got 29 percent of the popular vote; in Massachusetts, 28; in New York, 27; and in Wisconsin, 27 percent.

32. To Maria Buell, Nov. 27, 1848; to SFB, Dec. 7, 1848, BSI.

33. GPM to Mrs. E, Feb. 3, 1839; to Drake, Dec. 7, 1848; Rafn to GPM, July 21, 1848.

34. *BS,* Baltimore *Patriot,* and Boston *Courier,* quoted in *BDFP,* Jan. 17, June 15, Feb. 13, 1849.

35. C. C. Jewett to GPM, July 3, 1849. Marsh could never have been Speaker; when invited to preside in the chair, he asked "to be excused, because . . . his eyesight was so imperfect, that he was unable to distinguish members in their places" (May 9, 1846, *CG,* 29 Cong. 1 Sess., p. 782). For Hannegan, see Woollen, *Biographical and Historical Sketches,* pp. 211–22.

36. GPM to Mrs. E, May 29, 1849, in *LL,* p. 139; GPM in *BDFP,* Aug. 31, 1849; C. S. Daveis to GPM, April 9, 1849, Daveis Pap.; Solomon Foot to Zachary Taylor, May 30, 1849, U.S. Dept. State, Appointment Pap. See Hamilton, *Zachary Taylor,* pp. 26, 221; Poore, *Perley's Reminiscences,* I, 359–60. Marsh complained that Vermonters had "not made an effort for me"; if he received a post "I am not likely to owe it to the goodwill of the people of my own state" (to SFB, March 21, 1849). But the State Dept. Appointment Papers show he was wrong.

37. Fillmore to John M. Clayton, May 10, 1849, Clayton Pap.; *BDFP,* June 4, 1859; GPM to E, in *LL,* p. 137, and also to E, Oct. 22, 1849.

38. GPM to SFB, June 9, 1849, BSI; GPM in *BDFP,* Aug. 29, Sept. 25, 1849.

39. SM to Mrs. HPH, Oct. 15, 1849.

VI: CONSTANTINOPLE AND THE DESERT

1. GPM to E's, Oct. 22, 1849; to CM, Oct. 25, 1849, DCA.

2. To Lyndon Marsh, Nov. 9, 1849.

3. To SFB, Aug. 23, 1850; *LL,* p. 148.

4. GPM to CM, Feb. 3, 1850, DCA; GPM, "Notes on Vesuvius," *Amer. Journal of Science and Arts,* 2d ser., XIII (1852), 131–32.

5. GPM to SFB, Aug. 23, 1850, BSI.

6. GPM, "Supplementary Statement of Complaint," April 4, 1850, MS; Paine, *Tent and Harem,* pp. 6–8.

7. GPM, March 14, 1850, DD (Turkey, Vol. XII), No. 3; Carlisle, *Diary*, p. 46.

8. GPM to CM, July, 1850, DCA; GPM, Feb. 4, 1852, DD No. 26. For the situation in Turkey, see Lane-Poole, *Stratford Canning*, II, 206–16; GPM, "The Future of Turkey," *CE*, LXV (1858), 401-19.

9. GPM, Feb. 4, 1852, DD No. 26; GPM to FM, July 5, 1852, FC.

10. To SFB, Sept. 23, 1850, BSI; to SM, April 17, 1850, DCA; to FM, Dec. 20, 1852, FC.

11. To Drake, Aug. 3, 1850; GPM, Aug. 19, 1850, DD No. 13 (confidential).

12. To FM, April 26, 1852, FC. See GPM, Dec. 24, 1851, DD No. 24.

13. GPM to Robert C. Winthrop, June 4, 1850, Winthrop Pap.

14. Brown to GPM, May 26, Sept. 19, 22, 1850; Lewis Cass to GPM, Jan. 15, 1858.

15. Brown to H. A. Homes, April 10, 1851; Reshid Pasha to GPM, in GPM, Jan. 6, 1851, DD. See Gordon, *American Relations with Turkey*, espec. pp. 12–47.

16. GPM, April 18, 1850, Dec. 18, 1851, DD Nos. 5, 22; GPM, "Persia Treaty Negotiations," MS.

17. GPM to William Goodell *et al.*, Dec. 24, 1853; Hamlin, "Recollections of Turkey," undated MS, UV. See Hamlin, *Among the Turks*, pp. 218–19; missionaries to GPM, Sept. 22, 1853.

18. GPM, March 25, 1850, June 19, 1852, DD Nos. 4, 29.

19. GPM to Foot, Jan. 1, 16, 1855, MV.

20. GPM to Sublime Porte, May 13, 1852, Turkey, PR, Misc. Corr. No. 149; to E. S. Offley, June 1, 1852, PR, Misc. Corr. No. 156.

21. To Webster, Nov. 25, 1850, DD No. 16.

22. GPM, April 18, Aug. 19, 1850, DD Nos. 5, 12.

23. Clayton to GPM, Jan. 12, 1850, DI (Turkey, Vol. I) No. 3, p. 338; GPM, March 14, 25, 1850, DD Nos. 3, 4. See Curti, "Austria and the United States 1848-1852," *Smith College Studies in History*, XI (1926), 141–60.

24. Kossuth to GPM, Jan. 1, 1850, PR, Misc. Corr. Received; GPM to Kossuth, June 2, 1850, PR, Misc. Corr. No. 28.

25. GPM to Kossuth, June 2, 8, 1850, PR, Misc. Corr. Nos. 28, 29; GPM, May 15, July 4, 1850, DD Nos. 6, 10.

26. GPM, Nov. 18, 1850, DD No. 15; Webster, Feb. 28, 1851, DI No. 15, pp. 346–49.

27. GPM to Long and to C. W. Morgan, Sept. 5, 6, 1851, PR, Misc. Corr. Nos. 101, 103; U.S., *Kossuth and Captain Long*, 32 Cong. 1 Sess.,

H. Ex. Doc. 78; Long to GPM, Nov. 11, 1851; GPM to H. J. Raymond, April, 1852. See J. B. Moore, "Kossuth," *Political Science Quart.,* X (1895), 95–131, 257–91.

28. Poore, *Perley's Reminiscences,* I, 404–6; FM to GPM, Jan. 13, 1852, MLC.

29. GPM to Foot, April 26, 1852. Kossuth did eventually write Marsh, but only to ask a favor for a friend (Aug. 7, 1852, PR, Misc. Corr. Received).

30. GPM to Webster, Dec. 17, 1851, DD No. 21.

31. GPM to SFB, Aug. 23, 1850, BSI; to Drake, Aug. 3, 1850.

32. Markoe quoted in LW to CCM, Jan. 7, 1851; Foot to GPM, March 28, 1852.

33. GPM to Drake, Aug. 3, 1850; CCM, MS draft for *LL,* p. 163. For Greeley, see Van Deusen, *Horace Greeley,* pp. 126–28; *H. Journal,* 28 Cong. 2 Sess., pp. 446–47.

34. New York *Tribune,* June 28, 1850.

35. GPM to Drake, Aug. 3, 1850.

36. GPM to SFB, Aug. 23, 1850; to Webster, Sept. 24, 1850, DD No. 14; to FM, Sept. 25, 1850, FC, and Jan. 21, 1851, in Marsh letter-book, 1851–53; Webster to GPM, Jan. 25, 1851, DI No. 14, p. 344.

37. To Mrs. E, Jan. 21, 1851; to FM, Jan. 21, 1851; to H. A. Homes, Jan. 25, 1851. For Egypt, see Dodwell, *The Founder of Modern Egypt,* pp. 261–62; Malortie, *Egypt,* pp. 68–71; Cameron, *Egypt,* pp. 227–31.

38. GPM to J. G. Saxe, Feb. 7, 1851.

39. To Homes, Feb. 25, 1851. See Paine, *Tent and Harem,* pp. 94–104.

40. GPM to LW, May 3, 1851, WP; to E, May 28, 1851; to Dr. Taylor, Oct. 10, 1860, DCA.

41. GPM to SM, June 16, 1851.

42. GPM, *The Camel,* pp. 133–34.

43. GPM, "The Desert," *Amer. Whig Rev.,* XVI (1852), 49; 42. See Paine, *Tent and Harem,* pp. 237–41, for a less enthusiastic view of camels on this trip.

44. Paine, *Tent and Harem,* pp. 248–52; GPM, *The Camel,* pp. 73, 153–55.

45. GPM to E's, July 4, 1851.

46. GPM to SM, Aug. 23, 1851, DCA.

47. James W. Kimball to Lyndon Marsh, Sept. 16, 1851.

48. GPM to SM, Aug. 23, 1851, DCA; GPM to Rev. Adolf Biewend, Jan. 1, 1852, in Marsh letter-book, 1851–53.

49. *The Camel,* pp. 159–61.

50. GPM to E, Aug. 23, 1851; GPM to SFB, various dates, 1849–53, BSI. See GPM, "Notes on Vesuvius."

51. SFB to GPM, Feb. 9, 1851; GPM to SFB, Feb. 8, May 3, Nov. 18, 1851, BSI.

52. GPM to SFB, Aug. 4, 1852. Marsh's kegs of fish and reptiles are acknowledged in SI, *Sixth* and *Ninth Ann. Repts.* (*1851,* p. 61, and *1854,* p. 45).

53. To SFB, Jan. 14, March 21, 1854, BSI.

54. GPM to SM, Aug. 23, 1851, in Marsh letter-book, 1851–53; to Mrs. E, March 28, 1851.

55. GPM to E's, June 18, Aug. 23, 1851.

VII: DIPLOMATIC PROBLEMS AND PASTIMES

1. GPM to Clayton, April 25, 1850, DD; Brown to GPM, May 15, 1850; GPM, May 20, 1850, Nov. 5, 1851, DD Nos. 7, 19.

2. Dainese to W. L. Marcy, March 15, 1853, No. 115 in U.S., *Francis Dainese,* p. 72.

3. Homes to GPM, Aug. 5, 1851; March 20, DI No. 21; Aali Pasha to GPM, April 18/30, 1852, in GPM to Marcy, April 30, 1852, DD No. 27.

4. GPM, Dec. 15, 1853, DD No. 66.

5. GPM to FM, April 26, 1852, FC; FM to GPM, Jan. 13, 1852, MLC. See GPM, "American Diplomacy," New York *World,* June 30, 1860.

6. To SFB, May 24, Oct. 28, 1852, BSI. The article was "The Desert."

7. Webster to GPM, April 29, 1852, DI, in U.S., *Communications . . . Relative to . . . the Reverend Mr. King,* 33 Cong. 1 Sess., Sen. Ex. Doc. 67.

8. *Jeune Hellas* (Athens), July 12/24, 1852; GPM to SFB, Oct. 28, 1852; to FM, Dec. 20, 1852, FC. For King, see GPM to Commodore Stringham, Oct. 25, 1852; John Hill to GPM, Aug. 17, 1852; GPM to Hill, May 31, 1853; Hill *et al.* to Webster, April 6, 1852.

9. GPM to Webster, Aug. 21, 1852.

10. GPM to Marcy, Aug. 20, 1853, DD; to Paikos, May 17, 1853, in DD, June 2, 1853; to FM, Oct. 24, 1852, FC.

11. GPM to FM, Oct. 29, 1852, FC; to SFB, Oct. 28, 1852, BSI.

12. Everett to GPM, Feb. 5, 1853, DI No. 24, pp. 358–64.

13. GPM to Marcy, May 27, 1853, DD.

14. GPM to FM, Jan. 22, 1854, FC; to Marcy, June 2, 17 (in U.S.,

Communications . . . Relative to . . . the Reverend Mr. King, p. 162),
23, 24, 1853, DD.

15. Jonas King to GPM, May 5, 1854.

16. GPM to FM, Jan. 14, 22, 1853 [1854], FC; FM to GPM, Feb. 21,
1854. See GPM, June 23, July 6, 1853, DD; GPM to Carroll Spence,
Jan. 21, 1854.

17. To SFB, Sept. 23, 1853, BSI; to Marcy, June 16, 1853, DD; GPM,
"The American Image Abroad," *BDFP,* Sept. 21, 1854; GPM, "Oriental
Christianity and Islamism," *CE,* LXV (1858), 106.

18. GPM to CM, Sept. 8, 1852; CCM and GPM to LW, Sept. 13,
Oct. 10, 1852, WP.

19. GPM to CM, Oct. 28, 1852; to SFB, Oct. 28, 1852, BSI; to CCM,
Nov. 2, 1852; to LW, Nov. 14, 1852; to FM, Dec. 20, 1852, FC.

20. GPM to FM, Jan. 1, 1853, FC.

21. E. B. Browning to CCM, July 19, 1853. See E. B. Browning to
Miss Mitford, Feb., March 15, 1853, in Browning, *Letters,* II, 102–5;
LL, pp. 324–25.

22. Wise to GPM, March 26, 1853; Goldsborough to GPM, June 5,
1853.

23. GPM, "Martin Koszta and the American Legation at Constanti-
nople," MS, p. 4; Brown to Ingraham, June 28, Offley to Brown, July 4,
Ingraham to Schwarz, July 2, 1853, in U.S., *Martin Koszta,* 33 Cong. 2
Sess., Sen. Ex. Doc. 40, pp. 11, 20–22.

24. CCM to LW, July 13, 1853.

25. Ingraham to GPM, July 4, 1853; GPM to V. de Bruck, July 30,
1853; GPM to Marcy, July 7, Aug. 4, 17, 1853, DD Nos. 43, 48, 50 (in
U.S., *Martin Koszta,* pp. 23, 31–38, 44–45); de Bruck to GPM, Sept. 14,
1853; Marcy to GPM, July 26, 1853, DI No. 27, pp. 371–74.

26. GPM, "Martin Koszta," MS, p. 12; GPM to Offley, Sept. 26, Oct.
5, 1853; to Marcy, Oct. 20, 1853, DD No. 60 (in U.S., *Martin Koszta,*
pp. 58–59); Koszta to Offley, Oct. 14, 1853.

27. GPM to Offley, Oct. 20, 1853, PR, Misc. Corr.; GPM, "Martin
Koszta," MS, p. 15, in U.S., *Martin Koszta,* pp. 61–62; J. P. Brown to
GPM, Oct. 19, 1853. See *CG,* 33 Cong. 1 Sess., pp. 313, App., pp. 50–51,
79–84.

28. J. M. Gilliss to GPM, March 30, 1854.

29. To SFB, Oct. 28, 1852, BSI; to FM, Jan. 1, 1853, FC; to LW, Oct.
10, 1852, WP; to SM, Sept. 1, 1852.

30. To SFB, April 13, 1853, BSI; to FM, Jan. 14, 1854, FC.

31. Healy to GPM, Jan. 5, 1853. See De Mare, *G. P. A. Healy*, pp. 181, 208.

32. Homes to GPM, July 12, 1853; GPM, "Office-Holders Turned Out," MS.

33. "Oriental Question," *CE*, LXIV (1858), 393–97, 418. See B. D. Gooch, "Origins of the Crimean War," *AHR*, LXII (1956), 33–58.

34. GPM to Marcy, Aug. 14, 1853, DD No. 49.

35. "Oriental Question," pp. 399–411. "By the time [the Crimean War] was over the United States was the only nation in the world that was neither ashamed nor afraid to acknowledge boldly her friendship for Russia" (Golder, "Russian–American Relations during the Crimean War," *AHR*, XXXI [1926], 474). See Lane-Poole, *Canning*, II, 228–328; Dvoichenko, "Americans in the Crimean War," *Russian Rev.*, XIII (1954), 137–45.

36. GPM to FM, Aug. 5, 1855, FC.

37. Carlisle, *Diary*, p. 86. See Woodham-Smith, *Florence Nightingale*, pp. 304–5.

38. GPM to SFB, Sept. 25, 1853, BSI.

39. GPM to FM, Jan. 14, March 21, 1854, FC; to SFB, March 21, 1854, BSI.

40. GPM to FM, Jan. 22, 1854, FC; to LW, Jan. 26, 1854, WP.

41. GPM to FM, March 21, 1854, FC. See Lynch, *Van Buren*, pp. 526–27.

42. GPM to SFB, July 4, 1854, BSI.

VIII: MAKESHIFTS OF A BANKRUPT

1. *BDFP*, Aug. 24, 26, 1854.

2. GPM to CCM, Sept. 26, 1856. For the Vermont Central, Burlington affairs, and Marsh's financial problems, see *BDFP*, Dec. 26, 28, 1849, April 17, 18, 1852, July 17, 19, Oct. 10, 1854, Dec. 9, 1856; VC, *Proc. of the Stockholders;* VC, *Rept. of the Trustees,* Notes Receivable, p. 16; Kirkland, *Men, Cities and Transportation,* I, 169, 176–80, 436–44; R. E. Bassett, "A Study . . . of the Vermont Central Railroad"; William Warner to GPM, April 12, 1849; GPM to VC directors, Aug. 18, 1855; to Samuel Adams, Aug. 23, 1855; Adams to GPM, Sept. 22, 1855; Asa O. Aldis to GPM, Dec. 28, 1855; GPM to Wyllys Lyman, March 14, 1850, Dec. 17, 1851; HPH to GPM, Aug. 27, 1850, Feb. 17, 1851; GPM to CCM, Jan. 19, Sept. 8, 1855, Sept. 18, 22, 1856; *Life of T. H.*

360 NOTES TO VIII: MAKESHIFTS OF BANKRUPT

Canfield, pp. 12–13; Peck, *Genealogical History,* pp. 301–2; G. P. Mayo to GPM, Oct. 2, 1856; Paris Fletcher to GPM, Dec. 1, 1856; *Michigan State Bank* v. *John Peck et al.,* 28 Vt. 200 (1855); *H. B. Stacey* v. *VC,* 29 Vt. 39; GPM powers-of-attorney to Lyman, Jan. 24, Sept. 15, 1849, April 27, 1852, and mortgages, Nov. 1, 1852, Burl. Real Estate Rec., XXIII, 407, 410–12 (also XX, 336, and XXI, 159–60, 292–93); *Thaddeus Fletcher* v. *Lyman & Marsh & VC, John Peck* v. *Lyman & Marsh, Asahel Peck* v. *Lyman & Marsh & J. H. Peck,* Chittenden County Court Records, XXV, 131–33, and XXVI, 13, 14–15; Burl. Land Records, XXVIII, 152; Wyllys Lyman Estate, Chittenden Co. Probate Off., March 3, 1864, XLVIII, 423.

3. GPM to CCM, Sept. 26, 1856; GOM to CCM, "Sunday"; GPM to LW, Feb. 17, 1856, WP; CCM to GPM, Aug. 26, 1854, Dec. 7, 1856.

4. GPM to Francis Lieber, April 27, 1860.

5. GPM, *Memorial of George P. Marsh, of Vermont,* 33 Cong. 2 Sess., Sen. Misc. Doc. No. 8, pp. 1–2.

6. Hughes to Dainese, Oct. 12, in Dainese to Marcy, Oct. 15, 1853; Chandler and Douglas in the Senate, March 2, 1855, and House vote, March 3, 1855, *CG,* pp. 1090–93, 1165.

7. GPM to LW, Dec. 19, 1850, WP; to CCM, Dec. 17, 9, 1856; CCM to GPM, Feb. 24, 1856; Charlotte Bostwick Thrall to GPM, March 22, April 9, 1861, and to CCM, Sept. 24, 1884.

8. GPM to FM, Oct. 9, 1857, FC; Dainese in *American Organ* (Washington), Aug. 2, 1855; Foot and Brodhead in the Senate, April 25, 1856, *CG,* 34 Cong. 1 Sess., pp. 818–21, 1019–20.

9. Foot in the Senate, April 4, 25, 1856, *CG,* 34 Cong. 1 Sess., pp. 818–21, 1020–22; Brodhead in New York *Herald,* June 16, 1856.

10. GPM, *Reply to Mr. Brodhead's Remarks;* Pennington, in U.S., *Marsh Claim,* May 23, 1856, 34 Cong. 1 Sess., H. Rep. 166, pp. 4–5.

11. Dainese to Elisha Whittlesey (Treasury), Aug. 6, 1856; GPM to CCM, Aug. 10, 1856.

12. GPM to CCM, Aug. 19, 23, 1856; to SFB, March 16, 1857.

13. Dainese to President Pierce, April 30, 1853; to Whittlesey, Sept. 4, 1856; GPM to McConnell (Treasury), in U.S., *Francis Dainese,* pp. 255, 162, 102–4; Morrill to GPM, Jan. 18, 1858; FM to GPM, Feb. 2, 1858; GPM to Foot, Jan. 4, 1858, MV.

14. Royce, Comm. on Foreign Affairs, April 6, 1860, 36 Cong. 1 Sess., H. Rep. 350; FM to GPM, June 16, 1860; "An Act for the Relief of George P. Marsh," June 13, 1860, 124 *Stat. at Large* 857.

15. GPM to CCM, Sept. 7, 1856.

16. Samuel Marsh to GPM, Jan. 6, 1855; GPM to Lady E, March 31, 1857, in *LL*, p. 385; Powers to GPM, June 1, 1855; GPM to LW, Feb. 17, 1856, WP.

17. FM to GPM, March 22, 1855; GPM to FM, March 29, 1855, Galloway-Maxcy-Markoe Corr.

18. Ticknor to GPM, Feb. 5, 1855; Felton to GPM, Feb. 9, March 18, 1855. See James Walker to Ticknor, Feb. 16, 1855, College Letters, Vol. IV (1853–60), Harvard College Archives; Morison, *Three Centuries of Harvard,* pp. 291–93.

19. GPM to Ticknor, Feb. 10, 1855.

20. John Pennington to GPM, April 15, 1859; GPM to SFB, April 25, 1859, BSI. On the University of Vermont, see GPM, UV Library Rept., Nov. 27, 1855, MS; Asa O. Aldis to GPM, Aug. 14, Nov. 27, 1855; UV Records, Trustees Minutes, III, 155–63, 172–73.

21. SFB to GPM, May 6, 1854; Gilliss to GPM, June 12, 1853; FM to GPM, Sept. 18, 1854.

22. Gilliss to GPM, May 8, 1854; New York *Weekly Tribune,* Jan. 20, 1855; *SIJ,* pp. 102–17. See Borome, *Jewett,* pp. 81–94; Coulson, *Henry,* p. 213.

23. Gilliss to GPM, Nov. 23, 1854; GPM to SFB, Sept. 8, 1854, BSI; GPM, SI Affairs, draft of letter to C. W. Upham, Feb. 1855; Henry to GPM, Feb. 3, March 24, 1855.

24. Gilliss to GPM, Jan. 25, 1853.

25. FM to GPM, Jan. 22, 1853, Sept. 18, 1854; Gilliss to GPM, Jan. 25, 1853, March 30, 1854. On the mountain rule, Senator Ralph E. Flanders, personal communication, April 29, 1955. Much to Marsh's pleasure, hard-working Solomon Foot had succeeded hard-drinking S. S. Phelps in the Senate in 1850 (GPM to R. C. Winthrop, June 4, 1850, Winthrop Pap.); Phelps's new appointment was to the other seat.

26. To SFB, April 13, 1853, BSI; to Drake, Aug. 27, 1856; to Winthrop, Aug. 6, 1856, Winthrop Pap. For Council of Censors, see *BDFP,* March 29, 31, 1855; VSA, LXXIX, 46–65; Crockett, *Vermont,* III, 435–38.

27. GPM to CCM, Aug. 3, 16, 19, 23, 1856; to Foot, Aug. 18, 1856; Foot to GPM, Aug. 20, 1856; GFE to GPM, Oct. 8, Nov. 3, 1856. See also GPM to Charles Sumner, Sept. 1, 1856, Sumner Pap.

28. GPM to CCM, July 23, 1856; to SFB, Feb. 19, 1857.

29. GFE to GPM, March 8, 1858; GPM to Foot, March 23, 1858.

30. Sept. 17, 1857.

31. GPM to Alexander, July 11, 1855.

32. GPM to SFB, July 2, 1855, BSI; to FM, June 23, 1855, FC; GPM to Alexander, July 11, 1855; Alexander to GPM, Aug. 8, Nov. 21, 1855.

33. *Laws of Vermont*, 1855, Act No. 81, pp. 112–13. For Read, see *HVG*, I, 758–59; Gilman, *Bibliography of Vermont*, pp. 229–30.

34. GPM to Maria Buell, Oct. 1, 1855; to CCM, Sept. 13, 1855.

35. GPM to CCM, Sept. 11, 1855 (also Sept. 1, 1856, Nov. 10, 11, 1857); J. F. Flagg to Gilliss, in Gilliss to GPM, Dec. 3, 1857. For the marble quarry, see Hager, *Marbles of Vermont*, pp. 8–9; GPM to Read, Oct. 21, 1861, in Read, *Winooski Marble*, p. 8, and *ibid.*, pp. 6–7, 10.

36. GPM to CCM, Nov. 13, 1856; Boston *Herald*, Nov. 15, 1854; *BDFP*, Nov. 4, 13, 1854; *LL*, p. 377.

37. To CCM, March 30, 1855.

38. GPM to CCM, Jan. 17, 22, 20, 1855; to Maria Buell, Oct. 1, 1855. For discomforts on railroads in the 1850s, see Nevins, *Ordeal*, II, 232–33.

39. To Mrs. HPH, Jan. 10, 1855.

40. "American Image Abroad," *BDFP*, Sept. 21, 1854. See Curti, "The Reputation of America Overseas, 1776–1860," in his *Probing Our Past*, pp. 191–218; GPM, "American Representatives Abroad," New York *World*, June 21, 1860.

41. GPM to SFB, July 2, 1855, BSI; "Oration," N.H. Agric. Soc. *Trans., 1856*, pp. 35–89.

42. *Address . . . Agric. Soc. Rutland Co.* (1847), p. 16; "The Camel," in SI, *Ninth Ann. Rept. 1854*, pp. 116–18.

43. "The Desert," p. 48; "The Camel," pp. 119–20; *The Camel*, pp. 177–96, espec. p. 188.

44. Wayne to GPM, Oct. 4, Nov. 3, 1856; Fowler, *Camels to California*, espec. pp. 9–12, 18, 55–88; GPM, *The Camel*, pp. 26–27. For the camel experiments, see 35 Cong. 1 Sess., H. Ex. Doc. 124 (1858); Lewis, Gray, and Farquhar, *Camels in Western America*; Gray, "Camels in California," *Calif. Hist. Soc. Quart.*, IX (1930), 301–2; C. A. Carroll, "The Government's Importation of Camels," U.S.D.A., Bur. Animal Industry, Rept. No. 20, 1903, p. 392. Bonsal, *Beale*, pp. 199–200; Shaler, *Domesticated Animals*, pp. 125–27; Webb, *The Great Plains*, pp. 199–200.

45. *NAR*, LXXXIII (1856), 561; Alexander to GPM, July 7, 1856; GPM to Lanman, Sept. 21, 1856, in Lanman, *Haphazard Personalities*, p. 104.

46. GPM to CCM, May 9, 1856.

47. Gould and Lincoln to GPM, Oct. 13-14, 1856, March 17, 1860; GPM to CCM, Sept. 2, 1856. Like other writers, Marsh erred in believing that camels store water in their stomachs. The camel's stomach differs little from that of other ruminants. What enables camels to go so long without drinking is their low rate of water loss in urine and in sweat, their ability to withstand great dehydration, and their enormous and rapid drinking capacity (E. Schmidt-Nielson, "Animals and Arid Conditions," in *Future of Arid Lands,* pp. 372-76). For the Halligs, see Davis, "The Halligs," *GR,* XIII (1923), 99-106.

48. GPM to FM, Aug. 27, 1856, FC; to CCM, Nov. 12, Dec. 8, 1856; to FM, Nov. 8, 1856, FC.

49. To CCM, Feb. 1, 5[4], 5, 1857.

50. De Mare, *Healy,* pp. 175-83; GPM to CCM, Feb. 9, 1857; to Maria Buell, Oct. 1, 1855. For similar Yankee sentiments about Chicago, see Holbrook, *Yankee Exodus,* pp. 71-72.

51. GPM to CCM, Feb. 11, 1857; LW to CCM, March 8, 1857; GPM to CCM, Feb. 15, 18, 1857.

52. GPM to CCM, Feb. 28, 1857; LW to CCM, March 8, 1857; GPM to SFB, Feb. 19, 1857, BSI.

IX: VERMONT PUBLIC SERVANT

1. GPM to SFB, April 8, 1857, BSI; to LW, Aug. 20, 1857, WP.
2. To SFB, Nov. 6, 1857.
3. GPM, *Report, on the Artificial Propagation of Fish,* pp. 20-21.
4. *Ibid.,* pp. 12-16. See Z. Thompson, *Natural History of Vermont,* p. 19.
5. Oct. 13, 22, 1857, Vermont *House Journal,* pp. 67, 123; Baird, *Report of . . . Fish and Fisheries for 1872 and 1873,* pp. xlii, xlv; SFB to GPM, Dec. 12, 1874.
6. GPM to SFB, Aug. 12, 1858, BSI.
7. GPM to W. G. Shaw, March 8, 9, 1857, MV; to Drake, May 23, 1857.
8. Williams to GPM, Dec. 23, 1857; GPM *et al.,* Plan for the New State House, April 1, 1857, VSP, LXVI, 84; GPM, "Report of the Commissioners on Plan of the New State House."
9. T. E. Powers to GPM, July 20, 1858; T. W. Silloway to GPM, Aug. 7, Oct. 6, 1858; White, quoted in Hill, *The Winooski,* p. 206. See Powers to GPM, April 3, 1857; Silloway to GPM, various dates, 1857

and 1858; GPM to Powers, March 22, 1858; GPM to Silloway, June 9, 1857, and Feb. 11, 1859, in Silloway, *A Statement of the Facts;* Powers, *Report; Vermont Capitol and Star-Chamber.*

10. Collamer *et al.,* "Report of the Commissioners on Laws relating to Railroads," 1855 Vermont *House Journal,* App., pp. 642–49.

11. "Report of Commission on Roads on the Foregoing Bill . . . ," 1855 Vermont *House Journal,* App., pp. 650–52.

12. Linsley, "First Annual Report of the Railroad Commissioner," pp. 585–89; *BDFP,* Nov. 5, 6, 1857; GPM, address at Rutland Co. Agric. Soc. Fair, Oct. 3, in *BDFP,* Oct. 10, 1854; GPM, "Oration," N.H. State Agric. Soc., *Trans., 1856.*

13. GPM to CCM, Oct. 8, 1858, in *LL,* p. 400.

14. GPM, *Railroad Commissioner . . . Third Ann. Rept., 1858,* pp. 3–7, App. A. See Kirkland, *Men, Cities and Transportation,* I, 233, 241.

15. *Railroad Commissioner . . . Third Ann. Rept.,* pp. 7–9, 13–15.

16. *Railroad Commissioner . . . Fourth Ann. Rept., 1859,* pp. 5–6.

17. In Hill, *Winooski,* p. 277. See L. E. Chittenden, *Personal Reminiscences,* pp. 199–204; *BDFP,* April 7, 1851.

18. GPM, *Railroad Commissioner . . . Third Ann. Rept.,* pp. 9–15; *Fourth Ann. Rept.,* pp. 5, 9; Vermont Railroad Commissioner, *Seventh Ann. Rept.* (1862), pp. 10–11.

19. Rodney V. Marsh to GPM, Nov. 27, 1858; *BDFP,* Nov. 25, 1858. See L. E. Chittenden to GPM, Dec. 4, 1858; GFE to GPM, Oct. 16, 1858; 1858 Vermont *House Journal,* p. 294, *Senate Journal,* p. 259.

20. GPM to SFB, Jan. 8, 1866, BSI; GPM, *Railroad Commissioner . . . Fourth Ann. Rept.,* pp. 3, 10; Vermont Railroad Commissioner, *Fifth Ann. Rept.* (1860), p. 16. See Kirkland, *Men, Cities and Transportation,* I, 240–41, 254–64, 354–58, 432, 445–48.

21. *M & N,* pp. 53–55n.

X: THE ENGLISH LANGUAGE

1. Columbia Coll. Archives, Minutes of the Trustees, V (1856–58), 375–78; Ruggles to GPM, May 13, June 21, 1858.

2. GPM to CCM, Sept. 29, 1858.

3. GPM, *Lectures on the English Language,* pp. v, 3; GPM to CCM, Oct. 12, 1858; to Charles Folsom, June 22, 1859, Folsom MSS.

4. Lieber to GPM, Jan. 12, 1859; GPM to SFB, March 1, 1859, BSI. Lieber believed his audiences were small because he, like Marsh, refused to entertain; he "loathed that curse of American oratory . . . pityful

things to make the audience laugh" (in Freidel, *Lieber,* p. 297). But an eminent student recalled that "as a teacher he was a definite failure" (Burgess, *Reminiscences,* p. 70).

5. GPM to SFB, June 21, 1858, BSI; to CCM, Aug. 1, 1859.

6. GPM to CCM, July 26, 1859; Lieber to GPM, March 9, April 22, 1860; GPM to Lieber, April 12, 1860. See Freidel, *Lieber,* pp. 286–316.

7. GPM to Lieber, April 12, 1860; to CCM, July 25, 1859; to SFB, Jan. 3, Aug. 26, 1859, BSI.

8. GPM to Lieber, Jan. 4, 1860; CCM to LW, Dec. 7, 1859, WP.

9. Lieber to Ruggles, Feb. 17, 1860, Lieber Corr.; *Athenaeum,* Aug. 11, 1860; New York *Evening Post,* New York *Tribune, Atlantic Monthly* (April, 1860), *Universalist Quart.,* XVII (1860), 253–74 (all in Marsh scrapbook); *New Englander,* XLVIII (1860), 532–33; *Critic,* June 2, 1860, p. 684; *Saturday Rev.,* May 19, 1860, p. 644.

10. GPM to Felton, Jan. 10, 1860, Felton MSS; to George Ticknor, Feb. 20, 1860.

11. GPM, *New Dictionary by the Philological Soc.;* "Our English Dictionaries," *Christian Rev.,* CI (1860), 387–88; "Old English Literature," *Nation,* I (1865), 778. See GPM to J. S. Furnivall, Oct. 15, 1859; Alexander to GPM, Dec. 13, 1859; *New Englander,* XLVIII (1860), 224; GPM to Norton, June 2, 1860, Norton Pap.

12. Bryant, quoted in Mencken, *American Language,* p. 241.

13. GPM, "The Two Dictionaries," New York *World* (expanded in "Our English Dictionaries"); GPM to James R. Spalding, Oct. 15, 1860; Merriams to GPM, April 6, May 25, 1860; Noah Porter, 1864, in *Webster's Dictionary* (1880), p. vi.

14. GPM, "Our English Dictionaries," pp. 397, 404–5; GPM to Ticknor, Jan. 21, 1860; to Lieber, April 18, Sept. 6, 1860; to F. S. Child, July 26, 1862. See Sheldon & Co. to GPM, March 8, 15, 1860; Homes to GPM, April 7, May 22, Aug. 28, 1860; GPM to J. R. Lowell, Aug. 18, 1860, Lowell Pap.; Sophocles to GPM, Aug. 13, 1860; GPM to H. S. Dana, Feb. 15, March 5, 28, 1861; GPM, "A Glossary of Later and Byzantine Greek, by E. A. Sophocles," New York *World,* June 28, 1860.

15. GPM to Wedgwood, May, 1861; *Dictionary of English Etymology,* I, espec. 157–58, 174–75.

16. *Christian Rev.; NAR* (1862), p. 285. Several years later Marsh published some comments on words in the 2d and 3d vols. of Wedgwood's *Dictionary,* among them *empeach, filch, flesh* and *flitch, fling, haberdasher, harangue, lord, luke-warm, plough, provender, pry, queer, rogue, scabbard, scissors, shrewmouse, sir* and *sire, spick and span, spite,*

stain, and *popering-in-the-place (Notes on Mr. Hensleigh Wedgwood's Dictionary . . . ,* espec. pp. 2, 3, 13).

17. GPM to FM, March 19, June 20, 1860, Galloway-Maxcy-Markoe Corr.

18. GPM to FM, July 13, 1860, MLC; *LL,* p. 424; Everett, Journal, Nov. 22, 1860, Everett Pap., CLXXIX, 288.

19. Müller, *Lectures on . . . Language,* espec. pp. 45, 70–72, 84; Child to GPM, June 29, 1862; William Smith, Jr., ed., *Student's Manual.* See reviews in *NAR,* XCVI (1863), 264; *Cornhill Mag.,* VII (1863), 138–39.

20. GPM, *Lectures,* pp. 440–41; *Origin and History,* p. 565n.

21. GPM, *Lectures,* pp. 647–48; 224–25; 119–31.

22. *Ibid.,* pp. 15–16. For Marsh's attitude toward the "conservation" of English, see *ibid.,* pp. 645–65; GPM, "The Proposed Revision of the English Bible," *Nation,* XI (1870), 282.

23. Mencken, *American Language,* pp. 8–9 (also 215–16); GPM, *Lectures,* pp. 669–71. Some of Marsh's linguistic work is cited in Krapp, *English Language,* I, 46–47, and II, 19–22; Pooley, *Grammar and Usage,* p. 32, and *Teaching English Usage,* p. 111.

24. GPM to GOM, Feb. 22, 1861, May 19, 1860; GPM in *BDFP,* Nov. 9, 1860.

25. Schurz to J. F. Potter, Dec. 24, 1860, in Schurz, *Speeches,* I, 176; GPM to CCM, Sept. 14, 1856; to FM, Aug. 5, 1855, FC; to J. G. Saxe, Feb. 7, 1851; GPM, "American Image Abroad."

26. GPM to Norton, April 3, 1860; to Lieber, June 3, 1859. See his articles on Italy in New York *World,* June—July, 1860.

27. GPM to GFE, March 7, 1861, MV; Bryant to Lincoln, March 7, 1861, Collamer *et al.* to Lincoln, March 8, 1861, U.S. Dept. of State, Appointment Pap.; Botta to GPM, Feb. 9, 1861.

28. GPM to GOM, Feb. 22, 1861; to GFE, March 7, 1861; Foot to GPM, March 16, 1861.

29. GPM to Botta, Feb. 13, 1861, Norcross MSS; Guglielmo Cajani to GPM, March 19, 1861; Bertinatti to Seward, in Bertinatti to Cavour, dispatches nos. 70, 71, March 7, 16, 1861, quoted in Humphreys, "Le relazioni diplomatiche fra gli Stati Uniti e l'Italia del Risorgimento," Ch. 4; Lincoln to Seward, March 18, 1861, in Lincoln, *Complete Works,* VI, 218–19. See Botta to GPM, Feb. 24, 1861. Schurz got the mission to Spain, which he considered a "victory" and "better than the Turin mission" (to Mrs. Schurz, March 28, 1861, in his *Intimate Letters,* p. 253).

30. Lieber to GPM, March 19, 1861.

31. CCM to LW, March 20, 1861, WP; New York *Tribune* and Boston *Transcript* in *BDFP,* March 20, 22, 1861 (see *Vermont Standard,* March 29, 1861). GPM to LW, April 3, 1861. See GPM to Drake and to Ticknor, both April 1, 1861.

32. Lieber to GPM, March 19, 1861; Lowell to GPM, March 20, 1861; GPM to Norton, March 26, 30, 1861, Norton Pap. Marsh helped L. E. Chittenden get a Treasury job, secured the Burlington post office for George Benedict, recommended Charles Lanman as State Dept. Keeper of Rolls, put in a good word with Seward for D. W. Fiske, and aided Markoe, Schele de Vere, and Bayard Taylor.

33. R. H. Howard in *BDFP & Times,* Aug. 18, 1882; GPM in *BDFP,* April 18, 1861.

XI: RISORGIMENTO AND CIVIL WAR

1. Marsh served from March 20, 1861, until his death on July 24, 1882 (21 years, 4 months, 4 days). Only Edwin Vernon Morgan, Ambassador to Brazil from Jan. 18, 1912, to April 23, 1933 (21 years, 3 months, 5 days) approaches Marsh's record. Third longest tenure is that of Claude G. Bowers, Ambassador to Chile 1939–53. (U.S., *Register of Dept. of State,* pp. 572–97).

2. GPM to W. H. Seward, June 27, 1861, DD (Italy, Vol. X) No. 3; Cj, I, 1.

3. GPM, "The War and the Peace," *CE,* LXVII (1859), 273–74.

4. GPM, "Italian Independence," March, 1860, MS (abstract in *BDFP,* March 26, 1860), pp. 24, 36–37.

5. "The Future of Italy," New York *World,* July 9, 1860.

6. *Ibid.;* "The War and the Peace," pp. 268–71.

7. Marraro, *American Opinion on the Unification of Italy,* pp. 305–13. For developments in Italy, see Solmi, *Making of Modern Italy;* Stillman, *Union of Italy;* Whyte, *Evolution of Modern Italy;* Hales, *Pio Nono;* King, *Italian Unity.*

8. March 3, 1848, *CG,* 30 Cong. 1 Sess., p. 445; GPM to FM, n.d., in *LL,* p. 116. See Marraro, *American Opinion on the Unification of Italy,* pp. 5–15, 52–69, 123–54; Billington, *Protestant Crusade,* pp. 380–436.

9. "The War and the Peace," pp. 262–63, 280–82.

10. June 27, Oct. 28, 1861, Feb. 2, 1864, DD Nos. 3, 28, 83.

11. GPM to Sumner, July 26, 1861, Sumner Pap.

12. GPM to Seward, Sept. 4, 1861, Aug. 5, 1862, DD; Cj, II, 42.

13. Cj, II, 52; GPM to Seward, Aug. 5, 1862, DD No. 49. For Ricasoli, see Hancock, *Ricasoli*.

14. GPM to Seward, March 10, April 4, 1862, DD Nos. 39, 40.

15. GPM to Seward, Sept. 6, Oct. 8, 1862, DD Nos. 51, 52; Cj, VI, 20. See Cj, III, 65–66; Garibaldi to GPM, Oct. 7, 1862; Seward to GPM, Nov. 5, 1862, DI No. 57, pp. 163–64.

16. Seward to GPM, Jan. 7, Feb. 25, 1864, DI Nos. 88, 90, pp. 187–88; A. B. Crane to GPM, Nov. 1, 1880.

17. GPM to GFE, April 21, 1863.

18. All the foregoing in Cj, XI, 7, 9, XII, 25–26, and XVI, 29.

19. Godkin, "American Ministers Abroad," *Nation*, IV (1867), 132–34; Niles to John Forsyth, Feb. 18, 1838, in Marraro, "Nathaniel Niles' Missions at . . . Turin," *Vermont Quart.*, XV (1947), 14–18; Daniel, letter to Richmond *Examiner*, in Marraro, *American Opinion on the Unification of Italy*, p. 192.

20. CCM to Susan Edmunds, June 9, 1861; W. W. Story to Charles Sumner, Sept. 2, 1861, Aug. 9, 1863, Sumner Pap.

21. Cj, June 27, 1861, I, 13; GPM in Cj, March 29, 1862, IV, 10; GPM to GFE, June 8, 1861.

22. GPM to Dillon, April 29, 1862.

23. GPM to Seward, Feb. 6, 1862, confidential DD; Seward to GPM, March 8, 1862, DI No. 41, p. 151; GPM to Norton, June 12, 1862.

24. GPM to Seward, Feb. 16, March 21, 1863, DD Nos. 67, 70; GPM to GOM, Jan. 14, 1862; Cj, VIII, 64.

25. GPM to Seward, June 28, July 22, 1861, DD confidential and No. 7; Cj, II, 2; GPM to Monti, May 2, 1862, PR, Misc. Corr., I, 153. See GPM to Andrew Stevens, May 12, 1862, PR, Misc. Corr.; for Wheeler, see *National Cyclopaedia of Amer. Biog.*, XXV, 129, and Cj, VII, 28, XVI, 39.

26. To Seward, May 12, 1862, DD No. 45. See Stillman, *Autobiography*, I, 369–70, II, 388–91; Cj, II, 37–38, X, 67–69, XIII, 21–22. Marsh's advice had no bearing on the closing of the mission in 1868. See Marraro, *American Opinion on the Unification of Italy*, pp. 24–26, 64–65; Stock, *United States Ministers to the Papal States* and *Consular Relations;* Marraro, "Closing of the American Diplomatic Mission to the Vatican," *Catholic Hist. Rev.*, XXXIII (1948), 445–46.

27. W. B. Reed, *A Review of Mr. Seward's Diplomacy*, p. 19. For such activities, see Clapp, *Forgotten First Citizen*, pp. 149–61; Durden, *Pike*, Ch. 4.

28. GPM to Seward, May 29, 1861, DD No. 2; to Norton, June 12, 1862; to Seward, Feb. 2, 1864, DD No. 83; to Norton, Oct. 17, 1863, March 14, 1864 (CCM copy). See GPM to Harry Verney, May 13, 1861; Sandwith to GPM, May 4, Aug. 25–28, 1862; GPM to R. H. Dana, Jr., Dec. 21, 1865, Dana MSS.

29. GPM to Seward, March 30, July 20, 1863, DD Nos. 72, 76; to GFE, April 21, 1863.

30. GPM to Seward, June 27, Oct. 24, Nov. 1, 1861, DD Nos. 3, 25, 30; GPM to GOM, Jan. 14, 1862. See also GPM, DD Nos. 39, 75, 77; GPM to Ricasoli, Aug. 26, 1861; to D. H. Wheeler, Nov. 5, Dec. 15, 1861; W. T. Rice to GPM, Jan. 12, June 8, 1862; Gideon Welles to Commander Thatcher, Feb. 28, 1862, and Log of Raphael Semmes, C.S.S. *Sumter,* Jan. 4—June 20, 1862, in U.S., *Official Records of the Union and Confederate Navies,* I, 332, 638–86.

31. GPM to Norton, Sept. 16, 1861; to J. S. Pike, Sept. 14, 1861, Pike Pap. (courtesy of Robert Durden); to Norton, Jan. 22, 1864 (CCM copy).

32. GPM to Verney, May 13, 1861; to Pike, Nov. 21, 1861, Pike Pap.; to Norton, Sept. 16, 1861.

33. To F. S. Child, July 26, 1862; to Pike, Aug. 20, 1862, Pike Pap.; to Lieber, Aug. 22, 1862, LI 2783, HM.

34. GPM to CCM, Oct. 9, 1862; Cj, X, 29, 37, XVI, 14; GPM to Norton, March 14, 1864. Other American envoys echoed Marsh's views; see Clapp, *Forgotten First Citizen,* pp. 179–80; Randall and Current, *Lincoln the President,* pp. 83–84; Durden, *Pike,* p. 109.

35. GPM to SFB, Dec. 8, 1861, BSI; to D. H. Wheeler, Oct. 9, 1862; Cj, II, 36. See Seward to GPM, Sept. 21, 1861, DI No. 19, p. 133; GPM to Seward, Aug. 19, 1861, DD No. 10; Marraro, "Volunteers from Italy for Lincoln's Army," *South Atlantic Quart.,* XLIV (1945), 385–88. Marsh had little luck with his dilution. By 1880 there were only 44,000 Italians in the U.S., almost 1,900,000 Irish (U.S., *Historical Statistics,* pp. 32, 34).

36. Seward to Sanford, July 27, 1861; Sanford to Garibaldi, Aug. 20, 1861, in Sanford to Seward, Aug. 29, 1861: all in U.S. Dept. State, Belgium PR, Vol. VII.

37. Cj, Aug. 17, Sept. 3–9, 12, 1861, I, 31, 45–50, 55; Garibaldi to Sanford, Aug. 31, 1861, in Gay, "Lincoln's Offer of a Command to Garibaldi," *Century Mag.,* LXXV (1907), 68.

38. Sanford to Seward, Sept. 18, 1861, Belgium PR; GPM to Seward, Sept. 14, 1861, DD No. 19. See Sanford to GPM, Aug. 13, 17, 1861;

James Mortimer to GPM, Sept. 22, 27, 1861; W. L. Dayton to GPM, Sept. 21, 1861; Cj, II, 20. For the reaction in Washington, see Monaghan, pp. 136–37.

39. GPM to Baron ——, Aug. 31, 1862, in GPM to Seward, Oct. 6, 1862, DD No. 51; Garibaldi to GPM, Oct. 7, 1862, in GPM to Seward, Oct. 8, 1862, DD No. 52.

40. GPM to Garibaldi, Oct. 11 (also Nov. 28), 1862; Seward to GPM, Nov. 5, 1862, DI No. 57, pp. 163–64; Cj, VII, 6–7. According to Gay ("Lincoln's Offer," p. 73), the new offer to Garibaldi embarrassed the U.S.; if so, Marsh was not aware of it. For the 1862 negotiations, see Humphreys, "Le relazioni diplomatiche," Ch. 5; Marraro, "Lincoln's Offer of a Command to Garibaldi," *J. Ill. State Hist. Soc.,* XXXVI (1943), 255–70; Marraro, "American Opinion . . . Garibaldi's March on Rome, 1862," *J. Central European Affairs,* VII (1947), 143–61.

XII: TURIN

1. Cj, June 14, 1861, I, 5. See GPM to Mrs. J. S. Pike, June 19, 1861, Pike Pap.; Matthew Arnold to Mrs. Arnold, June 22, 1865, in M. Arnold, *Letters,* I, 329; James, "A European Summer," *Nation,* XV (1872), 332–33.

2. Cj, I, 7. For statesmen in Turin, see Howells, "Massimo d'Azeglio," *Nation,* II (1866), 202–4; Pasolini, *Giuseppe Pasolini;* Trollope, *What I Remember,* pp. 432–33.

3. Cj, III, 59. See Baruffi, *Saluzzo—Manta—Verzuola.*

4. "Viator" [GPM], "The 'Catholic Party' of Cesare Cantù and American Slavery," *Nation,* II (1866), 564–65.

5. GPM to Norton, March 14, 1864; to HPH, Jan. 14, 1862.

6. Cj, IV, 26–27, Jan. 2, 1864, XIII, 3.

7. Cj, III, 60–64, XIII, 19–20, 33; GPM to LW, Oct. 21, 1876. See Mackenzie-Grieve, *Clara Novello,* pp. 274–75, 302.

8. Cj, Jan. 23, 1862, III, 26, and June 22, 1863, X, 7–8.

9. Cj, IV, 15, III, 18.

10. Cj, II, 35, III, 5, 20, XIV, 26.

11. GPM to GFE, Nov. 26, 1861; Cj, II, 67, III, 35–36.

12. D. H. Wheeler, "Recollections of George P. Marsh," MS; Arnold to Mrs. Arnold, June 22, 1865, in *Letters,* I, 329; J. S. Pike, Notebook XVIII, 60, MS, Pike Pap.; Durden, "James S. Pike," *NEQ,* XXIX (1956), 363.

13. GPM to Mrs. J. S. Pike, June 19, 1861, Pike Pap.; to HPH's, Jan. 14, 1862.

14. GPM to Seward, May 12, 1864, DD No. 93; to D. H. Wheeler, July 4, 1862 (CCM copy). For examples, see GPM to CCM, Oct. 9, 1862; Ralph Keeler to GPM, Jan. 18, 1869; Keeler, *Vagabond Adventures,* dedication to GPM; Godkin, "American Ministers Abroad," pp. 132–33.

15. GPM to F. S. Child, Sept. 28, 1861.

16. *Ibid.;* GFE to GPM, April 28, 1862.

17. Scribner to GPM, April 25, 1861, Oct. 21, 1862, May 1, Dec. 1, 1863.

18. Child to GPM, April 14, Nov. 26, 1861; GPM to Child, Sept. 28, 1861, July 26, 1862. See Child, "Observations on the Language of Chaucer," AAA&S, *Memoirs,* VIII (1863), Part II, 455ff.

19. GPM to Child, Sept. 28, 1861; GPM, "Origin of the Italian Language," *NAR,* CV (1867), 1–41.

20. GPM to GFE, June 8, Nov. 26, 1861; to Child, Sept. 28, 1861.

21. R. S. Chilton to GPM, April 4, 1861; Seward Circular, No. 46, Feb. 6, 1864; Durden, "James S. Pike," pp. 359–60; GPM to J. S. Pike, May 12, 1864, April 30, 1862, Pike Pap.

22. Pike to GPM, June 9, 1862; GPM to CM, Oct. 25, 1862, DCA.

23. Cj, XI, 64–107; GPM to Norton, Oct. 17, 1863.

24. GPM to FW, July 4, 1864.

25. GPM to SFB, Nov. 21, 1864, BSI; to Susan Edmunds, July 30, 1863; to LW, Sept. 8, 1863, WP; to D. H. Wheeler, Aug. 19, 1864.

26. To SFB, Nov. 21, 1864, BSI; to Donald G. Mitchell, June, 1865, in Mitchell, *American Lands and Letters,* p. 43.

27. GPM to Mrs. Pike, Aug. 20, 1862, Pike Pap.

28. GPM to Seward, May 12, 1864, DD No. 93; to Wheeler, May 24, 1864.

29. GPM to GFE, June 8, 1861, Aug. 4, 1862.

XIII: MAN AND NATURE

1. Mumford, *Brown Decades,* p. 78. See also Mumford, *Condition of Man,* p. 80, and *Technics and Civilization,* p. 256. Mumford was probably the first in the United States to "rediscover" Marsh (W. L. Thomas, Jr., *Man's Role in Changing the Face of the Earth,* p. xxxn). But Marsh's work had been well known to Shaler and W. M. Davis in the 1900s. In

1933 a Dutch (now American) geographer noted Marsh's typically American pragmatism and pointed out that Marsh was "little if at all known" to American geographers (Broek, "Agrarische Opnemingen [Surveys] in de Vereenigde Staten," *Tijdschrift voor Economische Geographie,* XXIV [1933], 238n). J. R. Whitaker, "World View of Destruction and Conservation of Natural Resources," *AAAG,* XXX (1940), 143–62, discusses earlier European references to Marsh's work.

2. B. H. and F. P. Nash, "Notice of George Perkins Marsh," AAA&S *Proc.,* XVIII (1882–83), 456.

3. GPM to J. S. Pike, April 25, 1864, Pike Pap.; Humphrey Sandwith to GPM, Nov. 9, 1864.

4. GPM to SFB, March 6, May 21, 1860, BSI. See Guyot, *Earth and Man,* espec. pp. 29–34 and Chs. X–XII.

5. Cj, April 14, 1862, IV, 16.

6. Cj, Jan. 12, 1863, VII, 82–83. See also Cj, VII, 28–53, 62–64, 80, VIII, 4–7; B. Taylor, *At Home and Abroad,* I, 314.

7. Silliman, *Remarks Made on a Short Tour . . . in 1819,* p. 412; GPM to Asa Gray, May 9, 1849, with "Economy of the Forest," MS. Recalling his reconnaissance excursions with Captain Partridge in the Green Mountains, Marsh wrote that "physical geography has long been my favorite pursuit" (to Arnold Guyot, Oct. 27, 1857). See *Man and Nature* (hereafter *M & N*), p. 329n, and GPM, "Watershed," *Johnson's New Universal Cyclopaedia,* IV, 1299, for etymology of *watershed.* Zadock Thompson commented on the rapid transformation of Vermont from dense and unbroken forest to cleared and cultivated farms, the disappearance of trout and pickerel from the streams, and other changes in flora and fauna (*Natural History of Vermont,* pp. 15–19; see also Williams, *Natural and Civil History of Vermont,* I, 31–80; Gallup, *Epidemic Diseases in . . . Vermont,* p. 27; L. S. Hayes, *History of the Town of Rockingham, Vermont,* p. 3; BDFP, Feb. 28, March 3, 1857). For the Vermont background, see Lowenthal, "George Perkins Marsh and the American Geographical Tradition," *GR,* XLIII (1953), 208; Stilwell, *Migration from Vermont,* pp. 232–34; Swift, *History of . . . Middlebury,* pp. 96–98; J. M. Thomas et al., *Report . . . on Conservation of the Natural Resources of Vermont 1911–12,* pp. 33–36.

8. Allen quoted in Martin, *Thomas Jefferson: Scientist,* pp. 204–5; Franklin to Richard Jackson, May 5, 1753, in Franklin, *Writings,* III, 133. "In New England," Franklin illustrates his point, "they once thought *blackbirds* useless, and mischievous to the corn. They made

efforts to destroy them. The consequence was, the blackbirds were diminished; but a kind of worm, which devoured their grass, and which the blackbirds used to feed on, increased prodigiously; then, finding their loss in grass much greater than their saving in corn, they wished again for their blackbirds." For American attitudes toward, and modifications of, the environment at that time, see Boorstin, *Lost World of Thomas Jefferson;* R. H. Brown, *Mirror for Americans;* Chinard, "The American Philosophical Society and the Early History of Forestry in America," Amer. Phil. Soc. *Proc.,* LXXXIX (1945), 444–88, and "Eighteenth Century Theories on America as a Human Habitat," *ibid.,* XCI (1947), 27–57; Struik, *Yankee Science,* p. 168; Smallwood, *Natural History and the American Mind.* The idiom "to beat all nature" illustrates the typical American attitude (*Dictionary of Americanisms,* II, 1114).

9. *Address . . . Agric. Soc. Rutland County,* pp. 17–19.

10. To Gray, May 9, 1849; "Economy of the Forest," MS.

11. To SFB, Feb. 5, 1853, BSI.

12. *The Camel,* p. 16.

13. To C. S. Sargent, June 12, 1879. For the history of forests, see *M & N,* pp. 217ff, 278–328; J. Cameron, *Development of Governmental Forest Control in the U.S.,* pp. 5–67; Heske, *German Forestry;* Reed, *Forests of France;* Darby, "Clearing of the Woodland in Europe," in W. L. Thomas, Jr., ed., *Man's Role in Changing the Face of the Earth,* pp. 194, 199–204.

14. *M & N,* pp. 35, 43–44. See also Cj, XI, 65–80. For the development of forestry, see Fernow, *A Brief History of Forestry,* pp. 205–6; Sisam, "Principles and Practices of Forestry," in *World Geography of Forest Resources,* pp. 66–67, 79–80; Lowenthal, "Western Europe," in *ibid.,* pp. 275–76, 287–88, 293. The same year Marsh wrote this paragraph, Henry Adams expressed a similar doubt of man's future on earth: "Man has mounted science, and is now run away with. . . . Before many centuries more . . . the engines he will have invented will be beyond his strength to control. . . . The human race [may] commit suicide by blowing up the world" (to C. F. Adams, April 4, 1862, in Ford, ed., *A Cycle of Adams Letters,* I, 134–35).

15. *M & N,* Ch. 1; quotes from pp. 7, 42–43, 55–56.

16. *Ibid.,* pp. 58, 84.

17. To C. S. Sargent, June 10, 1879; *M & N,* p. 132.

18. *M & N,* p. 196.

19. *Ibid.*, pp. 214–17. See Davis, "Biographical Memoir of George Perkins Marsh," *NASBM* (1909), VI, 80; S. T. Dana, "Forest Influences," in *World Geography of Forest Resources*, espec. pp. 51–52.

20. *M & N*, pp. 327–29. "It is rare that a middle-aged American dies in the house where he was born," Marsh adds. "This life of incessant flitting is unfavourable for the execution of permanent improvements. . . . It requires a very generous spirit in a landholder to plant a wood on a farm he expects to sell. . . . But the very fact of having begun such a plantation would attach the proprietor more strongly to the soil for which he had made such a sacrifice."

21. *Ibid.*, p. 450.

22. *Ibid.*, p. 490. See Reed, *Forests of France*, pp. 253–66.

23. *M & N*, pp. 548–49.

24. GPM to GFE, April 21, 1863.

25. To SFB, Nov. 21, 1861, BSI. This was mere rhetoric; Marsh did not smoke. He considered the use of tobacco "the most vulgar and pernicious habit engrafted by the semi-barbarism of modern civilization upon the less multifarious sensualism of ancient life" (*M & N*, p. 63). For Piobesi, see Cj, VII, 83–85.

26. Letter to New York *Tribune*, quoted in *BDFP & Times*, May 1, 1883. See Cj, IX, 43–44, X, 39–40, 56–57, XI, 47–48.

27. CCM to LW, June 2, 1863, WP.

28. Cj, IX, 28, X, 17–18.

29. Murray to GPM, Sept. 28, 1863.

30. Scribner to GPM, Oct. 13, 1863; *M & N*, p. 54n. In one excised paragraph, Marsh railed against cotton as the "most virulent" of "vegetable poisons," which "crazes the brain of those who deal in it, benumbs their moral faculties, fills their hearts with a lying spirit" (MS for *M & N*, pp. 381–82).

31. GPM to Norton, March 14, 1864.

32. Scribner to GPM, Dec. 15, 1864; GPM to U.S. Sanitary Comm., Oct. 1864; John Sherwood to GPM, Jan. 25, 1865.

33. Scribner to GPM, Jan. 17, 1865; J. H. Allen in *CE*, LXXVII (1865), 65–73; J. R. Lowell in *NAR*, XCIX (1864), 320; *Round Table*, May 7, 1864(?), in Marsh scrapbook.

34. *Edinburgh Rev.*, CXX (1864), 469–82; *Nation*, XIX (1874), 243–44.

35. H. N. Smith, "Rain Follows the Plough," *Huntington Lib. Quart.*, X (1946–47), espec. 178–82, and *Virgin Land*, pp. 26–29, 128ff. Lillard errs in saying Marsh overstated the case for rainfall (*Great Forest*, pp.

258–60); Marsh thought it "improbable" that forests exercised "any appreciable influence on the total amount of precipitation," and thought the evidence for their local effect on rainfall "vague and contradictory" (MS, reply to Draper, "Has Our Climate Changed?" *Popular Science Monthly,* I [1872], 665–74). See GPM, *Earth as Modified by Human Action* (1874), p. 202.

36. H. A. Homes to GPM, July 31, 1872; Hough, "On the Duty of Governments in the Preservation of Forests," AAAS *Proc.,* XXII (1873), Part 2, 1–10; Hough, *Elements of Forestry,* p. 26; Hough, *Report upon Forestry,* pp. 76n, 268, 309; Hough to GPM, Oct. 28, 1873, April 9, 1878. Hough visited Marsh in 1881 to confer about forestry (Hough, "Experimental Plantation of the Eucalyptus Near Rome," *Amer. Journal of Forestry,* I [1882–83], 402–13. See GPM, *Earth as Modified* [1885 ed.], p. 383n). His admiration for Marsh was not reciprocated, however. "I hope Congress may do something for Forestry," wrote the Minister, "though I do not expect much from Dr. Hough" (to C. S. Sargent, March 25, 1880). See H. A. Smith, "Early Forestry Movement in the United States," *AH,* XII (1938), 343–45; H. A. Smith *et al., National Plan for American Forestry,* I, 743–44; J. Cameron, *Development of Governmental Forest Control.*

37. N. H. Egleston, *Arbor Day,* pp. 9–10; G. B. Emerson to GPM, Dec. 11, 1875; Rodgers, *Fernow,* p. 153; Fernow, "Do Forests Influence Rainfall?" *Garden and Forest,* I (1888), 489–90; Warder to GPM, Dec. 13, 1877; Sargent in the *Nation,* XXXV (1882), 136; Sargent, *A Few Suggestions on Tree-Planting,* pp. 3–18; Sargent, "Protection of Forests," *NAR,* CXXXV (1882), 401; Carstensen, *Farms or Forests;* Lapham *et al., Disastrous Effects of the Destruction of Forest Trees . . . in Wisconsin;* Starr, "American Forests: Their Destruction and Preservation" (1865), pp. 221, 226–29; F. V. Hayden to Susan Edmunds, Jan. 5, 1872; SFB to GPM, Dec. 21, 1872. But Hayden misinterpreted Marsh on the effect of tree planting upon climate. See Hayden, "Report on Nebraska Territory," pp. 155–60; H. N. Smith, "Rain Follows the Plough," *Huntington Lib. Quart.,* X (1946–47), 176–78; Rodgers, *Fernow,* pp. 148–49, 152.

38. Guyot to GPM, May 5, 1868; Davis, "Biographical Memoir of George Perkins Marsh," *NASBM* (1909), VI, 80.

39. March 6, 1868. See Reclus to GPM, various dates, 1868–70, and to CCM, Sept. 14, 1884; GPM to Reclus, Nov. 20, 1869; Reclus, *A New Physical Geography* (La Terre), p. 519; GPM, *Earth as Modified,* p. viii; Whitaker, "World View," *AAAG,* XXX (1940), 149; Girolamo

Boccardo to GPM, April 10, 1868; Lyell to GPM, Sept. 22, 1865; Lyell, *Principles of Geology;* Glacken, "Changing Ideas of the Habitable World," in W. L. Thomas, Jr., ed., *Man's Role,* p. 81; Dietrich Brandis to GPM, dated "Friday"; Yule to GPM, Jan. 15, 1878; J. C. Brown, comp., *Forests and Moisture. Man and Nature* was twice translated into Italian (*L'Uomo et la natura,* Florence, 1869, 1872); the first did not satisfy Marsh. A French translation under Reclus's guidance was never completed.

40. Pinchot, *Breaking New Ground,* pp. xvi–xvii, 4; GPM to SFB, Oct. 12, 1881, BSI. See also GPM to John Bigelow, Sept. 3, 1863, in Bigelow, *Retrospections,* II, 51.

41. Donne, *Devotions,* No. XVII; GPM, "Study of Nature," pp. 48–49. See GPM to Lady E, March 28, 1851, in Marsh letter-book, 1851–53; *M & N,* pp. 548–49.

42. GPM, Preliminary Notice to an English edition of Reclus's *La Terre,* MS; "Study of Nature," p. 44. See *M & N,* p. 8.

43. "Study of Nature," pp. 57–58. Marsh's reasoning follows that of James Marsh ("Additional Notes," in his edition of Coleridge, *Aids to Reflection,* pp. 292–94) and Bacon's argument: "It were better to have no opinion of God at all than such an opinion as is unworthy of him; for the one is unbelief, the other is contumely" (quoted in Bullett, *English Mystics,* p. 69).

44. James Marsh, "Preliminary Essay," in his edition of Coleridge, *Aids to Reflection,* pp. xl–xlii; GPM, *M & N,* p. iii; Scribner to GPM, July 7, 1863; GPM to Scribner, Sept. 10, 1863.

45. GPM, "Study of Nature," pp. 37, 40, 43–44. See Lowenthal, "George Perkins Marsh and the American Geographical Tradition," p. 212. Marsh's attitude toward nature was not always "practical." When he heard that the European scarlet poppy had become established in the United States as a weed in grainfields, he was not sorry: "With our abundant harvests of wheat, we can well afford to pay now and then a loaf of bread for the cheerful radiance of this brilliant flower" (*M & N,* p. 66n). Thoreau thought that "man's improvements, so called . . . simply deform the landscape and make it more and more tame and cheap" ("Walking," p. 602). But his description of man "at cross purposes with nature" is pungent: "The proprietor of a wood-lot commonly treats Nature as an Irishman does a horse,—by standing in front of him and beating him in the face all the way across a field" (*Journal,* XIV, 132). And Thoreau anticipated the time when America, like Europe, would have to plant trees to replenish natural forests (Whitford and Whitford,

"Thoreau: Pioneer Ecologist and Conservationist," in Harding, ed., *Thoreau*, p. 204). See also Thoreau, "Natural History of Massachusetts," *Dial*, III (1842), 19–40.

46. "Study of Nature," pp. 60; 58; 56; 61–62.

47. *Ibid.*, pp. 33–34. See *M & N*, p. v; Emerson, "The Man with a Hoe," *Complete Works*, VII, 135–54.

48. In the latter part of the nineteenth century, Lester Frank Ward, W J McGee, and N. S. Shaler were among the few who maintained a more balanced outlook (Hofstadter, *Social Darwinism*, pp. 57–64; Cross, "W J McGee and the Idea of Conservation," *Historian*, XV [1953], 158–62; Shaler, *Autobiography*, pp. 350, 354–56). The majority believed that with the frontier gone they were confined within "the stubborn American environment . . . with its imperious summons to accept its conditions" (Turner, "Significance of the Frontier in American History," p. 228). For the influence of Turner and the frontier hypothesis, see Malin, "Space and History," *AH*, XVIII (1944), 65–74, 107–26, and "The Turner-Mackinder Space Concept of History," in Malin, *Essays on Historiography*, Ch. 1. Malin has pointed out that Marsh, although fearful of man's destructive force, believed that he had a "counterbalancing capacity for amelioration" and "a power of and a responsibility for choices that might decide whether or not man survived. . . . Marsh . . . suspended judgment as his work applied to the ultimate issue" (*Contriving Brain and the Skillful Hand*, pp. 400–401). For the rationale of conservation philosophies, see Price, "Values and Concepts in Conservation," *AAAG*, XLV (1955), 64–84; Malin, *Grassland of North America*, pp. 331–35.

49. W. L. Thomas, Jr., ed., *Man's Role*, dedication, pp. v, xxviii–xxx, xxxv; Sauer, "The Agency of Man on the Earth," in *ibid.*, p. 49; Glacken, "Changing Ideas of the Habitable World," in *ibid.*, pp. 81–83. See Glacken, "Origins of Conservation Philosophy," *Journal of Soil and Water Conservation*, XI (1956), 66; Glacken, "Man and the Earth," *Landscape*, V, No. 3 (1956), 27; Frank and Netboy, *Water, Land, and People*, pp. 167–69; Brooks, "Influence of Forests on Rainfall and Runoff," Royal Meteorological Soc., *Quart. Journal*, LIV (1928), 1–17.

50. Leighly, "New Occasions and New Duties for Climatology," *GR*, XXIX (1939), 682; GPM, *M & N*, p. 24. Marsh objected to the notion that only measurable things were worth serious study: "The introduction of mathematical method into physical science . . . has impeded the progress of . . . Geography by discouraging its pursuit as unworthy of cultivation because incapable of precise results" (*Earth as Modified*

[1885 ed.], p. 14n). Many still gloomily regard geography as so hampered.

XIV: FLORENCE

1. Drouyn de Lhuys to the Italian Minister, quoted in Stillman, *Union of Italy*, p. 332. See Hales, *Pio Nono*, pp. 250–52; Cj, XV, 61–62.

2. GPM, Oct. 25, 1864, DD No. 108; to Norton, Jan. 16, 1865 (CCM copy). See Whyte, *Modern Italy*, p. 150; Cj, XV, 61, XVI, 1–3.

3. DD No. 102, Sept. 19, 1864.

4. GPM to Norton, Jan. 16, 1865.

5. GPM to Seward, Jan. 30, 1865, DD No. 112; Seward to GPM, Feb. 27, 1865, DI No. 126, pp. 213–14; GPM to Solomon Foot, March 21, 1865, MV.

6. U.S. Army, GOM Certificate of Discharge, Aug. 9, 1862, UV; Mrs. M. Brakeley to GPM, May 14, 1865; J. A. C. Gray to GPM, March 1, 1865.

7. Mrs. HPH to CCM, May 18, 1865; GFE to GPM, April 24, 1865; CCM to LW, Dec. 7, 1859, WP.

8. J. A. C. Gray to GPM, May 18, 1865; Mrs. M. Brakeley to GPM, May 14, 1865.

9. To Norton, March 29, 1865 (CCM copy); to LW, Oct. 29, 1869, WP; to SFB, Feb. 9, 1867, BSI; to Charlotte Thrall, April 24, 1868.

10. GPM to D. H. Wheeler, Jan. 4, 1866; GFE to GPM, May 10, July 2, 1866.

11. Morrill and GFE to Hamilton Fish, March 24, 1869, U.S. Dept. State, Appointment Pap.; Grant, quoted by CCM to GPM, Sept. 9, 1869; GFE to GPM, March 29, 1869. See GFE to Jacob Collamer, May 3, 1864, JCP; Solomon Foot to GFE, March 11, 1865; J. R. Young, *Around the World with General Grant,* I, 264–66; L. D. White, *Republican Era,* p. 6.

12. To Seward, Nov. 18, 1865, Jan. 18, 1868, DD Nos. 127, 199 (also Nos. 111, 187); to T. A. Trollope, Nov. 30, 1867, in Trollope, *What I Remember,* p. 449.

13. GPM to SFB, April 7, 1870, BSI; to Seward, Jan. 6, 1869, DD No. 239. See Solmi, *Modern Italy*, pp. 106–7.

14. GPM, MS, Milan, 1864; to W. M. Evarts, Dec. 10, 1878, DD No. 802. See also GPM, DD Nos. 111, 520, 865; Mario, "Right and Wrong in Italy," *Nation,* IX (1869), 48–49; GPM to John Bigelow, April 22, 1865, in Bigelow, *Retrospections,* II, 510.

15. GPM to Seward, Oct. 7, Nov. 2, Dec. 20, 1867, DD Nos. 191, 192; Garibaldi to GPM, Jan. 20, 1868. For this episode, see Gay, "Garibaldi's American Contacts," *AHR,* XXXVIII (1932), 13–19.

16. GPM to Carrie Marsh Crane, Sept. 7, 1870; to Seward, Nov. 23, 1870, DD No. 323. See also DD Nos. 407, 299–301, 309, 321, 329; Whyte, *Evolution of Italy,* pp. 152–59; Hales, *Pio Nono,* pp. 314–20.

17. To SFB, Sept. 21, 1871, BSI.

18. GPM to Seward, Nov. 28, 1866, DD No. 168; to Rufus King, Nov. 25, 1866, PR, Misc. Corr., II, 279–81; G. W. Moore, *Case of Mrs. Surratt,* pp. 75–77.

19. GPM to Seward, May 6, 1864, DD No. 92; Seward to GPM, Sept. 3, 1864, DI No. 110, p. 202; GPM to Fish, June 28, 1871, DD No. 361. For negotiations, see DD Nos. 92, 122, 142, 166, 171, 178, 200, 212, 221, 348, 357; DI Nos. 103, 158.

20. U.S., *Commercial Relations . . . 1882–83,* I, 550–54; GPM to Evarts, Dec. 17, 1877, DD No. 720; to George Opdyke, May 15, 1868.

21. GPM to F. W. Behn, Jan. 21, 1873, PR, Misc. Corr., IV, 123–24. See DD Nos. 214, 236, 237; DI No. 207; GPM, " 'Protection to Naturalized Citizens,' " *Nation,* III (1866), 115–16.

22. GPM press release, Jan. 7, 1873, in GPM to Fish, Jan. 9, 1873, DD No. 434. See Fish to GPM, Dec. 16, 1872, DI No. 363, pp. 409–410; Cj, II, 36.

23. Marraro, "Spezia: An Italian Naval Base, 1848–68," *Military Affairs,* VII (1943), 205–8; GPM to SFB, Jan. 8, 1866, BSI. For Smithsonian and related matters, see SI, *Ann. Rept. 1867,* p. 39, and *1870,* p. 25; DD Nos. 405, 688; Chersi, "Studies in the Diplomatic Relations of the United States and Italy," MS, p. 155.

24. GPM to D. H. Wheeler, Feb. 14, 1866 (also Nov. 9, 16, 1864); W. W. Story to J. R. Lowell, Feb. 11, 1853, in James, *Story,* I, 254–57; Preston Powers to GPM, Feb. 25, 1865; GPM to Powers, Feb. 29, 1865; Wurts to Fish, Aug. 11, 1874, DD No. 505; Fish to GPM, Sept. 3, 1874, DI No. 441, pp. 466–67. See GPM, DD Nos. 478, 522, 625; to H. A. Homes, March 17, 1879.

25. To J. G. Blaine, June 17, 1881, DD No. 976; to Rev. Moorehead, March 22, 1864. See DD Nos. 816, 858.

26. GPM to Fish, Sept. 12, 1870, DD No. 303, in U.S., *Foreign Relations . . . 1870,* p. 450; G. W. Wurts to CCM, Oct. 1, 1884. The incident caused quite a flurry in Washington; Fish thought he might have to move Marsh to Madrid (T. E. Vermilyen to Fish, March 4, 1872, Fish Corr.; CM to GPM, Jan. 22, 30, Feb. 12, 17, 1872; GPM to W. T. Sher-

man, Aug. 5, 1872, Sherman Pap.; to John Bigelow, March 2, 1872, in Bigelow, *Retrospections,* II, 19–20.

27. Trollope, *What I Remember,* pp. 488–90; Garibaldi to GPM, Jan. 20, 1868; Stillman, *Autobiography,* II, 390–91.

28. GPM to C. D. Drake, Dec. 30, 1867; GPM, "State Sovereignty" and "Were the States Ever Sovereign?" (GPM to R. H. Dana), both in *Nation,* Vol. I (1865).

29. GPM to Sumner, Aug. 1, 1864, Sumner Pap.; to Bigelow, April 22, 1865, in Bigelow, *Retrospections,* II, 510; to Drake, Sept. 30, 1867.

30. To Sumner, Feb. 17, 1868, Sumner Pap. See L. D. White, *Republican Era,* pp. 7–8, 366–67.

31. To SFB, Feb. 9, 1867, BSI; to Godkin, Sept. 20, 1870 (also Oct. 24, 1865), Godkin Pap.

32. Godkin to GPM, Aug. 8, 1867; Lowell to Godkin, Oct. 16, 1866, in Lowell, *Letters,* I, 372.

33. Godkin to GPM, Oct. 6, 1870; GPM, in *Nation,* I (1865), 778.

34. *Nation,* VII (1868), 420.

35. GPM, "Thoughts and Aphorisms," p. 7; GPM, "Old English Literature," *Nation,* I (1865), 778; James Murray to GPM, May 26, 1870, Oct. 22, 1879; *New English Dictionary,* I, iii; Phonetic Alphabet bill introduced in Senate, March 29, 1867, *CG,* 40 Cong. 1 Sess., p. 429; H. C. Lea to GPM, Dec. 20, 1869, Aug. 4, 1870; GPM to Nash, Dec. 22, 27, 1870.

36. GPM to Yule, dated only 1869. See Yule, *Marco Polo,* and GPM review, "Book of Marco Polo," *Nation,* XXI (1875), 135–37, 152–53.

37. Theodore Stanton, "Villa Forini," in New York *Semi-Weekly Tribune,* Jan. 23, 1885; Seward, July 27, 1871, in Seward, *Travels around the World,* p. 725; Trollope, *What I Remember,* p. 465.

38. GPM to SFB, March 14, 1868, BSI.

39. GPM to SFB, Dec. 26, 1867, BSI. See Sims to GPM, Sept. 6, 1866, Aug. 17, 1870; Harris, *Woman's Surgeon.*

40. To SFB, Jan. 8, 1866, BSI; to Henry Yule, July 21, 1869.

41. GPM to George Bancroft, Sept. 12, 1871, Bancroft MSS; to Yule, March 21, May 15, 1871; to SFB, Feb. 2, 1874, BSI.

42. To SFB, Feb. 2, 1872, BSI.

43. GPM to Fish, June 24, 1872, DD No. 407 (also Nos. 345, 363); to Yule, Dec. 17, 1871. See Stillman, *Union of Italy,* pp. 359–60.

44. GPM to Carrie M. Crane, Oct. 2, 1870; to CCM, Dec. 27, 1871; Fish to GPM, July 3, 1872, DI No. 346, p. 395.

XV: ROME

1. GPM to Evarts, April 23, 1877, Oct. 23, 1880, DD Nos. 662, 920; to Fish, Oct. 6, 1874, DD No. 520; to GFE, Jan. 29, 1878. The State Dept. kept Marsh without instructions for weeks, owing to "a terrific struggle with itself over . . . whether to call the new king, 'King Humbert' simply, or 'King Humbert *first*.' . . . After a due amount of incubation, however, it was decided to call him 'King' simply, leaving it to posterity to decide whether he is King Humbert 'first,' or 'last'" (GFE to GPM, Jan. 29, 1878).

2. GPM to Evarts, Jan. 26, 1880, Nov. 30, 1878, DD Nos. 865, 800.

3. To F. P. Nash, July 14, 1876.

4. *Ibid.;* to Norton, April, 1881; to Evarts, Dec. 1, 1880, to F. T. Frelinghuysen, Jan. 10, 1882, DD Nos. 928, 1015 (also Nos. 897, 920, 981). See Stillman, *Union of Italy,* p. 368.

5. To GFE, Dec. 30, 1877; to Nash, Aug. 3, 1877; to Sherman, Aug. 19, 1876, Sherman Pap.; to Fish through GFE, Oct. 27, 1876.

6. GPM to Yule, Oct. 28, 1878; to Frelinghuysen, Jan. 10, 30, 1882, DD Nos. 1015, 1016.

7. GPM to C. D. Drake, Feb. 20, 1869. For Wurts, H. S. Sanford to GPM, June 17, 1865; G. M. Wurts to GPM, Oct. 23, 1865; Caroline E. Crane, personal communication, summer 1951.

8. GPM to R. H. Dana, Jr., June 11, 1868, Dana MSS; GFE to GPM, June 11, 1868; GPM to Evarts, Jan. 23, 1879, DD No. 811; Eugene Schuyler to GPM, Dec. 17, 19, 1879.

9. GPM to Yule, Sept. 24, 1874; to Fish, Sept. 15, 25, 1874, DD Nos. 512, 513; 44 Cong. 1 Sess., Sen. Misc. Doc. 16 (Dec. 13, 1875). See GPM, Italo-Swiss Boundary Arbitration Report, MS.

10. GPM, "The Catholic Church and Modern Civilization," *Nation,* V (1867), 231; GPM to Bancroft, Aug. 3, 1869, Bancroft MSS. See Hales, *Pio Nono,* pp. 255–62.

11. GPM, *Medieval and Modern Saints and Miracles,* p. 122; Godkin to GPM, Feb. 10, 1874; Harpers to GPM, Jan. 11, 1881; *Harper's New Monthly Mag.,* LIII (1876), 787. See GPM to H. C. Lea, Aug. 16, 1874; A. B. Crane to GPM, various dates, 1875–76; GPM contract with Harpers, Jan. 20, 1876, cancellation, Jan. 25, 1882, statement, Jan. 8, 1884, Harper & Brothers Archives.

12. *Saints and Miracles,* pp. 18–21.

13. *Ibid.,* pp. 20, 214.

14. *Ibid.*, pp. 137; 98; 104.

15. *Ibid.*, pp. 200–201; 119.

16. To Nash, April 26, 1877; to W. J. Knapp, Jan. 29, 1880.

17. GPM to Gen. W. Cotton, March 9, 1874; GPM, *Irrigation*, pp. 3–4, 15–16. For background to irrigation controversy, see James Watts to GPM, May 21, 1873; J. A. Kasson to GPM, March 30, 1874; Gilpin, *Mission of the North American People*, espec. pp. 71–76, 89–90, for the classic statement of faith in the American "garden"; H. N. Smith, *Virgin Land*, pp. 35–43; Stegner, *Beyond the Hundredth Meridian*, pp. 1–8.

18. GPM, *Irrigation*, pp. 4–6.

19. *Ibid.*, pp. 15–17.

20. *Ibid.*, p. 19. See also GPM, "Irrigation," *Johnson's New Universal Cyclopaedia*, II, 1313.

21. SFB to GPM, Feb. 24, 1874; GPM to SFB, Feb. 2, 1874. See J. W. Powell, *Report on the Lands of the Arid Region*, pp. 83–84; Stegner, *Beyond the Hundredth Meridian*, pp. 301–55.

22. Sargent to GPM, Jan. 23, 1879; Sargent in *Nation*, XXXV (1882), 136.

23. *Earth as Modified by Human Action* (1885 ed.), pp. 320n, 35n.

24. *Ibid.*, pp. 605n, 587n, 473n. Marsh's discussion of how cities influence temperature is noted by Mumford ("Natural History of Urbanization," in W. L. Thomas, Jr., ed., *Man's Role*, p. 398).

25. *Earth as Modified* (1885), p. 46.

26. *Ibid.*, pp. 616–17n.

27. To Yule, Feb. 15, 1875; to Nash, Feb. 6, 1875. See A. J. Johnson and GPM, Agreement, Feb. 2, 1874; GPM to Johnson, Dec. 1875, Feb. 28, March 5, 1878; Johnson to GPM, April 4, 1878.

28. To Yule, Jan. 25, 1875, July 10, 1876.

29. GPM to Nash, March 25, 1875. See Whitney in *Nation*, XX (1875), 134; F. A. March, "Weisse's Origin of the English Language," *Nation*, XXVIII (1879), 153–54.

30. To Nash, Feb. 6, Dec. 27, 1875.

31. *Human Knowledge*, p. 42; "Ethan Allen Statue in Montpelier," VHS *Proc.*, n.s. II (1931), 144–45; J. N. Pomeroy to GPM, July 21, 1873.

32. GPM to GFE, Feb. 9, April 25, 1879, in Winthrop, *Addresses*, IV, 140–43; R. C. Winthrop *et al.*, Memorial to Congress, April 26, 1880, in Harvey, *Washington National Monument*, pp. 97–98. See Roberts, *Washington Monument*, p. 33.

33. GPM to Sherman, March 22, 1877, Sherman Pap. See Wittmann, "The Italian Experience," *American Quart.,* IV (1952), 4, 13.

34. James, "The After-Season at Rome," *Nation,* XVI (1873), 399–400; GPM to GFE, Feb. 15, 1879; to SFB, Feb. 21, 1872.

35. E. Clark, *Rome and a Villa,* p. 16; CCM to Susan Edmunds, Dec. 15, 1872; Arnold to Fanny Arnold, April 17, 1873, in Arnold, *Letters,* I, 112.

36. James, *William Wetmore Story,* I, 257–58; GPM to Charlotte Thrall, Jan. 1, 1880.

37. GPM to LW, Jan. 2, 1877 (CCM copy); to Yule, Dec. 25, 1872; to Sherman, Feb. 27, 1872, Sherman Pap.; to D. G. Mitchell, n.d., in Mitchell, *American Lands and Letters,* p. 43. It was a "great boon" to Marsh when the European countries decided to promote their envoys to Italy to the rank of ambassador. The United States did not follow suit, and as a mere Minister Plenipotentiary Marsh no longer served as dean of the diplomatic corps (Trollope, *What I Remember,* p. 448).

38. GPM to LW, Jan. 2, 1877 (CCM copy); to GFE, Dec. 30, 1877; to H. C. Lea, April 29, 1880; to LW, Feb. 25, 1880.

39. GPM to LW, May 10, 1879; to Charlotte Thrall, Jan. 1, 1880.

40. L. W. Mitchell to family, Dec. 16, 1876, courtesy of Dr. John K. Wright, Lyme, N.H.; Holmes to GPM, April 23, 1860; Norton to CCM, Aug. 5, 1882; GPM to LW, Nov. 9, 1875. See Seymour, "Lucy Myers Mitchell," *Critic,* XV (1888), 176; R. H. Dana, *Hospitable England,* pp. 243–46.

41. SFB to GPM, Feb. 4, 1854, in Dall, *Baird,* p. 316; Humphrey Sandwith to GPM, March 13, 1880; D. H. Wheeler, "Recollections of George P. Marsh," MS.

42. GPM to J. S. Pike, May 12, 1864, Pike Pap.; to GFE, Jan. 29, 1878; "Dry Wines," MS.

43. Carrie Crane to GPM, Feb. 2, 1872; GPM to Nash, Aug. 24, 1875.

44. GPM to LW, Oct. 21, 1876, WP; to Yule, June 17, 1876; Bessie Crane to A. B. Crane, Nov. 20, 1881.

45. GPM to Nash, Sept. 1877; to Fish, April 20, 1876, DD No. 602. See C. C. Andrews to GPM, April 26, 1876, AP; GPM to Andrews, Jan. 22, 1877.

46. To Charlotte Thrall, Jan. 1, 1880. After Marsh's death Carlo went to America with Caroline, was expelled from several schools and disappeared in the Middle West, reappearing occasionally to ask for money.

47. To Charlotte Thrall, Jan. 1, 1880.

48. To LW, Jan. 25, 1880; to Nash, April 26, 1877; A. B. Crane

to GPM, Nov. 1, 1880; CCM to LW, March 15, 1881, WP; GPM to Yule, Sept. 18, 1876.

49. Washington correspondent, Boston *Daily Transcript,* Jan. 11, 1873; Mrs. E. E. Evans to GPM, March 16, 1873, citing her reply in Boston *Evening Transcript,* Feb. 27, 1873. See J. R. Lowell to W. J. Hoppin, Nov. 22, 1881, in Lowell, *New Letters,* p. 259.

50. GPM to M. F. Force, May 5, 1877; GFE to GPM, May 10, 1877.

51. GFE to GPM, July 1, 1880, April 13, 1881; M. F. Force to GPM, Nov. 2, 1881. On Edmunds, see Selig Adler, "Senatorial Career of George Franklin Edmunds," MS; Austin, "Address"; Briggs, *Olivia Letters;* Badeau, *Grant in Peace,* pp. 536–37.

52. CCM and GPM to LW, March 15, 1881, WP.

53. GPM to GFE, April, 1881; Charles Marsh estate, April 14, 1874, Court of Probate, Dist. of Hartford, XXXII, 140. After all his fears, Marsh left his wife more than $54,000 (GPM, will and estate inventory, Probate Off., Burl., No. 4676, Chittenden Co., LX, 301–4, 384, 532, and LXI, 11).

54. GPM to Buckham, April 4, Sept. 23, 1881. See GPM to J. R. Lowell, Jan. 19, 1882, Lowell Pap.; UV, *Catalogue of the Library of George Perkins Marsh,* pp. v–viii. For Marsh's criticisms of American tinderbox building, see his "Fireproof Construction in Italy," *Johnson's New Universal Cyclopaedia,* II, 113–14.

55. To M. F. Force, May 5, 1877; to GFE, March 22, 1877.

56. To Sumner, Feb. 17, 1868, Sumner Pap.; to Sherman, March 18, 1876, Sherman Pap. For the decline in moral standards, see L. D. White, *Republican Era,* pp. 365–80.

57. GPM to Giuseppe Pasolini, May 29, 1875; GFE in the Senate, Jan. 14, 1887, *Cong. Record,* 42 Cong. 2 Sess., pp. 645–46.

58. To Sherman, Dec. 25, 1872, Sherman Pap.; to GFE, May 19, 1877.

59. To F. P. Nash, Aug. 9, 1879, March 28, 1877; to Pasolini, Sept. 11, 1876.

60. To Norton, April, 1881; GPM, "Aphorisms," MS; *Saints and Miracles,* pp. 184–86. Marsh considered "the reading of flashy novels the principal agency in the intellectual degradation" of England and America (to Norton, April, 1881).

61. "Study of Nature," p. 59; to C. D. Drake, Feb. 15, 1845; "Female Education in Italy," *Nation,* III (1866). See Ross, *Child of Destiny,* p. 136; Blackwell, *Pioneer Work for Women,* p. 101; Armstrong, *Fanny Kemble,* p. 278.

62. GPM to Horace Greeley, May 7, 1869, FC; to Norton, April, 1881. See Protestant Orphanage for Girls, *Report . . . 1882.*

63. GPM to Haynes, March 21, 1881; "Study of Nature," pp. 59–60; to C. C. Andrews, July 5, 1875, AP; "Aphorisms," MS.

64. Susan Edmunds to CCM, July 6, 1883; CCM, "To——," in *Wolfe of the Knoll,* pp. 324–37.

65. To Nash, Aug. 3, April 26, 1877.

66. To Nash, Sept. 1877; to LW and FW, Oct. 13, 1862, WP; to Nash, July 14, 1876; GPM, "England Old and New" (address at Middlebury, Vt., Dec. 1859), MS, p. 5; to LW and FW, July 25, 1862, WP; CCM to LW, July 25, 1862, WP.

67. GPM, "Thoughts and Aphorisms," pp. 2–3.

68. GPM to Nash, Aug. 3, 1877; CCM to S. G. Brown, n.d.

69. Story, *Vallombrosa,* pp. 8, 28, 69; James, *Story,* II, 330–37; Story to GPM, July 12, 1882.

70. Frelinghuysen to GPM, telegram July 7, July 18, DI No. 828, II, 206–9; GPM to GFE, Sept. 24, 1876; GPM in CCM, "Last Days of George P. Marsh," MS; G. W. Wurts to CCM, July 10, 1882. See Stillman, "The Late George P. Marsh," and "A Diplomatic Intrigue," *Nation,* XXXV (1882), 304–5, 529–30. Wurts rebuked Frelinghuysen for this act; he charged that at his death Marsh was preparing a dispatch "opposing this measure from which he considered he would be the greatest and first sufferer" (Wurts to Frelinghuysen, Sept. 15, 1882, DD No. 1044).

71. To Sargent, July 20, 1882. See Mitchell, *American Lands and Letters,* p. 36; Duncan, "Forest Practice at Vallombrosa," *Journal of Forestry,* XLIV (1946), 347–53; Kernan, "Trees of Vallambrosa [*sic*]," *American Forests,* LX, No. 7 (1954), 14–16, 44–45.

72. CCM, "Last Days of George P. Marsh," MS.

73. Mary Crane to LW, July 27, 1882, WP; CCM, "Last Days of George P. Marsh," MS.

74. Trollope, *What I Remember,* p. 530; Gay, *Protestant Burial Ground in Rome;* CCM to S. G. Brown, n.d.

XVI: A RETROSPECTIVE VIEW

1. F. A. March, "George Perkins Marsh" [review of *LL*], *Nation,* XLVII (1888), 214.

2. Schlesinger, "What Then Is the American, This New Man?" *AHR,* XLVIII (1943), 230.

Bibliography

THE MOST IMPORTANT SOURCE for this biography has been the Marsh manuscript collection at the University of Vermont. This collection, consisting of tens of thousands of letters to and from Marsh, in addition to many diaries, notebooks, and drafts of speeches, documents, and books, was presented to the University of Vermont between 1946 and 1950 by Caroline Crane Marsh's grandniece, the late Caroline E. Crane, of Scarsdale, N. Y. Of material still in Miss Crane's possession in 1950, Caroline Marsh's Italian diaries proved to be especially valuable. Other collections of primary importance were the Marsh letters at the Vermont Historical Society, the Dartmouth College Archives, the Baird correspondence at the Smithsonian Institution, the letters kindly loaned to me by Dr. Marsh Pitzman, of St. Louis, and Marsh's diplomatic dispatches in the National Archives, Washington, D.C.

Of published materials, Marsh's own extensive works and his great library at the University of Vermont necessarily formed the backbone for this study. Except for short sketches by W. M. Davis, H. L. Koopman, and Milburn McCarty, there have been no biographical studies of Marsh since Caroline Crane Marsh's *Life and Letters* of her husband, which ill-health prevented her from carrying beyond 1861. Many of the letters in her volume are bowdlerized or cut, and the work itself is highly eulogistic, but no student of Marsh can fail to be impressed by Mrs. Marsh's insight, by her clarity, and above all by her perspicacity in gathering together from all over the world the correspondence of her husband, the bulk of which must otherwise have been lost. Marsh himself despised both introspection and autobiography. "The best ordered life," he wrote, "is that which is least haunted by its own past."

MANUSCRIPT COLLECTIONS AND ARCHIVES

Samuel A. Allibone Papers. HL.

Anderson, Rasmus. Autobiography. MS, Wisconsin Historical Society.

C. C. Andrews Papers. Minnesota Historical Society.

Spencer F. Baird Correspondence. SI.

George Bancroft MSS. MHS.

Burlington, Vermont. Town Records.

—— Grand List, 1825–52.

—— Highway Rate Bill for District Number Two, 1831. UV.

—— Land List and Real Estate Assessment, 1837.

—— Land Records (real estate records), 1831–63.

Burlington MSS. UV.

Chittenden County. Court Records, 1825–58.

—— Probate Office. Wills of Ozias Buell, Wyllys Lyman, and George Perkins Marsh.

Green Clay MSS. Western Historical Manuscripts Collection, Univ. of Missouri Library.

John M. Clayton Papers. LC.

Jacob Collamer Papers. Mrs. William Clough, Woodstock, Vt.

Columbia College Archives, Minutes of the Trustees, Vol. V.

R. H. Dana, Jr., MSS. MHS.

Dartmouth College Archives. DC.

C. S. Daveis Papers. LC.

Drake, Charles D. Autobiography, MS. Missouri Historical Society.

R. W. Emerson Papers. HUL.

Edward Everett Papers. MHS.

C. C. Felton MSS. Harvard College Archives.

Hamilton Fish Correspondence. LC.

Willard Fiske Papers. Columbia University Library.

Charles Folsom MSS. Boston Public Library.

Ford Collection. New York Public Library.

Albert Gallatin Papers. NYHS.

Galloway-Maxcy-Markoe Correspondence. LC.

E. L. Godkin Papers. HUL.

Asa Gray Collection. Harvard University Herbarium.

Harper & Brothers Archives, New York.

Hartford, District of. Court of Probate, will of Charles Marsh.

Harvard College Archives.

Rush C. Hawkins Papers. Annmary Brown Memorial Library, Brown University.

Franklin B. Hough Papers. New York State Library.

Henry E. Huntington Library. Manuscripts.

Knollenberg Collection. YUL.

C. C. Jewett Papers. Boston Public Library.

Library of Congress, Letter Book of the Librarian of Congress, 1843–49. LC.

Francis Lieber Correspondence. LC.

Loomis Papers. UV.

James Russell Lowell Papers. HUL.

George P. Marsh Collection. UV.

Marsh MSS. VHS.

S. F. B. Morse MSS. LC.

Norcross MSS. MHS.

C. E. Norton Papers. HUL.

J. A. Pearce Papers. Maryland Historical Society.

J. S. Pike Papers. Calais Free Library, Calais, Maine (courtesy of Robert F. Durden).

Hiram Powers MSS. NYHS.

Carl Schurz Papers. Wisconsin Historical Society.

W. T. Sherman Papers. LC.

Smithsonian Institution Archives, Correspondence Received.

E. C. Squier Collection. LC.

Charles Sumner Papers. HUL.

Tappan, Benjamin. Senate Journal, MS. LC.

Bayard Taylor MSS. Columbia University Library.

Charles E. Tuttle Collection, Rutland, Vt. [GPM letters].

United States Department of State Papers, National Archives
    Appointment and Recommendation Papers.
    Belgium. Brussels Legation. Post Records, Vol. VII, 1861–63.
    Italy: Diplomatic Instructions. Vols. I–II, 1838–94.
        Diplomatic Despatches. Vols. X–XIX, 1861–83.
        PR, Miscellaneous Correspondence: Letters to Consuls and Others. Vols. I–VI, 1861–82. Serial Nos. 20–25.
        PR, Consular and Miscellaneous Letters Received. Vols. I–IX, 1861–82. Serial Nos. 39–47.
    Turkey: Diplomatic Instructions. Vol. I, 1825–59.
        Diplomatic Despatches. Vol. XII, 1849–53.

PR, Miscellaneous Correspondence of the Legation of the U.S. Letters Sent. 1849–59.

PR, Miscellaneous Correspondence Received. Vol. II, 1850–54.

University of Vermont Records, Trustees Minutes, Vol. III (1829–65).

Vermont State Archives. Office of the Secretary of State, Montpelier.

Vermont State Papers. Montpelier.

E. C. Washburne Correspondence. LC.

Alexander Wetmore Collection. YUL.

Windsor County (Vt.) Court Records, 1825. Woodstock, Vt.

R. C. Winthrop Papers. MHS.

Wislizenus Papers. Dr. Marsh Pitzman, St. Louis.

Woodstock, Vt., Land Records, Vols. I–II, 1793–96.

NEWSPAPERS

Athens, Greece	*Jeune Hellas,* 1852.
Boston	*Daily Advertiser,* 1847, 1854.
	Daily Transcript, 1873.
Burlington, Vt.	*Free Press* (after 1848, *Daily Free Press;* after 1868, *Daily Free Press & Times*), 1827–85.
	Sentinel (after 1830, *Northern Sentinel;* after 1844, *Sentinel and Democrat*), 1825–50.
Chicago and St. Louis	*Woman's Journal,* 1875.
Montpelier, Vt.	*Vermont Patriot,* 1843.
	Watchman & State Gazette (after 1837, *Watchman & State Journal*), 1835–44.
New York	*Christian Intelligencer,* 1877.
	Herald, 1856.
	Times, 1861–82.
	Tribune (weekly, semiweekly, daily), 1855–85.
	World, 1860.
Washington, D.C.	*National Intelligencer,* 1856.
Windsor, Vt.	*The Post Boy and Vermont and New Hampshire Federal Courier,* 1806.
	Spooner's Vermont Journal, 1813.
	Vermont Chronicle, 1844.
Woodstock, Vt.	*Northern Memento,* 1805.
	Observer, 1820–25.
	Vermont Mercury, 1844.
	Vermont Standard, 1857, 1861, 1882.

PUBLISHED MATERIAL BY GEORGE PERKINS MARSH

Address Delivered before the Agricultural Society of Rutland County, Sept. 30, 1847. Rutland, Vt., 1848.

Address [delivered before the American Colonization Society, Jan. 15, 1856], *African Repository*, XXXII (1856), 40–47; also American Colonization Soc., Thirty-ninth Annual Report (1856), pp. 10–17.

Address Delivered before the Burlington Mechanics Institute, April 5, 1843. *BFP* extra, June 2, 1843.

Address Delivered before the Graduating Class of the U.S. Military Academy at West Point, June, 1860. New York, 1860.

Address, Delivered before the New England Society of the City of New-York, Dec. 24, 1844. New York, 1845.

"Agriculture in Italy," *Nation*, II (1866), 183–84.

"American Diplomacy," New York *World*, June 30, 1860.

"American Heraldry," New York *World*, July 2, 1860.

The American Historical School: a Discourse Delivered before the Literary Societies of Union College. Troy, N.Y., 1847.

"The American Image Abroad," *BDFP*, Sept. 21, 1854.

"American Representatives Abroad," New York *World*, June 21, 1860.

An Apology for the Study of English; Delivered on Monday, Nov. 1, 1858; Introductory to a Series of Lectures in the Post-Graduate Course of Columbia College, New York. New York, 1859. [Rev. version is Ch. 1 of Lectures on the English Language.]

"The Aqueducts of Ancient Rome," *Nation*, XXXII (1881), 147–48.

"Biographical Sketch of the Author [J. G. Biernatzki]," in Caroline C. Marsh, The Hallig; or, The Sheepfold in the Water, pp. 17–24. Boston, 1856.

"The Biography of a Word," *Nation*, XXXII (1881), 88–89.

"Boccardo's Dictionary of Political Economy," *Nation*, XXII (1876), 65–66.

"The Book of Marco Polo," *Nation*, XXI (1875), 135–37, 152–53.

"The Camel," in Report of the Smithsonian Institution for 1854, pp. 98–122. 33 Cong. 2 Sess., Sen. Misc. Doc. 24. Washington, 1855.

The Camel; His Organization, Habits and Uses, Considered with Reference to His Introduction into the United States. Boston, 1856.

"The Catholic Church and Modern Civilization," *Nation*, V (1867), 229–31.

"The 'Catholic Party' of Cesare Cantù and American Slavery," *Nation*, II (1866), 564–65.

"A Cheap and Easy Way to Fame," *Nation,* I (1865), 778.

A Compendious Grammar of the Old-Northern or Icelandic Language: Compiled and Translated from the Grammars of Rask. Burlington, Vt., 1838.

"Cutting Metals with a 'Burr,'" letter to the New York *Tribune,* April 27, 1881.

"Departure of George P. Marsh.—The Meeting Last Night; Full Report of the Speeches of Prest. Pease and Geo. P. Marsh," Burlington *Daily Times,* April 19, 1861.

"The Desert: I. The Ship of the Desert; or, A Discourse of Camels, and Herein of Their Furniture, Diet, and Drivers," *American Whig Review,* XVI (1852), 39–51.

A Dictionary of English Etymology, by Hensleigh Wedgwood. Vol. I (*A–D*); with notes and additions by GPM. New York, 1862.

[Diplomatic Correspondence as Minister to Italy, 1861–82], in U.S. Dept. of State. Papers Relating to Foreign Affairs, 1861–83.

[Diplomatic Correspondence as Minister to Turkey, 1849–53], in the following U.S. documents (see under United States): Communications . . . Relative to the Case of the Reverend Mr. King; Francis Dainese; Further Correspondence . . . Relative to the Rev. Jonas King; Kossuth and Captain Long; Martin Koszta.

The Earth as Modified by Human Action. *See* Man and Nature.

"The Education of Women," *Nation,* III (1866), 165–66.

"The Excommunication of Noxious Animals by the Catholic Church," *Nation,* II (1866), 763–64.

"Female Education in Italy," *Nation,* III (1866), 5–7.

"The Future of Italy," New York *World,* July 9, 1860.

"The Future of Turkey," *CE,* LXV (1858), 401–19.

"A Glossary of Later and Byzantine Greek, by E. A. Sophocles" [review by GPM], New York *World,* June 28, 1860.

The Goths in New-England; a Discourse Delivered at the Anniversary of the Philomathesian Society of Middlebury College, Aug. 15, 1843. Middlebury, Vt., 1843.

"The Grammar of English Grammars, by Goold Brown.—A Treatise on the English Language, by Simon Kerl" [reviews by GPM], New York *World,* June 14, 1860.

Human Knowledge: a Discourse Delivered before the Massachusetts Alpha of the Phi Beta Kappa Society, at Cambridge, Aug. 26, 1847. Boston, 1847.

Irrigation: Its Evils, the Remedies, and the Compensations. (Rome,

July 24, 1873.) Feb. 10, 1874. 43 Cong. 1 Sess., Sen. Misc. Doc. 55.

"The Italian Cause and Its Sympathizers," New York *World*, July 7, 1860.

"Italian Nationality," New York *World*, June 14, 1860.

Johnson's New Universal Cyclopaedia . . . 4 vols. New York, 1874–78. The following articles: Amat (Felix de Torres), IV, 1560; Castanheda, de (Fernão Lopez), IV, 1573; Catalan Language and Literature, IV, 1573–74; Crichton (James), IV, 1584; D'Esclot . . . (Bernat), IV, 1591–92; Fireproof Construction in Italy, II, 113–14; Fréjus, Col de, Tunnel of, or Tunnel of Mont Cenis, II, 331; Fresco, or Fresco-Painting, II, 339; Fucino, or Celano, Lake and Tunnel of, II, 355; Genoa, II, 471; Girgenti, II, 556; Improvisation, II, 1129–30; Index, Concordance, Digest, Table of Contents, II, 1135–36; Index Librorum Prohibitorum, II, 1136–37; Inundations and Floods of Rivers, II, 1273–75; Irrigation, II, 1311–13; Italian Language and Literature, II, 1330–36; Jacme (Jayme or Jaume) En I., II, 1356; Legend, II, 1714–15; Lexicon, Dictionary, Thesaurus, Vocabulary, Glossary, II, 1751–52; Lombardini (Elia), III, 98; Lopes, or Lopez (Fernão), III, 112; Lull (Ramon), III, 147; March (Ausias), III, 294; Mulberry, III, 657–58; Muntaner Ramon, III, 668; Olive, III, 946–47; Po, III, 1298–99; Pontine Marshes, III, 1332; Romansch . . . , III, 1704–5; St. Gothard, Tunnel of, IV, 18–19; Sicilian Vespers, IV, 265; Sicilies, The Two, IV, 265–67; Sicily, Island of, IV, 267–69; Straw, Manufacture of, IV, 591–92; Tiber, IV, 853–54; Velvet, IV, 1712–13; Watershed, IV, 1299–1300; Well, IV, 1345–46.

"The Late General Estcourt," *National Intelligencer* (Washington, D.C.), Feb. 7, 1856. Also in *LL*, pp. 474–79.

Lectures on the English Language. New York, 1860; rev. and enlarged eds., First Series, 1861, 1872, 1885.

Man and Nature; or, Physical Geography as Modified by Human Action. New York, 1864.

The Earth as Modified by Human Action; a New Edition of Man and Nature. New York, 1874.

The Earth as Modified by Human Action; a Last Revision of Man and Nature. New York, 1885.

L'Uoma e la natura. Firenze, 1869, 1872.

"Marsh, James," in George Ripley and C. A. Dana, eds., New American Cyclopaedia, XI, 216–17. 12 vols. New York, 1859–61.

Medieval and Modern Saints and Miracles. Not ab uno e Societate Jesu. New York, 1876.

Memorial of George P. Marsh, of Vermont, Asking an appropriation for the compensation of his services as Minister Resident to the Ottoman Porte, under the Act of August 11, 1848, imposing judicial duties on the Minister, and of his services under a special mission to the government of Greece. Dec. 1, 1854. 33 Cong. 2 Sess., Sen. Misc. Doc. 8. [Reprint includes additional letter, GPM to Solomon Foot, Jan. 3, 1855.]

"Monumental Honors," *Nation,* I (1865), 491–92.

New Dictionary by the Philological Society of London. Burlington, Aug. 8, 1859.

Notes on Mr. Hensleigh Wedgwood's Dictionary of English Etymology, and on Some Words Not Discussed by Him. [London, 1864.]

"Notes on the New Edition of Webster's Dictionary," *Nation,* III (1866), 125–27, 147–48, 186–87, 225–26, 268–69, 288–89, 369, 408–9, 515–17; IV (1867), 7–9, 108–9, 127–28, 312–13, 373, 392–93, 516–17; V (1867), 7–8, 88–89, 208–9.

"Notes on Vesuvius, and Miscellaneous Observations on Egypt (from Letters to the Smithsonian Institution from a Traveller in the East)," *American Journal of Science and Arts,* 2d ser., XIII (1852), 131–34.

"Old English Literature," *Nation,* I (1865), 778.

"Old Northern Literature," *American Whig Review* [The American Review: a Whig Journal], I (1845), 250–57.

"Oration" [before the New Hampshire State Agricultural Society, Oct. 10, 1856], in N.H. State Agric. Soc., *Trans., 1856* (Concord, N.H., 1857), pp. 35–89.

"Oriental Christianity and Islamism" *CE,* LXV (1858), 95–125.

"The Oriental Question," *CE,* LXIV (1858), 393–420.

"The Origin and History of the Danish Sound and Belt-Tolls," *Hunt's Merchants' Magazine,* X (1844), 218–32, 303–8. Tr. from Schlegel's Danmark's og Hertugdommenes Statsret, 1827.

The Origin and History of the English Language, and of the Early Literature It Embodies. New York, 1862; rev. ed., 1885.

"The Origin of the Italian Language," *NAR,* CV (1867), 1–41.

"The Origin, Progress, and Decline of Icelandic Historical Literature, by Peter Erasmus Mueller . . . Translated, with Notes by George P. Marsh," *American Eclectic,* I (1841), 446–68; II (1841), 131–46.

"Our English Dictionaries," *Christian Review,* CI (1860), 384–415.

"Physical Science in Italy," *Nation,* VII (1868), 420–21.

"The Principles and Tendencies of Modern Commerce; with Special Reference to the Character and Influence of the Traffic between the

Christian States and the Oriental World," *Hunt's Merchants' Magazine,* XXXIII (1855), 147–68.

"The Proposed Revision of the English Bible," *Nation,* XI (1870), 238–39, 261–63, 281–82.

" 'Protection to Naturalized Citizens,' " *Nation,* III (1866), 115–16.

"Pruning Forest Trees," *Nation,* I (1865), 690–91.

Railroad Commissioner of the State of Vermont. Third Annual Report to the General Assembly, 1858. Burlington, Vt., 1858.

—— Special Report, October Session, 1858. Burlington, Vt., 1858.

—— Fourth Annual Report, 1859. Burlington, Vt., 1859.

Remarks on Slavery in the Territories of New Mexico, California and Oregon; Delivered in the House of Representatives, Aug. 3d, 1848. Burlington, Vt., 1848.

Reply to Mr. Brodhead's Remarks in the Senate on the Bill for the Relief of George P. Marsh, as Reported in the *Globe* of April 26, 1856. Washington, May 1, 1856.

"Report of the Commissioners on Plan of the New State House," in Annual Message of the Governor to the General Assembly of the State of Vermont, October Session, 1857, pp. 17–20. Montpelier, Vt., 1857.

Report on Durazzo Library. June 7, 1844. 28 Cong. 1 Sess., H. Rep. 553.

Report [on Memorial of] James A. Stevens. May 24, 1844. 28 Cong. 1 Sess., H. Rep. 510.

Report [on Memorial of] Joshua Dodge. April 26, 1848. 30 Cong. 1 Sess., H. Rep. 589.

Report [on Memorial of] P. J. Farnham and Jed Frye. March 3, 1849. 30 Cong. 2 Sess., H. Rep. 142.

Report [on Memorial of the National Institute for the Promotion of Science]. June 7, 1844. 28 Cong. 1 Sess., Sen. Doc. 368.

Report [on Petition of E. H.] Holmes and [W.] Pedrick. March 29, 1844. 28 Cong. 1 Sess., H. Rep. 389.

Report [on Petition of] Elisha H. Holmes. Jan. 30, 1846. 29 Cong. 1 Sess., H. Rep. 160.

Report [on Petition of] Elisha H. Holmes. Feb. 16, 1847. 29 Cong. 2 Sess., H. Rep. 62.

Report on Spirit Ration in Navy. Jan. 28, 1845. 28 Cong. 2 Sess., H. Rep. 73.

Report, on the Artificial Propagation of Fish. Made under the Authority of the Legislature of Vermont. Burlington, Vt., 1857.

[Report on the Education of the Deaf and Dumb], in Vermont General Assembly Journal, 1824, pp. 23–30.

"The River, from the Swedish of Tegner" [GPM, tr.], *American Whig Review,* II (1845), 357.

Speech on the Bill for Establishing the Smithsonian Institution; Delivered in the House of Representatives of the U. States, April 22, 1846. Washington, 1846.

Speech on the Mexican War, Delivered in the House of Representatives of the U.S., Feb. 10, 1848. Washington, D.C., 1848.

Speech on the Tariff Bill; Delivered in the House of Representatives of the United States, on the 30th of April, 1844. St. Albans, Vt., 1844.

Speech on the Tariff Question; Delivered in the House of Representatives of the U.S., June 30th, 1846. Washington, D.C., 1846.

"State Sovereignty" [entitled "The Sovereignty of the States" after the first installment], *Nation,* I (1865), 554–56, 648–50, 715–16, 776–77, 810–12.

"Statistics of the Mont Cenis Tunnel," *Nation,* V (1867), 259–60.

"The Study of Nature," *CE,* LXVIII (1860), 33–62.

"Summary of the Statistics of Sweden," *Hunt's Merchants' Magazine,* XXIV (1851), 194–99.

"Swedish Literature: 1. Olof Rudbeck the Elder and His Atlantica; 2. The Life and Works of the Painter Hörberg," *American Eclectic,* I (1841), 63–81, 313–32.

"Thoughts and Aphorisms," in T. Adolphus Trollope, ed., In Memoriam: a Wreath of Stray Leaves to the Memory of Emily Bliss Gould ob: 31st Aug. 1875. Rome, 1875.

"Translations from the German [Claudius' Rhine-Wine Song; Matthisson's The Gnomes and The Fairies]," *American Whig Review,* II (1845), 256–58.

"Trieste, and the Participation of Austria in the Commerce of the World, 1832–41; Translated from the Austrian Lloyd's Journal," *Hunt's Merchants' Magazine,* X (1844), 495–521.

"The Two Dictionaries," New York *World,* June 15, 1860.

"The War and the Peace," *CE,* LXVII (1859), 260–82.

"Waterglass," *BDFP,* July 13, 1857.

"Were the States Ever Sovereign?" *Nation,* I (1865), 5–8.

"What American Diplomacy Might Do," New York *World,* July 2, 1860.

SELECTED UNPUBLISHED PAPERS BY
GEORGE PERKINS MARSH

"Aphorisms" [in notebook]. About 1875.

"Broussa." About 1855.

[Campagna of Rome]. 1881.

"Constantinople and the Bosphorus." About 1855.

"Domestic Life and Arts of the Greeks and Romans." Burl. Lyceum, March 12, 1832.

"Dry Wines." From Paris *American Register*, 1877 or 1878.

"Economy of the Forest." With letter to Asa Gray, May 9, 1849.

"England Old and New." Address at Middlebury, Vt., Dec. 1859.

[Independence Day Oration. Burlington, July 4, 1829 (?)]. (In praise of American institutions.)

[Independence Day Oration. Burlington, July 4, 1843]. (On British institutions and aggressions.)

[Independence Day Oration. Woodstock, July 4, 1857 (?)]. (On changes in the American scene since the Revolution.)

"Indian Corn and the Pellagra." About 1875.

"Italian Independence." March, 1860. Abstract in *BDFP*, March 26, 1860.

[Italo-Swiss Boundary Arbitration Report]. 1874.

"Martin Koszta and the American Legation at Constantinople." Draft of letter to Mr. Benedict, signed "Mediterranean." 1853.

"Messina to Catania." About 1855.

Morse's New Atlas.

"Office-Holders Turned Out." 1854.

"The Old World and the New." Written for the *North American Review*. 1865 or 1866.

"Persia Treaty Negotiations." 1852.

Petition from Citizens of Burlington for Erection of a New State House, Oct. 17, 1832, VSA, LXVI, 39.

Phraseology of Paul Louis Courier. Collection of organized notes. N.d.

Plan for the New State House. April 1, 1857, VSP, LXVI, 84.

Preliminary Notice [to an English edition of Élisée Reclus's *La Terre*]. About 1865.

"Relations between Commerce and Civilization." After 1870.

SI Affairs. Draft of letter to C. W. Upham, Feb. 1855.

"Supplementary Statement of Complaint" (about Dubois' Hotel). April 4, 1850.

UV Library Report. Nov. 27, 1855.
Zoology: Linnaeus's system. About 1816.

OTHER SOURCES

Adams, John Quincy. Memoirs of John Quincy Adams, Comprising Portions of His Diary from 1795 to 1848. Charles Francis Adams, ed. 12 vols. Philadelphia, 1874–77.

Adler, Cyrus. "The Smithsonian Library," in G. Brown Goode, ed., The Smithsonian Institution 1846–1896, pp. 265–302. Washington, D.C., 1897.

Adler, Selig. "The Senatorial Career of George Franklin Edmunds, 1866–1891." Ph.D. thesis, MS, University of Illinois, 1934.

Allen, Charles E. About Burlington, Vermont. Burlington, Vt., 1905.

Allen, J. H. [Review of Marsh's Origin and History of the English Language], CE, LXXIV (1863), 448–49.

Amiens, E., ed. Un Salotto fiorentino. Firenze, 1902.

Andover. Biographical Catalogue of the Trustees, Teachers and Students of Phillips Academy Andover 1778–1830. Andover, Mass., 1903.

—— Catalogue of the Trustees, Instructors and Students of Phillips Academy, Andover. Andover, August, 1816. Oliver Wendell Holmes Library, Andover, Mass.

"Angelico." Letters from Florence, in New York Times, Nov. 30, 1866; June 5, 30, July 25, Aug. 5, 1867.

Armstrong, Margaret. Fanny Kemble: a Passionate Victorian. New York, 1938.

Arnold, Josias Lyndon. Poems. Providence, R.I., 1797.

Arnold, Matthew. Letters of Matthew Arnold 1848–1888. G. W. E. Russell, coll. 2 vols. New York, 1895.

Atwater, Caleb. Mysteries of Washington City, during Several Months of the Session of the 28th Congress. Washington, D.C., 1844.

Auden, W. H. "Njal's Saga," New Statesman and Nation, LII (1956), 551–52.

Auld, Joseph. Picturesque Burlington: a Handbook of Burlington, Vermont, and Lake Champlain. Burlington, Vt., 1893.

Austin, Warren F. "Address," in George F. Edmunds Centenary Exercises 1828–1928, pp. 1–28. Burlington, Vt., 1928.

Ausubel, Herman. Historians and Their Craft: a Study of the Presidential Addresses of the American Historical Association, 1884–1945. New York, 1950.

Badeau, Adam. Grant in Peace; from Appomatox to Mount McGregor: a Personal Memoir. Hartford, Conn., 1887.

Bailey, Harold L. "Vermont's State Houses; Being a Narration of the Battles over the Location of the Capitol and Its Construction," *Vermont Quarterly*, XII (1944), 135–56.

[Baird, S. F.] Report of the [United States] Commissioner [of Fish and Fisheries] for 1872 and 1873. 42 Cong. 3 Sess., Sen. Misc. Doc. 74. Washington, D.C., 1874.

Ball, John. Autobiography of John Ball. Kate Ball Powers, Flora Ball Hopkins, and Lucy Ball, comp. Grand Rapids, Mich., 1925.

Barnard, J. G. "Memoir of Joseph Gilbert Totten, 1788–1864," *NASBM* (1877), I, 35–97.

Barrett, James. Memorial Address on the Life and Character of the Hon. Jacob Collamer. Rutland, Vt., 1868.

—— Memorial Address on the Life and Character of the Hon. Charles Marsh, LL.D. (From VHS *Proc.*, 1870.) Montpelier, Vt., 1871.

Baruffi, Giuseppe. Saluzzo-Manta-Verzuolo nell' ottobre dell' anno 1863. Passeggiata autunnale. Torino, 1864.

Bassett, Raymond E. "A Study of the Promotion, Building, and Financing of the Vermont Central Railroad to July 1, 1853." M.A. thesis, MS, University of Vermont, 1934.

Bassett, T. D. Seymour. "A Case Study of Urban Impact on Rural Society: Vermont, 1840–80," *AH*, XXX (1956), 28–34.

—— "The Rise of Cornelius Peter Van Ness 1782–1826," VHS *Proc.*, n.s. X (1942), 3–20.

Beard, Charles A., and Mary R. Beard. The American Spirit; a Study of the Idea of Civilization in the United States. New York, 1942.

Beard, Charles A., and Alfred Vagts. "Currents of Thought in Historiography," *AHR*, XLII (1937), 460–83.

Beck, Richard. "George P. Marsh and Old Icelandic Studies," *SS*, XVII (1943), 195–203.

Beck, Thor J. Northern Antiquities in French Learning and Literature (1755–1855): a Study in Preromantic Ideas. 2 vols. New York, 1934.

Benson, Adolph B. "The Beginning of American Interest in Scandinavian Literature," *SS*, VIII (1925), 133–41.

Bigelow, John. Retrospections of an Active Life. 5 vols. New York, 1909–13.

Billington, Ray Allen. The Protestant Crusade 1800–1860; a Study of the Origins of American Nativism. New York, 1938.

Blackwell, Elizabeth. Pioneer Work for Women. London, 1895.

Bonsal, Stephen. Edward Fitzgerald Beale: a Pioneer in the Path of Empire, 1822–1903. New York, 1912.

Boorstin, Daniel. The Lost World of Thomas Jefferson. New York, 1948.

Borome, Joseph A. Charles Coffin Jewett. Chicago, 1951.

Boynton, Henry. "Woodstock, Vermont," *New England Magazine*, n.s. XVIII (1898), 65–84.

Briggs, Emily E. The Olivia Letters: Being Some History of Washington City for Forty Years . . . New York, 1906.

Broek, J. O. M. "Agrarische Opnemingen (Surveys) in de Vereenigde Staten," *Tidjschrift voor Economische Geographie*, XXIV (1933), 232–44.

Brooks, C. E. P. "The Influence of Forests on Rainfall and Run-off," Royal Meteorological Society *Quarterly Journal*, LIV (1928), 1–17.

Brown, Ernest Francis. Raymond of the Times. New York, 1951.

Brown, John C., comp. Forests and Moisture; or, Effects of Forests on Humidity of Climate. Edinburgh, 1877.

Brown, Ralph H. Mirror for Americans: Likeness of the Eastern Seaboard 1810. American Geographical Society Special Publ. No. 27. New York, 1943.

Brown, Samuel Gilman. A Discourse Commemorative of the Hon. George Perkins Marsh, LL.D. Burlington, Vt., 1883.

—— The Works of Rufus Choate, with a Memoir of His Life. 2 vols. Boston, 1862.

Browning, Elizabeth Barrett. The Letters of Elizabeth Barrett Browning. F. G. Kenyon, ed. 2 vols. New York, 1898.

Bryan, Wilhelmus B. A History of the National Capital from Its Foundation through the Period of the Adoption of the Organic Act. 2 vols. New York, 1914–16.

Buckham, Matthew H. "George Wyllys Benedict," in Services in Remembrance of Rev. Joseph Torrey, D.D., and of George Wyllys Benedict, LL.D., Professors in the University of Vermont, pp. 44–52. Burlington, Vt., 1874.

Bullett, Gerald. The English Mystics. London, 1950.

Burgess, John W. Reminiscences of an American Scholar, the Beginnings of Columbia University. New York, 1934.

Burlington *Free Press*. Index, 1848–1861. Historical Records Survey. 4 vols. Montpelier, Vt., n.d.

Busey, Samuel C. Pictures of the City of Washington in the Past. Washington, D.C., 1898.

Byington, Ezra H. Biographical Sketch of Rev. John Wheeler, D.D., 1798–1862, President of the University of Vermont 1833–1848: a Biographical Sketch. Cambridge, 1894.

Cameron, Donald A. Egypt in the Nineteenth Century; or, Mehemet Ali and His Successors until the British Occupation in 1882. London, 1898.

Cameron, Jenks. The Development of Governmental Forest Control in the United States. Baltimore, 1928.

Carlisle, George W. F. H. Diary in Turkish and Greek Waters. C. C. Felton, ed. Boston, 1855.

Carman, Ezra A. "Special Report on the History and Present Condition of the Sheep Industry of the United States," 52 Cong. 2 Sess., H. Misc. Doc. 105. (U.S. Dept. of Agriculture, Bureau of Animal Husbandry.) Part I, Ch. 4, pp. 217–348. Washington, D.C., 1892.

Carroll, Charles A. "The Government's Importation of Camels: a Historical Sketch." U.S.D.A., Bureau of Animal Industry, Rept. No. 20, 1903, pp. 391–409. Washington, D.C., 1904.

Carroll, Daniel B. "The Unicameral Legislature of Vermont." Ph.D. thesis, MS, University of Wisconsin, 1930.

Carstensen, Vernon. Farms or Forests: Evolution of a State Land Policy for Northern Wisconsin, 1850–1932. Madison, Wis., 1958.

Cheever, George B. Characteristics of the Christian Philosopher; a Discourse Commemorative of the Virtues and Attainments of Rev. James Marsh, D.D. . . . New York, 1843.

Chersi, Livio. "Studies in the Diplomatic Relations of the United States and Italy." M.A. thesis, MS, Louisiana State Univ., 1936.

Child, F. S. "Observations on the Language of Chaucer," AAA&S Memoirs, VIII, Part 2 (1863), 455ff.

Chinard, Gilbert. "The American Philosophical Society and the Early History of Forestry in America," American Philosophical Society Proc., LXXXIX (1945), 444–88.

—— "Eighteenth Century Theories on America as a Human Habitat," American Philosophical Society Proc., XCI (1947), 27–57.

Chittenden, L. E. Personal Reminiscences, 1840–1890 . . . New York, 1893.

Chittenden County. Court Calendar for the County of Chittenden, October Term, 1843. Burlington, Vt., 1843.

Churchill, G. A., and N. W. Churchill. "Churchill Family in America." MS, Norman Williams Library, Woodstock, Vt.

Clapp, Margaret. Forgotten First Citizen: John Bigelow. Boston, 1947.

Clark, Eleanor. Rome and a Villa. New York, 1952.

Clough, Wilson O., ed. "A Journal of Village Life in Vermont in 1848," *NEQ*, I (1928), 32–40.

Collamer, J., Daniel Kellogg, and Hiland Hall. "Report of the Commissioners on Laws relating to Railroads," Vermont House Journal, 1855, App., pp. 642–49.

Conant, H. J. "Imprisonment for Debt in Vermont: a History," *Vermont Quarterly,* XIX (1951), 67–80.

Connecticut Historical Society, Collections (1903), IX, 249.

Connecticut. The Public Records of the Colony of Connecticut, from May, 1757, to March, 1762, inclusive, Vols. IX (1880) and X (1881). Charles J. Hoadley, ed. Hartford, Conn.

Coulson, Thomas. Joseph Henry: His Life and Work. Princeton, 1950.

[Crane, Elizabeth Greene]. Caroline Crane Marsh: a Life Sketch. N.d., n.p.

Crockett, Walter H. Vermont: the Green Mountain State. 5 vols. New York, 1921.

Cross, Whitney R. "W J McGee and the Idea of Conservation," *Historian,* XV (1953), 148–62.

Cuningham, Charles E. Timothy Dwight 1752–1817; a Biography. New York, 1942.

Curti, Merle. "Austria and the United States 1848–1852: a Study in Diplomatic Relations," *Smith College Studies in History,* XI (1926), 141–206.

—— Probing Our Past. New York, 1955.

—— The Roots of American Loyalty. New York, 1946.

Dall, William H. Spencer Fullerton Baird: a Biography. Philadelphia, 1915.

Dana, Henry Swan. History of Woodstock, Vermont. Boston, 1889.

Dana, John Cotton. "George P. Marsh, 1820," *Dartmouth Alumni Mag.,* XII (1920), 874–81.

Dana, Richard H. Hospitable England in the Seventies: the Diary of a Young American, 1875–1876. Boston, 1921.

Dana, Samuel T. "Forest Influences," in A World Geography of Forest Resources (*q.v.*), Ch. 3, pp. 49–63.

Darby, H. C. "The Clearing of the Woodland in Europe," in W. L. Thomas, Jr., ed., Man's Role in Changing the Face of the Earth (*q.v.*), pp. 183–216.

Dartmouth College. Course of Instruction, &c. at Dartmouth College. Hanover, N.H., 1822.

Dartmouth College and Associated Schools. General Catalogue 1769–1940. Hanover, N.H., 1940.

Darwin, Charles Galton. The Next Million Years. London, 1952.

Davis, William Morris. "Biographical Memoir of George Perkins Marsh 1801–1882," *NASBM* (1909), VI, 71–80 (read April 18, 1906).

—— "The Halligs, Vanishing Islands of the North Sea," *GR,* XIII (1923), 99–106.

De Mare, Marie. G. P. A. Healy: American Artist. New York, 1954.

A Description of the State Houses of Vermont. Montpelier, Vt., 1896.

Dewey, John. "James Marsh and American Philosophy," *JHI,* II (1941), 131–50.

Dictionary of American Biography. Allen Johnson, Dumas Malone, and H. E. Starr, eds. 21 vols. New York, 1928–44.

A Dictionary of Americanisms on Historical Principles. Mitford M. Mathews, ed. 2 vols. Chicago, 1951.

Dictionary of National Biography. Leslie Stephen and Sidney Lee, eds. 24 vols. London, 1937–39.

The Dobbs Family in America by Our Own "Special" Correspondent. London, 1865.

Dodwell, Henry. The Founder of Modern Egypt: a Study of Muhammad 'Ali. Cambridge, Eng., 1931.

Donne, John. Devotions upon Emergent Occasions, John Hayward, ed., in Complete Poetry and Selected Prose. London, 1932.

Draper, Daniel. "Has Our Climate Changed?" *Popular Science Monthly,* I (1872), 665–74.

Duncan, D. P. "Forest Practice at Vallombrosa in Central Italy," *Journal of Forestry,* XLIV (1946), 347–53.

Dunn, Waldo H. The Life of Donald G. Mitchell, Ik Marvel. New York, 1922.

Dunne, Finley Peter. Observations by Mr. Dooley. New York, 1906.

Dupree, A. Hunter. Science in the Federal Period; a History of Policies and Activities to 1940. Cambridge, 1957.

Durden, Robert F. "James S. Pike: President Lincoln's Minister to the Netherlands," *NEQ,* XXIX (1956), 341–64.

——James Shepherd Pike: Republicanism and the American Negro, 1850–1882. Durham, N.C., 1957.

Dvoichenko-Markov, Eufrosia. "Americans in the Crimean War," *Russian Review,* XIII (1954), 137–45.

Dwight, Timothy. Travels in New-England and New-York. 2 vols. New Haven, 1821–22.

Edmunds, George F. The Life, Character and Services of Solomon Foot. Montpelier, Vt., 1866.

Eggleston, Edward. "Formative Influences," *Forum,* X (1890), 279–90.

Egleston, N. H. Arbor Day: Its History and Observance. U.S. Dept. of Agriculture. Washington, D.C., 1896.

Einarsson, Stefán. History of Icelandic Prose Writers, 1800–1940. *Islandica,* Vols. XXXII–XXXIII. Ithaca, N.Y., 1948.

Ekirch, A. A. The Idea of Progress in America, 1815–1860. New York, 1944.

Eldridge, Charles William. "Journal of a Tour through Vermont to Montreal and Quebec in 1833," VHS *Proc.,* n.s. II (1931), 53–82.

Ellis, William A. Norwich University 1819–1911; Her History, Her Graduates, Her Roll of Honor. 3 vols. Montpelier, Vt., 1911.

Emerson, Ralph Waldo. "English Traits" and "The Man with a Hoe," in Complete Works. Cambridge, 1903. Vol. V, Ch. 4, "Race," and VII, 135–54.

Enciclopedia Italiana di Scienze, lettere ed arti . . . 36 vols. Roma and Milano, 1929–39.

"Episcopus." Remarks on an Address Delivered before the New England Society of the City of New York. Boston, 1845.

"The Ethan Allen Statue in Burlington," VHS *Proc.,* n.s. II (1931), 144–45.

Fairbanks, Edward T. The Town of St. Johnsbury, Vt.;—a Review of One Hundred Twenty-five Years to the Anniversary Pageant 1912. St. Johnsbury, Vt., 1914.

Falnes, Oscar J. "New England Interest in Scandinavian Culture and the Norsemen," *NEQ,* X (1937), 211–42.

Fernow, Bernhard. A Brief History of Forestry in Europe, the United States, and Other Countries. 3d rev. ed., Washington, D.C., 1913.

—— "Do Forests Influence Rainfall?" *Garden and Forest,* I (1888), 489–90.

Feuer, Lewis S. "H. A. P. Torrey and John Dewey: Teacher and Pupil," *American Quarterly,* X (1958), 34–54.

—— "James Marsh and the Conservative Transcendentalist Philosophy: a Political Interpretation," *NEQ,* XXXI (1958), 3–31.

Fisher, Dorothy Canfield. Vermont Tradition: the Biography of an Outlook on Life. Boston, 1953.

Flint, K. R. B. "Alden Partridge," in Walter H. Crockett, ed., Vermonters; a Book of Biographies, pp. 165–68. Brattleboro, Vt., 1932.

Ford, W. C., ed. A Cycle of Adams Letters, 1861–1865. 2 vols. Boston, 1920.

Fowler, H. D. Camels to California: a Chapter in Western Transportation. Stanford, Calif., 1950.

Frank, Bernard, and Alexander Netboy. Water, Land, and People. New York, 1950.

Franklin, Benjamin. The Life and Writings of Benjamin Franklin. Albert H. Smyth, coll. and ed. 10 vols. New York, 1905–7.

Freidel, Frank. Francis Lieber, Nineteenth Century Liberal. Baton Rouge, La., 1947.

Fuess, Claude M. Daniel Webster. 2 vols. Boston, 1930.

—— An Old New England School: a History of Phillips Academy, Andover. Boston, 1917.

—— Rufus Choate, the Wizard of the Law. New York, 1928.

Fulton, John F., and Elizabeth H. Thomson. Benjamin Silliman, 1779–1864: Pathfinder in American Science. New York, 1947.

Gallatin, Albert. The Writings of Albert Gallatin. Henry Adams, ed. 3 vols. New York, 1879.

Gallup, Joseph A. Sketches of Epidemic Diseases in the State of Vermont; from its First Settlement to the Year 1815 . . . Boston, 1815.

Gay, H. Nelson. "Garibaldi's American Contacts and His Claims to American Citizenship," *AHR*, XXXVIII (1932), 1–19.

—— "Lincoln's Offer of a Command to Garibaldi: Light on a Disputed Point of History," *Century Mag.*, LXXV (1907), 63–74.

—— The Protestant Burial Ground in Rome; a Historical Sketch. London, n.d.

—— "Le relazioni fra l'Italia e gli Stati Uniti," *Nuova Antologia*, CCXI (1907), 657–71.

Gilman, M. D. The Bibliography of Vermont; or, A List of Books and Pamphlets Relating in Any Way to the State, with Biographical and Other Notes. Burlington, Vt., 1897.

Gilpin, William. Mission of the North American People, Geographical, Social, and Political. Philadelphia, 1873.

Glacken, Clarence J. "Changing Ideas of the Habitable World," in W. L. Thomas, Jr., ed., Man's Role (*q.v.*), pp. 70–92.

—— "Man and the Earth," *Landscape,* V, No. 3 (1956), 27–29.

—— "The Origins of Conservation Philosophy," *Journal of Soil and Water Conservation,* XI (1956), 63–66.

Glick, Wendell. "Bishop Paley in America," *NEQ,* XXVII (1954), 347–54.

Godfrey, William S. "Vikings in America; Theories and Evidence," *American Anthropologist,* LVII (1955), 35–43.

[Godkin, E. L.] "American Ministers Abroad," *Nation,* IV (1867), 132–34.

—— "The Pope and the Catholic Nations," *Nation,* V (1867), 375–76.

Golder, Frank A. "Russian–American Relations during the Crimean War," *AHR,* XXXI (1926), 462–76.

Gooch, Brison D. "A Century of Historiography on the Origins of the Crimean War," *AHR,* LXII (1956), 33–58.

Gooch, G. P. History and Historians in the Nineteenth Century. Rev. ed., London, 1952.

Goode, G. Brown. "The Genesis of the U.S. National Museum." A Memorial of G. Brown Goode, Together with a Selection of His Papers on Museums and on the History of Science in America, SI Ann. Rept., 1897, pp. 83–192. Washington, D.C., 1901.

—— "The Three Secretaries," in G. Brown Goode, ed., The Smithsonian Institution 1846–1896, pp. 115–234. Washington, D.C., 1897.

Goodrich, John E. "Immigration to Vermont," VHS *Proc.,* 1908–9, pp. 63–86.

Gordon, L. J. American Relations with Turkey, 1830–1890; an Economic Interpretation. Philadelphia, 1932.

La Grande Encyclopédie. . . . André Berthelot et al., eds. 31 vols. Paris, 1886–1902.

Gray, A. A. "Camels in California," *California Historical Society Quarterly,* IX (1930), 299–317.

Gridley, John. History of Montpelier. Montpelier, Vt., 1843.

Griswold, R. W. "George P. Marsh," in his The Prose Writers of America, pp. 414–16. Philadelphia, 1847.

Grøndal, Benedikt, ed. Breve fra og til Carl Christian Rafn, med en Biografi. Kjöbenhavn, 1869.

Guyot, Arnold. The Earth and Man: Lectures on Comparative Physical Geography in Its Relation to the History of Mankind, tr. C. C. Felton. New York, 1889 [first published 1849].

Hager, Albert D. The Marbles of Vermont. Burlington, Vt., 1858.

Hale, E. E. [Review of Marsh's Lectures on the English Language], *CE*, LXIX (1860), 1–18.

Hales, E. E. Y. Pio Nono, a Study of European Politics and Religion in the Nineteenth Century. London, 1954.

Hamilton, Holman. Zachary Taylor: Soldier in the White House. Indianapolis, 1951.

Hamlin, Cyrus. Among the Turks. New York, 1878.

Hancock, W. K. Ricasoli and the Risorgimento in Tuscany. London, 1926.

Handlin, Oscar. Boston's Immigrants, 1790–1865: a Study in Acculturation. Cambridge, Mass., 1941.

Harris, Seale. Woman's Surgeon: the Life Story of J. Marion Sims. New York, 1950.

Harvey, F. L. History of the Washington National Monument and the Washington National Monument Society. 57 Cong. 2 Sess., Sen. Doc. 224. Washington, 1903.

Hayden, F. V. "Report on Nebraska Territory," in Report of the Commissioner of the General Land Office 1867, pp. 152–205. 40 Cong. 2 Sess., H. Doc. 1. Washington, 1867.

Hayes, Lyman S. The Connecticut River Valley in Southern Vermont and New Hampshire. Rutland, Vt., 1929.

—— History of the Town of Rockingham, Vermont . . . 1753–1907. Bellows Falls, Vt., 1907.

Hayes, Rutherford B. Diaries and Letters of Rutherford Birchard Hayes. . . . Charles R. Williams, ed. 5 vols. Columbus, Ohio, 1922–26.

Hemenway, Abby Maria, ed. Vermont Historical Gazetteer. 5 vols. Various places, 1862–82.

Henderson, Daniel. The Hidden Coasts: a Biography of Admiral Charles Wilkes. New York, 1953.

Hermannsson, Halldór. "Willard Fiske and Icelandic Bibliography," Bibliographical Society of America, *Papers*, XII (1918), 97–106.

Herodotus. "The Persian Wars," in The History of Herodotus, George Rawlinson, tr. 4 vols. New York, 1909. Vol. IV.

Heske, Franz. German Forestry. New Haven, 1938.

The Hickok Family in Burlington, Vermont. N.p., 1882.

Hilen, Andrew. Longfellow and Scandinavia: a Study of the Poet's Relationship with the Northern Languages and Literature. New Haven, 1947.

Hill, Ralph Nading. The Winooski: Heartway of Vermont. New York, 1949.

Hofstadter, Richard. Social Darwinism in American Thought 1860–1915. Philadelphia, 1944.

Holbrook, Stewart H. The Yankee Exodus: an Account of Migration from New England. New York, 1950.

Hone, Philip. The Diary of Philip Hone, 1828–1851. Bayard Tuckerman, ed. 2 vols. New York, 1889.

Hough, Franklin B. The Elements of Forestry. Cincinnati, 1882.

—— "Experimental Plantation of the Eucalyptus Near Rome," *American Journal of Forestry*, I (1882–83), 402–13.

—— "On the Duty of Governments in the Preservation of Forests," AAAS *Proc.*, XXII, Part 2 (1873), 1–10.

—— Report upon Forestry. Washington, D.C., 1878.

Howells, W. D. "Massimo d'Azeglio," *Nation*, II (1866), 202–4.

Humphreys, Sexson E. "Le relazioni diplomatiche fra gli Stati Uniti e l'Italia del Risorgimento (1847–1871)." Dottore in lettere, MS, Università degli Studi, Roma, 1945.

—— "Two Garibaldian Incidents in American History," *Vermont History*, XXIII (1955), 135–43.

Hurd, Charles. Washington Cavalcade. New York, 1948.

James, Henry. "The After-Season at Rome," *Nation*, XVI (1873), 399–400.

—— "A European Summer; VI: From Chambery to Milan," *Nation*, XV (1872), 332–34.

—— "From Lake George to Burlington," *Nation*, XI (1870), 135–36.

—— William Wetmore Story and His Friends . . . 2 vols. Boston, 1903.

Jewett, C. C. "Report of the Assistant Secretary in Charge of the Library of the Smithsonian Institution, for the Year 1850," Fifth Annual Report of the SI . . . 1850, pp. 28–41. Washington, D.C., 1851.

J. L. D. Woodstock, Vt.: a Few Notes, Historical and Other, concerning the Town and Village. Woodstock, Vt., 1910.

Jones, L. R. "Notes on the Trees of Burlington and Vicinity," in Contributions to the Botany of Vermont, pp. 87–97. Burlington, Vt., 1902.

"Journal of an Excursion to Manchester, Vermont, by a Party of Norwich Cadets, 1823," in VHS, ed., Essays in the Social and Economic History of Vermont, pp. 185–99. Montpelier, Vt., 1943.

Kane, Kate Morris. "The Revolutionary History of a Vermont Town," *Vermont Antiquarian*, I (1902), 1–28.

Keeler, Ralph. Vagabond Adventures. Boston, 1870.

Kelly, Mary Louise. Woodstock's U.S. Senator: Jacob Collamer. Woodstock, Vt., 1944.

Kernan, Henry. "The Trees of Vallambrosa [sic]," American Forests, LX, No. 7, (1954), 14–16, 44–45.

Kerr, J. A., G. B. Jones, and W. E. McLendon. "Soil Survey of Windsor County, Vermont." U.S.D.A., Bureau of Soils, Field Operations 1916, XVIII, 175–94. Washington, D.C., 1921.

King, Bolton. A History of Italian Unity. 2 vols. London, 1899.

Kirkland, Edward C. Men, Cities and Transportation: a Study in New England History, 1820–1900. 2 vols. Cambridge, Mass., 1948.

Kliger, Samuel. "Emerson and the Usable Anglo-Saxon Past," JHI, XVI (1955), 483–86.

—— "George Perkins Marsh and the Gothic Tradition in America," NEQ, XIX (1946), 524–31.

—— "The 'Goths' in England: an Introduction to the Gothic Vogue in Eighteenth-Century Aesthetic Discussion," Modern Philology, XLIII (1945), 107–17.

—— The Goths in England: a Study in Seventeenth and Eighteenth Century Thought. Cambridge, Mass., 1952.

Koopman, Harry L. "George P. Marsh." An Address in the Marsh Library of the University of Vermont, before the New England College Librarians, May, 1926. MS, UV.

——, comp. Bibliography of George Perkins Marsh. Burlington, Vt., 1892 [reprint from UV, Catalogue of the Library of George Perkins Marsh, q.v.].

Krapp, George Philip. The English Language in America. 2 vols. New York, 1925.

Kraus, Michael. A History of American History. New York, 1937.

—— The Writing of American History. Norman, Okla., 1953.

Lane-Poole, Stanley. The Life of the Right Honourable Stratford Canning, Viscount de Redcliffe. 2 vols. London, 1888.

Lanman, Charles. Haphazard Personalities; Chiefly of Noted Americans, pp. 91–108 [on Marsh]. Boston, 1886.

—— Letters from a Landscape Painter. Boston, 1845.

Lapham, I. A., J. G. Knapp, and H. Crocker. Report on the Disastrous Effects of the Destruction of Forest Trees Now Going on So Rapidly in the State of Wisconsin. Madison, Wis., 1867.

Larned, Ellen D. History of Windham County, Connecticut. 2 vols, Worcester, Mass., 1880.

Latimer, W. J., *et al*. Soil Survey (Reconnaissance) of Vermont. U.S.D.A., Bureau of Chemistry and Soils, Series 1930, no. 43. Washington, D.C., 1937.

Lea, Henry C. A History of the Inquisition of the Middle Ages. 3 vols. rev. ed., New York, 1922.

Leighly, John B. "Inaccuracies in Longfellow's Translation of Tegnér's 'Nattvardsbarnen.'" *SS*, XXI (1949), 171–80.

—— "New Occasions and New Duties for Climatology," *GR*, XXIX (1939), 682–83.

Leopold, Richard W. Robert Dale Owen: a Biography. Cambridge, Mass., 1940.

Lewis, W. S., A. A. Gray, and F. P. Farquhar. Camels in Western America: a Contribution towards the Bibliography of the Camel. San Francisco, 1930.

Life of Thomas Hawley Canfield. Burlington, Vt., 1889.

Lillard, Richard G. The Great Forest. New York, 1947.

Lincoln, Abraham. Complete Works of Abraham Lincoln. James G. Nicolay and John Hay, eds. 12 vols. New York, 1905.

Lincoln, Benjamin. An Exposition of Certain Abuses, Practised by Some of the Medical Schools in New England; and Particularly, of the Agent-Sending System, as Practised by Theodore Woodward, M.D. Burlington, Vt., 1833.

Lindsay, Julian I. Tradition Looks Forward; the University of Vermont: a History, 1791–1904. Burlington, Vt., 1954.

Linsley, Charles. "First Annual Report of the Railroad Commissioner," Vermont House Journal, 1856, pp. 583–92.

Long, Clement. Serving God with the Mind: a Discourse Commemorative of the Rev. Roswell Shurtleff, D.D., Late Professor Emeritus of Moral Philosophy and Political Economy in Dartmouth College. Concord, N.H., 1861.

Longfellow, Samuel. Life of Henry Wadsworth Longfellow, with Extracts from His Journals and Correspondence. 2 vols. Boston, 1893.

Lord, John K. A History of Dartmouth College, 1815–1909. Concord, N.H., 1913.

Lord, Russell. Behold Our Land. Boston, 1938.

Lowell, James Russell. Letters of James Russell Lowell. Charles Eliot Norton, ed. 2 vols. New York, 1894.

—— New Letters of James Russell Lowell. M. A. De Wolfe Howe, ed. New York, 1932.

—— [Review of Marsh's *Man and Nature,*] *NAR,* LXCIX (1864), 318–20.

Lowenthal, David. "George Perkins Marsh and the American Geographical Tradition," *GR,* XLIII (1953), 207–13.

—— "G. P. Marsh and Scandinavian Studies," *SS,* XXIX (1957), 41–52.

—— "Western Europe," in A World Geography of Forest Resources (*q.v.*), Ch. 13, pp. 269–302.

Ludlum, David. Social Ferment in Vermont 1791–1850. New York, 1939.

Lyell, Charles. Principles of Geology. 2 vols. London, 1830–32.

Lynch, Denis T. An Epoch and a Man, Martin Van Buren and His Times. New York, 1929.

McCarty, Milburn. "Forgotten Dartmouth Men: Greatest Scholar— George Perkins Marsh," *Dartmouth Alumni Magazine,* XXVIII, No. 4 (1936), 18, 68.

—— George Perkins Marsh (A Biographical Sketch). Hanover, N.H., 1935. MS, DCA.

McDaniels, J. H. "Francis Philip Nash," *Hobart College Bulletin,* IX, No. 4, supplement (1911), 1–23.

McDill, John H. "The Billings Farm: a Brief Historical Sketch." Woodstock, Vt., 1948. MS, Norman Williams Library, Woodstock, Vt.

Mackenzie-Grieve, Averil. Clara Novello, 1818–1908. London, 1955.

Malin, James C. The Contriving Brain and the Skillful Hand in the United States. Lawrence, Kans., 1955.

—— The Grassland of North America: Prolegomena to Its History. Lawrence, Kans., 1947.

—— "Space and History: Reflections on the Closed-Space Doctrines of Turner and Mackinder and the Challenge of Those Ideas by the Air Age," *AH,* XVIII (1944), 65–74, 107–26.

—— "The Turner-Mackinder Space Concept of History," in his Essays on Historiography. Rev. ed., Lawrence, Kans., 1955. Ch. 1.

Mallery, Arlington H. "The Pre-Columbian Discovery of America: a Reply to W. S. Godfrey," *American Anthropologist,* LX (1958), 141–50.

Malortie, Karl von. Egypt: Native Ideas and Foreign Interference. London, 1882.

March, F. A. "George Perkins Marsh" [review of *LL*], *Nation,* XLVII (1888), 213–15.

—— "Weisse's Origin of the English Language," *Nation,* XXVIII (1879), 153–54.

Mario, Jesse White. "Italian Finances," *Nation,* II (1866), 369–70.

—— "Right and Wrong in Italy," *Nation,* IX (1869), 48–49.

—— "The Volunteers of 1867," *Nation,* VI (1868), 208–9.

Marraro, Howard R. "American Opinion and Documents on Garibaldi's March on Rome, 1862," *Journal of Central European Affairs,* VII (1947), 143–61.

—— American Opinion on the Unification of Italy, 1846–1861. New York, 1932.

—— "The Closing of the American Diplomatic Mission to the Vatican and Efforts to Revive It, 1868–1870," *Catholic Historical Review,* XXXIII (1948), 423–47.

—— "Lincoln's Offer of a Command to Garibaldi: Further Light on a Disputed Point of History," *Journal of the Illinois State Historical Society,* XXXVI (1943), 237–70.

—— "Nathaniel Niles' Missions at the Court of Turin (1838; 1848–50)," *Vermont Quarterly,* XV (1947), 14–32.

—— "Spezia: an American Naval Base, 1848–68," *Military Affairs,* VII (1943), 203–8.

—— "Volunteers from Italy for Lincoln's Army," *South Atlantic Quarterly,* XLIV (1945), 384–96.

Marsh, Caroline Crane [Mrs. George P. Marsh]. The Hallig; or, The Sheepfold in the Waters. A Tale of Humble Life on the Coast of Schleswig. Tr. from the German of Biernatzki. Boston, 1856.

—— "Last Days of George P. Marsh," MS.

—— Life and Letters of George Perkins Marsh. 2 vols. (Vol. II never published). New York, 1888.

—— Wolfe of the Knoll, and Other Poems. New York, 1860.

Marsh, Charles. An Essay on the Amendments Proposed to the Constitution of the State of Vermont, by the Council of Censors. Hanover, N.H., 1814.

Marsh, Dwight Whitney, ed. Marsh Genealogy, Giving Several Thousand Descendants of John Marsh of Hartford, Ct., 1636–1895. Amherst, Mass., 1895.

Marsh, James, ed. Aids to Reflection, by S. T. Coleridge . . . Together with a Preliminary Essay [pp. xiii–xlvi], and Additional Notes, by James Marsh. Burlington, Vt., 1829.

Marsh, Leonard. The Apocatastis; or, Progress Backwards: a New "Tract for the Times." Burlington, Vt., 1854.

—— A Bake-Pan for the Dough-Faces. By One of Them. Burlington, Vt., 1854.

Martin, Edwin T. Thomas Jefferson: Scientist. New York, 1952.

Mason, Jeremiah. Memoir, Autobiography and Correspondence of Jeremiah Mason. G. J. Clark, ed. Kansas City, Mo., 1917.

Meader, L. H. "The Council of Censors in Vermont," in Early History of Vermont, pp. 155–287. VHS, ed. Montpelier, Vt., 1943.

Mencken, H. L. The American Language: an Inquiry into the Development of English in the United States. New York, 3d ed., 1930; 4th ed., 1936.

Mierow, Charles C., ed. The Gothic History of Jordanes in English Version. Princeton, 1915.

Milham, W. I. "The Year 1816—the Causes of Abnormalities," *Monthly Weather Review*, LII (1924), 563–70.

Miller, Perry, ed. The Transcendentalists: an Anthology. Cambridge, 1950.

Mitchell, Donald Grant. American Lands and Letters; Leatherstocking to Poe's Raven, pp. 35–45, in his Works, Vol. XV. 15 vols. New York, 1907.

Monaghan, Jay. Diplomat in Carpet Slippers: Abraham Lincoln Deals with Foreign Affairs. New York, 1945.

Montesquieu, Charles de Secondat, Baron de. The Spirit of Laws. Thomas Nugent, tr.; J. V. Prichard, rev., 1748. In Great Books of the Modern World, Vol. XXXVIII. Chicago, 1952.

Moore, Guy W. The Case of Mrs. Surratt . . . Norman, Okla., 1954.

Moore, John Bassett. "Kossuth: a Sketch of a Revolutionist," *Political Science Quarterly*, X (1895), 95–131, 257–91.

Morison, Samuel Eliot. Three Centuries of Harvard, 1636–1936. Cambridge, Mass., 1936.

Müller, Friedrich Max. Lectures on the Science of Language: First Series. Rev. ed., New York, 1874.

Mumford, Lewis. The Brown Decades: a Study of the Arts in America, 1865–1895. New York, 1931.

—— The Condition of Man. New York, 1944.

—— "The Natural History of Urbanization," in W. L. Thomas, Jr., ed., Man's Role in Changing the Face of the Earth (*q.v.*), pp. 382–98.

—— Technics and Civilization. New York, 1934.

Mussey, Barrows. "Yankee Chills, Ohio Fever," *NEQ*, XXII (1949), 435–51.

Nash, B. H., and F. P. Nash. "Notice of George Perkins Marsh," AAA&S *Proc.*, XVIII (1882–83), 447–57.

The *Nation*. Index of Titles and Contributors, Vols. I–CV. Daniel Haskell, ed. New York, 1951.

National Cyclopaedia of American Biography. 41 vols. New York, 1893–1956.

Neilson, Joseph. Memories of Rufus Choate . . . Boston, 1884.

Nevins, Allan. Ordeal of the Union. 2 vols. New York, 1947.

A New English Dictionary on Historical Principles, Vol. I. James A. H. Murray, ed. 10 vols. Oxford, 1888–1928.

Nicolay, Helen. Our Capital on the Potomac. New York, 1924.

Nicolson, Marjorie. "James Marsh and the Vermont Transcendentalists," *Philosophical Review,* XXXIV (1925), 28–50.

Nye, Mary Greene. Vermont's State House. Montpelier, Vt., 1936.

Odgers, Merle M. Alexander Dallas Bache: Scientist and Educator, 1806–1867. Philadelphia, 1947.

Oehser, Paul H. Sons of Science: the Story of the Smithsonian Institution and Its Leaders. New York, 1949.

Paine, Caroline. Tent and Harem: Notes of an Oriental Trip. New York, 1859.

Pasolini dall' Onda, P. D. Giuseppe Pasolini, 1815–1876: Memorie raccolte da suo figlio. 4th ed. 2 vols. Torino, 1915.

Peck, Ira B. A Genealogical History of the Descendants of Joseph Peck . . . Boston, 1868.

Perkins, Nathan. A Narrative of a Tour through the State of Vermont from April 27 to June 12, 1789. Woodstock, Vt., 1920.

Perrin, Porter Gale. The Life and Works of Thomas Green Fessenden, 1771-1837. Orono, Maine, 1925.

Phelps, Samuel S. Mr. Phelps' Appeal to the People of Vermont, in Vindication of Himself . . . Middlebury, Vt., 1845.

—— To the People of Vermont. Mr. Phelps' Rejoinder to Mr. Slade's "Reply." [Washington, D.C., 1845.]

Pierce, C. H. Surface Waters of Vermont. U.S. Geological Survey, Water-Supply Paper 424. Washington, D.C., 1917.

Pickard, Madge E. "Government and Science in the United States: Historical Backgrounds," *Journal of the History of Medicine and Allied Sciences,* I (1946), 254–89, 446–81.

Pinchot, Gifford. Breaking New Ground. New York, 1947.

Pochmann, Henry A. German Culture in America: Philosophical and Literary Influences, 1600–1900. Madison, Wis., 1957.

Pooley, Robert C. Grammar and Usage in Textbooks on English. Univ.

of Wisconsin, Bureau of Educational Research, Bull. No. 14. Madison, Wis., 1933.

—— Teaching English Usage. New York, 1946.

Poore, Benjamin Perley. Perley's Reminiscences of Sixty Years in the National Metropolis. 2 vols. Philadelphia, 1886.

Porter, E. G. "Speech at the Presentation of Marsh Portrait," in Speeches at the First Annual Dinner of the Phillips Andover Academy Alumni Association, Parker House, Boston, March 24, 1886, pp. 31-35. Boston, 1886.

Powell, J. H. Richard Rush, Republican Diplomat, 1780–1859. Philadelphia, 1942.

Powell, J. W. "The Personal Characteristics of Professor Baird," SI Ann. Rept. 1888, pp. 739–44. Washington, D.C., 1890.

—— Report on the Lands of the Arid Region of the United States, with a More Detailed Account of the Lands of Utah. 2d ed., Washington, D.C., 1879.

Powers, T. E. Report of the Hon. Thomas H. Powers, Superintendent of Construction of the State House. Oct. 18, 1858. Montpelier, Vt., 1858.

Price, Edward T. "Values and Concepts in Conservation," *AAAG,* XLV (1955), 64–84.

Proceedings and Address of the Vermont Republican Convention Friendly to the Election of Andrew Jackson to the Next Presidency of the United States, Holden at Montpelier, June 27, 1828. Montpelier, Vt., 1828.

Protestant Orphanage for Girls (Collegio Ferretti). Report of the Executive Committee for the Year 1882. Florence, 1883.

Raeder, Ole Munch. America in the Forties: the Letters of Ole Munch Raeder. Gunnar J. Malmin, ed. and tr. Minneapolis, 1929.

Rafn, C. C., ed. Antiquitates Americanae . . . Kjöbenhavn, 1837.

Randall, J. G., and Richard N. Current. Lincoln the President: Last Full Measure. New York, 1955.

Read, David. Report and Statements concerning the Winooski Marble, at Mallett's Bay, near Burlington, Vermont. Boston, 1866.

Reclus, Élisée. A New Physical Geography [La Terre]. New York, 1874.

Reed, J. L. Forests of France. London, 1954.

[Reed, W. B.]. A Review of Mr. Seward's Diplomacy. By a Northern Man. [Philadelphia? 1862].

Rhees, W. J., ed. The Smithsonian Institution: Documents Relative to

Its Origin and History. SI. Misc. Coll., Vol. XVII. Washington, D.C., 1879.

—— ed. The Smithsonian Institution: Journals of the Board of Regents, Reports of Committees, Statistics, Etc. SI Misc. Coll., Vol. XVIII. Washington, D.C., 1879.

Rice, John L. "Dartmouth College and the State of New Connecticut, 1776–1782," Connecticut Valley Historical Soc., *Papers and Proc.* (1876–81), I, 152–206.

Richardson, Leon Burr. History of Dartmouth College. 2 vols. Hanover, N.H., 1932.

Roberts, Chalmers. The Washington Monument, the Story of a National Shrine. Washington, D.C., 1948.

Robinson, James Harvey. The New History . . . New York, 1912.

Rodgers, Andrew Denny, III. Bernhard Eduard Fernow: a Story of North American Forestry. Princeton, N.J., 1951.

Ross, Ishbel. Child of Destiny: the Life Story of the First Woman Doctor. New York, 1949.

Rostlund, Erhard. "Twentieth Century Magic," *Landscape,* V, No. 3 (1956), 23–26.

Sargent, Charles Sprague. A Few Suggestions on Tree-Planting. Boston, 1876.

—— in *Garden and Forest,* I (1888), 25, 505.

—— [George Perkins Marsh], *Nation,* XXXV (1882), 136.

—— "The Protection of Forests," *NAR,* CXXXV (1882), 386–401.

Sauer, Carl O. "The Agency of Man on the Earth," in W. L. Thomas, Jr., ed., Man's Role in Changing the Face of the Earth (*q.v.*), pp. 49–69.

—— "Foreward to Historical Geography," *AAAG,* XXXI (1941), 1–24.

Saveth, Edward N. American Historians and European Immigrants, 1875–1925. New York, 1948.

Saxe, John G. The Money-King and Other Poems. Boston, 1860.

Schlesinger, Arthur M. "What Then Is the American, This New Man?" *AHR,* XLVIII (1943), 225–44.

Schmidt-Nielson, Knut. "Animals and Arid Conditions: Physiological Aspects of Productivity and Management," in Gilbert F. White, ed., The Future of Arid Lands: Papers and Recommendations from the International Arid Lands Meetings, pp. 368–82. AAAS Publ. No. 43. Washington, D.C., 1956.

Schurz, Carl. Intimate Letters of Carl Schurz, 1841–1889. Joseph Schafer, tr. and ed. Wisconsin Hist. Soc., *Coll.,* Vol. XXX. Madison, Wis., 1928.

—— Speeches, Correspondence, and Political Papers of Carl Schurz. Frederic Bancroft, ed. 6 vols. New York, 1913.

Seward, W. H. William H. Seward's Travels around the World. Olive R. Seward, ed. New York, 1873.

[Seymour, T. D.] "Lucy Myers Mitchell," *Critic,* XV (1888), 176.

Shaler, Nathaniel Southgate. The Autobiography of Nathaniel Southgate Shaler. Boston, 1909.

—— Domesticated Animals: Their Relation to Man and to His Advancement in Civilization. New York, 1895.

Sherman, Ernest L. "Meet Charles Marsh," Kimball Union Academy (Meriden, N.Y.), *Alumni Bulletin* (March, 1947), pp. 6–10.

Shirley, John M. The Dartmouth College Causes and the Supreme Court of the United States. St. Louis, 1877.

Siebert, Wilbur H. Vermont's Anti-Slavery and Underground Railroad Record. Columbus, Ohio, 1937.

Silliman, Benjamin. Remarks Made on a Short Tour between Hartford and Quebec, in the Autumn of 1819. New Haven, 1824.

Silloway, T. W. A Statement of the Facts, concerning the Management of Affairs, Connected with the Rebuilding of the Capitol, at Montpelier, Vermont. Burlington, Vt., 1859.

Sisam, J. W. B. "Principles and Practices of Forestry," in A World Geography of Forest Resources (*q.v.*), Ch. 4, pp. 65–82.

Slade, William. Gov. Slade's Reply to Senator Phelps' Appeal. Burlington, Vt., 1846.

—— To the People of Vermont. N.p., Oct. 10, 1846.

Smalley, Margaret T. "Notes on Early Vermont Artists," VHS *Proc.,* n.s. XI (1943), 146–68.

Smallwood, William Martin. Natural History and the American Mind. New York, 1941.

Smith, Henry Nash. "Rain Follows the Plough; the Notion of Increased Rainfall for the Great Plains, 1844–1880," *Huntington Library Quarterly,* X (1946–47), 169–93.

—— Virgin Land; the American West as Symbol and Myth. Cambridge, Mass., 1950.

Smith, Herbert A. "The Early Forestry Movement in the United States," *AH,* XII (1938), 326–46.

Smith, Herbert A. *et al.* A National Plan for American Forestry. 73 Cong. 1 Sess., Sen. Doc. 12. 2 vols. Washington, D.C., 1933.

Smith, William, Jr., ed. The Student's Manual of the English Language. London, 1863.

Smithsonian Institution. Annual Reports of the Board of Regents. Washington, D.C., 1847–1955.

Solmi, Arrigo. The Making of Modern Italy. New York, 1925.

Somervell, D. C. English Thought in the Nineteenth Century. London, 1929.

Squier, E. G., and E. H. Davis. Ancient Monuments of the Mississippi Valley; Comprising the Results of Extensive Original Surveys and Explorations. Smithsonian Inst. Contributions to Knowledge, Vol. I. Washington, D.C., 1848.

Stanton, Theodore. "The Villa Forini," New York *Semi-weekly Tribune,* Jan. 23, 1885 [reprinted as "The Italian Home of George P. Marsh," *Vermont Alumni Weekly,* XIV (1934), 43–44].

Starr, Frederick. "American Forests; Their Destruction and Preservation," in Report of the Commissioner of Agriculture for the Year 1865, pp. 210–34. 39 Cong. 1 Sess., H. Ex. Doc. 136. Washington, D.C., 1866.

Stegner, Wallace. Beyond the Hundredth Meridian: John Wesley Powell and the Second Opening of the West. Boston, 1953.

Stevens, William O. Washington, the Cinderella City. New York, 1943.

Stevenson, Elizabeth. Henry Adams: a Biography. New York, 1955.

Stillman, William James. The Autobiography of a Journalist. 2 vols. Boston, 1901.

—— "A Diplomatic Intrigue," *Nation,* XXXV (1882), 529–30.

—— "The Late George P. Marsh," *Nation,* XXXV (1882), 304–5.

—— The Union of Italy, 1815–1895. Cambridge, Eng., 1899.

Stilwell, Lewis D. Migration from Vermont. Montpelier, Vt., 1948.

Stock, Leo F., ed. Consular Relations between the United States and the Papal States: Instructions and Despatches. Washington, D.C., 1945.

—— United States Ministers to the Papal States: Instructions and Despatches 1848–1868. Washington, D.C., 1933.

Story, William Wetmore. Vallombrosa. Edinburgh, 1881.

Stowell, E. S. "Merino Sheep Industry," in Third Biennial Report of the Vermont State Board of Agriculture, Manufactures, and Mining for the years 1875–76, pp. 199–226. Rutland, Vt., 1876.

Struik, Dirk J. Yankee Science in the Making. Boston, 1948.

Sturtevant, Albert M. "An American Appreciation of Esaias Tegnér," *SS*, XVI (1941), 157–64.

Swift, Samuel. History of the Town of Middlebury, in the County of Addison, Vermont. Middlebury, Vt., 1859.

Taft, Russell F. "The Supreme Court of Vermont," *The Green Bag: an Entertaining Magazine of the Law* (Boston), V (1893), 563–64; VI (1894), 16–35, 72–91, 122–41, 176–92.

Taylor, Bayard. At Home and Abroad; a Sketch Book of the Life, Scenery, and Men. 2 vols. New York, 1860.

Taylor, Isaac. Words and Places; or, Etymological Illustrations of History, Ethnology, and Geography. 4th rev. ed., London, 1873.

Thomas, J. M., C. P. Smith, and F. S. Billings. Report of the Committee on the Conservation of the Natural Resources of the State of Vermont 1911–12. Rutland, Vt., 1912.

Thomas, William L., Jr., ed. Man's Role in Changing the Face of the Earth. Chicago, 1956.

Thompson, Daniel P. History of the Town of Montpelier . . . Montpelier, Vt., 1860.

Thompson, Zadock. A Gazetteer of the State of Vermont . . . Montpelier, Vt., 1824.

—— Ed. The Iris; or, Semi-Monthly Literary and Miscellaneous Register. Burlington, Vt., 1828–39.

—— Natural History of Vermont. Burlington, Vt., 1853.

Thoreau, Henry David. *Journal*, B. Torrey, ed., in The Writings of Henry David Thoreau . . . Vols. VII–XX. 20 vols. Boston, 1906.

—— "The Natural History of Massachusetts," *Dial*, III (1842), 19–40.

Ticknor, George. Life of William Hickling Prescott. Boston, 1864.

Torrey, Joseph. The Remains of the Reverend James Marsh, D.D., with a Memoir of His Life. New York, 1845.

Townsend, George A. Washington, Outside and Inside . . . Cincinnati, 1874.

Tracy, Joseph. A Discourse Commemorative of Rev. John Wheeler, D.D., Late President of the University of Vermont. Cambridge, Mass., 1865.

Trollope, T. Adolphus. What I Remember. New York, 1888.

Tucker, William H. History of Hartford, Vermont . . . Burlington, Vt., 1889.

Tupper, Frederick. "George Perkins Marsh," in Walter H. Crockett, ed., Vermonters: a Book of Biographies, pp. 151–54. Brattleboro, Vt., 1932.

Turner, Frederick Jackson. "The Significance of the Frontier in American History," in The Early Writings of Frederick Jackson Turner, pp. 183–229. Madison, Wis., 1938.

Tyler, Mary Palmer. Grandmother Tyler's Book: the Recollections of Mary Palmer Tyler (Mrs. Royall Tyler) 1775–1866. Frederick Tupper and Helen Tyler Brown, eds. New York, 1925.

United States. Annals of Congress, 1815–17.

—— Biographical Directory of the American Congress 1774–1949. Washington, D.C., 1950.

—— Census. Heads of Families at the Second Census of the United States Taken in 1800: Vermont. Montpelier, Vt., 1930.

—— Commercial Relations of the United States with Foreign Countries during the Years 1882 and 1883. Washington, D.C., 1884.

—— Communications . . . relative to the Case of the Reverend Mr. King. May 24, 1854. 33 Cong. 1 Sess., Sen. Ex. Doc. 67.

—— Congressional Directory, 13–15, 27–31 Congresses. Washington, various dates.

—— Congressional Globe, 1843ff.

—— Congressional Record, 1887.

—— Francis Dainese. Feb. 26, 1857. 34 Cong. 3 Sess., H. Ex. Doc. 82.

—— Foreign Relations of the United States, 1870. pp. 448–52. 41 Cong. 3 Sess., H. Ex. Doc. 1. Washington, D.C., 1871.

—— Further Correspondence . . . Relative to the Rev. Jonas King. Dec. 19, 1854. 33 Cong. 2 Sess., Sen. Ex. Doc. 9.

—— Historical Statistics of the United States 1789–1945. Washington, D.C., 1949.

—— House Journal, 1843–61.

—— Kossuth and Captain Long. Feb. 20, 1852. 32 Cong. 1 Sess., H. Ex. Doc. 78.

—— [Marsh claim for extra compensation]. Feb. 20, 1855, 33 Cong. 2 Sess., Sen. Ex. Doc. 40. May 23, 1856, 34 Cong. 1 Sess., H. Rep. 166. Dec. 22, 1857, 35 Cong. 1 Sess., Sen. Rep. 2. March 12, 1858, 35 Cong. 1 Sess., H. Rep. 168. April 6, 1860, 36 Cong. 1 Sess., H. Rep. 350. 12 Stat. at Large 857.

—— [Martin Koszta.] March 2, 1854. 33 Cong. 1 Sess., Sen. Ex. Doc. 40.

—— Official Records of the Union and Confederate Navies in the War of the Rebellion. Series I, Vol. I. Washington, D.C., 1894.

—— [Presents to Marsh]. Hamilton Fish to Sen. George F. Edmunds, Nov. 19, 1875. 44 Cong. 1 Sess., Sen. Misc. Doc. 16.

—— Register of the Department of State. Washington, D.C., 1950.

—— State Department. Papal States, see Stock, Leo F., ed.

—— Statutes at Large.

—— Supreme Court. The President, Directors, and Company of the Bank of the U.S. v. Wyllys Lyman and Others. Dec. 1851. 12 How. (53 U.S.) 225. Fed. Case 924, 1 Blatchford 297.

University of Vermont. Catalogue of the Library of George Perkins Marsh. Burlington, 1892.

Van Deusen, Glyndon G. Horace Greeley: Nineteenth Century Crusader. Philadelphia, 1953.

Vann, Richard T. "The Free Anglo-Saxons: a Historical Myth," *JHI*, XIX (1958), 259–72.

Vermont. Directory and Rules of the House of Representatives, for the Present Session. Montpelier, 1835.

—— General Assembly Journal, 1823–35.

—— House Journal, 1836–83.

—— Joint Assembly Journal, 1857.

—— Laws of Vermont, 1835–60.

—— Railroad Commissioner. Annual Reports, 1856–62.

—— Senate Journal, 1857–60.

—— Supreme Court. Vermont Reports (Records of the Supreme Court of the State of Vermont), Vols. I–XXVIII, 1828–55.

—— Supreme Executive Council. Records of the Council of Safety and Governor and Council of the State of Vermont, E. P. Walton, ed. 8 vols. Montpelier, Vt., 1873–80.

Vermont: a Guide to the Green Mountain State. American Guide Series. Boston, 1937.

Vermont Capitol and the Star Chamber. Testimony and Defense of the Superintendent of Construction. Oct., 1858. Montpelier, Vt., 1858.

Vermont Central Railroad. Proceedings of the Stockholders . . . at Northfield, Vt., May 4, 5, 1852. Montpelier, Vt., 1852.

—— Reports of the Trustees, 1849, 1851.

Very, Jones. Essays and Poems. Boston, 1839.

Webb, Walter P. The Great Plains. Boston, 1931.

Webster's American Dictionary of the English Language. Rev. ed. by Noah Porter. Springfield, Mass. 1880.

Wells, Ronald V. Three Christian Transcendentalists: James Marsh, Caleb Sprague Henry, Frederic Henry Hedge. New York, 1943.

Wheeler, David Hilton. "Recollections of George P. Marsh," MS.

Whipple, J. R. "Imprisonment for Debt in Vermont," *Vermonter*, XLII (1937), 23–24.

Whitaker, J. R. "World View of Destruction and Conservation of Natural Resources," *AAAG*, XXX (1940), 143–62.

White, George L., Jr. "Longfellow's Interest in Scandinavia during the Years 1835–1847," *SS*, XVII (1942), 70–82.

White, Horatio S. Willard Fiske: Life and Correspondence; a Biographical Study. New York, 1925.

White, John. The Planters Plea; Or, the Grounds of Plantations Examined and Usuall Objections Answered (London, 1630), in Peter Force, ed., Tracts and Other Papers, Relating Principally to the Origin, Settlement, and Progress of the Colonies of North America, Vol. II, no. 3, Washington, D.C., 1838.

White, Leonard D. The Republican Era, 1869–1901; a Study in Administrative History. New York, 1958.

White, Pliny H. "Early Poets of Vermont," VHS *Proc.*, 1917–18, pp. 93–125.

White, Richard Grant. Words and Their Uses, Past and Present; a Study of the English Language. Rev. ed., Boston, 1901.

Whitford, Philip, and Kathryn Whitford. "Thoreau: Pioneer Ecologist and Conservationist," in Walter Harding, ed., Thoreau, a Century of Criticism, pp. 192–205. Dallas, Texas, 1954.

Whitney, William Dwight. Language and Its Study, with Especial Reference to the Indo-European Family of Languages. 2d ed., London, 1880.

—— [on Marsh's linguistic work], *Nation*, XX (1875), 134.

Whyte, A. J. The Evolution of Modern Italy. Oxford, 1944.

Wilgus, William J. The Role of Transportation in the Development of Vermont. Montpelier, Vt., 1945.

Williams, Samuel. The Natural and Civil History of Vermont. 2 vols. 2d rev. ed., Burlington, Vt., 1809.

Wilson, Rufus R. Washington, the Capital City, and Its Part in the History of the Nation. 2 vols. Philadelphia, 1901.

Winthrop, Robert C. Addresses and Speeches on Various Occasions. 4 vols. Boston, 1886.

Winthrop, Robert C., Jr. A Memoir of Robert C. Winthrop. Boston, 1897.

Wislizenus, Frederick A. A Journey to the Rocky Mountains in the Year 1839. St. Louis, 1912.

Wittke, Carl. Refugees of Revolution: the German Forty-Eighters in America. Philadelphia, 1952.

Wittmann, Otto, Jr. "The Italian Experience (American Artists in Italy, 1830–1875)," *American Quarterly*, IV (1952), 3–15.

Wood, Frederic J. The Turnpikes of New England and Evolution of the Same through England, Virginia, and Maryland. Boston, 1919.

Wood, Henry. Sketch of the Life of President Brown. Boston, 1834.

Woodham-Smith, Cecil. Florence Nightingale 1820–1910. London, 1950.

Woollen, W. W. Biographical and Historical Sketches of Early Indiana. Indianapolis, 1883.

A World Geography of Forest Resources. Stephen Haden-Guest, John K. Wright, and Eileen M. Teclaff, eds. American Geographical Society Special Publ. No. 33. New York, 1956.

Wright, John Kirtland. Geography in the Making: the American Geographical Society 1851–1951. New York, 1952.

Wright, Walter L., Jr. "George Perkins Marsh," in *Dictionary of American Biography,* XII, 297–98.

Young, Augustus. Preliminary Report on the Natural History of the State of Vermont. Burlington, Vt., 1856.

Young, J. R. Around the World with General Grant . . . 2 vols. New York, 1879.

Yule, Henry, tr. and ed. The Book of Ser Marco Polo the Venetian, concerning the Kingdoms and Marvels of the East. London, 1875.

Index